The International Library of Sociology

THE SOCIAL SERVICES
OF MODERN ENGLAND

Founded by KARL MANNHEIM

The International Library of Sociology

PUBLIC POLICY, WELFARE
AND SOCIAL WORK
In 18 Volumes

THE SOCIAL SERVICES OF MODERN ENGLAND

by

M. PENELOPE HALL

Routledge
Taylor & Francis Group

LONDON AND NEW YORK

First published in 1952 by
Routledge

Reprinted 1998, 2001 by
Routledge
2 Park Square, Milton Park, Abingdon, Oxon, OX14 4RN

Simultaneously published in the USA and Canada by Routledge
711 Third Avenue, New York, NY 10017

Transferred to Digital Printing 2007

Routledge is an imprint of the Taylor & Francis Group, an informa business

First issued in paperback 2013

© 1959 , 1960 M. Penelope Hall

All rights reserved. No part of this book may be reprinted or reproduced
or utilized in any form or by any electronic, mechanical, or other means,
now known or hereafter invented, including photocopying
and recording, or in any information storage or retrieval system, without
permission in writing from the publishers.

The publishers have made every effort to contact authors/copyright holders
of the works reprinted in *The International Library of Sociology*.
This has not been possible in every case, however, and we would
welcome correspondence from those individuals/companies
we have been unable to trace.

British Library Cataloguing in Publication Data
A CIP catalogue record for this book
is available from the British Library

The Social Services of Modern England

ISBN 978-0-415-17725-2 (hbk)
ISBN 978-0-415-86860-0 (pbk)

Publisher's Note
The publisher has gone to great lengths to ensure the quality of this
reprint but points out that some imperfections in the original
may be apparent

To
ELLINOR I. BLACK
Teacher, Colleague and Friend

PREFACE

D
URING the closing years of the Second World War and the period of reconstruction which followed, our social services —embracing social insurance and assistance, health, housing, education, the care of old people and of deprived children—which had been expanding and developing during the previous half-century, were examined, evaluated and reconstituted. Their scope was widened to include the whole population, and the benefits provided were made more far-reaching and comprehensive. To-day their cost forms an important item in the national budget, thousands of officials and social workers are employed in administering them, and the concept of the 'Welfare State', of which they are the concrete embodiment, is a challenge to our social and political thinking. Yet surprisingly little has been written about them. As it is less than four years since the 'appointed day' (5th July 1948) on which much of our present social legislation became operative, and as since then economic and technical difficulties have resulted in delays and shortcomings, it is still rather soon for a major analysis and evaluation of the social services to be undertaken. At the same time, judging by my teaching experience, both within a university department of social science and with extra-mural students, there appears to be a real need for a book which gives a general description of the principal social services, outlines their development and considers their present functions in relation to the needs of the individuals and groups for whose benefit they were brought into being. This is the kind of book I have tried to write. It is based in the main on published material, and is intended to serve as an introduction to, and not as a substitute for, the study of Government publications and other original and specialist writings.

The scope of the book is wide, and I fully realise that each of its twenty-three chapters could have been written by a person more knowledgeable about that particular service or branch of social work than I am myself. Consequently, I am particularly grateful to my colleagues in the Universities of Liverpool and Manchester who specialise in the subjects dealt with here, and to my friends whose task it is to administer the social services I have described, for their constructive and helpful criticisms. The suggestions made

PREFACE

by Miss C. S. Blackburn, Miss E. K. Blackburn, Dr. D. Chapman, Mrs. J. Cole, Miss D. M. Deed, Mr. W. Duncan, Miss M. Irvine, Mrs. A. M. Pearson, Miss V. D. Pearson, Miss M. Price, Miss D. B. Read, Mr. and Mrs. B. N. Rodgers, Mrs. T. S. Simey, Mr. and Mrs. F. D. Weeks and Miss J. Woodward have done much to enrich and improve the work. I should also like to thank the authors and publishers who have given me permission to quote from their books and other writings. These are referred to in the text and full details are given in the bibliography at the end. In these acknowledgments I must include Messrs. Secker and Warburg Ltd., who have agreed to my using a sentence from Lewis Mumford's book *The Condition of Man* as a chapter heading; Mr. T. S. Eliot and Messrs. Faber and Faber, who have allowed me to quote from the former's poem *The Rock*, and Messrs. A. and C. Black, who have given me permission to use the quotation from Albert Schweitzer.

This book contains a good deal of material based on articles in periodicals and other writings published by voluntary and professional associations and I should like to record my thanks to the following organisations for the help I have received from their publications: The Institute of Almoners, Family Service Units, The Family Welfare Association, The National Association of Girls' Clubs and Mixed Clubs, The Society of Housing Managers, The British Medical Association, The National Association for Mental Health, the Nuffield Foundation, Political and Economic Planning, the Institute of Personnel Management, The Association of Psychiatric Social Workers, The National Council of Social Service, The Manchester and Salford Council of Social Service, and The National Council for the Unmarried Mother and her Child.

The secretarial work involved in the preparation of this book has been carried out by Miss D. Coleman and Miss B. Gilley, who have patiently dealt with its successive drafts. I am also grateful to Miss E. Eaves for reading and correcting a portion of the typescript, and to my sister Mrs. W. J. Simmons for helping to correct the proofs.

Finally, I should like to record my indebtedness to Professor T. S. Simey, without whose inspiration I should probably not have undertaken this task, and whose continued counsel and encouragement has helped me carry it through.

January 1952   M. PENELOPE HALL

PREFACE
TO THE FOURTH EDITION

A writer rash enough to call her book *The Social Services of Modern England* is in the position of Alice in the grip of the Red Queen. Run as hard as this unfortunate child might, still the Queen cried 'Faster! Faster!' and when at last they paused, and she was able to look around, she found herself in exactly the same place as before. 'If you want to get anywhere else you must run twice as fast as that,' remarked the Red Queen acidly. Similarly at the end of each successive attempt to catch up with current legislation and research, I find myself, as always, a little behind the times, conscious that, like its predecessors, the newly revised edition contains statements of fact that were correct when the manuscript was written but which have become out of date during printing, and opinions which might have been modified had the findings of a government enquiry or piece of current research been available a little earlier. The way out of this dilemma is with the reader. If he wishes, as he should, to get 'anywhere else' he must himself consult the government publications and other original and specialist writings to which, as stated in the Preface to the First Edition, this book is intended as an introduction.

The present revision has been more thorough and extensive than previous ones and several chapters have been entirely re-written. I am grateful to those colleagues and friends who have helped me with it by their advice, criticism and encouragement. For the errors and inadequacies which still remain despite their generous help I must take full responsibility, and can but trust that they will be rectified by the student's further reading, observation and practical experience.

September 1958   M.P.H.

PREFACE
TO THE FIFTH EDITION

IT is just over a year since the preface to the last edition was written. Still running faster, I have managed to catch up with the Mental Health Act, 1959, and I have rewritten Chapter XX so as to incorporate this important new legislation, though it is too soon as yet to assess its effects. I have also rewritten that part of Chapter IX which deals with child adoption so as to incorporate the changes brought about by the Adoption Act, 1958, and included in Chapter III references to the National Insurance Act, 1959, the Act which introduces graded retirement pensions. References to the recommendations of the Young-husband, Crowther and Albemarle Committees have also been incorporated in the appropriate chapters. The report of the Ingleby Committee should be available shortly after this edition is published, and this may act as a reminder to the student that it is his responsibility to carry on from the point at which I have, perforce, left off if his knowledge of the social services is to be up to date.

October 1960   M.P.H.

CONTENTS

CONTENTS

PART IV. THE AGED AND HANDICAPPED

PART V. COMMUNITY SERVICE

INTRODUCTION

'In the end all our contrivances have but one object: the continued growth of human personalities and the cultivation of the best life possible.'

LEWIS MUMFORD

CHAPTER I

THE DEVELOPMENT OF THE SOCIAL SERVICES

THE terms 'social service' and 'the social services' are relatively modern, having come into general use with the multiplication of public and voluntary provisions to further the well-being of members of the community which is one of the outstanding characteristics of our times. They are terms which are sometimes used rather vaguely, and there is no general agreement as to which services should be classified as 'social'.[1] Some vagueness is inevitable, and may even be desirable, in a sphere in which growth and change are continually taking place, but the establishment of criteria by which the social services can be distinguished from other forms of public and voluntary effort contributing to the general good is essential if the words are to have any meaning at all.

The generally accepted hall-mark of social service is that of direct concern with the personal well-being of the individual. Thus, Gertrude Williams, discussing 'The Recruitment and Training of Social Workers', postulates that the essence of social work is that it involves personal relationships, and illustrates this by pointing out that although a public utility service is undoubtedly for the public benefit, the main concern of the officer in charge is 'to see that the facilities provided are adequate in amount and efficient in operation. . . . His interest is in the object provided and not in the people who make use of it.'[2] The social worker, on the other hand, is concerned not only with the efficient administration of a particular service, but with the effects of its use on the personalities and relationships of the people taking advantage of it. Social service is essentially 'the manifestation of a personal interest in a human situation',[3] a recognition both of

---

[1] The inconsistencies contained in the Treasury classification are exposed by Professor R. M. Titmuss in *The Social Divisions of Welfare*, Eleanor Rathbone Memorial Lecture, 1956, pp. 10–11. Reprinted in *Essays on the 'Welfare State'*, 1958.

[2] Gertrude Williams, 'The Recruitment and Training of Social Workers', in Henry Mess and others, *Voluntary Social Services since 1918*, p. 227.

[3] The phrase is taken from a pamphlet entitled *Goodwill in a Great Society*, by Arthur Radford, late Professor of Social Administration, University of

3

the uniqueness and value of the individual and of our common humanity.

The basis of social service is then to be found in the obligation a person feels to help another in distress which derives from the recognition that they are in some sense members one of another. This sense of community and consequent obligation may be narrowly restricted to the family, tribe or neighbourhood, and the needs of all outsiders disregarded, or it may be widened to embrace mankind itself, and lead an Albert Schweitzer to abandon a brilliant career in Europe to give medical care to the primitive people of Central Africa, or a Father Damien to devote his life to the lepers of a remote Pacific island. In its simplest form it manifests itself in neighbourly action, but, as civilisation has advanced and life become more complex, its scope has widened, and its mode of expression become more varied and elaborate. In particular, the transformation, wherever and whenever it has occurred, from an agricultural society made up of close-knit and almost self-contained family groups living in isolated local communities, each responsible for the care of its own poor and unfortunate, to a highly industrialised urban society, has necessitated a complete rethinking of the implications of the question 'Who is my neighbour?' and its answer 'He that showed mercy unto him'.

But this is not all. As Roger Wilson has reminded us, 'There is a subtle but absolutely real difference between the social services and social service,'[1] and the social services are not simply the outgrowth or institutionalisation of private philanthropy or Christian charity. While this element, as exemplified in achievements in social reform as well as in personal service of such men and women as Lord Shaftesbury, Octavia Hill and Benjamin Waugh, cannot and should not be discounted, philanthropy was but one of the influences which, as the nineteenth century moved on and the long-term social effects of industrialism were perceived and documented, led to increased concern about the condition of the people and provided the tools with which to tackle the situation. While humanitarians, of whom Lord Shaftesbury is an outstanding example, and writers such as Charles Dickens and Mrs. Gaskell, brought the cry of exploited factory hands and workhouse children to the ears of public and Parliament, that able administrator and utilitarian Edwin Chadwick had realised that there was a

---

Nottingham (National Council of Social Service, 1948, p. 12). Professor Radford uses it as a definition of voluntary social service, but it appears from the context that he is using the term 'voluntary' to describe a method of approach rather than in the usual sense of 'non-statutory'. The pamphlet is now out of print.

[1] *Social Work in a Changing World*, Family Welfare Association, 1950, p. 1.

significant relationship between squalor, disease and destitution, and, backed by sanitarians such as Dr. Southwood-Smith, had begun the long-drawn-out campaign for cleansing the towns in the interests of public health, assisted by recurrent outbreaks of cholera, and it was the gradual realisation of the economic advantages which would follow from the greater efficiency of a literate, if not necessarily educated population, which helped to bring a measure of public support to those, such as Sir James Kay-Shuttleworth, who had begun the long slow task of the education of the populace. Apart from education, the chief efforts of the nineteenth-century social reformers to improve the condition of the people were directed towards creating passable environmental conditions in factory, mine and town, to protecting the weak, in particular factory children, from gross exploitation, and to guarding the people from infectious disease. These efforts led to the emergence of 'environmental' services whose objective was 'to improve the sanitary (or, generally speaking, the physical) surroundings of the individual, and thus indirectly to lead to better public health or greater amenities of life'. But alongside these environmental services, and overshadowing them in public interest as the nineteenth century gave way to the twentieth, have developed others, such as the 'personal' health services, education with its related welfare provisions, the care and protection of deprived and delinquent children, the care and training of the permanently handicapped, for example, in which the aim is 'to provide the individual, *as an individual*, with the precise form of assistance he needs'.[1] These services, which have as their objective the enhancement of the well-being of the individual citizen,[2] and which in some measure at any rate, recognise his uniqueness, and deal with him as an individual, even when meeting the needs he has in common with others, are the services described in this book. They may be provided by the State, by voluntary organisations, or, as, for example, occupational pensions, by private individuals or companies, but, during the last half-century, it is the statutory services whose development has been the most spectacular. To-day social services, provided by statute and administered either directly by central government departments or through local authorities, impinge on the life of the individual from the time of his entry into the world assisted by a midwife employed by the local health authority as one of its duties under the National Health Service Act, until his burial in a municipal cemetery, his funeral expenses met by a death grant from the National Insurance Fund.

[1] T. S. Simey, *Principles of Social Administration*, p. 4. Author's italics.
[2] The phrasing is based on the definition of a 'social service' given in *Political and Economic Planning*, 'Report on the British Social Services', 1937, p. 10.

5

INTRODUCTION

This assumption of statutory responsibility for the well-being of the individual citizen has been accompanied by a change in the scope of the social services. In a simple society with few class distinctions 'social service' is simply the help given by a man to his neighbour in difficulty, but in a society where there are extremes of wealth and poverty it becomes 'charity' or 'philanthropy', the assistance given by the rich to the poor. Thus the division of Victorian society into Two Nations, the Rich and the Poor, was reflected in its division into Givers and Receivers. The Rich were expected to give of their wealth and their leisure, the Poor to receive these gifts gratefully, and order themselves lowly and reverently to all their betters. To-day we are moving towards a more equalitarian society, and the principal social services are provided and paid for by the community as a whole for the benefit of all its members. Thus a universal scheme of social insurance has replaced the Poor Law, hospitals are no longer places where the sick poor obtain the medical and nursing care they cannot afford to obtain privately, but centres of specialised medical treatment for all, and, whereas in 1833 the Government made a grant to the National Society for the Education of the Poor in the Principles of the Established Church, to-day there is a Minister of Education charged with the promotion of the education 'of the people of England and Wales'.[1]

There were signs of this change in the scope of the social services, with the change of outlook it implies, in the years before the Second World War, but the real change in attitude came about with the war itself. As Professor Titmuss has shown in his survey of the developments in social policy during this period, the administrators who were entrusted with making preparations to meet the social chaos likely to be caused by aerial attack were so imbued with the tradition which placed the 'poor' and the 'fortunate' in separate categories that they failed to realise that total war is no respecter of persons. Hence they made the 'fundamental error' of assuming that the relief of the victims of air raids could be administered on Poor Law principles, and much misery and confusion was caused thereby.[2] However, under the stress of bombardment, and as a result of the drawing together of all members of the community in the face of a common danger, this attitude was profoundly modified and the way prepared for transforming the social services into a nation-wide scheme of mutual assistance and care.

The two modern developments just discussed, namely the increasingly important part played by the State in the furtherance of the well-being of the individual citizen, and the increase in the

[1] Education Act, 1944. Section I (1).
[2] R. M. Titmuss, *Problems of Social Policy*, H.M.S.O., 1950, pp. 250–256.

6

scope of the social services so that they cover the whole population, have been accompanied by a significant change of outlook on the part of both their administrators and their users. Social service benefits are now regarded as among the rights of citizenship, the citizen need not be ashamed of availing himself of them, nor may the administrator withhold them on the ground that the recipient is undeserving. This change in outlook has released many from the burden of shame and guilt which intensified the misery of unavoidable poverty and dependence on statutory or voluntary assistance in the days when this meant the forfeiture of self-respect, and it was almost a crime to be poor, but over-emphasis on rights has its own dangers, although these may be exaggerated. The belief that the extension and multiplication of statutory social services has led to a serious decline in personal initiative and family responsibility is widespread, but it has not been substantiated by social investigation.[1] The continuing existence of the supine and inadequate with their chronic tendency to dependence should not be discounted but there is no reliable information which goes to show that the development of the social services has added considerably to their numbers. Those who laboured to create the social services hoped rather that by freeing men and women from excessive anxiety and preoccupation with the struggle to obtain the bare necessities of life, they would provide them with opportunities for a more fruitful exercise of their talents and greater fullness of life, and the ordering of our social life so as to achieve this is one of the challenges of our times.[2]

A further problem arising from the greatly increased scope of the social services, and associated with the assumption of statutory responsibility for them, is the danger of their depersonalisation. It was stressed at the beginning of this chapter that social service is essentially personal in character, concerned with meeting the needs of the individual as such, but the social services have grown so vast and complicated that he may easily become a cipher, his needs assessed according to a formula. This tendency, together with the emphasis on 'right', has been carried furthest in the national insurance scheme, where benefits are obtained on a contractual basis, but it can be discerned in other services too, and, as Professor Radford has pointed out,[3] is not confined to the statutory services, but threatens all large organisations. It is one of the fundamental problems of the Great Society, and its manifestation

---

[1] See, for example, the discussion in Chapter XVIII of family responsibilities for the care of old people.

[2] Cf. Lord Beveridge, *Social Insurance and the Allied Services*, Cmd. 6404, 1942, p. 170, par. 455. This question is discussed further in Chapter XXIII.

[3] Op. cit., p. 10.

in the social services can be paralleled by similar developments in industrial and other relationships. In part it is a technical or administrative problem, but it is surely not beyond the wit of man to overcome the administrative difficulties of dealing with large numbers, given the right attitude of mind. This attitude was well expressed by the Rt. Hon. Lord Soulbury, then Chairman of the Assistance Board, in a speech made at a conference convened by the National Council of Social Service in 1941. 'Welfare provisions in various statutes', he said, 'show that the State has now accepted the view that social legislation should not be confined to money payments and legal safeguards, but should seek the good life of its citizens. . . . The good administrator must realise that every citizen is an individual with his own life to live and particular needs to satisfy, that he is a unique thing with a spirit indestructible and imperishable, and never a mere cipher in a mass of figures.' If means can be found to give expression to this ideal in the day-to day work of the vast army of social servants of the State, then one of the most difficult problems of the modern social services will have been solved.

At the same time as the social services have been extending their scope and coverage, social workers and administrators have been paying increased attention to complexities of human motivation and relationships, since, only if these are taken into account, can the services function effectively. Many of the problems encountered in administering the social services are problems of social and psychological maladjustment, which may or may not be associated with difficulties of meeting material needs, and these are problems which must be handled with understanding and delicacy using personal rather than mass techniques. Some students of social affairs consider that this is the point at which the voluntary organisations, with their smaller case loads and greater flexibility than the statutory services, have their special contribution to make, and the recommendations of the Denning and Harris Committees on the provision of a marriage guidance service, are examples of this type of thought.[1] But, important as is the contribution of the voluntary case work organisations, the State cannot solve its problems by handing over all cases demanding individual care to them. Some situations in which the psychological aspect is crucial, in which personal relationships are most important, and co-operation between client and worker fundamental if a readjustment between

---

[1] Final Report of the Committee on Procedure in Matrimonial Causes, Cmd. 7024, 1947. Report of the Departmental Committee on Grants for the Development of Marriage Guidance, Cmd. 7566, 1948.

For further discussion of the Reports of these Committees, see Chapter IX, and of the role of voluntary services in the welfare state, see Chapter XXII.

the individual and society is to be made, also necessarily involve an element of compulsion in the interests of both the individual and the community. In these cases, for example, cases of delinquency or more serious breakdowns in mental health, the State cannot abrogate its responsibility to voluntary bodies, but must itself evolve the techniques necessary to meet the situation. The shifting of the emphasis in social work from satisfying the material needs of those unable to provide for themselves to the adjustment of personal relationships and the integration of the maladjusted individual into society, is a challenge to all concerned with the development of the social services, both statutory and voluntary. It demands from the worker not only imaginative sympathy and patience, but also wisdom and understanding, including some knowledge of the human mind and its working and of the culture of the society of which the individual is a member.

The change of emphasis just described is one of the reasons for the increasing importance attached to the selection and training of social workers. It is now realised that in the delicate task of adjusting human relationships an insensitive or unskilled worker, however well-meaning, may do harm rather than good. Hence, although there is still room for the voluntary or untrained worker, responsible positions should be held by those who are devoting their lives to the work, and who have received special training, including both theoretical instruction and practical experience under careful supervision, designed to widen their knowledge and understanding. Some of the most important developments in social service in modern times have been in connection with the training of social workers, the emergence of the various social work professions, and their gradual recognition.

An important modern development which has profoundly affected the scope and character of the social services is the application of scientific method to the study of social problems. The efficient and energetic disciples of the political philosopher, Jeremy Bentham, were among the first to utilise this approach, and such reports as the Report on the Sanitary Condition of the Labouring Population, which was prepared at the request of the Poor Law Commission of which Chadwick was secretary, and published in 1842, marked a real advance in technique. The study of society began to claim a place among the sciences, and the need for an objective study of the facts of the situation as a preliminary to social action became more widely recognised.[1] This attitude found its most important nineteenth-century expression in Charles

---

[1] These developments are described in an article by O. R. McGregor, 'Social Research and Social Policy in the Nineteenth Century', *The British Journal of Sociology*, June 1957, pp. 146–157.

Booth's monumental survey, *The Life and Labour of the People of London*, and the conclusions reached as a result of this survey, and the little classic which followed it—B. Seebohm Rowntree's detailed study of York, *Poverty, a Study in Town Life*—revolutionised men's ideas as to the extent and causes of poverty, and prepared the way for much of the social legislation of the first decade of the twentieth century.[1]

Booth and Rowntree set a fashion in social surveys, and during the first half of the twentieth century a number of areas were studied in this way. The surveys were usually undertaken by a university or similar disinterested body, and set out to throw as much light as possible on economic and social conditions in a particular area. In general, they were confined to those aspects of social life which are most amenable to statistical treatment, and accumulated material on such objective facts as the extent and causes of poverty or overcrowding, rather than attempting to discover people's reactions to them. Recent social research is much more concerned with the attitudes of people to social conditions, and relationships between individuals and groups. This type of investigation demands great tact and skill on the part of the investigator, and great care is needed in the interpretation of the data thus obtained, but in the long run the findings of modern research workers may be as important in their influence on the next generation's approach to social problems and policy as the findings of Booth and Rowntree were in their day.

The development of social research is one aspect of the growth of the scientific attitude towards social questions, but this attitude also influences the whole approach of the social worker and administrator. The young social worker of to-day has to a large extent abandoned the moralistic judgments of his predecessors, and thinks instead in terms borrowed from medicine or psychiatry. In many respects this approach is an advance. From the patient labours of psychologists and psychiatrists social workers have gained much in increased understanding and the ability to deal sympathetically yet objectively with difficult situations and relationships, and have begun to realise that the sociologists' discoveries about the functioning of society may be as relevant to their work as knowledge of individual motivation and behaviour. But this increased toleration and understanding, vital as it is, does not release the social worker, nor for that matter the sociologist, from the obligation to consider the ethical values underlying his work. Rather, since increased knowledge brings increased power, it may be said to impose a greater obligation. As Karl Mannheim has pointed out, the crisis through which western civilisation is

[1] See Chapter II, pp. 15–17.

passing is essentially a crisis of valuation, and in the social, as in the natural, sciences there is always the danger that developments in technique may outstrip growth in spiritual and moral stature and ultimately result in disintegration instead of more abundant life. 'What is the good of developing child guidance, psychiatric social work, psychotherapy, if the one that is to guide is left without standards?'[1]

The more important modern developments in social service and the social services which have led up to the situation to-day are then, the increasingly active and prominent part played by the State, which has gradually assumed responsibility for meeting the basic needs of all its citizens; the widening of the scope of the social services to include the whole community, without distinction of social or economic class; the acceptance of the benefits they confer as rights; the increasing importance attached to the adjustment of relationships as well as of meeting material needs; the increased and increasing influence of the scientific attitude and the development of social research, and the growth of professionalism. The body of this book will, it is hoped, illustrate these developments and their implications in different fields. The section which follows describes the social services which have been evolved to meet man's basic material needs, that is those services which aim at the maintenance of a minimum economic standard when the family is unable to do this unaided, the provision of adequate health and medical care and of housing accommodation which makes possible the creation of a home. But fundamental as these services are, they are insufficient in themselves, and the multiplication of services designed to raise the standard of life of the whole community has been accompanied by the development of social case work and counselling which help the individual to overcome his personal difficulties and make constructive use of the more general services. This is described in Part II. The two following Parts deal with the efforts made by the community to meet the needs of those of its members who need special care and for whom it has a continuing responsibility, namely children and young people, the aged and the handicapped. The book ends with a discussion of neighbourhood work and of the development and possibilities of co-operation between the different forms of social service, and some further consideration of the broader issues associated with the assumption by the community of responsibility for the social well-being of its members.

[1] K. Mannheim, *Diagnosis of Our Time*, p. 25. See also Charles Vereker, 'By Whose Authority?', *Moral Welfare*, January 1958.

PART ONE

MEETING BASIC NEEDS

'Really I think that the poorest he that is in England hath a life to live as the greatest he.'—THOMAS RAINBOROUGH, 1647.

'Everyone has the right to a standard of living adequate for the health and well-being of himself and of his family, including food, clothing, housing and medical care and necessary social services, and the right to security in the event of unemployment, sickness, disability, widowhood, old age or other lack of livelihood in circumstances beyond his control.'—*Universal Declaration of Human Rights*, adopted and proclaimed by the General Assembly of the United Nations on the tenth day of December 1948, Article 25.

CHAPTER II

FAMILIES IN POVERTY

'They that are snarled and entangled in the utter lack of things needful for the body cannot set their minds on Thee as they ought to do, but when they are deprived of the things they so greatly desire, their hearts are cast down and quail for grief.'—*A Prayer for those that be in Poverty.* LUDOVICUS VIVES, 1492–1540.

T HE complexity of modern economic and social life is matched by the elaborate ramifications of its social services, but just as the primitive needs of food, clothing and shelter remain in the most refined and mechanised society, so must the guarantee that no member of the community perish from cold or hunger for lack of succour from his fellows remain the basic obligation of the Welfare State. 'Freedom from Want' is not the same thing as social security, in the full meaning of these words, and it is unfortunate that the two are identified in the minds of many people, but the one contributes to the other, and measures to secure minimum economic standards for all families at all times are basic to any comprehensive social policy. Moreover, to be effective such measures must be based on a real understanding of the reasons why individuals and families fail to reach this standard unaided.

A great advance towards the understanding of the extent and causes of poverty resulted from the researches of Charles Booth and B. Seebohm Rowntree. The former published the first of his seventeen volumes surveying *The Life and Labour of the People of London* in 1889; the latter's detailed investigation of social conditions in York, *Poverty, a Study in Town Life,* was published in 1901. Both investigators chose as their standard of poverty a bare sufficiency of the means of livelihood,[1] and Rowntree endeavoured to make this definition as precise as possible by working out as scientifically and objectively as he could a 'physical efficiency' standard based

[1] Booth describes this standard as follows: 'By the word "poor" I mean to describe those who have a sufficiently regular though bare income, such as 18s. or 21s. a week for a moderate family, and by the "very poor" those who fall much below this standard.' Charles Booth, *Life and Labour of the People of London,* Poverty Series, Vol. I, p. 33; cf. B. Seebohm Rowntree—*Poverty, a Study in Town Life,* ch. iv, pp. 86 ff. As a result of careful inquiry Rowntree suggests 21s. 8d. as the minimum necessary expenditure for physical efficiency for a family of man, wife and three children, which corresponds very closely with Booth's 18s.–21s. for a 'moderate' family. Corresponding figures for families of differing sizes are set out on p. 110 of *Poverty, a Study in Town Life.*

15

on the incomes required by families of different sizes to provide the minimum of food, clothing and shelter needed 'for the maintenance of merely physical health'. Families whose income failed to reach this level were regarded as living in 'primary poverty' or below the poverty line, and a house-to-house survey made in 1899 revealed that 15·46 per cent of the wage-earners or 9·9 per cent of the total population of York were in this position—that is, the income coming into the home was so small that even if every penny were spent on physical necessities it would still be inadequate to meet the family's needs.[1]

In addition to these families in primary poverty were those 'whose total earnings would be sufficient for the maintenance of mere physical efficiency were it not that some portion of it is absorbed by other expenditure either useful or wasteful'. Rowntree described the poverty falling under this head as 'secondary' poverty.[2] It was far more difficult to measure objectively and accurately than primary poverty. In the end all that he could claim was that, judging 'partly by appearance and partly by information given', he was able 'to arrive at a fair estimate of the total number of persons living in poverty in York'. From these he subtracted the number in primary poverty, the difference represented those in secondary poverty. By these not very accurate means he estimated that 43·4 per cent of the wage-earning class or 27·84 per cent of the total population of the city were living in poverty. Deducting the 9·91 per cent in primary poverty, this left 17·93 per cent in 'secondary' poverty.[3]

The extent of poverty revealed by the investigations of Booth and Rowntree caused some concern, especially as it was claimed that the findings of the two investigations were strikingly similar. In London 30·7 per cent, in York, 'a typical provincial town', 27·84 per cent of the population were in poverty, and so 'we are faced by the startling probability that from 25 to 30 per cent of

[1] 'And let us clearly understand what "merely physical efficiency" means. A family living on the scale allowed for in this estimate must never spend a penny on railway fare or omnibus. . . . They must write no letters to absent children, for they cannot afford to pay the postage. They must never contribute anything to their church or chapel, or give any help to a neighbour which costs money. They cannot save, nor can they join a sick club or Trade Union because they cannot pay the necessary subscriptions. The children must have no pocket money for dolls, marbles or sweets. The father must smoke no tobacco and must drink no beer. . . . Should a child fall ill it must be attended by the parish doctor, should it die, it must be buried by the parish. Finally, the wage-earner must never be absent from his work for a single day. If any of these conditions are broken the extra expenditure involved is met, *and can only be met*, by limiting the diet, or in other words by sacrificing physical efficiency.' B. S. Rowntree, op. cit., pp. 133–134. Author's italics.
[2] Op. cit., pp. 86–87.   [3] Op. cit., pp. 117–118.

the town populations of the United Kingdom are living in poverty.[1] But these overall totals, immediately disturbing as they were, were, in fact, not as objectively assessed as was commonly supposed, nor was the attempt to estimate the extent of primary and secondary poverty taken together as far-reaching in its effects on social policy as the distinction Rowntree made between primary and secondary poverty and his measurement of the extent and his analysis of the causes of the former. It was this which constituted the real challenge to current beliefs about and attitudes towards the poor.

Legislators and philanthropists of the Victorian era had emphasised the personal element in the causation of poverty. It was assumed that with hard work, thrift and sobriety a workman should be able to keep himself and his family, put by sufficient to cover periods of sickness or unemployment, and save for his old age, when in any case his children would contribute to his support. Failure to achieve and maintain this financial independence, which was regarded as the basis of self-respect, was believed to be due to exceptional misfortune, or to deplorable weakness on the part of the individual or family concerned, and hence the Victorians relied on the painstaking case work of the Charity Organisation Society and kindred organisations to relieve the distress of the 'helpable' and 'deserving'[2] and consigned the remainder to the harsh mercies of a deterrent Poor Law. But it had now been shown that nearly ten per cent of the population were living on incomes insufficient to maintain them in a state of 'bare physical efficiency' even if carefully and wisely spent, and when Rowntree went on to analyse the causes of this 'primary' poverty his findings, confirmed a few years later by the investigations of Professor A. L. Bowley and Mr. A. R. Burnett-Hurst in five English towns of varying size and industrial character[3] demonstrated conclusively that, while personal factors might be present, poverty in the early years of the twentieth century was due in the main to factors which were beyond the control of the individual concerned. These factors were earnings so low or so irregular as to be insufficient to meet the family's needs, families so large that their needs could not be met by wages which were sufficient to keep average families above the 'poverty line', and interruptions of earnings through sickness, unemployment, old age or premature death, which the family

[1] Ibid., p. 301.
[2] These case work methods and the principles underlying them are described in Chapter VII, while the relationship between the voluntary organisations and the Poor Law is described in Chapter XXII.
[3] A. L. Bowley and A. R. Burnett-Hurst, *Livelihood and Poverty*, 1915. The five towns investigated were Northampton, Warrington, Stanley (a mining town in Co. Durham), Reading and Bolton.

had not the resources to meet, as the low wages earned during employment precluded saving. At the conclusions of his 'Five Towns' survey Bowley wrote, 'Of all the causes of primary poverty which have been brought to our notice, low wages is by far the most important. To raise the wages of the worst-paid worker is the most pressing social task with which the country is confronted to-day.'[1]

This sums up the position at the end of the first decade of the twentieth century. Twenty or thirty years later the situation had altered in some important respects. The total amount of dire poverty had declined. This was shown, for example, by a second survey of York which Rowntree undertook in 1935, and which demonstrated that the number of persons living below the 'physical efficiency standard' of 1889[2] had decreased from 15.46 per cent of the working class or 9.91 per cent of the whole population of York to 6.8 per cent of the working class or 3.9 per cent of the total population of the city. This was an advance, but further investigations revealed that 31.1 per cent of the working class or 17.7 per cent of the total population of York were in receipt of incomes which, although they might reach the 'physical efficiency' level, were insufficient to reach a slightly less austere standard based on 'human needs'. This standard allowed each family an income which, in addition to paying the rent and providing a bare sufficiency of food, clothing, warmth, light and household necessities, left a small margin to cover such items of personal expenditure as bus fares, burial clubs, tobacco, trade union subscriptions, newspapers and the wireless licence, items which although not essential for physical survival were regarded as necessary components of civilised living.[3] The results of other investigations made during the inter-war years varied slightly according to the precise standards by which human needs were assessed, the character of the area and the state of trade when the survey was made, but they were sufficiently close to demonstrate that even if standards had risen since the beginning of

[1] Op. cit., p. 42. Rowntree's survey of York revealed that the immediate cause of poverty was lowness of wage in 51.96 per cent of the total number of those living in primary poverty. He concludes, 'It is thus seen that the wages paid for unskilled labour in York are insufficient to provide food, shelter and clothing adequate to maintain a family of moderate size in a state of bare physical efficiency'. *Poverty, a Study of Town Life*, pp. 131 and 133.

[2] Allowances were, of course, made for the rise in prices during the intervening years. The equivalent of the 17s. 8d. (exclusive of rent) considered in 1899 to be adequate to meet the 'physical efficiency' requirements of a man, wife and three children was 30s. 7d. in 1936 prices. *Poverty and Progress*, pp. 102 ff.

[3] Rowntree has described the methods he used to arrive at his 'human needs' standard in a little book called *The Human Needs of Labour*, which was published in 1937. A man, wife and three dependent children were allowed 43s. 6d. exclusive of rent; cf. 30s. 7d. on the 'physical efficiency' standard.

the century, as late as the 1930's a disquietingly large proportion of the citizens of this country were without adequate resources to meet their basic human needs.[1]

Just as Booth and Rowntree had analysed the causes of the poverty they uncovered, so the later investigators attempted to assess the contributions made by various economic and social factors to the new situation. The decline in the amount of dire poverty was attributed in the main to the increases in the wages of unskilled workers brought about by the 1914–18 war, while the declining birth-rate with its consequent reduction in the numbers of families with large numbers of young children was considered to be a contributory factor. At the same time the wages paid in some occupations were still too low to meet the needs of the wage-earner with several children to maintain, while owing to the prolonged trade depression of the inter-war years, which hit certain occupations and areas particularly hard, poverty due to the interruption of earnings, particularly as a result of unemployment, was widespread. By this time social insurance schemes were well established, but the benefits received, while they were sufficient to prevent destitution, were inadequate to meet the 'human needs' of their recipients. The situation was summed up by Sir William (now Lord) Beveridge at the beginning of his *Report on Social Insurance and the Allied Services*: 'During these years [i.e. the years immediately preceding the Second World War] impartial scientific authorities made social surveys of the conditions of life in a number of the principal towns in Britain, including London, Liverpool, Sheffield, Plymouth, Southampton, York and Bristol. They determined the proportions of people in each town whose means were below the standard assumed to be necessary for subsistence, and they analysed the extent and causes of that deficiency. From each of these social surveys the same broad result emerges. Of all the want shown by the survey, from three-quarters to five-sixths, according to the precise standard chosen for want, was due to interruption or loss of earning power. Practically the whole of the remaining one-quarter to one-sixth was due to failure to relate income during earning to the size of the family . . . abolition of want requires a double redistribution of income through social insurance and by family needs.'[2]

[1] For example, 16 per cent of the families included in the Merseyside Survey made in 1929 were found to be living below a poverty line slightly more austere than Rowntree's 'human needs' standard; 15·4 per cent of the Sheffield working class families surveyed in 1931–2 and 10·7 per cent of the Bristol families investigated in 1937 were similarly placed. (*Survey of Merseyside*, Vol. I, p. 153; A. D. K. Owen: *Survey of the Standard of Living in Sheffield*, p. 24; Herbert Tout: *The Standard of Living in Bristol*, p. 24.)

[2] *Social Insurance and the Allied Services*, Cmd. 6404, 1942, par. 11, p. 7.

The need for some form of family or children's allowances to overcome the poverty caused by the failure to relate income during earnings to family needs had been urged by a group of reformers, prominent among whom was Miss Eleanor Rathbone,[1] for many years before Lord Beveridge insisted that no scheme of social security would attain its end without them. Their adoption was advocated on three main grounds.

In the first place, it had long been common knowledge and experience that if wage rates remained unchanged, the wages of the unskilled labourer reached their maximum in his early manhood. Consequently, as the number of children increased the standard of living of the family tended to decline, and if wages were low to start with it was in danger of sinking below the poverty line with the coming of two or three children. This was confirmed by the findings of both earlier and later social surveys.[2] For example, Rowntree in his earlier study showed that the life of a labourer was marked by five alternating periods of want and comparative plenty. During three of these periods he was in poverty, in childhood when his constitution was being built up, in early middle life and in old age.[3] Thirty-seven years later, as the result of the 1935 survey he showed that 52·5 per cent of the working-class children under one year of age were living below the human needs standard; that 47 per cent would probably remain in poverty as defined for five years or more, and 31·5 per cent for ten years or more.[4] The results of the Bristol Survey made in 1937 were similar—10·7 per cent of the families surveyed were below the minimum standard, but these included more than 20 per cent of the children under 15, and the author comments: 'It is an appalling fact that one working-class child in every five comes from a home where the income is inadequate to provide a bare minimum standard according to the austere survey rules.'[5] Thus it was clear that poverty was bearing hardest on those who, in the interests of the future well-being of the community, as well as for their own sakes, should be the first to be protected from it, that is the children and the mothers who were bearing them and caring for them.[6]

[1] Her book, *The Disinherited Family*, first published in 1924, is the classic statement of the case for family allowances. A new edition, with an Epilogue by Lord Beveridge, and a chapter on 'The Family Allowances Movement, 1924–1947', by Eva M. Hubback, was published in 1949. See also Mary Stocks, *Eleanor Rathbone*, particularly ch. viii.

[2] *Social Insurance and the Allied Services*, Cmd. 6404, 1942, par. 11, p. 7.

[3] *Poverty, a Study of Town Life*, pp. 136–137.

[4] *Poverty and Progress*, p. 459.   [5] H. Tout, op. cit., p. 36.

[6] This was recognised during the war, when it was generally accepted that expectant and nursing mothers and young children should receive priority allocations of milk, eggs, and other essential foods.

Moreover these conditions meant that many more people than were shown by the surveys to have been in poverty at a particular time must have suffered from it at one or more periods in their lives, and might be feeling its effects for the remainder of them.

The relatively high incidence of primary poverty among families where there were several young children was perhaps the strongest argument which could be brought forward in support of family allowances. Another contention which carried some weight during the years between the wars was that such allowances would encourage people to have more children. The decline of the birthrate was becoming a matter of national concern, and it was recognised that it was due mainly to voluntary family limitation, which in its turn could be attributed, in part at least, to the increasing costs of rearing children, and the economic disadvantages suffered by parents of large families compared with the single or childless in the same social class.[1] It was acknowledged that family limitation was more widely practised among the middle and upper classes than among the semi-skilled and unskilled workers, to whom family allowances would bring the greatest proportionate increase in income, and some feared that the proposed allowances might be dysgenic in their effect, but the advocates of the allowances urged that at least they would be concrete evidence of the community's recognition of the importance of family life and the status of motherhood.

The third consideration put forward by its advocates in support of a scheme of family allowances was the unsatisfactory relationship between income during earning and the provisions made from public funds to cover periods when earnings were interrupted. These provisions included dependants' allowances, and in spite of the inadequacy of the insurance and assistance payments to bring the families benefiting from them above the 'human needs' standard, it might happen that a man whose family was large, but whose wages were small, could obtain more than he normally earned from State or social insurance funds when out of work. This was an obviously undesirable situation, and in order to prevent it, a 'wages stop', which meant that the assistance given would not be allowed to rise beyond the man's normal earnings, even if his family's needs entitled him to a larger sum, was operated by the Unemployment Assistance Board. It provided no real solution, however, as it simply meant that the body administering statutory relief to large families 'must in certain cases penalise children by underfeeding them, because in certain circumstances these children

[1] This issue is discussed by the Report of the Royal Commission on Population, 1949, ch. xiv, particularly pars. 366–369.

would again be underfed'.[1] As social insurance and assistance became more comprehensive it became increasingly clear that any system granting an income sufficient for subsistence when earnings were interrupted could only operate successfully as part of a policy of ensuring that the money coming into the house was also sufficient when the head of the household was in work. Suggestions that a national minimum wages policy would solve the problem were put forward from time to time, and minimum wage scales are actually enforced in certain occupations by means of 'wages councils'.[2] It was generally recognised, however, that this was not the real answer to the problem, for 'a national minimum for families of every size cannot in practice be secured by a wage system, which must be based on the product of a man's labour and not on the size of his family'.[3] The only way out of the impasse was by the introduction of family allowances, and this was finally accomplished by the Family Allowances Act 1945, the first of the postwar 'social security' measures to become law.

It is significant that the Act is the 'Family' and not the 'Children' Allowances Act. Allowances are 'for the benefit of the family as a whole',[4] not to meet the specific needs of the individual child on whose behalf they are paid, and they are payable to private families only and are not to public authorities or voluntary organisations caring for children.

Special provisions have been made to cover cases where the children are living apart from or have been removed from the care of their parents. Children removed from their homes by order of the juvenile court and detained in remand homes or approved schools, or committed to the care of a local authority as a 'fit person' cease to count for family allowance purposes, and the same applies to children over whom the local authority has assumed parental rights.[5] On the other hand children away from home in

[1] Joan Simeon Clarke, 'The Assistance Board' in William A. Robson, *Social Security*, p. 156. Third edition, 1947.

[2] Joint councils of workers and employers, together with a proportion of independent members. They were originally known as 'trade boards' and were first set up in 1909 to cover certain 'sweated' industries. Their scope has been extended by successive enactments, the latest major one being the Wages Councils Act, 1945. The minimum wages decided on by wages councils can be enforced by prosecution in the criminal courts.

[3] Beveridge, op. cit., p. 154, par. 411; cf. the words of Sir W. Jowett (then Minister of National Insurance) when introducing the second reading of the Family Allowances Act: 'Under any wage system as I conceive it, whether in a capitalist or socialist society, the remuneration which a worker gets must depend on the service he renders. It cannot depend on the size of his family.' Parliamentary Debates, Official Reports, Fifth Series, 1944–5, Vol. CCCCVIII, col. 2262.

[4] Family Allowances Act, 1945, s. 11.

[5] A child home on licence from an approved school, or allowed by the local

22

hospital or school may continue to be included in their parents' family for allowances purposes even though their absence be prolonged and no contribution is made towards their support, but the child placed in the care of the local authority children's department or a voluntary organisation by arrangement with his parents, ceases to count for allowances purposes at the end of four weeks unless the claimant is contributing at least eight shillings a week towards his support. The allowances are inalienable, however, so that it is not possible for the parent to authorise the organisation caring for the child to draw it on his behalf.

Claims for family allowances may be made on two grounds, the ground of 'issue', that is that the claimant is the parent or treated as the parent of the child, or on grounds of 'maintenance', that is that the claimant is providing more towards the cost of keeping the child than any other person. Married couples living together may claim for stepchildren (unless they are children of an earlier marriage which has been ended by divorce) and legally adopted children as 'issue'. Children of separated or divorced parents may be claimed for by either parent according to the circumstances, but only one claim can be made in respect of each child and if the parents cannot agree on this point the Minister of Pensions and National Insurance may decide. The mother of an illegitimate child may include him in her family provided that he is living with her, or she is contributing an amount, equal to the allowance, towards his maintenance.

Allowances are payable in respect of second and subsequent children. A child ceases to count for allowances purposes when he reaches the upper limit of school-leaving age unless he is undergoing full-time instruction in school or is an apprentice, in which case he continues to count until he has attained the age of eighteen years. As laid down by the original Act, a child still attending school or apprenticed ceased to count on the 31st July following his sixteenth birthday, but this penalised families whose children remained at school after passing the General Certificate of Education at 'Ordinary' level. In 1954 the Central Advisory Council for Education (England), after investigating the reasons why children able to profit from more advanced work left school prematurely, issued a Report in which they pointed out that there are strong financial inducements to withdraw boys and girls from school

authority which has assumed parental rights over him to return home for a limited period or remain with a relative or friend, may have an allowance claimed in respect of him. Family Allowances Act, 1945, Section 11, as amended by the Family Allowances and National Insurance Act, 1956, Section 5.

before the age of eighteen and that the choice of sixteen as the maximum age for family allowance purposes was 'not only arbitrary, but from the educational point of view, most unfortunate, as it gives the impression that the State takes for granted a normal leaving age of sixteen for those who stay at school beyond fifteen,[1] and they recommended that the upper age limit for inclusion in the family for allowances purposes should be raised to eighteen. This was accomplished by the Family Allowances and National Insurance Act, 1956.

Family allowances are financed by the Exchequer and there is neither a needs nor an insurance contribution test. The only tests are those of nationality and domicile.[2] This means that they are payable to families where the income reaches a high level and these families also benefit substantially from the tax reliefs which are granted in respect of dependent children. Indeed, a family where income tax is paid at standard rate gains little from the receipt of family allowances compared with its gain from tax remission, especially as allowances are taxed.[3] It has therefore been suggested that family allowances might be withdrawn from families benefiting from income tax relief and that the consequent loss to families near the bottom of the tax scale, who would be most likely to suffer hardship by such a change, could be avoided by suitable adjustments to the income tax codes. An alternative might be to retain allowances and amend income tax codes so as to reduce concessions for dependent children in the upper income limits.[4]

The article suggesting that family allowances might well be withdrawn from families benefiting from tax remission in respect of their children ends by remarking that if this were done it might then be possible to give more to poorer families whose income is below the taxable limit. This raises the issue of the adequacy or otherwise of the rates at which family allowances are paid. Originally paid at a rate of 5s. a week, this amount was raised to 8s. in 1952, while the Family Allowances and National Insurance Act, 1956, increased the amount payable in respect of the third and

[1] Ministry of Education, *Early Leaving*, H.M.S.O., 1954, para. 11, pp. 41–2.
[2] Family Allowances Act, 1945, Section 24; Family Allowances (Qualifications) Regulations, 1946.
[3] It has been pointed out that for a family which pays income tax at the standard rate, the allowance for the second child is worth only £13 18s. 5d. a year, those for the third and subsequent children are worth £15 10s. 0d. each. The tax reliefs are worth, for each child (including the first), £42 10s. 0d. a year if the child is under eleven, £53 12s. 6d. if the child is over eleven and under sixteen, and £63 15s. 0d. if over sixteen and still at school or college. Leading article in *The Manchester Guardian*, January 11, 1958.
[4] The grading of family allowances is discussed in Joan Barnes, *Family Allowances*. Conservative Political Centre, 1958.

24

subsequent children to 10s. a week. These amounts are well below subsistence level, as may be seen by comparing them with the National Assistance Board scales.[1] This raises the question as to whether it is desirable social policy for the State to relieve parents of the whole of their financial responsibility for rearing their children. Both the Beveridge Report and the Report of the Royal Commission on Population contend that the cost of a child's maintenance should be borne in part at least, by his parents. The Royal Commission on Population was quite emphatic on this point, 'We think it only right,' it is stated, 'that some substantial part of the cost of a family and each addition to it should be borne by the individual parents directly concerned.' 'A readiness to incur reasonable financial sacrifice for one's children is in our view an indispensable element in the responsible code of values which must form the basis of a successful population policy; and to attempt to build on the assumption that parents cannot be expected to make such sacrifices would be a profound psychological mistake.'[2] Family allowances may be used to help raise the standards of families with children nearer to those of families without, but not to equate the two. In any case, they are not the only contribution made by the community to the costs of child-raising. Income tax reliefs have already been mentioned, and in addition to these financial measures are the community provisions such as school meals and welfare foods. The Swedish sociologist, Alva Myrdal, argues that in so far as the aim is to meet the needs of the children, provision in kind is cheaper and more efficient than the granting of cash allowances, and 'when society intervenes by placing an economic burden on other income receivers and thus compels them to participate in the cost of child-bearing, it is also reasonable that society shall reserve the aid for the children and shall keep control of its utilisation'.[3] She also thinks that cash allowances tend to encourage the less responsible rather than the more responsible elements in the population. In favour of cash grants it can be argued that communal services involve heavier administrative costs than cash grants, and the latter, by leaving her more freedom of choice as to how she will feed, clothe and care for her child, stress the mother's close relationship with him.

In the first draft of the 1945 Act made payable to the father as the person responsible for the maintenance of the family, family

[1] Since 27 January 1958 these have been 20s. a week for a child between eleven and sixteen years, 17s. for a child five to eleven years, and 14s. 6d. a week for a child under five years of age. (National Assistance (Determination of Need) Amendment Regulations, 1957.)

[2] Report of the Royal Commission on Population, Cmd. 7695, 1949, par. 452, p. 168. Cf. the Beveridge Report, par. 417, p. 156.

[3] Alva Myrdal, *Nation and Family*, p. 144.

allowances were in the end made the property of the mother, who signs the claim form, although either parent may draw the allowance. This is a public recognition of both her status in the home and her responsibility for the housekeeping, and was largely due to the efforts of women members of Parliament. The originators of the campaign for family allowances were not only deeply concerned about the health and welfare of the family, but also about the effects of her financial dependency on the married woman's position and outlook. They realised that the great majority of wives were indifferent to or apathetic about their dependent status, but believed that there were a 'very large and growing number [of working-class wives] either consciously or subconsciously in revolt'.[1] These women, it was said, felt that society, while paying tribute 'in plenty of sugary phrases' to the value of their services, paid for them in nothing else, and it was believed that the endowment of motherhood would enable wives and mothers to feel they had some share in the wealth of the community which depends on them for its very existence. The rapid extension of married women's work outside the home during and since the Second World War has radically altered the position compared with the early twenties, and the payment of the allowance to the mothers probably has less status value now than it would have had then, but it is still of practical and psychological significance. Family allowances, as well as being an essential element in the social security scheme, have played their part in raising the position of the married woman from that of dependant to that of partner.

[1] E. F. Rathbone, *The Disinherited Family*, 1924, pp. 82 ff.

CHAPTER III

SOCIAL INSURANCE

THE investigations into the extent and causes of poverty made between the close of the nineteenth century and the Second World War showed that it had two main causes, namely failure to relate income during earning to the size of the family and interruption or loss of earning power. In the chapter just concluded we have been considering the cash allowances and other provisions made by the community to overcome the want due to failure to relate income during earning to family size and to benefit all families with children. The measures taken to support families whose incomes have been interrupted or discontinued form the subject of this and the following chapter. They consist of a nation-wide scheme of social insurance, covering the whole population and providing maternity, widowhood, sickness, unemployment, and industrial injury benefits, retirement pensions and a death grant, supplemented by a State scheme of social assistance providing for those whose needs cannot be met, or are inadequately met, by social insurance.

The underlying principle of social insurance is that all persons within its scope contribute at an agreed rate to an insurance fund, to which employers and the State also contribute, on the understanding that if certain contingencies befall them they can claim benefits from the fund at standard rates, without any test of need. The benefits are claimed as a right provided that the requisite number of contributions have been paid.

This method of providing against contingencies to which all are liable was widely adopted by trade unions and friendly societies during the nineteenth century. It was first applied on a national scale in this country by Mr. Lloyd George, who introduced it in 1911 as a means of providing against temporary interruption of earnings by sickness or unemployment. The first health and unemployment insurance schemes were very limited in scope, but they were subsequently widened to include sickness and unemployment benefits for all manual workers and for non-manual workers with limited incomes.[1] In time a contributory scheme providing for

[1] Certain categories of workers such as private domestic servants and nurses of the sick were excluded from unemployment insurance, while teachers, civil

widows, orphans and old people was linked with National Health Insurance. The loss of income resulting from injury at work was not covered by social insurance, but was met by a scheme of 'workmen's compensation' by which individual employers were legally bound to compensate employees for the loss of earning power resulting from injuries sustained 'out of or in the course of employment', or from certain specified industrial diseases.

The pre-war social insurance schemes thus made some provision to meet the main contingencies of life, but they were insufficient in themselves as a safeguard against want. Only persons working 'under a contract of service or apprenticeship' were included, so that the small trader and others working on their own account were not protected, unless they joined a limited scheme providing health and pensions benefits to voluntary contributors introduced in 1938. Moreover, the benefits received were inadequate to meet the needs of many families, particularly the sickness and disablement benefits, which did not include dependants' allowances, and the old age pensions, which only amounted to 10s. for the pensioner and 10s. for his wife. Further, there were many people in need but unable to claim insurance benefit, either because they failed to satisfy the contribution test, or had exhausted their right to benefit, or were faced with a difficulty not provided for in any scheme of social insurance.

The needs of individuals and families who had not qualified for benefit, or for whose needs the current rates of benefit were inadequate, or who were outside the scope of the social insurance schemes, were met by the various forms of social assistance. Thus there were non-contributory old age pensions for old people over seventy who had not qualified for the contributory pensions, and a nationally financed and administered scheme (Unemployment Assistance) for the able-bodied unemployed who had exhausted their right to benefit from the Unemployment Insurance Fund or had never qualified for it, while Public Assistance, the lineal descendant of the Elizabethan Poor Law, provided assistance in cash or kind to destitute individuals and families unable to obtain help from any other source. In practice, it catered for a miscellaneous collection of unfortunates ranging from the respectable family, unable to manage on sickness or disablement benefit, to vagrants and unemployables. It also provided institutional care for orphans and other destitute children, and for the old and infirm who had no one to care for them. In all forms of social assistance the financial help given consisted of grants from public funds,

---

servants, local government officials and certain other workers were excluded from both schemes as provision was made for them in other ways.

national or local, to individuals and families because they were in need and according to their need. Consequently the giving of relief was preceded by an investigation of the applicant's[1] needs and resources, and the relief given was calculated on a scale designed to provide a bare maintenance, but no more.

Taken together, the social insurance and assistance schemes in operation on the eve of the Second World War were comprehensive and far reaching, and Lord Beveridge wrote at the beginning of his Report that 'provision for most of the many varieties of need through interruption of earnings and other causes that may arise in modern industrial communities has already been made on a scale not surpassed and hardly rivalled in any other country in the world'.[2] But reasonably good as they might be, they were far from perfect. They had grown up piecemeal, and there was little co-ordination between different schemes, which were administered by a medley of different government departments,[3] not to mention the local authorities, who under the general direction of the Ministry of Health, were responsible for the administration of the Poor Law. There were differences in contribution and benefit rates which led to serious hardships and anomalies,[4] and, while the benefits and allowances were sufficient to enable the families concerned to obtain the bare necessities of physical existence, they were insufficient to meet their human needs as measured by the austere standards of the social investigators of the time. It was *in spite of* these elaborate provisions that in the thirties between 10 per cent and 15 per cent of working-class families in England and Wales were living in primary poverty, and three-quarters to five-sixths of this poverty was due to interruption of earning power.[5]

The Second World War, like the First, acted as a stimulus to social and economic planning, and hardly was the immediate danger of invasion past when far-seeing administrators began to consider what measures should be taken to prepare for the social

---

[1] Notice the term used. An insured persons *claims benefit*—it is his right, by contract; a person in need *applies* for *assistance* and can only obtain it if the official investigating the application is satisfied that the need is real and cannot be met in any other way. However, if need is proved, the applicant has a right to the assistance, and it cannot be refused on the grounds that he is 'undeserving'.

[2] Op. cit., par. 3.

[3] The most curious historical anomaly was, perhaps, the administration of non-contributory old age pensions by the Department of Customs and Excise.

[4] The most notorious of these was the absence of dependants' allowances from the National Health Insurance Scheme so that families with no other resources had to apply for Public Assistance as supplementary relief.

[5] An excellent critical description of the social insurance and assistance services at the time of the issue of the Beveridge Report is contained in William A. Robson (ed.), *Social Security*, Pt. I, first published 1943, second edition 1947.

advance which it was hoped would follow a victorious peace. As part of this planning Mr. Arthur Greenwood, who was then Minister without Portfolio, and in charge of reconstruction plans, set up a committee under the chairmanship of Sir William (now Lord) Beveridge 'to undertake, with special reference to the interrelation of schemes, a survey of existing national schemes of social insurance and the allied services including workmen's compensation, and to make recommendations'. The Report was issued eighteen months later, in December 1942, and proved to be a much more imaginative and far-reaching document than its somewhat uninspiring terms of reference would suggest. It was no less than a comprehensive plan to secure that all members of the community would at all times be free from want, and even this was regarded as part of a much wider and far-reaching programme, for 'Want is only one of five giants on the road of social reconstruction and in some ways the easiest to attack. The others are Disease, Ignorance, Squalor and Idleness.'[1] A concerted attack on all these giants was required if real progress was to be achieved, and Beveridge made it clear that, in his view, the comprehensive insurance and assistance services proposed in the Report could only be fully effective if their introduction were accompanied by the introduction of children's allowances, if health and rehabilitation services were available to all members of the community, and if the mass unemployment of the inter-war years were avoided in future.[2] Given all this, the proposed provisions to secure the maintenance of an adequate income if earnings were interrupted or brought to an end would fit into their proper place as part of a comprehensive scheme of social security.

The Beveridge Report was accepted in principle both by the National Government which was in power when it was published and the Labour Government which succeeded it, and within two years steps were taken to implement it. The first necessity was a unified system of administration, and in November 1944 the Ministry of National Insurance was created and made responsible for the administration of the social insurance and assistance services including family allowances. At that time war pensions and related services were the responsibility of a separate ministry, the Ministry of Pensions, but by an Act passed in 1952 the Minister of National Insurance assumed these responsibilities and became the Minister of Pensions and National Insurance. Meanwhile the Family Allowances Act had been passed in 1945, the National Insurance

[1] Beveridge, op. cit., par. 8, p. 6.
[2] These are the 'three assumptions' underlying the Social Security Plan. They are discussed in some detail in Part VI of the Report, pars. 409-43, pp. 153-65.

and National Insurance (Industrial Injuries) Acts in 1946, and the National Assistance Act followed two years later in 1948. With the exception of the Family Allowances Act, which became operative in 1946, the 'appointed day' on which these enactments, together with the National Health Service Act and the Children Act, came into operation was 5 July 1948.

The social insurance and assistance services brought into being by the legislation listed above embodied the main recommendations of the Beveridge Report, but with some important modifications which will be discussed later. The intention of both the Beveridge Plan and subsequent legislation was that a comprehensive system of social insurance, which according to the Plan was to provide benefits at subsistence level, should cover the main contingencies likely to lead to interruption or cessation of earning power, and that this should be supplemented by an equally comprehensive national assistance service for those whose contingencies were not covered or whose needs not fully met by social insurance. Hence separate schemes of insurance against unemployment and sickness, old age and widowhood were replaced by a unified scheme covering loss of income through inability to earn, and providing additional payments to meet the extra expenditure attendant on birth and death.

With certain specified exceptions national insurance is universal in scope. 'Subject to the provisions of this Act, every person who on or after the appointed day, being over school-leaving age and under pensionable age, is in Great Britain, and fulfils such conditions as may be prescribed as to residence in Great Britain, shall become insured under this Act and thereafter continue throughout his life to be insured.'[1] The exceptions are persons with an income of less than £156 a year, who, if they are not employed under a contract of service, may claim exemption from paying contributions, although this naturally involves loss of benefit rights,[2] and married women for whom special arrangements have been made.

The position of a married woman varies according to her status. A woman who is an employed person, that is, works for gain for an employer, is insurable under the scheme, but may, if she wishes, claim exemption from paying contributions. In this case she will receive none of the social insurance benefits in her own right, but

[1] National Insurance Act, 1946, Section I (1).

[2] The position of such persons was reviewed by the National Insurance Advisory Committee in 1954. At that time, when the income limit for exception was £104, they numbered about 200,000, 28 per cent of whom were engaged in household duties for parents or relatives, 23 per cent invalids living with relatives, 10 per cent widows with 10s. pensions, 10 per cent members of religious communities. About 30 per cent were in receipt of national assistance. Cmd. 9432, par. 14.

must rely on those to which she is entitled by virtue of her husband's insurance. The exemption of the woman from the payment of contributions does not excuse the employer from paying his share, nor does it exempt either the woman or her employer from contributing to the Industrial Injuries Insurance Fund. A married woman who is working on her own account, for example as a music teacher or milliner, is insured under the Act, but is excepted from the payment of contributions unless she chooses to pay them, in which case she is entitled in her own right to the benefits available to this category of persons. The married woman who was not insured when the scheme started, and has not worked for gain since, is not insured under the scheme, but she is entitled to a wide range of benefits from her husband's insurance. However, if prior to her marriage she was insured as an employed or self-employed contributor, she may elect to pay contributions as a 'non-employed' person and in this way receive certain benefits in her own right, the most important of which is the retirement pension. Alternatively, she may elect to remain in the insurance scheme without paying contributions. If she does this she retains her legal status as an insured person, and continues to be entitled to benefits for a limited period.

Apart from these two categories all persons over school-leaving age and under pensionable age are compulsorily included in the scheme whatever their occupation, income or social class. Participation is not only a right but an obligation, and the obligation overshadows the right in that while the payment of contributions is enforced, the choice as to whether or not he will claim benefit rests with the insured person himself. Contributions and benefits are at a flat rate, that is they do not vary with income,[1] but, for the purposes of the scheme, insured persons are divided into three categories, 'employed', 'self-employed' and 'non-employed'.

Employed persons are those who work 'under a contract of service or apprenticeship' for another person or organisation. They include wage- and salary-earners of all kinds, and their employers have to pay part of the contributions which are paid into the fund for their benefit. Employed persons qualify for all benefits under the general scheme, and are also insured under the National Insurance (Industrial Injuries) Act.

Self-employed persons work for gain, but on their own account, and include shopkeepers, farmers, solicitors, and other business and professional men who are not under the control of an employer. They are responsible for paying their own contributions, and are entitled to all benefits except unemployment benefit.

[1] The National Insurance Act, 1959, introduces graded superannuation benefits. See below, pp. 40–41.

Non-employed persons do not work for gain. They may do a great deal of work voluntarily, but the income which they receive is not a direct reward for their work and is not dependent on it or related to it. They contribute at a lower rate than the other two classes, but are not entitled to sickness or unemployment benefit. They are, however, entitled to maternity benefit, widow's benefit, retirement pensions and the death grant.

Contributions are paid into the Insurance Fund out of which benefits are paid at a known rate in virtue of the claimant having fulfilled the contribution conditions laid down in the Act.[1] In general these are twofold. In the first place a minimum number of contributions must have been paid since the entry of the claimant into insurance, and, in addition, a specified number must have been paid or credited[2] during the contribution year prior to the claim.[3] Entitlement to widow's benefit or to a retirement pension depends, not on the record of the previous contribution year, but on the average number of contributions paid or credited since entry into insurance. These conditions imply, as do all the arrangements connected with the collection of contributions and the payment of benefits, that the insured person, when claiming his benefit, is drawing out what he and his fellows have paid in, that is that benefits have been 'earned', and this goes a long way to explain the general acceptance of the scheme. As applied to a comprehensive social security scheme for the whole nation this insurance principle presents serious difficulties, however, and these difficulties are increased when contributions and benefits are payable at flat rates regardless of income.

When the original health insurance scheme was being worked out by Lloyd George and his advisers prior to the passing of the Act of 1911, one of the major problems which had to be settled was whether the scheme should be a true insurance founded on actuarial principles, or a superficially more attractive scheme whereby accumulation of funds would be kept to a minimum, and the Societies operating the scheme would rely on attracting year by year a sufficient number of young members to provide the cash to cover the benefits of older members whose benefits would be likely to exceed their contributions. In the end, we are told, Lloyd George 'decided to be virtuous', an attempt was made to relate con-

---

[1] National Insurance Act, 1946. Third Schedule, 'Contribution Conditions'.

[2] Contributions are credited to an insured person for weeks of certified sickness or registered unemployment or during the receipt of maternity or injury benefit. During these times he is not required to pay contributions himself.

[3] For a quarter of the insured population this starts in March, for a quarter in June, for a quarter in September, and for a quarter in December.

tributions paid to estimated risk, and reserves were accumulated.[1] Sound finance had won the day, and W. G. Braithwaite recorded, 'It was a very great decision, and meant everything to the financial success of the Health Insurance, and the whole difference between success and failure.'[2] But, as future events were to show, the real problem postulated by social insurance is that of reconciling sound actuarial finance and social needs, and the problem is intensified if the scheme is dependent on flat rate contributions, which are limited to amounts which even an unskilled worker can afford to pay, while at the same time it is expected to provide benefits which will make a substantial contribution towards the maintenance of the claimant and his family when earning power is interrupted or has ceased. This problem became more complicated as the years went on and the scheme became more comprehensive, until the question had to be faced as to whether the Beveridge Plan, which sought by means of an insurance scheme to provide a wide range of benefits at subsistence level covering the whole population, was in fact a workable method of ensuring freedom from want.

One drastic modification in the Beveridge Plan was made at the start. Benefits have never been paid at subsistence level. Beveridge regarded this modification of his scheme as disastrous. For him the payment of social security benefits as of right at subsistence level was an objective which 'should appeal to anyone who believes in individual responsibility and freedom. For assistance subject to a means test is assistance on condition of being poor, is discouragement to thinking and saving for oneself. Insurance benefit as a right without inquiry into means is a floor below inequalities. Assistance subject to a means test is a ceiling above which no one may rise.'[3] He recognised that the application of this principle raised subsidiary issues, for example the question as to whether insurance payments should be adjusted to cover inequalities of rent, either between family and family or between one part of the country and another,[4] but he was sure of his objective, which was that 'every citizen willing to serve according to his powers has at all times an income sufficient to meet his requirements',[5] and he

---

[1] The story of this controversy is told in *Lloyd George's Ambulance Wagon*, the Memoirs of William J. Braithwaite, 1911–12. These were published in 1957, with an Introduction by Sir Henry N. Bunbury, from which the above quotations are taken. It is prefaced by a valuable Commentary by Professor Titmuss.

[2] Op. cit., p. 127.　　　　　　　　　　[3] Article in *The Times*, 9 November 1953.

[4] The problem of rent is discussed in par. 193 of the Report. In the end he decided against varying rent allowances according to regions on the grounds that inequalities of rent are a housing problem and should be dealt with as such and not concealed by insurance benefits. In his autobiography, *Power and Influence*, p. 305, he describes this as 'an outstanding victory of advisers over chairman'.

[5] *Social Insurance and the Allied Services*, Cmd. 6404, 1942, p. 165, par. 444.

intended that when earning power was interrupted this income should be guaranteed by insurance benefits. However, the Government of the day finally concluded 'that the right objective was to give a rate of benefit which provided a reasonable insurance against want and at the same time took account of the maximum contributions which the great body of contributors could properly be asked to pay',[1] and the initial benefit rates fixed by the National Insurance Act, 1946, were somewhat below those proposed in the Beveridge Report, which were based on a careful calculation of the amounts required for subsistence at 1938 prices with an addition of 25 per cent to cover the increased cost of living.[2]

During the years which have elapsed since the Act became operative the problem of benefit rates has been further complicated by the rapidly rising cost of living, a rise which has been much steeper and higher than was anticipated by Beveridge, and although successive Acts have been passed increasing benefit rates they still remain below subsistence level. This is shown by the fact that, according to the latest available report of the National Assistance Board, in December 1958 the proportion of households receiving insurance benefits which also received assistance was in the case of retirement pensions, 20·4 per cent, in the case of sickness benefit 11·6 per cent, in the case of widow's benefit 11·6 per cent, and in the case of unemployment benefit 19·1 per cent. These percentages are somewhat lower than in previous years and the position has been described as one in which 'a compulsory universal insurance scheme provides a grant-in-aid towards the maintenance by national assistance under a means test of those who lose other sources of income'.[3] It can be defended on the grounds that in return for his contribution the insured person obtains a reasonable cover in times of interruption or loss of earning power, particularly if the interruption is of relatively short duration, and that, if National Assistance scales are generous, they will cover the areas of greatest need which are the areas on which resources should be concentrated, while if the inquiries are conducted in the spirit of the Act, the dislike of the 'means', or as it should more correctly be termed the 'needs', test will lessen as bitter memories of the Poor Law die away. It is, however, a pattern of social security which should not be accepted without careful examination of its implications and of the alternatives which might be substituted for it.

In his commentary on W. G. Braithwaite's Memoirs, Professor R. M. Titmuss has pointed out that the risks covered by the present

---

[1] Harold E. Raynes, *Social Security in Britain*, p. 21.
[2] *Social Insurance and the Allied Services*, Part III, Section 1.
[3] Iain Macleod and J. Enoch Powell, *The Social Services, Needs and Means*, Conservative Political Centre 1951, p. 31.

social security scheme fall into two distinct categories. On the one hand there are the long-term and 'desirable' risks of which the two main ones are a quiverful of children and survival to a ripe old age, on the other the short-term 'undesirable' risks of sickness, industrial injury and unemployment.[1] One of these 'desirable' risks, that of having a number of dependent children to support, is met by a system of family allowances financed wholly out of taxation, and is right outside the social insurance scheme. Old age pensions were excluded from the proposed contributory insurance schemes in 1911, but in 1925 this decision was reversed by the Widows, Orphans and Old Age Contributory Pensions Act, and this, in the opinion of Professor Titmuss, contributed largely to 'the gradual transformation of a contribution to a sickness and unemployment club to a system of taxation to support a variety of social policies'.[2]

The Beveridge Report and the legislation which followed retained survival beyond working age as one of the contingencies to be covered by a comprehensive system of social insurance, and now the problem of providing adequate retirement pensions without imposing too great a burden on the Insurance Fund is proving the most obstinate of all our social security problems, while our present uncertainties about pension policies demonstrate only too clearly the difficulty, if not the impossibility, of reconciling sound insurance finance and social need in old age. The nature and extent of this difficulty is seen when we consider the relationship between contributions paid and benefits received, particularly in the case of late entries into the scheme. In working out the contributions needed to cover retirement pensions under the National Insurance Act it was assumed that the average insured person enters into insurance at the age of sixteen, but since contributory pensions were not introduced until 1926, no one retiring at the present time has paid contributions for the whole of his working life, and still less has he paid the higher contribution rates introduced in 1948; and this position will continue for a number of years. Moreover, while increases in pension rates, such as those that have been taking place at frequent intervals since 1948, can, and usually are, accompanied by increases in the contributions payable, such contribution increases are not retrospective, they apply to the future and not to the past, and hence in a period of inflation there will always be a tendency for benefits to be at a higher rate than the claimant's contributions warrant. Figures published in the Phillips Committee Report show a discrepancy between the accumulated value of contributions since 1 January 1926 and the capital value of a pension payable on 1 January

[1] *Lloyd George's Ambulance Wagon*, Commentary, pp. 49–50.
[2] Ibid., p. 51.

SOCIAL INSURANCE

1954, of £700 in the case of a single man, £1,440 in that of a married man with a wife of the same age, and £1,025 in that of a single woman.[1] The present financial position is made even more difficult by the number of middle-aged men and women who had not previously been insured who were brought into the scheme in 1948. These were only required to pay contributions for ten years in order to obtain full pension rights, and their contributions therefore only constitute a small portion of what, given normal survival, they will receive in benefits. Meanwhile men and women over pensionable age are increasing both in numbers and in proportion to the working population,[2] and, although estimates vary, it appears inevitable that the cost to the nation of national insurance pensions will increase and there will be a growing deficit on the working of the National Insurance Fund.[3] The simplest solution to these financial problems would be to remove provision for retirement from the national insurance scheme altogether and finance it out of taxation. 'In a sentence', to quote Professor Titmuss, 'the obvious answer is that these costs—the long term and foreseeable dependencies of old age—should be shouldered by progressive taxation just as the long-term dependencies of childhood are.'[4]

But obvious as this remedy may appear to Professor Titmuss, it is not, as yet, widely accepted. For example, both the Phillips Committee and the sponsors of the 1958 Labour Party memorandum on security in old age wished to retain the insurance principle, though for different reasons. The Phillips Committee advocated its retention on three grounds. First, they did not think that 'a system under which constantly mounting charges had to be met from taxation would continue to be tolerated without the introduction of some form of income test (Family allowances are not subject to an income test, but the amounts involved in providing for retirement would be much larger); secondly, they considered that 'contributions provide an important measure of social discipline since everyone is aware that higher rates of pension must be at once accompanied by higher contributions'; and thirdly, they thought that the existence of an accepted actuarial basis 'is a useful basis when benefits are under consideration', since it imposes some

[1] Report of the Committee on the Economic and Financial Problems of the Provision for Old Age (Cmd. 9333), 1954, Table XIV, p. 41.
[2] This increase is considered in more detail in Chapter XVII.
[3] The Phillips Committee reporting in 1954 estimated that even if there were no increases in benefit rates this deficit would amount to £126m. in five years' time and £364m. in twenty-five years' time. The Labour Party booklet, *National Superannuation*, estimates £145m. in 1960, £295m. in 1970, and £424m. in 1980. Table V, p. 113. See also *Provision for Old Age*, Cmnd. 538, pp. 6-7.
[4] R. M. Titmuss, 'Pension Systems and Population Change', *Political Quarterly*, Vol. XXVI, 1955, p. 161.

check on reckless increases, and to some extent removes the difficult question of rates of contribution from the arena of political
controversy.[1] The objections made by the Labour Party to the
financing of old age pensions by taxation are rather different.
They are based partly on 'the very real limit to the amount which
the taxpayer—and that includes the working-class taxpayer—is
prepared to pay in taxes' (though, in fact, income tax is much
more equitable in its incidence than flat rate insurance contributions), and partly on the 'legitimate fear among trade unionists
that if the State took over the whole responsibility for financing
social security benefits, then the State might one day slash those
benefits in order to weather an economic storm. As long as the
benefits are earned by payment of contributions and financed out
of an Insurance Fund, they are felt to be something which the
worker receives as a right and which no politician can take away
from him.'[2]

It would seem, then, that there is every likelihood that retirement pensions will be retained among the national insurance benefits at any rate for some time to come, but this does not rule out
possible modifications designed to ease the financial situation. One
such modification suggested by the Phillips Committee, was to
raise the minimum pensionable age. At present this is 65 for men
and 60 for women, but elderly persons are encouraged to continue
working after this age by being awarded an extra 1s. 6d. a week
for each six months further employment, an inducement which is
continued until the age of 70 for men and 65 for women. The
limited extent to which this inducement operates was revealed in
the course of investigation made by the Ministry of Pensions and
National Insurance in 1954 into reasons for retiring or continuing
at work. While the great majority of the 12,009 men questioned
said that they knew that a higher rate of national insurance pension could be obtained by staying on at work only seven in a
thousand said that this was their reason, although one in four said
that knowledge of the arrangement had influenced them in making their decision.[3] The Phillips Committee, with two dissentients,
recommended that provisions should be made to raise the minimum pensionable ages to 68 for men and 63 for women, though
they agreed that 'to avoid hardship a substantial interval must
elapse before an increase in the minimum pension ages can come
into force'. They estimated that, despite the longer than average
periods of sickness and unemployment that these older men and

---

[1] Report, p. 44, par. 167.
[2] *National Superannuation*, Labour's policy for Security in Old Age, p. 10.
[3] *Reasons given for Retiring or Continuing at Work*—Report of an Inquiry by
the Ministry of Pensions and National Insurance, 1954, par. 30, p. 8.

women would be likely to experience, there would be an appreciable net saving, and they considered that such hardships as were likely to result from this change could be adequately mitigated.[1] Nevertheless, they said that they were 'fully conscious that any such proposal is likely to meet with strenuous and sincere opposition', and so perhaps were not altogether surprised that it was not accepted by the Government.

Since most people expect to, and do, live a number of years after retirement, benefit rates matter more to them than they do to insured persons experiencing relatively short interruptions of earning power, and, as we have seen, the proportion of households receiving insurance benefits and also receiving National Assistance, is higher among retirement pensioners than among any other group. The problem is not only one of subsistence, however, though living at subsistence level is difficult enough for an old person. Hardship is also caused by the drop in income consequent on retirement which may be very considerable and is keenly felt.[2] The problem is one of relative, not simply of absolute poverty, and it is difficult to see how a universal and compulsory national insurance scheme based on flat-rate contributions and benefits can overcome it.

In recent years the problem of income maintenance during retirement has been eased for a large and increasing number of employed persons because of their entitlement to an occupational pension of one sort or another. A survey made by the Government Actuary in 1958 indicated that about $6\frac{1}{2}$ million people in industry and commerce belonged to such schemes, 5 million more than in 1936.[3] Such schemes may be contributory or non-contributory and may or may not include a lump sum or ex-gratia payment among the advantages they offer. Their growth has been encouraged by the Government, and, on the principle that income should only be taxed once, money set aside by firms under a properly constituted pension scheme is exempt from taxation. Taxation is levied on the pension or annuity when it is paid, but it is beneficially treated as earned income, while lump sums are tax free, and Professor Titmuss suggests that these occupational pensions may in this way result in a greater loss to the Exchequer, and so be more 'costly' than national insurance pensions. They also have the two further disadvantages in that, if limited to particular firms, they discourage industrial mobility,[4] while they may be used as a reason for not engaging elderly workers, though this difficulty can be overcome.

[1] Report, pars. 182–191, pp. 47–51.
[2] See below, Chapter XVIII.
[3] Ministry of Pensions and National Insurance, *Provision for Old Age*, Cmnd. 538, p. 7.   [4] 'Pension Systems and Population Change', op. cit., pp. 164–165.

But, as Professor Titmuss sees it, these disadvantages are not so serious as the schemes' long-term effect. To him 'the outlines of a dangerous social schism are clear, and they are enlarging; . . . Already it is possible to see two nations in old age; greater inequalities in living standards after work than in work; two contrasting social services for distinct groups based on different principles, and operating in isolation from each other as separate autonomous instruments of social change'.[1]

In May 1958 the Labour Party set out its proposals for dealing with this situation in a booklet *National Superannuation*, which outlined a scheme for wage-related pensions. All insured workers, while continuing to contribute towards, and in time be eligible for, a flat-rate pension as at present, would, in addition, participate in a new National Superannuation Scheme with contributions and benefits on a percentage basis, subject to a floor and a ceiling. This, it was claimed, 'would satisfy the social requirements of the second half' of the twentieth century just as flat-rate pensions suited the first half.[2] The Government proposals contained in *Provision for Old Age*[3] issued six months later by the Ministry of Pensions and National Insurance were similar in many respects to those of their rivals. They were given legislative sanction by the National Insurance Act, 1959.[4] When this Act becomes operative, in April 1961, flat-rate insurance contributions, which will be at a new and slightly lower rate than at present, will be supplemented in the case of employed persons aged 18 and over whose remuneration exceeds £9 a week and who have not been contracted out because they belong to non-participating employments, by graduated contributions. These will consist of contributions from both employer and employee, the amount due from each being 4¼ per cent of any amount up to £6 by which the remuneration exceeds £9.

All insured persons, including those who pay graduated contributions, will remain covered for flat-rate pensions and other existing National Insurance benefits such as sickness and unemployment benefit. Those who have paid graduated contributions will, when they retire, receive in addition a graduated benefit equal to sixpence for each contribution unit paid. The contribution units are to be £7 10s. for men and £9 for women when the scheme first comes into operation but quinquennial increases in contributions are envisaged and these will, in turn, affect the

[1] Ibid., p. 166.
[2] *National Superannuation*, p. 17.
[3] Cmnd. 538.
[4] An outline of the provisions of this Act in as far as they are concerned with graduated pensions is contained in the Ministry's leaflet N.I. 111, July 1959, *Outline Guide to the New Graduated Pension Scheme*.

benefits paid. To be recognised as a non-participating employment, the employment concerned must have a superannuation
scheme providing retirement benefits as favourable as those
derived from graduated contributions.

These proposals represent an important departure in social
policy, at least as far as pensions are concerned. The State's financial responsibility is no longer limited to guaranteeing minimum
subsistence, as proposed in the Beveridge Plan. In future older
citizens will be helped, to a limited extent at any rate, to maintain
the economic and social standards to which they were accustomed.

The problems posed by making provision for retirement are so
serious and complex, and the number of pensioners, both present
and future, so large, that, of recent years, more attention has been
paid to the retirement pensions than to any other insurance benefit. But the major problem posed by retirement pensions, that of
framing a scheme covering the whole population which will provide benefits which will go at least some way to meeting the claimant's financial needs, and be sufficiently varied to cover major
differences in circumstance, and which, at the same time, will be
both equitable and actuarily sound, occurs in connection with
other benefits also. It is met, for example, in connection with
maternity benefits. A 'maternity grant', a lump sum of (in 1958)
£12 10s. for each child born, is paid to any woman, married or
single, who has either satisfied the contribution conditions herself
or can claim by virtue of her husband's insurance. In addition,
although both she and the woman whose child is born in hospital
or other public institution have both paid the same contribution,
an additional 'home confinement' grant of £5 is paid to the
woman whose child is born at home or in a nursing home or other
institution not financed out of public funds. This is because the
woman confined in hospital is maintained there free of charge as
well as receiving medical treatment.[1] Special provision is also made
for the woman wage-earner. It takes the form of a maternity
allowance, at present £2 10s. a week for eighteen weeks, beginning
eleven weeks before the expected date of the confinement. It is
paid to women who have themselves paid twenty-six Class 1
(employed person) or Class 2 (self-employed person) contributions in the fifty-two weeks ending thirteen weeks before the
expected week of the confinement, and (in order to get the allowance at the full rate) have paid or been credited with at least fifty
contributions during that same fifty-two weeks. These allowances
were designed primarily to help 'the working woman who will
return to work a comparatively short time after her confinement

[1] Women confined in hospital in an emergency may receive a home confinement grant.

and who needs an insurance benefit to assist her in view of her loss of earnings during her absence from employment',[1] and their introduction was intended to protect both mother and child from the undesirable consequences of over-long continuance at work in the weeks before the confinement takes place. In point of fact, however, many women employed during pregnancy do not return to gainful employment after the baby's birth.[2] On reviewing the situation, the National Insurance Advisory Committee concluded, however, that while the position was not satisfactory, 'If, in ensuring that the allowance is paid to these women (i.e. those for whom it was designed) it is found that the allowance is also paid to other women for whom it was not designed—because they do not intend to return to work at the end of the allowance period—that is an inevitable result of making title to benefit depend on the position of the woman at the beginning of the period for which benefit is payable,'[3] and they did not consider that there was any escape from this dilemma. A benefit which was, in intent, a maintenance benefit has become for many women an additional source of income used to help them meet the special expenses attendant on the birth of the child, such as provision for the baby's needs,[4] but it is retained because for other women, interruption of earning power because of pregnancy and child birth creates serious financial problems and a maternity allowance to cover this period is of great benefit to both mother and child.

The treatment of widows is more flexible under the present scheme than it was under the former Widows, Orphans and Contributory Old Age Pensions Act. Under that Act the widow of an insured person received 10s. a week for life, and small additional payments if there were dependent children. The contribution conditions and benefit rates meant that a young able-bodied woman, quite capable of self-support, could claim what was in effect pocket money for the rest of her life if she lost her husband within a few years of marriage, while a widow with children, or an elderly or incapacitated woman, without other resources, had to apply for Public Assistance to supplement a pension which was quite inadequate for her needs. Present-day legislation provides continuing

[1] Ministry of National Insurance, *Maternity Benefits*. Report of the National Insurance Advisory Committee. Cmd. 8446, 1952, par. 67, p. 18.

[2] Inquiries made by the Ministry revealed that, out of 2,300 recipients of maternity allowance who were interviewed from two to eight months after confinement, only one-quarter had gone back to work or registered for employment; two-fifths had no intention of doing so; and the rest either spoke of going back later, or had not made up their minds. Ibid., par. 64, p. 17.

[3] Ibid., par. 67, p. 18.

[4] For evidence of this see Griselda Rowntree, 'The Finances of Founding a Family', *Scottish Journal of Political Economy*, October 1954, p. 226.

benefits for widows unable to support themselves either because they are elderly or infirm or have young children to care for, but, after an initial period to enable her to readjust herself to changed circumstances, the young, able-bodied widow without children is expected to support herself.

A widow obtains benefit by virtue of her husband's insurance. He must have paid at least 156 contributions into the insurance fund, and the yearly average of contributions paid or credited since entry into insurance must have been at least fifty. With the successive increases granted since 1946 to the present day, a widow receives a widow's allowance of £3 10s. a week for the first 13 weeks after her husband's death, together with £1 for the first child under school-leaving age, and a supplement of 12s. to the family allowance of each of the younger children. At the expiration of this period she receives no further widow's benefit unless she is over fifty, or is the mother of a child or children under school-leaving age. In the latter case she is entitled to a 'widowed mother's allowance'. This was originally £1 6s. a week for the woman herself and 7s. 6d. for the eldest child—younger children being excluded from insurance payments on the ground that they were benefiting from the family allowance scheme. Moreover, the widowed mother could not earn more than £1 10s. a week without corresponding reductions being made in her allowance. Legislation passed since has improved the widowed mother's position. The allowance for herself and her first child is increased to £3 10s., and weekly allowances of 12s. in addition to the family allowances are payable for each of the younger children. Further, the amount which a widowed mother can earn before her allowance is affected is greater than the amount allowed to a retirement pensioner or elderly widow without dependent children. It is £5 a week without any deduction, 6d. for each 1s. earned from £5 1s. to £6 a week, and 1s. for each 1s. earned thereafter.[1] If a widowed mother is over forty when she ceases to be entitled to a widowed mother's allowance, that is normally when the youngest child reaches school-leaving age, she can claim a pension of £2 10s. a week until she reaches the age of sixty when a retirement pension will be substituted. An elderly widow who was between fifty and sixty at the date of her husband's death, and who at that time had been married at least three years, is entitled to claim a widow's pension of £2 10s. a week. Women whose husbands died before the introduction of the new scheme continue to receive the old pension of 10s. a week, but it has been increased to £2 10s., with the addition of children's allowances at standard rates for those who

---

[1] National Insurance (Earnings) Regulations, 1960.

43

have young children, and to £2 10s. for the elderly or infirm,
Widow's benefit ceases to be payable if the woman marries again.
or while she is cohabiting.[1]

Guardian's allowances of 27s. 6d. a week are payable in respect
of an orphan child one of whose parents was insured.

One of the many improvements brought about by the National
Insurance Act, 1946, is that contribution and benefit rates for
sickness and unemployment now correspond. In either case the
claimant must have paid not less than twenty-six contributions
between entry into insurance and the date of his claim, and must
have at least fifty contributions of the appropriate class credited to
him for the contribution year prior to his claim. Benefit does not start
until the fourth day of sickness or unemployment, but a claimant
will receive back pay for the first three days if he is sick or unemployed on twelve days during the period of thirteen weeks beginning
with the first day. The disqualifications contained in the previous
schemes are continued. For example, unemployment benefit is not
payable if the unemployment is directly due to a trade dispute, and
it may be disallowed for a maximum period of six weeks if the
claimant left work of his own accord, or was dismissed for misconduct or if he refuses suitable work, while sickness benefit may
be forfeited for a maximum period of six weeks if the claimant
refuses medical examination or fails to submit himself for treatment
without good cause, or does not comply with certain prescribed
rules of behaviour.

The standard weekly rate of sickness and unemployment benefit
for persons over eighteen is £2 10s. for the single person and £4
for a married man. Children's allowances of 15s. for the eldest and
7s. each for subsequent children are also payable. If 156 contributions have been paid, sickness benefit continues indefinitely; otherwise it is limited to 312 days. There is no reduction for the first
eight weeks in hospital, although the sick person is receiving free
board, lodging and treatment under the National Health Service
Act, but at the end of this period benefit is reduced by 10s. a
week if the claimant has dependants, if not, by 20s. a week. There
is no further reduction for the in-patient with dependants, provided he arranges that all but 10s. a week (which he is allowed for
his own personal expenditure) is paid to his dependants, but the
patient without dependants has his benefit reduced to 10s. a week
after a year in hospital (15s. in cases of respiratory tuberculosis).
These reductions also apply to widows' and retirement pensions.

Unemployment benefit normally continues for 180 days, but

[1] The present provisions for widows are critically discussed in a book which
was published in 1958: Peter Marris, *Widows and their Families*, a Survey by the
Institute of Community Studies.

44

this period may be extended if the claimant has a good insurance record up to a maximum of 492 days (nineteen months). Under the National Insurance Act, 1946, a special 'extended unemployment benefit' was payable, on the recommendation of a local insurance tribunal, to persons who had exhausted their statutory right to benefit. This was discontinued in July 1953, since the contingency of exceptional unemployment against which it was originally provided had not materialised.

The death grant is the only complete innovation among the benefits of post-war social insurance legislation, the others being extensions or modifications of existing provisions. Its introduction was welcomed by social workers and others, who were aware of the sacrifices made by many families to maintain their weekly payment to the 'burial club' so as to be sure of a decent funeral for themselves and their loved ones. Lord Beveridge estimated that the administration costs of the Industrial Life Offices which conducted the greater part of this business were as high as 7s. 6d. in the £,[1] and pointed out that a large number of policies lapsed each year as the owner was unable to keep up the premiums.[2] These considerations led him to recommend that grants, adequate to cover the cost of a simple but seemly funeral, be included among the benefits of the proposed social insurance scheme, and this recommendation was adopted. The death grant is payable in respect of an insured person, or his wife, child, or widow, and ranges in amount from £25 for an adult to £7 10s. for a child under three years.

The National Insurance Act thus provides cash benefits for insured persons and their dependants when they are faced with a reduction in income or increase in expenditure caused by the birth of a child, the death of a husband or father, the sickness, unemployment or retirement of the chief wage-earner. A separate but linked scheme makes special provision for persons injured at work, or suffering from diseases directly attributable to the nature of their employment. This scheme, which is embodied in the National Insurance (Industrial Injuries) Act, 1946, makes a complete break with previous methods of dealing with these particular misfortunes. Before it came into operation industrial injuries were outside the scope of social insurance. Each employer was legally liable to pay compensation to any workman injured during the course of his employment, the amount paid being related not to

[1] Beveridge, *Social Insurance and the Allied Services*, par. 157, p. 66.

[2] In each of the three years just before the war the number of policies in six of the largest offices which, after some premium had been paid on them, ended prematurely, by lapsing, surrender for cash, or being made free for a reduced sum, was about two-thirds of the total number of policies issued and taken up in the year, more than half of these two-thirds were forfeited completely.' Ibid., par. 186, p. 73.

the extent of the injury,but, subject to a statutory minimum, and after 1940 including dependants' allowances, to the workman's earnings. The onus of making and enforcing his claim, if need be in court, rested with the injured person, who, unless he was backed by a powerful trade union, or able to obtain legal aid in some other way, might be at a serious disadvantage owing to his ignorance of the law, which, although apparently simple, was exceedingly difficult to interpret, and to his unfamiliarity with court procedure. The scheme was concerned solely with monetary compensation for loss of earning power, and was not associated with any measures of rehabilitation. In general it was unsatisfactory from the point of view of both worker and employer.

The present scheme is a form of social insurance, administered by the Ministry of Pensions and National Insurance. Workers, employers, and the State all contribute to a common fund, the contribution rates being 9d. from employer and 8d. from worker for an adult man, 5d. from worker and 6d. from employer for an adult woman, 4d. for a boy and 3d. for a girl under eighteen. The benefits are payable any time after a person enters employment—there is no contribution test—and are of three kinds, injury benefit, disablement benefit, and death benefit.

Injury benefit is payable for six months at the rate of £4 5s. a week for an adult, with reduced benefits for younger workers. If a child under school-leaving age is injured at work injury benefit is paid to his parent or guardian, the amount depending on whether he is in full- or part-time employment. Dependants' allowances are paid at the usual rates, and persons under eighteen with dependants are entitled to benefit at the full adult rate.

At the expiration of six months, injury benefit is replaced by disablement benefit provided that a Medical Board is satisfied that there is likely to be a permanent loss of physical or mental faculty. In the case of a minor injury this may take the form of a lump sum gratuity, not exceeding £280, but where the disablement is more serious it consists of a weekly pension assessed, not in relation to the worker's previous earnings, but according to the extent to which he is disabled 'by comparison with a normal healthy person of the same age or sex'. It is not affected by subsequent earning, though an 'unemployability supplement' of £2 10s. a week is payable if the injured person is permanently incapable of work, or of earning more than £52 a year. 'Special hardship' and 'constant attendance' allowances are also payable. These arrangements recognise 'a certain similarity between the position of the soldier wounded in battle and that of a man injured in the course of his productive work for the community. Neither is liable to have his pension reduced on account of what he may earn after the injury;

each is compensated not for loss of earning capacity but for whatever he has lost in health, strength and the power to enjoy life.'[1] Dependants' allowances are payable if the beneficiary is entitled to an unemployability supplement or is receiving approved hospital treatment.

The National Insurance Act, 1951, made concessions to widowed mothers, but the childless widow of a man killed in an industrial accident or dying as the result of an industrial disease fares better than the woman whose husband has died a natural death. The widow considered able to earn her own living receives a pension of £1 a week; the one who has children to look after £2 16s. a week, together with an allowance of 15s. for the eldest child and 7s. for each of her subsequent children. In either case her pension ceases on remarriage, but she then receives a gratuity equal to fifty-two times the weekly pension to which she was entitled.

Provision is made under the Act to enable the parents, and under certain conditions other relatives, of a person killed at work to obtain benefit if they were maintained by him at the time of death.

The administration of the industrial injuries scheme necessarily involves numerous decisions, both administrative and medical. In general, claims for benefit and questions arising out of such claims are dealt with by the local Insurance Officer, but he may refer the case, or appeals may be made from his decision, to a local appeal tribunal, and from there to the Industrial Injuries Commissioner, whose decision is final. Medical Boards and a Medical Appeal Tribunal assess the degree of disability resulting from the disease or accident and deal with other medical questions.

One of the criticisms made of the old workmens' compensation system was that it did not contribute in any way to the rehabilitation of the injured workman, and might indeed be said to discourage him from doing all in his power to speed his own recovery, since he feared the loss of his compensation rights. Present legislation, by dissociating industrial injury and disablement benefits from earning power, and expressedly providing that disablement pensions are not affected by subsequent earnings, encourages an injured person to fit himself for work again as quickly as possible. Facilities for rehabilitation, and if necessary, retraining, have been established under the Disabled Persons (Employment) Act,[2] and the National Insurance (Industrial Injuries) Act includes provisions designed to encourage injured workers to take advantage of these facilities.

[1] Ministry of Reconstruction, *Social Insurance*, Part II, 'Workmen's Compensation. Proposals for an Industrial Injury Insurance Scheme', Cmd. 6551, 1944.
[2] Discussed in Chapter XIX.

The industrial injuries scheme thus makes comprehensive provisions to meet the needs of persons injured at work or suffering from diseases resulting from the nature of their employment, but this does not release employers, workers and the State from their responsibility for doing all in their power to reduce the number of such accidents or the incidence of these diseases. This is recognised by a clause in the Act[1] which enables the Minister of National Insurance to promote research into the causes, incidence and methods of prevention of industrial disease or accidents, either by conducting such research himself or contributing to it.

Taking into account the Industrial Injuries as well as the National Insurance Scheme, the benefits provided, if not adequate for subsistence, are comprehensive in the contingencies they cover as well as being universal in scope. They are paid for, as we have seen, by contributions from insured persons, and in the case of those employed, from their employers also, and are supplemented by the Exchequer to the extent of one-seventh of the total. Like benefits, contributions are paid at a flat rate regardless of income, and, as they are increased to help meet the cost of increasing benefits, so does the question as to the equity of this 'regressive tax' become more acute, since flat rate contributions place a disproportionate burden on the lowest paid worker,[2] and take no account of family responsibilities. But, as was shown when discussing pensions, resistance to change is still strong, and it can be argued that, from the fiscal point of view alone, 'it would be unwise to abandon revenue from a freely accepted, but regressive tax in favour of one which is socially more just but less acceptable'.[3]

Although some of its salient characteristics have remained, the British system of social insurance has developed almost out of recognition since it was introduced in 1911. During this period it has become universal in scope, more comprehensive in range of contingencies covered, and much more particular in application as shown, for example, in the differential provisions that have been

[1] Section 73.

[2] This point was made when the Minister of Pensions and National Insurance announced the increases in contribution and benefit the Government proposed to make in the House of Commons in November 1957. Mr. Marquand suggested that the value of a weekly insurance stamp now represented about seven per cent of the wages of the lowest paid worker. In reply, Mr. Boyd Carpenter pointed out that, when the National Insurance Act came into operation in 1948 the percentage was 6–7 per cent. In 1912, the employer's weekly contribution represented 1·9 per cent of average weekly earnings in industry; in 1938 it was 2·3 per cent, in 1955 3·3 per cent. R. M. Titmuss in *Lloyd George's Ambulance Wagon*, p. 56.

[3] Gertrude Williams in W. A. Robson (ed.), *Social Security*, 1943, p. 56. The scheme for graduated pensions discussed above will constitute a modification of this.

made for insured persons with and without dependants and the differentiated maternity and widow's benefits. Meanwhile economic and social conditions such as population structure, wage rates and standards of living have all been changing too, and to a greater extent than hitherto the State has accepted responsibility for the welfare of its citizens. From a note to his private secretary written in March 1911,[1] it appears that Lloyd George regarded insurance as a 'necessarily temporary expedient', and he believed that 'gradually the obligation of the State to find labour or sustenance will be realised and honourably interpreted'. How this can be done, not only honourably, but also acceptably, without insurance has not yet emerged, however. Meanwhile, despite the criticisms which are and can be made of their deficiencies and inadequacies, social insurance benefits, particularly the long-term ones, such as widows' and old age pensions, continue to enhance in some measure at least the extent to which their recipients feel secure and independent, and hence they serve a valuable social purpose.

[1] Quoted in *Lloyd George's Ambulance Wagon*, p. 24.

CHAPTER IV

SOCIAL ASSISTANCE

THE provisions made by the National Insurance and National Insurance (Industrial Injuries) Acts described in the last chapter form the first line of defence against want. But strong as this defence is, it has its loopholes, and if all members of the community are to be protected from want in all circumstances there must be a reserve in the form of a scheme of social assistance as comprehensive and universal in its scope as the insurance service. This need is met by the National Assistance Act, 1948, the passing of which meant the replacement of the Poor Law and the existing specialised assistance services for the old, the long-term unemployed, the blind and the tuberculous by a unified national scheme of financial assistance to all in need. Part III of the Act contains provisions making local authorities responsible for residential accommodation and welfare services for the aged and handicapped, and these services are discussed in later chapters.[1]

Since the National Assistance Act came into force financial assistance to those in need has been given from national funds, and the administration of this relief is in the hands of the National Assistance Board. The Board was constituted in 1934 to administer a state system of relief to able-bodied unemployed men and women who had exhausted their right to benefit from the insurance fund, or whose needs were not met by unemployment benefit. Its scope was gradually widened, and during the war it became responsible for the administration of a wide variety of schemes of monetary assistance to persons in need. The original title of Unemployment Assistance Board ceased to be appropriate, and in 1940 it was rechristened the Assistance Board, a title retained until the implementation of the National Assistance Act in 1948, when it became the National Assistance Board.

The Unemployment Assistance Board was established at a time of bitter controversy about the treatment of the unemployed, and the Board was deliberately constituted in such a way as to make it independent of direct Parliamentary control and so to keep the administration of relief free from political pressure, a policy which has been continued up to the present. Hence members of the

---

[1] Chapters XVIII and XIX.

Board are appointed by Royal Warrant for specified periods, their salaries are charged to the Consolidated Funds, and they are precluded from becoming members of the House of Commons.[1] Parliamentary questions about the Board's work are addressed to the Minister of Pensions and National Insurance to whom the Board must submit an annual report for presentation to the House. The Beveridge Report envisaged that one department would administer both social insurance and social assistance,[2] but this recommendation was not accepted, and the administrative distinction remains between the Ministry of Pensions and National Insurance, which through its Minister is directly answerable to Parliament, and the National Assistance Board.

The policy of the Board is carried out by civil servants, who staff a network of regional and area offices. Direct contact with the public is made through more than 400 area offices, while the eleven regional officers supervise and co-ordinate the work in their respective regions.

Though open to criticism in some respects, this administrative set-up works reasonably smoothly and well, and the increasing responsibilities given to the Board can be regarded as a measure of the growth of public confidence in the ability of its officers to administer a wide range of relief services with efficiency and humanity.[3]

In order that the Board may benefit from local knowledge and experience, local advisory committees have been set up in different parts of the country.[4] They deal with general questions such as rent allowances, and not with individual cases. For this latter purpose they appoint sub-committees, one for each area office, whose function it is to advise the Area Officer about difficult or special cases. They have no administrative responsibility, and in the main a sub-committee's work is limited to dealing with a few selected applicants, often those who have exhausted the patience and ingenuity of everyone else, and whose prognosis is bad, if not

---

[1] These conditions are laid down in the First Schedule of the Act which also decrees that the Board shall consist of a Chairman, Deputy Chairman and from one to four other members. One member must be a woman.

[2] Beveridge, op. cit., p. 141, par. 369.

[3] In addition to its own special work of assisting persons in need the Board makes investigations into circumstances on behalf of other Departments. For example, the Legal Aid Act, 1948, provides for free or assisted legal aid to persons whose 'disposable incomes' are below a certain level. These cases are investigated by the National Assistance Board. See Chapter IX.

[4] These are provided for in Section 3 of the National Assistance Act which lays it down that: 'For the purpose of securing that full use is made of the advice and assistance, both on general questions and on difficult individual cases, of persons having local knowledge and experience in matters affecting the functions of the Board, the Board shall arrange for the establishment of advisory committees . . . to act for such areas as the Board think fit.'

hopeless. Nevertheless, constructive work may often be done,[1] and the existence of the advisory committees and sub-committees means that men and women from industry, local government and the related social services, who are willing to undertake this service and are selected for it, gain some insight into the day-to-day work of the Board. They also gain some understanding of the problems, particularly the more intractable ones, with which its officers have to deal, of the ways in which these are being met, and the difficulties which have to be surmounted. In their turn the committee members can give the Board's officers the benefit of their knowledge of local conditions and of their experience in related fields of work. Moreover, however imperfectly they may function, advisory committees are at least an official recognition by Parliament and the Board that, although national assistance is centrally administered, the real work is carried out in the local offices, and it should be the concern of local people and related to local conditions and other services in the area.

Like the National Insurance Act, the National Assistance Act is universal in scope. Any person in Great Britain over the age of sixteen may apply for assistance, and the amount granted will be sufficient to meet both his needs and those of his dependants. Children under the age of sixteen not in the care of parents or guardians are not assisted under this Act, but special provision is made for them by the Children Act which came into operation at the same time.[2] The Board is also precluded from giving general assistance to persons in full-time employment, except in emergencies, but it may help them to tide over the first few days in work after a spell of unemployment, and continuing assistance may be given to a disabled person not working under a contract of service whose earning power has been substantially reduced in comparison with others doing similar work.[3] Legislation imposing charges for dentures, spectacles, surgical appliances and prescriptions obtained through the National Health Service authorises the Board to assist people in need of these appliances, but unable to afford them, even if they are in full-time work.[4] National Assistance may not be given to a person directly participating in a trade dispute unless he is destitute, although the requirements of his dependants may be met if need is proved.

[1] This is described in the Board's annual reports. See especially the Report for 1950 (Cmd. 8276) which describes their work in some detail.
[2] These provisions are discussed in Chapter XIV.
[3] National Assistance Act, 1948, Section 9.
[4] National Health Service (Amendment) Act, 1949, s. 16; National Health Service Act, 1951, s. 4; National Health Service Act, 1952, s. 7. Of the £1,829,000 refunded in 1957 only £115,000 consisted of grants to persons not already drawing national assistance.

SOCIAL ASSISTANCE

Since, apart from the exceptions just mentioned, anyone in need can obtain help from the National Assistance Board, the variety of cases dealt with is very large. The Board's clients include persons who have failed to qualify for insurance benefit, or who have exhausted their right to benefit, or for whose needs the standard benefit is insufficient. There are also a number of cases outside the scope of the insurance scheme, for example, the deserted wife unable to go out to work as she has young children to care for, the wife and children of a man serving a term of imprisonment, the unmarried mother and her young child. Old people over seventy who are not entitled to retirement pensions and blind persons over forty can claim special non-contributory pensions, provided that they can satisfy a test of need, nationality and residence, and these pensions are administered by the Board, which has also taken over from the local authorities the responsibility for making special allowances to needy blind persons and to persons who have suffered a loss of income as a result of undergoing treatment for pulmonary tuberculosis. Allowances for blind and tuberculous persons are at a special rate.

Assistance is normally given in cash, although under special circumstances it may be given in kind. Except in cases of emergency it cannot be granted without a prior investigation by an officer of the Board into the applicant's needs and resources, and regulations, approved by Parliament,[1] determine the scale on which relief shall be given. The 'needs test' is a personal one, and the only legal obligations to support relatives recognised by the Act are those of a man to maintain his wife and children, and a woman to maintain her husband and children, including her illegitimate children.[2] Although, in general, assistance has to be given on the scale laid down, the Board's officers have discretionary powers which enable them to meet the special needs of individual cases, such as, for example, those of an infirm old person who may require an additional allowance to enable him to obtain domestic help or pay for laundry. Further, the Board is empowered to make lump-sum payments to meet exceptional needs, such as clothing, tools to enable an unemployed man to take a particular job, bedding so that a tuberculous person can sleep alone, or fares to enable parents to visit a child in a distant hospital. Until recently the Board was precluded from meeting any medical needs, but, as we have already seen, it can now make payments to persons

[1] The National Assistance (Determination of Needs) Regulations, 1948. Statutory Instrument, 1948, No. 1334, as amended by the various National Assistance (Determination of Needs) Amendment Regulations, which have been passed since.

[2] National Assistance Act, 1948. Section 42. Cf. the provisions of the Poor Law concerning liable relatives.

53

requiring dentures, glasses or surgical appliances, but unable to afford the charges authorised by the National Health Service Acts. Should an applicant be dissatisfied with the Board's officer's determination of his needs he may appeal to an Appeals Tribunal. Such tribunals consist of three members, two appointed by the Minister of Pensions and National Insurance and one by the Board from a panel nominated by the Minister to represent workpeople. The decisions of these tribunals are final.

The main function of the National Assistance Board is thus to give assistance to persons in need. It is essentially an income-maintenance service, but in providing this service the Board and its officers are expressedly required to 'exercise their functions in such a manner as shall best promote the welfare of the persons affected, that is the welfare of the persons assisted and their dependants',[1] and it is significant that this direction is given right at the beginning of the National Assistance Act before any of the Board's specific functions are laid down. Since the passing of the Act there has been a good deal of discussion as to what is implied by this clause. It has been taken by the Board as meaning that the officer handling a case should have a real concern for the well-being of the applicant, but not that an applicant for assistance is necessarily in need of comprehensive care. The Board proceeds on the assumption that persons in receipt of assistance are in the main competent to manage their own affairs, and differ only from others in point of income.[2] One senior official has pointed out, moreover, that applicants are driven to approach the Board by financial necessity, and this same financial necessity prevents them from breaking off the relationship even should they so wish. She considers that 'the application of a means test, the necessarily close inquiry which is involved into financial resources and physical conditions, would certainly be made *less*, and not *more*, acceptable to the great majority concerned, if it came to be thought that an application for national assistance might involve inquiries into the private or emotional life, as well as into the financial affairs, of the applicant'.[3] It has been noted by an American visiting social worker that the attitude towards independence and self-development exemplified here is one of the factors differentiating social work in Britain and America. 'Given the tools such as the various social security measures, it is assumed in Britain that people,

---

[1] Section 2 (1).

[2] Report of the National Assistance Board for the year ended 31 December 1949, Cmd. 8030, p. 16. Cf. the Report for 1955, where the question is discussed again and the same point made, Cmd. 9781, p. 19.

[3] J. Hope-Wallace, 'The Caseworker, the Welfare Officer, and the Administrator in the Social Services', II, *The Boundaries of Casework*, a Symposium published by the Association of Psychiatric Social Workers, p. 90.

individually or in groups, should be able to manage their own affairs.' In the United States, with its development of casework as a method of helping people to make the most of their capacities, actual or potential, the aim of public assistance is generally to determine, not only the person's need and eligibility for assistance, but also the causes which lead him to be in need.[1]

The National Assistance Board considers that its primary responsibility is to meet the financial needs of each of the 2,000,000 and more persons who may apply for assistance in any one year[2] as speedily and effectively as possible and this must receive priority over the more intensive work implied in the American objective. Nevertheless it is recognised that, in a minority of cases, financial need is but one symptom of general social maladjustment, and, in dealing with these cases, unless financial relief is accompanied by some attempt at social rehabilitation, no improvement in their condition is possible. This is not regarded as the proper function of the Board's officer, however, since 'he will not have the skill for some tasks or the time for others'. 'To the minority—still a large number—whose needs are not only financial, [he] can be of help mainly in recognising the nature of their special needs and advising them what steps to take, or putting them in touch with some other body which can give them the help they need.' This may be far from easy, for the most difficult task of the welfare worker is often to diagnose what is really wanted, and before he can do this, 'he must learn how to gain the confidence of those with whom he is dealing'.[3] He must also be familiar with the working of the statutory and voluntary social services in his area, and be ready to consult, and able and willing to co-operate with, those responsible for administering them. Moreover, although the social rehabilitation of an individual or family in serious difficulties may not be the responsibility of the National Assistance Board officer, financial assistance, administered with tact and discretion and adjusted as far as possible to the family's special needs, may be a potent factor in this rehabilitation.

Apart from these specially difficult cases, the Board's officers are daily confronted with a great variety of different people presenting a range of human needs so great that they can only be met by the exercise of tact, resource and initiative combined with sympathy and understanding and the wide use of discretionary powers. This

[1] Arlien Johnson in *Some Impressions of Social Services in Great Britain by an American Social Work Team*, 1956, pp. 11 and 24.

[2] In 1958 2,161,000 applicants were dealt with (apart from applications to meet Health Service charges). In December 1958 1,649,000 weekly allowances were current, making provision for 2,361,000 persons. Report, 1958, Cmnd. 781, June 1959.

[3] Report of the National Assistance Board, 1955, Cmd. 9781, p. 29.

MEETING BASIC NEEDS

being the case, the quality and outlook of these officers, and especially those who are in direct contact with members of the public, are particularly important. This appears to be receiving increasing recognition from the Board itself, for of recent years a good deal of attention has been paid both to the training of new recruits and to the provision of special courses, frequently by arrangement with extramural departments of universities, for more experienced officers. In addition, the Board is seconding a few carefully selected officers each year to universities to take generic casework courses, a recognition of the fact that although it does not itself attempt to provide a casework service, some understanding of casework concepts is relevant to its work.

In addition to the general duty to treat all clients in such a manner as shall best promote their welfare, the Board has special welfare responsibilities for two groups. These are the long-term unemployed who appear to have lost or to be losing, if they ever had, the will and capacity to work, and persons without a settled way of living or vagrants, as they were described in the days of the Poor Law.

The long-term unemployed present a small but difficult probblem to the Board and its officers, and in 1956 a special inquiry, the details of which are given in Appendix VIII of the Board's report for that year, was undertaken with the object of obtaining fuller information about them. The conclusions reached as the result of this inquiry were that 'There seems to be little doubt that at least three-quarters of those interviewed were at a disadvantage from a physical or mental point of view in getting a job, and the physical disadvantage was all the greater where, as in the vast majority of cases, they could be considered only for unskilled (which often means laborious) work.' 'Wilful idleness, as distinct from physical or mental disability or other causes, would seem to account for the lengthy unemployment in very few cases indeed.'[1] By Section 16 of the Act the Board may, subject to the approval of the Minister of Pensions and National Insurance, provide centres for the 're-establishment' of persons in need thereof through lack of regular occupation or of instruction or training. The Board has established one such centre at Henley-in-Arden, near Birmingham, and another has been started in Co. Durham. These centres are intended to 'provide unemployed men who, though capable of work have become unaccustomed to it, with opportunities of building up their strength in healthy surroundings and acquiring habits of regular employment'.[2] Such men may go to a re-establishment centre 'voluntarily', that is on the advice of,

[1] Report of the National Assistance Board for the year ended 31 December 1956, Cmnd. 181, pp. 42 and 43.
[2] Report of the National Assistance Board, 1954, Cmd. 9530, p. 21.

and possibly under pressure from, the Board's officers or local
advisory committees, or, if it is considered necessary in the man's
own interests, may be directed there under Section 10 of the Act.
This Section provides that if a person, not being in receipt of unemployment benefit, appears to the Board to be refusing or neglect-
ing to maintain himself, the matter may be reported to a local
appeal tribunal, and the applicant directed to a re-establishment
centre instead of being granted an allowance in money. The
Board's report for 1956 claims that 'nearly all the men who go to
the Centre do so voluntarily and co-operate to the best of their
ability in the arrangements made for them',[1] and, considering the
problems presented, the Board regards the result of this work as on
the whole encouraging.[2]

The number of persons without a settled way of living is also
small.[3] It is the duty of the Board 'to make provision whereby
persons without a settled way of living may be influenced to lead
a more settled way of life', and to this end it must provide and
maintain 'reception centres' for their temporary board and lodging.[4] The Board may, and does, require the councils of counties
and county boroughs to exercise these functions on its behalf, and
in certain cases, the assistance of voluntary bodies specially concerned with the rehabilitation of such wayfarers may be sought.
At the reception centres efforts are made in all likely cases to
influence the person concerned to abandon the way of life he has
adopted and settle down to work, and some men are sent on to
one or other of the re-establishment centres. In some cases the
Board's efforts at rehabilitation have met with gratifying success,
'but unfortunately the failures . . . far outnumber the successes',
and it is recognised that, 'the chances of reclaiming a casual are
best where it is possible to tackle his problems before he has been
too long on the road'.[5]

The National Assistance Act completes the legislation designed
to secure a subsistence income for all families in all circumstances,
and before concluding this review of the social security services it
is pertinent to consider to what extent these services have, in fact,
achieved this objective. The results of a third survey of York, made

[1] Report for 1956, Cmnd. 181, p. 17.
[2] Report for 1955, Cmnd. 9781, p. 31. Inquiries made at the end of 1955 into
the circumstances of the 110 men discharged from the Centre during the twelve
months ending the previous August showed that over half were not receiving
assistance, 29 were known to be working, 22 were presumed to be, and nine
others, although unemployed, had worked long enough to qualify for benefit.
[3] The average numbers in the Board's reception centres for these persons
varied during 1956 from 1,626 in July to 1,929 in February.
[4] National Assistance Act, 1948, Section 17.
[5] Report for 1955, p. 34; Report for 1956, p. 19.

in 1950, were, on the face of it, encouraging. Taking as their criterion a 'human needs' standard comparable with that laid down in 1936 the two investigators, B. Seebohm Rowntree and G. R. Lavers, found that 1·66 per cent of the total population of York, or 2·77 per cent of the working class, were in poverty compared with 17·7 per cent of the population or 31·1 per cent of the working class in 1936. Old age was the determining factor in 68·1 per cent of the 846 families in poverty, sickness in 21·3 per cent, and in not a single case was the poverty due to the unemployment of an able-bodied wage-earner. An attempt was made to assess the contribution made by the welfare services to the improvement that had taken place since 1936, and the result of the investigators' calculations was that had welfare legislation remained unchanged during the intervening years, the percentage of working-class families in poverty would have been, not 2·77 per cent, but 22·18 per cent.[1]

The conclusions drawn from this survey have been criticised in some detail in a broadsheet published by Political and Economic Planning,[2] where it is argued that the balance of evidence suggests that the numbers living below the poverty line in 1950 were substantially greater than the figure given by Rowntree and Lavers suggests. P.E.P. would substitute 4·64 per cent of working-class families in poverty for Rowntree and Lavers' 2·77 per cent, but even with this adjustment, the decline in poverty as measured by the authors' standard was very considerable. What is being asked now, however, is whether the definitions of poverty and the scales by which it was measured, which were hammered out in the early years of the century and again in the years of economic depression and extensive unemployment between the wars, are appropriate to-day.

One criticism that is made of the classic method of measuring poverty by establishing a minimum subsistence standard based on what are regarded as the necessities of life is that this standard bears little or no relation to working-class spending. It has been pointed out, for example, that during the 1951 trade recession in Lancashire families who were forced to reduce their expenditure as the wage earners were out of work cut down their spending not only on drink, cigarettes, newspapers and periodicals and confectionery, but also on meat, butter, milk, food and clothing. Hire-purchase (especially on furniture) and private insurance payments, almost as much as rent and rates, were regarded as first claims

---

[1] B. Seebohm Rowntree and G. R. Lavers, *Poverty and the Welfare State*, 1951, pp. 34 and 38.

[2] PEP, 'Poverty, Ten Years after Beveridge', *Planning*, Vol. XIX, No. 344, 4 August 1952, pp. 26–27, and Appendix I.

upon income, which is understandable, as if abandoned the loss might be permanent, and spending on some form of entertainment was regarded as essential even by those in poverty.[1] The fact that families in poverty spend money on items other than those regarded by the investigator as essential was known to Rowntree when he was making his first survey, and he was concerned lest it should be deduced from this that he was exaggerating the extent and seriousness of the problem.[2] In the climate of opinion at that time, only a standard that was both austere and rigid would convince the sceptical of the existence of widespread poverty beyond the power of the persons concerned to alleviate. But attitudes have now changed, and the concern expressed in the two P.E.P. broadsheets is lest those who calculate 'subsistence' needs, whether for purpose of estimating the extent to which poverty still exists, or of making assessments for assistance grants, take too little account of expenditure on articles which are not strictly speaking essential if basic needs alone are considered, but which are generally regarded as necessary for the maintenance of an acceptable standard of life. They urge a more thorough investigation than has hitherto taken place into how families in the lower income groups actually do spend their money, as they believe this would be a guide in assessing the level at which payments should be made to meet family needs. It is recognised, however, that in determining the level at which social assistance payments should be made, levels and patterns of working-class expenditure cannot be the sole deciding factor. 'Knowing what people actually spend does not explain what they ought to spend' and in the last resort decisions as to the level of social assistance 'must be based on contemporary views about the lowest living conditions that are tolerable in the community'.[3] As the standard of living of the community as a whole, rises these will rise also, and the opinion has been expressed that 'it is not unreasonable to suggest that the level [of what is regarded as reasonable subsistence] will rise faster than our standard of living'.[4] At present this does not seem to be the case, however, and the gap between the levels of insurance and assistance payments and average wages is wider now than before the war. Hence strong representations have been made that in framing social security policies we should seek to ensure that families where the head is no longer able to earn, whether temporarily or permanently, should

[1] PEP, 'Social Security and Unemployment in Lancashire', *Planning*, Vol. XIX, No. 349, December 1952, p. 122.

[2] *Poverty*, A Study in Town Life, p. 135, footnote.

[3] *Poverty, Ten Years after Beveridge*, pp. 35 and 36.

[4] Walter Hagenbuch, 'The Rationale of the Social Services', *Lloyds Bank Review*, July 1953, p. 10.

not be forced down to a 'subsistence' level which bears no relation to their accepted standard of living.[1]

In its commentary on the Beveridge Report made in 1943, P.E.P. expressed what was probably the accepted opinion of the day when it declared that, 'To provide less than a subsistence minimum is indefensible, to provide more is unnecessary, probably dangerous.'[2] Fifteen years later the Labour Party, in its plan for security in old age, described the drop in standards of life consequent on retirement, and went on, 'This is poverty. No arbitrary or sophisticated attempt to draw lines of minimum subsistence could supply a better definition.'[3] These two quotations, placed in juxtaposition, demonstrate the difficulty of finding an equitable and acceptable basis for income maintenance during interruptance of earning power. The State has accepted the responsibility for, and during the last fifty years we have gone a long, though not the whole way towards, overcoming want in the sense of the lack of all things needful during periods of sickness and unemployment and in old age, but by many people this is no longer regarded as sufficient. When we try to make provision beyond subsistence level, however, it becomes increasingly difficult to find a criterion by which we can decide a just apportionment to individuals and families unable temporarily or permanently to support themselves, for we must bear in mind that this involves a redistribution of community resources on which there are other claims equally valid from the point of view of human need.[4] We are here involved in problems of social equity which go beyond the social insurance and assistance services, and whose consideration must be deferred until a later chapter.

[1] For example in the Labour Party pamphlet, *National Superannuation*, discussed above, pp. 39–40. The hardships suffered by families where the breadwinner is incapacitated or has died leaving a widow with dependent children are brought out in a report presented by the Department of Economics (Social Studies Section), University of Bristol, to the Joseph Rowntree Charitable Trust in 1958: *A Study of Families in which Earnings are Interrupted by Illness, Injury or Death.*

[2] 'After the Beveridge Report', *Planning*, No. 205, 20 April 1943. Quoted in 'Poverty, Ten Years after Beveridge', *Planning*, August 1952.

[3] *National Superannuation*, p. 30.

[4] E.g. those of the National Health Service, the finances of which are discussed in Chapter VI.

CHAPTER V

THE DEVELOPMENT OF THE HEALTH
SERVICES

'An immortal work, since man cannot more nearly imitate the Deity than in bestowing health.'—*Inscription on the stone erected to the memory of Sir Hugh Middleton, who in the reign of James I brought a fresh supply of clean water to London.*

ON 5 July 1948 the National Health Service Act, an Act 'to promote . . . a comprehensive health service designed to secure improvement in the physical and mental health of the people of England and Wales, and the prevention, diagnosis, and treatment of illness'[1] became operative. It was just a hundred years since that Parliament, by passing the Public Health Act of 1848, had first affirmed the State's responsibility for securing minimum conditions of health for the people, and a comparison between the scope and character of the two measures brings out the advances in technique and changes in outlook of the intervening century.

The National Health Service Act, 1946, sets out to co-ordinate the personal health services and establish them on a national basis, and deals with such questions as medical treatment, at home and in hospital, health care for mothers and children, the provision of drugs and appliances and the setting up of health centres. It takes for granted the existence of a central government department which can take responsibility for the service as a whole, an ordered and reasonably efficient system of local government, and of measures to ensure a sufficiently healthy environment, such as a good supply of clean water, an efficient method of sewage disposal and of cleansing and draining the streets. These prerequisites of the personal health services, the pride of the twentieth century, were created by the sanitary reformers of the nineteenth, and their labours not only helped to make life in the great towns, brought into existence by the Industrial Revolution, tolerable, but probably saved the developing urban civilisation from being ravaged, and possibly destroyed, by infectious disease.

Some idea of the magnitude and complexity of the tasks which confronted Edwin Chadwick, Southwood Smith, their colleagues

[1] National Health Service Act, 1946, Section (1).

and supporters, can be gained by reading the Report on the Sanitary Condition of the Labouring Population of Great Britain, published in 1842, and other contemporary documents.[1] Not only had they to tackle the vast technical problems involved in cleansing, sewering, paving, and lighting the towns, for sanitary engineering was still in the experimental stage, but also to contend with the inefficiency and apathy of many of the local authorities,[2] and the chaotic state of local government, particularly in the areas outside the incorporated boroughs which were not affected by the Municipal Corporations Act of 1835, and further to face active opposition on the part of the many vested interests, concerned to preserve the *status quo*. The main need was for the establishment of efficient administrative machinery, both centrally and locally; a central body which would inspire, encourage, advise and, if necessary, coerce the responsible local authorities into an efficient discharge of their duties, and local bodies which would be responsible for all the sanitary services within their respective areas.

The first attempt to create this administrative framework by the establishment of a General and Local Boards of Health was ill-conceived and unsuccessful,[3] and the subsequent reaction probably delayed the development of the public health services for a number of years, but even after the abolition of the General Board of Health and the retirement of Chadwick, statesmen and administrators were not allowed to repudiate entirely the responsibility for the health of the nation they had reluctantly and half-heartedly assumed in 1848. Recurrent outbreaks of cholera; the patient work and example of medical officers of health, of whom Sir John Simon was the greatest,[4] and of statisticians such as Dr. William

[1] Extracts are given in most social histories of the period, e.g., J. L. and Barbara Hammond, *The Bleak Age*, chs. iv and vii.

[2] Not all, however. Some were in advance of the general standards of the time and used what powers they had to improve the sanitary conditions in their areas. For example, Liverpool, after obtaining a special Act giving it what were for the period drastic powers, appointed the first Medical Officer of Health in the country in 1847, and a Borough Surveyor and Inspector of Nuisances at the same time.

[3] The General Board of Health was controlled by a nominated President who was not necessarily a Minister of the Crown. Under certain circumstances it could turn a Town Council into a Board of Health against its will and yet it had no powers to appoint its own permanent inspectors. Sanitary measures which were urgently needed were carried out in different parts of the country as a result of the passing of the Act and the work of the Board; but its bias towards centralisation and Chadwick's tactlessness roused so much antagonism that in 1854 the Board was reconstituted (without Chadwick), and its medical duties were transferred to the Privy Council in 1858.

[4] For some years he was Medical Officer of Health to the City of London, he then became attached to the General Board of Health, and for fourteen years

THE DEVELOPMENT OF THE HEALTH SERVICES

Farr;[1] the work of Florence Nightingale both in insisting on sanitary reforms in the army and establishing nursing as a profession for educated women; and the increasing efficiency and enterprise of local authorities, together with advances in medical knowledge as to the cause and prevention of disease, all combined to keep the issue alive. As a result of all these efforts successive measures, culminating in the comprehensive Public Health Act of 1875, at length established the environmental health services on a firm basis. Even this Act did not satisfactorily solve the problem of central government administration, however, as it combined public health and poor law administration in the Local Government Board, and the spirit of the Poor Law was dominant for many years. It was not until the close of the First World War that the Ministry of Health was created and Chadwick's main task completed.

However, by the end of the nineteenth century the State had accepted responsibility for ensuring a reasonably healthy environment for its citizens both at home and, through the factory legislation whose growth had paralleled that of the public health services, at work. The foundations had been laid and reformers could begin the building of a superstructure of personal services, designed not only to maintain, but to improve, the health of the nation. It was already recognised that this largely depended on the health care of the mothers and children, and when once the most urgent problems of sanitation and the control of infectious disease had been met, those concerned with public health could turn their attention to the special needs of these groups. Voluntary organisations, such as the Manchester and Salford Ladies' Sanitary Reform Association, which established the first health visiting service in the country, and progressive medical officers of health, such as Dr. F. Drew Harris, of St. Helens, who established the first infant milk depot, and Dr. James Kerr of Bradford, who was inspecting school children and experimenting with a school clinic in the nineties, had already pioneered in this field, and their experience was invaluable to later legislators and administrators. By the first decade of the twentieth century the time was ripe for government action to secure an improvement in the national standard of physical efficiency, and public opinion, shocked by the revelations

was Medical Officer to the Privy Council. His reports to the Privy Council, and his book *English Sanitary Institutions* are classics.

[1] Appointed Compiler of Abstracts to the General Register Office 1839, retired 1879. He has been described as 'the greatest medical statistician who has ever lived'. 'But for the work of Farr, the efforts of the sanitary reformers would have lacked direction and it would have been impossible to assess the value of the successive steps taken during the second half of the nineteenth century to reduce mortality'. W. M. Frazer, *History of English Public Health 1834–1939*, p. 22.

as to the number of army recruits rejected on grounds of physical unfitness during the South African War, was ready to accept it.

The first personal health legislation passed was designed to minimise the risks of child-bearing by securing that only properly trained and qualified individuals should 'habitually and for gain' attend women in childbirth. This was accomplished by the Midwives Act, 1902, which, by the creation of the Central Midwives Board to be an examining and supervising body, and by directing that after 1905 no woman could enter the profession unless certified and registered, established a minimum standard of professional efficiency. In general, midwives remained independent private practitioners, however, and it was not until 1936 that local authorities were made responsible for ensuring that there was an adequate number of trained midwives practising in their respective areas and available when required. They could do this either by employing them themselves or coming to an agreement for their services with a voluntary organisation such as the local district nursing association. In this way domiciliary midwifery became in the main a public service under local authority control. One advantage of this was the possibility of closer association between the midwife and those responsible for the ante-natal and post-natal supervision of the mother and the welfare of the infant, provisions for which had been increasing since the beginning of the century.

The objects of the maternity and child welfare service are the maintenance and improvement of the health of both mother and child. Although certain forms of treatment are available, for instance dental treatment for the mother, and the treatment of minor ailments in the child, the service is principally concerned with preventive measures and health education. It provides for the medical supervision of the mother before and after the birth of the child and for the regular examination of the infant at a clinic or centre; the visiting of mother and child at home by a properly trained and qualified health visitor, and the meeting of the special food requirements of the expectant and nursing mother and young child. Its slow but steady growth was due to a combination of voluntary effort, the enterprise and persistence of local medical officers of health and encouragement from enlightened administrators at the centre, particularly Sir Arthur Newsholme, who, when he became Medical Officer to the Local Government Board in 1908, made a special study of the nation's infant mortality rate and did all in his power to reduce it.[1] The First World War was followed by an increased recognition of the value of maternity and child welfare work, and the need for its establishment on a national basis, and

[1] The history of the maternity and child welfare services is told by Dr. G. F. McCleary, *The Maternity and Child Welfare Movement*, 1935.

the Maternity and Child Welfare Act, 1918, empowered local authorities to make arrangements for safeguarding the health of expectant mothers and children under five. Central government grants were made available to assist the local authorities in this task, but the Act laid it down that the authorities who undertook it should appoint special maternity and child welfare committees —with at least two women members—to carry it out.

A necessary prerequisite of the efficient care of mother and child is that all births shall be notified to the local medical officer of health, and since 1915 this has been compulsory throughout the country.

The legislation just described stimulated local authorities to develop their maternity and child welfare work, and in spite of certain shortcomings it has become widely recognised as one of the most valuable of the health and social services.[1]

The spectre of physical deterioration which haunted the public in the early years of the twentieth century, and whose role in the development of the personal health services can be compared with that played by the recurrent outbreaks of cholera in reconciling people to the limitations imposed on them in the interests of sanitation in the first part of the nineteenth, was a precipitating factor in the enactment of legislation to ensure the physical well-being of school children. The need for such action had long been apparent to those in direct contact with the schools in the poorer areas, for the physical condition of many of the children compelled to attend school by the Education Acts of the closing years of the nineteenth century was such that they could have received little benefit from the instruction they were given. They came to school ill-nourished, dirty, insufficiently clad and often suffering from preventible defects, as much in need of medical attention and social care as instruction.

Efforts to meet these needs were made by enlightened school boards, such as that at Bradford, by voluntary bodies, and sometimes by the teachers themselves, but the State took no action until after the publication of the Report of the Interdepartmental Committee on Physical Deterioration in 1904. This Committee's recommendations included the feeding of necessitous school children and school medical inspection, and these recommendations were carried into effect by the Education (Provision of Meals) Act, 1906, and the Education (Administrative Provisions) Act, 1907. The first of these Acts empowered local authorities to provide meals for necessitous children, while the latter made medical inspection a duty and treatment permissive. From the time of their inception,

[1] The maternity and child welfare and related services are discussed in more detail in Chapter X below.

these provisions for preserving and improving the health of school children have been recognised as part of the nation's educational service. Legislative enactments under which they operate to-day are to be found, not in the National Health Service Act, 1946, but in the Education Act, 1944,[1] and the National Health Service Act is silent on the subject of the health of the school child. The acceptance in principle of a comprehensive national health service has, however, inevitably raised the question of the transfer of the school health services in whole or in part from the control of the education authorities and their incorporation into a general health service. Thus the White Paper in which the National Government of the war years set out its proposals for a National Health Service suggests that while inspection should remain a function of the local education authority, 'as from the time when the new health service is able to take over its comprehensive care of health, the child will look for its treatment to the organisation which that service provides and the education authority, as such, will give up responsibility for medical treatment'.[2] Arrangements are now in operation for promoting co-operation between school doctors, general practitioners and the consultants and other staff of the regional hospital boards in connection with the treatment of schoolchildren, and these are discussed in a later chapter.[3]

So far, this chapter has been devoted to the consideration of the development of the services which are designed to safeguard the health of the people and aim at improvements in general standards of health and well-being rather than the care or treatment of the sick. But the treatment of the sick, whether at home or in hospital, is now also recognised as a public responsibility, an integral part of any comprehensive health service, and the historical background of this modern assumption must now be considered.

Before 1911 the relationship between doctor and patient was for the great majority of people a matter of personal arrangement at private cost. The Poor Law Medical Service met the needs of those who would otherwise be destitute of medical care, but the remainder of the population made their own arrangements with whichever doctor they had chosen, or whose services they had been able to obtain. The State gave powerful assistance to the medical profession in its efforts to maintain and raise its own standards by prohibiting practitioners not on the Medical Register kept by the General Medical Council from signing death certificates, suing for payments or getting their prescriptions made up by chemists, but it left undisturbed the independent status of the general prac-

---

[1] Section 48. They are discussed in detail in Chapter XI below.
[2] Ministry of Health and Department of Health for Scotland, *A National Health Service*. Cmd. 6502/44, p. 39.   [3] Chapter XII.

titioner, who obtained the fees for his services in his own way as best he could. This frequently entailed some hardship both to the weekly wage-earner living on the margin of poverty and to those doctors who practised in working-class areas. Some doctors employed collectors on a commission basis to call weekly on those families who could not manage to pay the fee in a lump sum, while the more provident workers formed themselves into medical clubs or joined friendly societies, subscribing a few pence each week to be sure of being able to receive medical attention during sickness without incurring debt. Dispensaries set up by the charitable in some of the large cities catered for the very poor, who also crowded into the out-patient departments of the hospitals, particularly in London, and hindered them from carrying out their proper work of specialised diagnosis and treatment.

A radical change took place when Mr. Lloyd George's National Health Insurance Act was placed on the statute book in 1911. This Act entitled insured persons not only to weekly payments to help maintain a minimum income level during sickness, but also to free doctoring from the doctor of their choice, provided he was among those who had agreed to participate in the scheme. The doctors were paid on a *per capita* basis. The 'panel doctor' was thus brought into being, and as the scope of National Health Insurance was extended, an increasing proportion of the population became his patients.

National Health Insurance had advantages for both doctor and patient. The doctor was assured of regular payments on behalf of his panel patients, and thus could count on a fairly stable nucleus income, while the wage-earner knew that if he fell ill he would not be burdened with a doctor's bill in addition to his loss of earnings and his other expenses. There were, however, limitations to the usefulness of the scheme. For example, it was confined to the insured workers themselves, and did not cover their dependants, a limitation which bore particularly hardly on the wives of the lower-paid workers. These women, often ignorant and prejudiced, overburdened with the task of meeting the needs of their families with inadequate resources, and creating some sort of a home in spite of deplorable housing conditions, sure that the whole structure of home and family would collapse if they were laid up or sent to hospital, were still further discouraged from seeking medical advice by the knowledge that it must be paid for out of the housekeeping money, already strained to its limits.[1] Others excluded

---

[1] This is discussed at some length by Margery Spring-Rice in *Working-class Wives* (a survey of the conditions of 1,250 married women based on information collected by the Women's Health Enquiry Committee), 1939, ch. iv. She quotes a letter from a district nurse in a rural area, part of which runs 'Fathers and

from the benefits of free doctoring were the small traders and independent workers, often as badly, if not worse, off than the insured worker.

While National Health Insurance eased the financial difficulties of the doctor striving to establish himself in private practice, it could not and did not provide a solution to other problems of which he and the public became increasingly conscious as time went on and standards of medical treatment for the whole population were raised. Thus he often remained an isolated unit chronically overworked and overstrained yet unable to take time off to obtain adequate holidays owing to the difficulties of finding and paying for a locum. He had great difficulty in finding the time to keep abreast with contemporary advances in scientific and medical thought and practice, and usually worked in his own home without the equipment and auxiliary staff which would render his task easier and enable him to perform it more efficiently and increase the scope of his work. Moreover, not only were the conditions under which individual general practitioners were working unsatisfactory, but their distribution throughout the country was in no way related to the need for their services, so that, for instance, just before the war Hastings had one general practitioner for every 1,178 persons, in South Shields there was one for every 4,105. Yet, in spite of all these difficulties, and of the inroads of the growing public health and specialist provisions, the importance of the service rendered by the general practitioner—ideally not only 'a specialist in primary diagnosis giving first line treatment of all kinds', but also the health adviser of the families who chose to make him their confidant[1]—was increasingly recognised as vital, and when, after the publication of the Beveridge Report, the idea of a comprehensive medical service for all citizens began to take shape it was clear that one of its objects must be to ensure that these services would be available for all the families of the nation.

Skilled medical attention is the first essential in sickness, but it has oft-times been rendered ineffective by lack of proper nursing care. Among the first to realise this, and to appreciate the difficulties that the poor and ignorant had in providing it in their own homes, was William Rathbone, a Liverpool merchant who, in 1859, started a system of district nursing by trained nurses in his native city. The success of this experiment led to its being adopted

children at work come under the N.H.I., but very seldom the mothers. It is the mother who gets left out as far as treatment goes. . . . She may get the family doctor for herself as well as the children if she is on the club. . . . If she does not pay in she carries on as long as she possibly can without advice or treatment. . . . She will not start a doctor's bill for herself if she can possibly stand on her feet'.
[1] P.E.P., 'Medical Care for Citizens', *Planning*, No. 222, June 1944, p. 8.

in both towns and cities throughout the land, and before long the district nurse became an established institution. Her work has been particularly valuable in rural areas where other medical and social services are scanty or wanting, and as the personal health services developed, the most practical and economical way of extending them to those areas where the population was too scattered to justify separate provision, was found to be by enlisting the co-operation of the local district nursing association, and extending the scope of the nurse's work. Consequently, in many areas she became health visitor, midwife, child-life protection visitor, tuberculosis visitor and school nurse, as well as attending to the sick. Moreover, a wise and sympathetic nurse is, in time, accepted as adviser and friend on all family and personal problems, a travelling citizens' advice bureau, as well as a travelling clinic.[1]

As time went on it was recognised that hospital training was an inadequate preparation for the multifarious demands made on the district nurse, and the Queen's Institute of District Nursing was established to co-ordinate the work of the separate voluntary committees in the different districts and to ensure that a good standard of nursing was maintained, and it arranges training courses for those nurses who wish to take up this branch of the profession.[2]

Skilled medical diagnosis and treatment and nursing care in the patient's own home together form the basis of medical care, but they are insufficient in themselves for the successful treatment of many conditions. These require the specialist skills and equipment which only a hospital can give, and which it is now its function to provide. From being 'asylums' for the sick poor the hospitals have changed and developed into centres where the resources of medical science are concentrated, to be expended freely for the benefit of the patient whatever his status in the world outside, and of recent years this spirit has penetrated even to those last refuges of the pre-scientific era, the 'chronic' wards, now being transformed into geriatic units.[3] These developments have inevitably affected and been affected by methods of administration, and during the years before the recent war two questions which exercised the minds of

[1] 'It is wonderful how one finds out, and without asking, their joys and troubles, all their aches and pains, all their hopes and family histories. They expect advice about baby's rash, what to do with granny, father's false teeth, Johnny's boots... Lily's love affairs... and so on.'—Letter from district nurse quoted above.

[2] This originated as the Queen Victoria Jubilee Institute for Nurses, the founding of which was made possible by the decision of Queen Victoria to devote the money which the women of the nation collected to celebrate her Jubilee in 1887 to the purpose. The name was changed in 1925. See Mary Stocks, *A Hundred Years of District Nursing*, 1960.

[3] See below, Chapter XVIII.

many concerned administrators were how far existing methods were adequate to meet the needs of the developing situation, and along what lines changes should be made.

At that time there were two distinct hospital systems, the voluntary and the municipal, separately and differently organised and financed, and each with its own traditions and fund of experience. The voluntary hospitals, some of which, like St. Thomas's and St. Bartholomew's, could trace their history back to the Middle Ages, were independent organisations administered by their own governing bodies or boards of trustees. They varied greatly in size and efficiency, from the large general hospitals of 200 or more beds in London and the big cities with their distinguished consultants and modern equipment, to the small 'cottage hospitals' served by local general practitioners.[1] There was also considerable variation in function as, while the majority were general hospitals, accepting a wide range of surgical and medical cases, others specialised in particular diseases or conditions. In general, however, the voluntary hospitals tended to accept only acute cases needing active treatment, leaving to the municipal hospitals the care of the chronic sick.

Municipal hospitals, for which the local authorities were directly responsible, were of two kinds, the infectious diseases hospitals and the general hospitals. The latter had originated as Poor Law infirmaries, provided by the boards of guardians, for the 'destitute sick'. In many such infirmaries standards of care were, in the first instance, very low, but conditions improved after the middle of the century when 'Nightingale' nurses took the place of the able-bodied paupers who had hitherto 'nursed' their fellows,[2] and enlightened administrators gradually placed more emphasis on the noun 'sick' than the adjective 'destitute'. Finally, in 1929, the twenty-year-old recommendations of the Royal Commission on the Poor Law were put into operation, the boards of guardians were abolished, and it became an accepted principle that 'general hospital care was a proper activity of the major local health authorities rather than of the Poor Law machinery'.[3] During the

[1] Just before the war, of the 700 or so voluntary hospitals in England and Wales for which particulars were available, some 75 had more than 200 beds, 115 had 100 to 200 beds each, over 500 had less than 100 beds and more than half of these had less than 30. Ministry of Health, op. cit., p. 58.

[2] The first qualified nurse to be appointed to a poor law infirmary was Agnes Jones, who, as a result of the efforts of the same William Rathbone who started district nursing in the city, was put in charge of the male wards of the Brownlow Hill Institution, Liverpool, in 1864. She compared the place as she found it to Dante's *Inferno*, but gradually brought about considerable improvements. Her devotion to duty undermined her health, and she died of typhus a few years after her appointment.

[3] Ministry of Health, op. cit., p. 56.

next few years local health committees gradually 'appropriated' the old infirmaries and began the slow and difficult process of converting them into modern hospitals. Although handicapped by unsuitable buildings and the poor law atmosphere, good progress was being made by many local authorities in the years immediately preceding the war. Some authorities not only modernised old hospitals, but built new ones, and at the outbreak of war many health committees had hospitals under their control of which they were justly proud.[1]

But while much good, and even invaluable, work was done in connection with both the voluntary and municipal hospital service the position, taken as a whole, was far from satisfactory. 'Britain had hospitals, but no hospital system', and nobody had the power or responsibility to combine the separate units into a planned and co-ordinated service based on a consideration of the needs of all sections of the population.[2] Like doctors, hospitals were unevenly distributed, and in some areas the provision was inadequate for the needs of the population, many were too small for efficient working, and in many voluntary hospitals and some local authority areas finance presented a serious problem and held back improvements. The lack of co-ordination meant that there could be two hospitals in the same area close to each other, one in debt, the other well endowed, one with a long waiting list, the other with empty beds.

As medical science developed and standards of hospital care rose, the disadvantages of this lack of co-ordination and administrative inefficiency became more and more evident, and the need for closer co-operation was increasingly recognised. The King Edward Hospital Fund for London, started in 1897 by Edward VII when Prince of Wales as the Prince of Wales Hospital Fund, was the first step in this direction. But it only touched the fringe of the problem. Many years later the voluntary hospitals in certain provincial cities, such as Liverpool and Bristol, took the much bolder step of forming themselves into hospital units, and the possibility and desirability of regional co-operation began to be seriously considered. Then came the Second World War, and the prospect of many casualties, both from the battle zones and as a result of air raids, made planning on a national scale essential. So the Emergency Medical Service came into being, and brought

[1] Just before the war the local authorities of England and Wales had nearly 70,000 beds in 140 general hospitals maintained by public health committees, and nearly 60,000 more in 400 hospitals and institutions still administered under the Poor Law by public assistance committees.

[2] Cf. P.E.P., *Planning*, No. 222, June 1944, 'Medical Care for Citizens', p. 41, and Ministry of Health, op. cit., p. 56, where the hospital services are described as 'everybody's business, but nobody's full responsibility'.

with it improvements in many hospitals, but 'above all experience of what it means to translate a collection of individual hospitals into a related hospital system'.[1] This having been achieved, a return to the previous inchoate state of affairs was unthinkable and the creation of a national hospital service was clearly the next step forward.

Thus, as with social insurance and assistance, so with provisions for medical care, the time was ripe for the creation of a unified national service based on the varied developments of the previous half-century. In February, 1944, the National Government published a White Paper outlining its proposals for a comprehensive service which would 'bring the country's full resources to bear on reducing the ill-health and promoting the good health of its citizens',[2] and which would ensure that in future every man, woman and child in the country could rely on getting the advice and treatment needed in matters of personal health, irrespective of ability to pay. The proposals contained in the White Paper had not yet been given legislative form and passed through Parliament when the general election of 1945 took place, and the Labour Government took over this task. Mr. Aneurin Bevan, who became Minister of Health, made several changes in the White Paper proposals, but the underlying purpose remained the same, and in November 1946, after eighteen months of negotiation and controversy, the National Health Service Act, 'to provide for the establishment of a comprehensive health service for the people of England and Wales', was placed on the statute book.

[1] Ministry of Health, op. cit., p. 7. For a discussion of the working of this scheme see R. M. Titmuss, *Problems of Social Policy*. The scope and quality of the service are assessed in ch. xxiii, pp. 466–89. The following chapter, ch. xxiv, deals with the effect of the war on hospitals for the sick.

[2] Ministry of Health, op. cit., p. 5.

CHAPTER VI

THE NATIONAL HEALTH SERVICE

THE object of the National Health Service Act, 1946, was to create an administrative framework in which a health service universal in scope, comprehensive in character, and free to the user could be built up. The task was not an easy one. The State was assuming responsibility for the medical care of all within its borders, whether living in town or country, in densely or sparsely populated areas, in metropolitan or remote regions, hence adequate provision must be available everywhere. The service was designed to 'secure improvement in the physical and mental health of the people of England and Wales, and the prevention, diagnosis and treatment of illness'; hence not only must there be specialist provision for all manner of mental and physical diseases, but the health needs of differing age and social groups must be met. Moreover, in planning the service regard had to be paid to the traditions and interests of established and functioning institutions and to the professional outlook of the men and women who were being asked to enter and operate the new service. This meant taking cognisance of the desire of the teaching hospitals to retain their identity, the private practitioners' fear of becoming servants of a central government department or local authority, the value of maintaining services created and maintained by enterprising and conscientious local authorities.

The attempt to achieve these ends and reconcile these interests has resulted in a complicated administrative set-up. Ultimate control rests with the Minister of Health. He is, of course, responsible to Parliament and thus to the people, but within the framework of the Act his powers are very considerable. An advisory body, the Central Health Services Council, has been created to advise him on professional and technical questions and to keep the general development of the service under review. The forty-one members are either members of the medical and kindred professions or people with special experience in local government, hospital management or mental health. With the exception of holders of certain specified offices, such as the President of the Royal College of Surgeons, who serve *ex officio*, members are appointed by the Minister after consultation with the relevant professional bodies.

The Council's functions are purely advisory, and the Minister is not bound to take its advice, but he is required by the Act to lay its annual report before Parliament,[1] and in this way the views of the Council become known even if they differ from those of the Minister. On the recommendation of the Council nine standing advisory committees, Medical, Dental, Pharmaceutical, Ophthalmic, Nursing, Maternity and Midwifery, Tuberculosis, Mental Health and Cancer and Radiography have also been established, and from time to time the Council has set up its own special committees to consider questions of immediate interest and importance. Since it came into being special committees of this kind have considered such diverse questions as hospital supplies, general practice, health centres and the welfare of children in hospital.

The services provided under the National Health Service Act are administered in three separate groups, the hospital and specialist services form one group, the personal practitioner services the second, and the services administered by local authorities the third. Two major health responsibilities remain outside the National Health Service, the health of the school child and the health of the worker. The School Health Service developed as a part of the educational system, and remains the responsibility of the Ministry of Education and the local education authorities, though there are links with the National Health Service. The State has not yet accepted responsibility for the creation of a unified industrial health service to function alongside the general health service, though enactments designed to protect the health and safety of the worker cover mines and quarries, factories, shops and other work places, and are enforced by central government or local authority inspectors, while many large firms have developed their own health services which go far beyond minimum legislative requirements. A Committee of Inquiry, which met under the chairmanship of Judge Edgar T. Dale to examine the relationship between the general health and industrial health services, considered that it was desirable that 'eventually' there should be some comprehensive provision for occupational health covering both industrial and non-industrial occupations, but thought that more experience would have to be gained from future surveys and experiments before such provision could be made effectively.[2]

The hospital, specialist and ancillary services include all forms of general and special hospital provision, both in-patient and out-patient, and specialist advice either in hospital, in a health centre

---

[1] National Health Service Act, Section 2 (5). The Minister may refrain from publishing anything in the Report if, after consulting the Council, he is satisfied that it would be contrary to the public interest to do so. This is a normal legal safeguard. [2] Cmd. 8170, 1951.

74

or, if necessary, at the patient's own home. These services are directly under the control of the Minister of Health and are organised regionally, the country being divided into fifteen hospital regions, in such a way that the hospital service in each region is associated with a university having a school of medicine.[1] Each region has its own regional hospital board, which is responsible, as the agent of the Minister, for the planning, provision and supervision of the hospital services in its region. The regional boards decide major issues of policy, but the day-to-day administration of the hospitals is in the hands of the hospital management committees, each of which is responsible, as an agent of its board, for a single hospital or group of hospitals, The thirty-six 'teaching hospitals', that is, hospitals or groups of hospitals which provide facilities for undergraduate or post-graduate clinical teaching, are administered separately by their own boards of governors appointed by the Minister and directly responsible to him. A small number of voluntary hospitals, about two hundred in all, have chosen to remain outside the health service. They are chiefly hospitals with religious or sectional affiliations, such as certain hospitals run by religious orders, 'The Retreat', the mental hospital at York carried on by the Society of Friends, and Manor House Hospital, which is maintained by the trade union movement.

The nationalisation of the vast majority of the former municipal and voluntary hospitals, their grouping into regions and management by appointed boards and committees was the most drastic and far reaching change brought about by the National Health Service Act. The hospital service thus created is large,[2] widely dispersed, and its member units differ considerably in tradition and standards. Many of the buildings taken over were obsolete and inappropriate, and there were grave staff shortages. Hence there were many difficulties of organisation and administration to overcome. Nevertheless the bold experiment appears to be succeeding. At the end of the first year's working, *The Practitioner* recorded that the regional organisation of the service had given general satisfaction to the medical profession, and its advantages from the point of view of the efficient planning of the specialist services had quickly become manifest.[3] Eight years later the Acton Society Trust, having made an objective investigation into the

[1] The number of regions was increased from 14 to 15 in 1960.

[2] The Acton Society Trust points out that, with its nearly half-a-million employees, the hospital service is the third largest organisation in the country, surpassed only by the British Transport Commission and the National Coal Board. *Hospitals and the State*, 1, 'Background and Blueprint', p. 3.

[3] *The National Health Service Act in Great Britain, A Review of the First Year's Working*, p. 5.

working of the hospital service, concluded that 'so far as its institutions are concerned the structure of the service is basically sound'.[1] Nor did the Guillebaud Committee, reporting about the same time, wish to introduce any great changes, although some of their witnesses were critical of the regional structure, and one of their members, Mr. E. Maude, dissented from his colleagues on this issue.

One of the major criticisms which have been made of the structure of the hospital service is that it is organised from above, in that regional boards are appointed by, and are agents of, the Minister, while management committees are agents of the boards. Neither boards nor committees are responsible directly to the electorate, nor are they responsible for finding the money they spend.[2] Members of boards and committees are appointed as individuals and are unpaid. The Act provides for the inclusion on each board of persons appointed after consultation with the associated universities and local health authorities in the region, organisations representative of the medical profession and 'such other organisations as appear to the Minister to be concerned',[3] but this does not imply that the persons so appointed are in any way representatives or delegates of these bodies. They serve in their personal capacities. It has been pointed out that 'in a basically democratic country nomination from above can only be justified if it can secure better people and more balanced committees without sacrificing that responsiveness to local needs and opinion which is the hallmark of elected representation',[4] and the question arises as to whether this is the case in the hospital service. In a study of the part played by voluntary effort in this service sponsored by the National Council of Social Service and King Edward's Hospital Fund for London, Mr. John Trevlyan implicitly claims that it is. He contends that the assumption that a committee can only be democratic if it consists of elected representatives is 'a narrow interpretation of the term'. 'It is our belief', he continues, 'that the true democratic element, which defies precise description, is maintained through the voluntary status of members of boards and management committees irrespective of method of appointment, and that the members of voluntary boards and committees entrusted with statutory responsibilities are, except in the method of their appointment, representative of

---

[1] *Hospitals and the State*, 4, Groups, Regions and Committees. Part II, Regional Hospital Boards, p. 54.

[2] Report of the Committee of Enquiry into the Cost of the National Health Service. Cmd. 9663, pp. 55. Reservation by E. J. Maude, pp. 274–286.

[3] National Health Service Act. Section 11(1) and Third Schedule.

[4] P.E.P. *The Hospital Service*, I. The System of Management. *Planning*, Vol. XVI, No. 303. September 1949.

the people whose interests they serve.'[1] In support of this he points out that an analysis made of the membership of hospital boards and committees revealed that the composition of regional hospital boards did not differ greatly in quality or type of members from that of the major local authorities, except for 'a substantial and effective' representation of the medical profession and the universities.[2] After reviewing the whole situation the Guillebaud Committee concluded that Ministers of Health 'must reserve to themselves the sole right to decide who shall be appointed to the regional boards, and members must be selected solely for the contribution they can make to the efficient running of the hospital service'.[3]

Various alternatives to the hierarchical regional structure set up by the Act were put forward by some witnesses to the Guillebaud Committee. The most feasible of these was the suggestion that the administration of the service be transferred to the local health authorities who would establish joint authorities to provide for regional development. This broadly speaking, was the plan put forward by the National Government in 1944,[4] but never implemented. The majority of the Guillebaud Committee decisively rejected any attempt to revive it on the grounds that local authority areas are, in general, wholly irrelevant to the administrative needs of the hospital service and their standards are uneven; past experience had suggested that joint boards would be unlikely to work effectively or smoothly; the return of the hospitals to the local authorities would impose an intolerable burden on the local rates; and, finally, such a transfer would not be acceptable to the medical profession.[5] In their view, the present administrative system has 'greatly improved and levelled up the general standard of hospital services throughout the country', and apart from Mr. Maude, they had no wish to alter it.

From the above discussion it would appear likely that the present regional organisation of the hospitals is generally accepted and is here to stay. Within its broad framework there is room for considerable variation in procedure and relationships, and the last twelve years have been years of growth and experiment, during which the functions of regional boards and management committees

[1] National Council of Social Service and King Edward's Hospital Fund for London. *Voluntary Service and the State*, pp. 35–36.

[2] National Council of Social Service and King Edward's Hospital Fund for London. *Voluntary Service and the State*, p. 37. The results of the analysis are given in Appendix I.

[3] Cmd. 9663, p. 96, par. 256.

[4] Ministry of Health and Department of Health for Scotland, *A National Health Service*, Cmd. 6502, 1944.

[5] Cmd. 9663, pp. 56–58.

have been slowly clarified and established, and individual hospitals and their staffs have adjusted themselves to the new order. Each regional hospital board is responsible, as an agent of the Minister and in collaboration with the boards of governors of the teaching hospitals in its area, for the planning, provision and supervision of a hospital and specialist service for its region.[1] It is thus both a planning authority and supervisory authority, and in each of these capacities has complex problems to solve.

In the exercise of their functions as planners, regional boards have been handicapped ever since the inception of the service by shortage of capital. When they took over in 1948 the state of the hospitals was far from satisfactory, yet, allowing for increased prices, annual capital expenditure in the years which followed was only about one-third that of the years just before the war.[2] In February 1955 the Minister of Health and Secretary of State for Scotland announced plans for financing certain new building projects and for allocating a further sum for plant replacement and deployment as a result of which the total annual capital expenditure increased from £13 million in 1956–7 to well over £20 million in 1958–9. This is still well below the £30 million annually the Guillebaud Committee considered desirable,[3] and until further resources are made available for replacements and renewals, let alone expansion, the service must continue to operate under an increasing handicap as buildings and equipment deteriorate and become more and more out of date.

Financial stringency accentuates the need for careful planning so that available resources are utilised to the best advantage, and, as the Acton Trust points out,[4] boards, in their planning, cannot take into account only current needs, they have also to try to estimate future trends in demand. This involves consideration both of changing incidence and methods of treating differing diseases (for example the declining demand for beds for tuberculosis and other infectious illnesses) and changing economic and social conditions (for example, age structure and marital status of the population). These questions demand serious and continued study and thought, and hence it is important that those who undertake the onerous work which the development of the hospital

[1] National Health Service Act, ss. 11 and 12.

[2] B. Abel-Smith and R. M. Titmuss, *The Cost of the National Health Service in England and Wales*. The authors estimated that in 1938–39 hospital capital expenditure amounted to £32m. in 1952–53 prices. In 1952–53 it was £10·2m. i.e. 32 per cent of the 1938–39 expenditure. Quoted in the Guillebaud Report, p. 33, par. 64.

[3] Cmd. 9663, pp. 113–117, pars. 313–319.

[4] *Hospitals and the State*, Groups, Regions and Committees, Part 11, Hospital Boards, p. 25.

service on sound yet imaginative lines involves have the time and ability to give it.

It has been pointed out already that members of regional hospital boards and management committees serve as part-time volunteers. 'It is the distinctive feature of the national hospital plan that the responsibility for handling expenditure of public funds exceeding £300 millions annually is delegated to voluntary unpaid committees.'[1] This is in line with the tradition already well established in local government and applies to a new situation the principle that ultimate administrative control shall rest, not with a small group of professional administrators, but with a body of citizens acting on behalf of their fellows. The problem is, however, to find a sufficient number of persons with capacity and judgment to exercise the large and intricate responsibilities that hospital administration involves, and sufficient time to undertake them. To quote the Acton Society Trust once again, 'one of the most important questions which hangs over the future of the National Hospital Service is whether it will always be possible to find enough people of the right kind to carry the burden of work and leadership required, especially in those posts which involve much more than occasional attendance at committee meetings.'[2]

Final responsibility may rest with the voluntary members of regional hospital boards and management committees, but the main burden of administration is carried by the permanent officials, particularly those in senior positions. Hence the importance of recruiting and training for the service men and women of intelligence, integrity and initiative, and of giving them scope for the exercise of their talents and satisfactory career prospects. The possibility of developing a national scheme of recruitment and training for hospital administration was already being discussed when the Guillebaud Committee reported, and in its report recommended that such provision should be made 'at the earliest possible date'.[3] The Ministry of Health has now sponsored a plan for a three-year training course for selected candidates, and it is being operated at two centres, King Edward's Hospital Fund Administrative Staff College and Manchester University. It is also hoped to supplement and develop further such opportunities as now exist for refresher courses and part-time training for the men and women already in the service.

The second major division of the National Health Service consists of the personal practitioner services, that is the services of the general practitioner or family doctor, together with those of the dentist and pharmacist and the supplementary ophthalmic

[1] Acton Society Trust, op. cit., p. 46.
[2] Ibid., p. 50. [3] Cmd. 9663, p. 140, par. 394.

service. The key position here, and in some respects in the health service as a whole, is occupied by the general practitioner, 'for only general practice can ensure that the patient is treated both as an individual and in relation to his family background, and it alone provides for continuity of treatment at all times by one doctor', while 'the general practitioner by the exercise of his responsibility for the patient, can link together preventive, social and curative medicine'.[1] The problem facing the planners of the health service was to make the general practitioner service available to the whole population and at the same time preserve the doctor's clinical freedom, freedom of choice for both doctor and patient and a satisfactory doctor-patient relationship. These three conditions were regarded by doctors as essential for the proper practice of their profession, and rightly or wrongly, they believed that they would be endangered if medical practice became a salaried service directly under State or local authority control. So fearful were they that such control would be introduced by ministerial regulation that they brought pressure to bear on the Minister to make such action impossible, and the National Health Service (Amendment) Act, 1949, contains a clause designed to allay these fears.[2]

The personal practitioner services are administered by local executive councils. Each council consists of twenty-five members of whom eight are appointed by the local health authority, five by the Minister and the remainder by the doctors, dentists and pharmacists practising in the area. This means that, if all those appointed attend regularly, a balance is maintained between lay and professional representation and thus the interests of both the profession and those of the public are safeguarded. There is an executive committee for each county and county borough except where, as in eight areas, one council covers the areas of two local authorities. Equating areas in this way makes it easier to bring about and maintain co-operation between the personal practitioner services and those of the local health authority and was endorsed by the Guillebaud Committee.[3] Moreover, local executive councils have taken over several of the functions formerly exercised by the local insurance committees, which had been established in each county and county borough in connection with the National Health Insurance scheme, and thus continuity with an established and accepted service has been ensured.

Doctors and dentists intending to practise in a particular area contract with their local executive council, but in order to bring

[1] Central Health Services Council. Report of the Committee on General Practice within the National Health Service, H.M.S.O., pp. 2–3.
[2] Section 10.　　　　　　　　　　　[3] Op. cit., p. 155, par. 443.

about a more even distribution of doctors throughout the country two Medical Practices Committees, one for England and Wales and one for Scotland, have been established. Their approval must be obtained before a doctor can attempt to build up a new national health service practice in an area, or succeed to a place in a partnership or fill a vacancy caused by death or retirement. The powers of these committees are wholly negative, however. They can refuse permission for the establishment of a new practice or the filling of a vacancy if they consider that the number of doctors in the area is sufficient, but they cannot direct a doctor to a particular area, however great the need there. In order to attract practitioners to under-doctored areas or areas which present special difficulties, 'initial practice allowances' are granted to doctors who set out to establish single-handed practices in areas which have been designated by the Medical Practices Committee as requiring additional doctors, while 'inducement payments' may be made in suitable cases to help doctors practising in areas which are sparsely populated or, for some other reason fail to provide sufficient income in the ordinary way. The numbers of practitioners affected by such payments appear to be few.[1] However, the Guillebaud Committee considered that since the 'appointed day' doctors had become more evenly distributed over the country as a whole, and a more reasonable balance had been struck between over-doctored and under-doctored areas, although there was still room for improvement.[2] The Report of the Ministry of Health for the year ended 31 December 1956 notes that by far the greater part of the population is now living in adequately doctored areas, and while there is still room for further improvement, 'it is clear that there has been a steady and satisfactory improvement in the distribution of doctors'.[3]

It was suggested in the previous chapter that before 1948 the work of many general practitioners was rendered more difficult and less effective by their isolation, the unsuitable premises many of them occupied and the general lack of facilities for diagnosis. The remedy proposed by the Act was the establishment by local authorities throughout the country of health centres which, it was hoped, would become 'a main feature of the personal practitioner service'.[4] In those centres, so the planners intended, group practice would be developed, scientific aids to diagnosis provided, and ancillary workers would be in attendance. For various reasons,

[1] During the year 1958 only twenty-seven inducement payments were made.
[2] Op. cit., p. 165, par. 478.
[3] Op. cit., p. 53.
[4] National Health Service Bill, Summary of the Proposed New Service. Cmd. 6761, p. 9.

including shortages of money, materials and manpower, very few health centres have been established, but during the last ten years the medical profession has been making its own adjustments to changing conditions and demands, and the Committee on General Practice reported in 1954 that 'one of the encouraging developments in the National Health Service has been increasing co-operation between doctors'.[1] This has manifested itself in the increase in the number of partnerships and of group practices, that is, practices 'carried on by several general practitioners working together in close association, consulting one another about their patients and doing their surgery work in whole or in part in a common building controlled by the doctors'.[2] The formation of such practices which, 'besides lightening the burden of a doctor's life and enormously facilitating co-operation with his colleagues also opens the door to co-operation in other spheres',[3] has been encouraged by the setting aside of £100,000 annually since April 1953 to form a Group Practice Loan Fund, out of which interest-free loans, intended for doctors wishing to establish or improve central surgery premises from which to carry on group practice, are provided. By the end of 1958 323 applications had been received, of which 144 had been approved.[4]

The crucial issue in general practice is the relationship between doctor and patient, 'the true basis of the family doctor's life and often his chief reward',[5] and at the time of the inception of the service many doctors feared lest the new administrative arrangements would tend to destroy a relationship which, although tenuous in many large industrial practices, has remained one of the ideals of the profession. The Committee on General Practice, taking into account both survey material made available to them, and the evidence of individual doctors, concluded that, in general, the advent of the National Health Service had not disturbed the relationship between doctors and patients, 'in some respects, indeed, it was found to be better than before'. This was ascribed to the absence of the money bar and to increased co-operation between doctors.[6] The Guillebaud Committee, while admitting

[1] Report, p. 5.   [2] Ibid., p. 17.
[3] Minister of Health (Mr. Robert H. Turton) in an address to the Annual Meeting of the Executive Council's Association (England), on 21 October 1955. Quoted in the Annual Report of the Ministry of Health, 1955. Cmd. 9857, p. 51.
[4] Report of the Ministry of Health for the year ended 31 December 1958. Cmnd. 806, p. 100.
[5] Paper by Dr. A. Talbot Rogers, 'Some Administrative Problems of the General Practitioner' printed in *The Health Services, Some of their Practical Problems*. Institute of Public Administration, 1951, p. 53.
[6] Op. cit., p. 13.

that one or two of their witnesses expressed a contrary opinion, concurred with this conclusion which, they said, was in a line with the great volume of the evidence received.[1]

There has been some increase in the services given by general practitioners to their patients since the inception of the service, but this increase has not been very great. One effect of the extension of the right to free medical attention from the doctor of one's choice to the whole population has been an increase in the number of consultations by women and children.[2] While this may be due in some measure to women preferring their own doctor to the ante-natal or child welfare clinic, and therefore is to be set against the decline in the number of attendances at those clinics, a question to be considered later,[3] at the same time the greater availability of medical services to, and use by these most vulnerable groups should, in the long run, lead to improvements in the health of the nation.

Among the benefits to which the patient became entitled by the National Health Service Act, 1946, was the free provision of such drugs and appliances as were required for his treatment. During the early years of the service both the number of prescriptions dispensed and their total cost rose rapidly,[4] and it was widely believed both that a good deal of this expenditure was unnecessary and that doctors and patients were taking advantage of the service.[5] Successive governments became concerned about the increasing and possibly excessive cost of prescriptions and the apparent ease with which certificates authorising the free provision of medical and surgical appliances were issued, and in June 1952 a charge was imposed of one shilling for each National Health Service prescription form dispensed, an amount which has since been increased to one shilling for each item. At the same time a charge of up to £1 was imposed for dental treatment for patients other than young persons under twenty-one, expectant mothers, and mothers with children under a year old, while both young and old pay up to £4 5s. for the cost of dentures. Payments must also be made for surgical appliances such as boots, supports and elastic hosiery, as well as for spectacles. These charges do not apply to hospital in-patients, patients in receipt of National Assistance, or war pensioners in respect of their accepted war disabilities. Other persons not able to afford the charges may apply to the National Assistance Board for a grant towards them, and in these cases the

---

[1] Op. cit., p. 165, par. 476.
[2] Report of the Committee on Medical Practice, p. 10, par. 34.
[3] Chapter XI. [4] Cmd. 9663. Table 45, p. 161.
[5] This is discussed by François Lafitte writing in *The Health Services, Some of their Practical Problems*, p. 106.

Board is empowered to waive its general rule of not assisting persons in full employment.

The charges listed in the previous paragraph were imposed in order to reduce the cost of the Health Service to the nation by both yielding revenue and reducing surplus demand. In 1957–8 payments for drugs and appliances amounted to slightly less than £10,800,000, payments for dental treatment and dentures to slightly more than £8,100,000, and for glasses slightly more than £5,200,000.[1] The extent to which charges have reduced demand, and whether and to what extent persons in genuine need of drugs or dental treatment or appliances have been deterred by the charges from obtaining them are matters less easy to ascertain. The conclusions the Guillebaud Committee reached about the charge for prescriptions (at that time one shilling for each prescription and not for each item), were that while the evidence was not wholly conclusive, there was no reason to think that the charges hindered the proper use of the service by at least the great majority of its potential users, nor did they think that its removal would improve the working of the service to an extent commensurate with its cost.[2] On the other hand they did not think that a case had been made for increasing the charges. Charges and demand apart, the cost of this particular service has continued to rise owing to the increased use of new and expensive drugs, including proprietary drugs, and, while much of this has been necessary and beneficial, the Ministry of Health has evolved machinery designed to keep a careful check on such prescribing.[3]

There was some evidence that the demands on the dental service were already declining up before charges were imposed as the large arrears of unmet needs were made, and the same applies to the ophthalmic services. The Guillebaud Committee considered that the charge for dental treatment as it is now imposed hinders people from making the best use of the service by attending regularly and so obtaining early conservative treatment, and they 'would regard the reduction of the incidence of this charge as having the highest priority when additional resources become

[1] Report of the Ministry of Health for 1958, pp. 5–6. In addition it is estimated that payments amounting to approximately £50,000 were made for repairs and replacements of dentures and spectacles where the loss was due to the patient's own carelessness.

[2] Report, p. 195, par. 590.

[3] The Guillebaud Committee quote estimates attributing 36 per cent of the increased cost of the pharmaceutical service to an increase in the amount prescribed, 35 per cent to the changed composition of proprietary and nonproprietary articles and 40 per cent to other factors, including the use of new and expensive drugs. Report, p. 47. Cf. the conclusions of the study made by J. P. Martin, *Social Aspects of Prescribing*, 1957.

available'. They also favoured a proposal put forward by the British Dental Association that persons who had received comprehensive treatment and thereafter sought treatment regularly should have the treatment charge refunded, and so contract into a free dental service. They considered that this would be an effective contribution to preventive health.[1] As a second priority the Committee recommended a substantial reduction in the amount charged for spectacles.

The third major grouping within the National Health Service consists of the services for which the local authorities are responsible. The local health authorities for the purposes of the Act are the county councils and the county borough councils, but joint boards may be formed where it is considered expedient. These same authorities are also responsible for the administration of the welfare services for aged and handicapped persons provided for by Part III of the National Assistance Act, and in some areas the health committee of the council has assumed responsibility for both health and welfare services. Even where they are administered separately, close co-operation between the administrators of the two groups of services is essential, since their functions interlock and their users are frequently the same people. The assignment of all powers and duties under the National Health Service Act to the counties and county boroughs has deprived the minor authorities of the responsibilities, particularly in connection with maternity and child welfare, which they had carried for many years, and thus caused some regrets. However, county and county borough councils, with their generally larger resources and wider powers, are in a better position than the smaller authorities to plan their services comprehensively and relate them to other health and social provisions. Decentralisation is possible in the county areas as they may be subdivided 'according to local health requirements', and sub-committees of the county health committee, on which the councils of the county districts in the subdivision are represented, may be set up in each area. These sub-committees undertake the day to day administration of the services delegated to them, but the county council, as local health authority, retains responsibility for general policy and finance.[2]

The services assigned to the local authorities are mainly preventive in character, that is, they are concerned with the maintenance and improvement of health rather than with the treatment of illness. In connection with the latter the functions of the

[1] Report, pp. 192–193, pars. 578–582.
[2] Ministry of Health Circular, 118/47. The National Health Service Act, 1946. Health Services to be provided by Local Authorities under Part III of the Act, par. 20, p. 8.

local health authorities, although important, are ancillary; in connection with the former they are primary. Among the most important are those laid down in Sections 21–4 of the Act, which are designed to safeguard and improve the health of mothers and young children. These services, which include the care (including dental care) of expectant and nursing mothers, the provision, either by direct employment or by arrangement with regional hospital boards or voluntary organisations, of an adequate number of midwives to meet the needs of the area, and the provision of health visitors, were already undertaken by many local authorities before 1948, but the Act has turned what had been powers into duties, and so has ensured nation-wide coverage. Other duties which must be undertaken by local health authorities are the provision of home nurses (whether by making arrangements with a voluntary organisation or themselves employing them), making arrangements with medical practitioners for vaccination against smallpox and immunisation against diphtheria[1] and any other disease if so directed by the Minister. They also provide ambulances 'and other means of transport' for the conveyance of sick or mentally defective persons or expectant mothers to places 'in or outside' their area.

In addition to these duties local authorities have wide permissive powers in connection with the prevention of illness, the care of persons suffering from illness or mental defect and the after-care of such persons, and these powers become duties 'to such extent as the Minister may direct'.[2] He has directed that arrangements must be made for the care and after-care of persons suffering from tuberculosis and to prevent the spread of this disease.[3] One of the useful services undertaken by local authorities exercising these powers is the loan of sick-room requisites, not only to patients to whom a nurse has been called in, but also to those being cared for wholly by relatives. This loan service is one of the few services not free to the user under the original Act, local authorities having discretionary powers to make whatever charges they consider reasonable, having regard to the means of the persons using the service.

Charges for services rendered may also be levied by a local authority providing a domestic help service in accordance with Section 29 of the Act. This section gives general powers to local health authorities 'to make such arrangements as the Minister may approve for providing domestic help for households where such help is required owing to the presence of any person who is

[1] Although arrangements must be made for these services to be available, no one is compelled to make use of them. The Vaccination Acts have now ceased to have effect.
[2] National Health Service Act, 1946, Section 28.
[3] For the position with regard to the mental health services see Chapter XX.

ill, lying-in, an expectant mother, mentally defective, aged or a child not over school age within the meaning of the Education Act, 1944'. All local health authorities are now operating approved schemes, chiefly with the assistance of part-time staff, and the service is meeting a real need especially in maternity cases, for the aged, and where chronically sick persons are being nursed at home. Two recent developments are the use by certain authorities of selected home helps to assist in the rehabilitation of problem families,[1] and the provision in some areas of night services of 'sitters-up', to relieve friends and relatives caring for aged or chronically sick persons and to help in cases where there are no friends or relatives available.

Having now described the structure of the National Health Service it remains to examine its working. The first major question to be considered is that of co-ordination. It has already been shown that, owing to the complexities of the administrative problems presented, and to differing traditions and outlook embedded in its component parts, what was intended to be essentially a unified service has been divided administratively into three, and, in some cases, the new lines of demarcation have made it more, rather than less difficult to provide continuous care for the patient and to link prevention and after-care with treatment. This is seen, for example, if we consider the provisions made for the prevention and treatment of tuberculosis. Of recent years the decline both in deaths from and notifications of this disease has been rapid,[2] owing partly to the improved economic and social conditions and partly to advances in chemotherapy, but for many years it was, in its social effects and implications, one of the gravest of all diseases, and even now it still ranks as 'by far the chief of the group of infectious diseases, especially in the most productive years of life'.[3] The need for a comprehensive tuberculosis service, which would include provisions directed both towards the prevention and the treatment of the disease, was brought to the notice of the public by the issue, just before the First World War, of the Interim and Final Reports of the Departmental Committee on Tuberculosis,[4] which recommended that county councils and county borough councils should draw up plans for preventive and treatment services in their areas. The Interim Report suggested that these

[1] Discussed below, p. 156.
[2] In 1948 there was a mortality rate of 21,993, while notifications numbered 52,576. In 1958, the mortality was 4,480, notifications 29,838.
[3] Report of the Ministry of Health, 1955. Part II, 'On the State of Public Health'. Cmnd. 16, p. 97. In 1955 it caused 67 per cent of all deaths due to infection and 78 per cent of those in the age group 15–39 years.
[4] The Committee was set up in February 1912, the Interim Report was published later in the same year, the Final Report in 1913.

provisions should include the setting-up of dispensaries, that is local centres of diagnosis and treatment through which all cases of tuberculosis would pass, at which the examination of contacts would take place and from which educational work and after-care would be carried out. The need for adequate sanatorium and hospital accommodation was also stressed. During the years following the publication of the reports, local authorities began putting these recommendations into practice, and the Tuberculosis Act, 1921, made their implementation a statutory duty for all county councils and county borough councils. This meant that, in the years between the wars, a unified system for the prevention and treatment of tuberculosis existed in each local authority area, and, although standards varied, these services gradually became more comprehensive and effective.

The National Health Service Act made radical changes in the administration of the tuberculosis service. Hospitals and sanatoria were taken over by the regional hospital boards, and with them went the dispensaries, now transformed into or replaced by 'chest clinics'. The local health authorities retained their responsibilities for the control of tuberculosis by such means as the supervision of notifications, health education, and the examination of contacts. Mass radiography units are operated by the regional hospital boards, however, while, on the other hand, immunisation is a local health authority responsibility and B.C.G. vaccination may be carried out by chest physicians on behalf of the county council or county borough council. The health authorities are responsible for the social care of patients awaiting places in sanatoria, and for their after-care on return from treatment, that is, for providing under Section 28 of the Act, 'a care and after-care organisation which will co-operate with, but not overlap the treatment services, and whose basic function will be to help to solve the special problems of the tuberculous household and so relieve domestic difficulties and worry'.[1] This means not only providing special tuberculosis welfare services and marshalling those general services of the local health authorities such as district nurses and home helps which are immediately concerned, but also invoking the help of other statutory and voluntary organisations such as the National Assistance Board (which body not only assists tuberculous persons at a special scale rate but may also make cash grants for extra nourishment), and the rehabilitation services of the Ministry of Labour.[2]

[1] Lancashire County Council. Report of the Medical Officer of Health for the year 1956, p. 90.
[2] For a fuller discussion of these questions see H. Coltart, H. Raine and E. Harrison, *Social Work in Tuberculosis*, 1959.

THE NATIONAL HEALTH SERVICE

One of the chief advantages of the administrative arrangements now in operation for the control and treatment of tuberculosis would appear to be the possibility of a closer link between the tuberculosis service and general hospital service, and it is the policy of regional hospital boards to attach chest clinics to hospital out-patients departments and employ hospital staff on the purely clinical duties.[1] Another is the extension of this service to cover other diseases of the chest.[2] On the other hand the new set-up has been criticised on the grounds that 'no disease has wider social implications than tuberculosis and the application of the principle of the unity of clinical medicine to the staff working in this field has raised more problems than it has solved',[3] a criticism re-enforced if 'the increasing preoccupation of chest physicians with the clinical and curative aspects of tuberculosis to the detriment of the preventive services which are the concern of the Medical Officer of Health'—one of the complaints made to the Guillebaud Committee[4]—is well-founded. Only close co-operation between preventive and treatment services, so that, for example, the chest physicians employed by the hospital boards spend part of their time on duties for the local health authority, advising on problems of prevention, care and after-care, and working in collaboration with the staff of the authority, can overcome these administrative difficulties, and deal effectively not only with the disease itself, but also with its social accompaniments.

Tuberculosis is an outstanding example of a disease in which prevention, treatment and after-care interlock, and must be considered as parts of a single process, but the same interdependence between hospital treatment and community care exists in connection with other medical conditions. This has been demonstrated by Professor T. Ferguson and Dr. A. N. MacPhail in a survey made of the subsequent histories of 705 unselected male patients discharged from a general medical ward in each of two Glasgow teaching hospitals, and in each of two provincial hospitals some miles from the city.[5] The clinicians in charge of those cases discharged 9·3 per cent of them as 'cured', and a further 73 per cent of them as 'improved', many requiring only a period of convalescence to consolidate their improvement. Yet two years later[6]

[1] Lancashire County Council Report, p. 89.
[2] British Medical Association, *Tuberculosis and the National Health Service*. Report of the Tuberculosis and Diseases of the Chest Group Committee, approved by the Council of the Association, November 1950, pars. 4 and 5.
[3] Institute of Public Administration, *The Health Services, Some of their Practical Problems*, p. 91.   [4] Report, par. 615, p. 202.
[5] T. Ferguson and A. N. Macphail, *Hospital and Community*, published for the Nuffield Provincial Hospitals' Trust by the Oxford University Press, 1954.
[6] There was an intermediate investigation three months after discharge, the findings of which are cited in the report.

171 had died, 60 could not be traced, and, of the 474 men who
had been seen by the investigators in their own homes, only
111 could be regarded as cured. One hundred and ninety-three
had continued to maintain the improvement effected in hospital,
106 had not improved, and 64 were obviously worse. That is, only
'about two-thirds of those still alive two years after leaving hospital could be regarded as having derived substantial and lasting
benefit from hospital care'. After studying the circumstances of the
men concerned, the investigators concluded that 'the transition
from the sheltered atmosphere of the modern hospital wards to the
icy chill of the workaday world is indeed a testing time, and it is
not surprising that many soon break down'.[1] Only 4 per cent of
the cases studied enjoyed a spell of convalescent care before re-
turning home, far too many returned to work 'which could hardly
fail to precipitate another breakdown in the not-far-distant
future',[2] while instead of having the 'benevolent background that
is so helpful in consolidating recovery'[3] many patients came from
'a social background which would daunt the stoutest heart'. Professor Ferguson's and Dr. MacPhail's final summing-up of the
position was that 'without more help in the transition from hospital to everyday life, without decent living conditions and reasonably suitable work to which the patient can return on leaving hospital, even the most careful and enlightened treatment is not likely
to achieve a full measure of lasting benefit'.[4]

It will be seen that some of the conditions likely to facilitate
complete recovery listed by Professor Ferguson and Dr. MacPhail
involve community action outside the scope of the health service,
and the promotion of the health of the community requires not
only better co-ordination between the different parts of the health
service itself, but developments in related social services. Some of
these developments, for example the provision of better houses and
measures taken by the Ministry of Labour to assist in the rehabilitation and resettlement of disabled persons, are discussed later in
this book, others such as the reduction of atmospheric pollution, are
outside its scope. All of them should, in the long run, help to reduce the burden on hospital accommodation and family practitioner
services. But developments such as these, important as they are,
do not diminish the need for those concerned with the health service itself to achieve closer co-operation, pay more attention to the
prevention of illness and achieve higher standards of care, more
particularly of domiciliary care. This is recognised by the Guillebaud Committee which in this connection draws attention to the
value of what has been called the 'domiciliary team'. The aim of
these teams is 'to place at the disposal of the patient in his home

[1] Op. cit., p. 137.   [2] Ibid., p. 141.   [3] Ibid., p. 143.   [4] Ibid., p. 144.

equally with the patient in hospital a co-ordinated team acting under the clinical guidance of his personal medical attendant'.[1] Ideally this team should be composed of the general practitioner the home nurse, the health visitor, midwife and domestic help and work in close association with maternity and child welfare clinics and, through the almoners and consultant staff, with the local hospitals. Another method of co-operation, developed in some areas, is the establishment of liaison committees on which both general practitioners and public health workers are represented, and at which matters of common interest are discussed.[2] The degree and methods of co-operation between the curative and preventive services vary from area to area, and the Guillebaud Committee sums up the position by saying 'What is needed is a greater interest in this aspect of social medicine, a greater will to co-operate, and readiness on the part of the local authorities to provide domiciliary services on the scale required. . . . These are matters for arrangement locally between general practitioners, hospital staff and the officers of local authorities who are directly concerned.' Whatever schemes are adopted they should ensure that co-operation goes further than the Health Service itself, so that close links are maintained with such local authority departments as the children's department and, where this is not administered as part of the work of the local health authority, the social welfare department, as well as with the rehabilitation services of the Ministry of Labour and with appropriate voluntary organisations.

Having emphasised this need and the difficulties created by the division of the service into its three parts, one must, in concluding this discussion on co-ordination, refer to the progress that has been made and which the Health Service itself has helped to bring about. Thus, Dr. Stephen Taylor considers that since the advent of the National Health Service the gap between general practitioners and local authority services has been getting less,[3] and the Guillebaud Committee remarks that 'too little credit may have been given in the past to the degree of integration achieved through the introduction of the Health Service itself in 1948, and through the steps subsequently taken by the statutory authorities

---

[1] Op. cit., par. 617, p. 204.

[2] One such committee in a county borough is described in Dr. Stephen Taylor's report, *Good General Practice* (O.U.P., 1954), p. 365. It consisted of five representatives of the general practitioners, the Medical Officer of Health, the two senior medical officers for maternity and child welfare and school health. It met every two or three months and discussed, for example, T.B. after-care, toddlers' clinics and the examination of school children. Unfortunately the hospital doctors were 'too busy' to attend.

[3] *Good General Practice*, p. 134.

concerned to improve co-ordination in all three branches of the service.'[1] Good progress has indeed been made, but better co-ordination is still needed at all levels: at the policy-making level at the centre, in the hospital regions and local authority areas where national policies are applied to local circumstances, and finally at the personal level where individual workers combine, or should combine, to meet the needs of particular patients. Given the will to co-operate at all these levels and the thought and imagination to see how best this can be done, then even that vast and complicated machine, the National Health Service, can function smoothly and efficiently and so achieve its aim of providing an all-embracing service to maintain and improve the nation's health.

No organisation can function properly if the money to maintain and develop it is lacking or inadequate, nor, on the other hand, can it be regarded as efficient if the resources which are available to it are being wasted or improperly used. Ever since its inception, there has been considerable concern about the cost of the National Health Service, both the high overall cost and the allocation of the available resources between the three parts. Overall costs exceeded the original estimates even in the early years of the service and have increased steadily ever since. As an extreme example of the fears these increasing costs have engendered we may cite the book published by Dr. Ffrangcon Roberts in 1952, *The Cost of Health*. In this book the author traces the increasing cost of the treatment of sickness not solely, or even mainly to the National Health Service, although he considers that this has encouraged more profligate expenditure, but 'primarily and paradoxically to the advancement of medicine, which is spurred to perpetual acceleration by the perpetual acceleration of scientific discovery'. Dr. Roberts can see no end to this process except that imposed by limitations of available resources.[2] He contends, moreover, that this increasing expenditure on medical treatment is not, as might be expected, likely to increase general health and productivity, for its main consequence would seem to be the prolongation of life for old people and sufferers from chronic diseases, which may be to the detriment of the community. Dr. Ffrangcon Roberts urges that the long-term consequences of this must be faced, and, 'since our resources are insufficient to enable us to treat all diseases with the efficiency which, under more fortunate conditions, the advance of science would make possible, we are compelled to reach a just balance between the short-term direct benefits to the individual and the long-term benefits reflected back to the individual'. That is, if sacrifices have to be made, 'as they undoubtedly will', priority should be given, even if individuals

[1] Op. cit., par. 707, p. 235.   [2] Op. cit., p. 191.

suffer thereby, to the treatment of diseases which can be cured, and, if not cured, would be disabling, and to those in which treatment, while not resulting in cure would enable the patient to maintain his efficiency and independence, rather than to those diseases in which medical treatment results in prolongation of life with no hope of cure or substantial amelioration and no likelihood of increased capacity for productive work. 'This is a hard saying,' he concludes, 'but we live in a hard world.'[1]

Although to few people can the problem which appeared to be posed by expenditure on medical treatment have presented itself in such stark terms as it has done to Dr. Ffrangcon Roberts, yet taken in conjunction with the overall economic and financial position of the country, it seemed, by the early fifties, sufficiently serious to warrant investigation, and in May 1953 the Minister of Health and the Secretary of State for Scotland, acting jointly, set up a Committee with Mr. C. W. Guillebaud, a Cambridge economist, as chairman. Its terms of reference were 'To review the present and prospective cost of the National Health Service; to suggest means . . . of ensuring the most effective control and efficient use of such Exchequer funds as may be made available; to advise how . . . a rising charge upon it can be avoided while providing for the maintenance of an adequate service; and to make recommendations.' The Committee wisely asked for a statistical analysis of expenditure on the National Health Service in England and Wales during the period 1948–54, as an essential background to its discussions, and the picture presented as a result of this analysis proved to be very different from that anticipated by those who had been looking only at rising monetary costs.[2] It showed that, far from becoming an increasing drain on the resources of the community, the National Health Service was absorbing a smaller proportion of those resources in 1953–4, when the proportion of the current net cost of the Service to the gross national product was $3\frac{1}{4}$ per cent, than in 1949–50, when the proportion was $3\frac{3}{4}$ per cent. The net cost to public funds per head of the population was highest in the year 1950–1 (£8 19s. at the 1948–9 prices), while the gross cost was highest in 1953–4 (£9 7s. at 1948–9 prices), but the movement was small and 'Contrary to public opinion since the net diversion of resources to the National Health Service since 1949–50 has been of relatively insignificant proportions.'[3]

[1] This seems to be the general argument of ch. xi, 'National Health and National Wealth', of the book. The quotations are taken from pp. 136–137.

[2] This analysis was undertaken by Professor R. M. Titmuss and Mr. B. Abel-Smith, and its results have been published as *The Cost of the National Health Service in England and Wales* (Cambridge, 1956).

[3] Op. cit., p. 67. Quoted in the Guillebaud Committee. Report, par. 24, pp. 11–12.

But four years is a relatively short time, and it was not only current costs but their possible increase as the result of the changing age composition of the population and widespread 'medicated survival' which was causing alarm. Hence Professor Titmuss and Mr. Abel-Smith were asked to consider the possible effects of projected size and age structure of the population on the cost of the Health Service. In view of the many variables involved, this was, as the authors recognised, a hazardous undertaking, and, in making their tentative predictions, they limited themselves to 'certain estimated population changes', assuming for the purposes of the analysis that the incidence and character of sickness, standards of diagnosis, and quality of treatment, the provision of resources in goods and services, the present level of unsatisfied demand and the present proportionate distribution of consumer use of the Service by age, sex and many other factors would all remain unchanged. On this admittedly somewhat unrealistic basis the authors concluded that, 'On the basis of what is known at present about age and sex differences in demand (which, incidentally, is lamentably little), there is no justification for the alarm that has been expressed about the impact of "an ageing population" on the cost of the National Health Service. Changes in age structure by themselves are calculated to increase the present cost of the Service to public funds by $3\frac{1}{2}$ per cent by 1971–2. A further increase of $4\frac{1}{2}$ per cent (making a total of 8 per cent in all) is attributable to the projected rise in the total population of England and Wales (using the official projection figures).'[1] In making this prediction they admit that 'in the absence of representative studies' they were unable to take into account the heavier demands which, it is generally accepted, older men and women make on the services of the general practitioner, nor could they take into account the fact that, compared with the rest of the population, this age group is at present receiving a lower standard of service, and there is a substantial area of unmet need among them. Another social factor which, the authors point out, is likely to influence the extent to which the ageing of the population will increase the cost of the Health Service is the proportion of married to single persons in the population, for an analysis made of the hospital population on the night on which the 1951 Census was taken revealed that compared with the demands made by single men and women (and to a lesser extent the widowed), the proportion of married men and women in hospital even at the age of sixty-five and over is extremely small. They reached the conclusion that 'Marriage and its survival into old age appears to be a powerful safeguard against admission into

[1] Ibid. p. 69, Guillebaud Report, par. 81, p. 40.

hospital in general and to mental and "chronic" hospitals in particular.'[1] Hence such factors as the abnormally high number of marriages broken by the early death of the husband during the First World War, the numbers of women of that generation remaining single, also as a result of deaths during that war, the decline in family size and increased number of childless couples during the inter-war years, all influence current demands for hospital care. In the same way, to-day's higher marriage rate and greater likelihood of both man and wife surviving into old age will in their turn influence future demand. Faced with all these imponderables the Guillebaud Committee could only make the not very helpful inference that 'in considering the more distant future there are a large number of factors at work, some of which will lead to an increase in the cost of the Service, while others operate in the opposite direction'.[2]

Nor did the inclusion of the phrase 'an adequate Service' in their terms of reference make the task of the Committee any easier, particularly in view of the growth of medical knowledge which, like Dr. Ffrangcon Roberts, they admitted 'adds considerably to the number and expense of treatments, and, by prolonging life also increases the incidence of slow-killing diseases'. They decided therefore to base their recommendations on the assumption that 'In the absence of an objective and attainable standard of adequacy, the aim must be . . . to provide the best service possible within the limits of available resources. . . . The development of the National Health Service is one among many public tasks in which objectives and standards must be realistically set and adjusted, as time goes on, both to means and to ends.[3] The choice of priorities was a task for the Government. They were, however, quite definite that 'The rising cost of the Service in real terms during the years 1948–54 was within narrow bounds; while many of the services provided were substantially improved and expanded during the period. Any charge that there has been widespread extravagance in the National Health Service, whether in respect of the spending of money or the use of manpower, is not borne out by our evidence.'[4]

Having exposed the limited extent to which national resources are being expended on the National Health Service at present, having considered some very tentative propositions regarding trends affecting future demands on them, and having referred back to the Government the policy decision as to how much money, manpower and materials can be allotted to the Service in view of competing demands for those resources, the Guillebaud

[1] Op. cit., p. 71. Guillebaud Report, Par. 84, p. 41.
[2] Par. 735, p. 269.　　[3] Pars. 95 and 98, p. 50.　　[4] Par. 735, p. 269.

Committee went on to review the distribution of Health Service expenditure between its different branches and to consider whether the money allocated was being spent to the best advantage. The most expensive branch of the Service is the hospital service, expenditure on which has not only risen steadily, but become larger in proportion to the total cost.[1] Nevertheless, even here, increased current costs which were largely due to increases in staff (mainly nurses and domestic staff) and, to a lesser extent, increases in medical supplies, had to be balanced against the increased amount of work done by the hospitals for an increasing total population during the period,[2] and the Guillebaud Committee has no major criticisms to make, or changes to recommend. When they came to consider the question of capital expenditure the criticism made was, as we have already seen, of under- rather than of over-expenditure, and they recommended a desirable rise in capital expenditure of up to £30 million per annum over the seven years succeeding the year 1957–8.

Thus, by and large, the findings of the Guillebaud Committee were that, while the cost of the National Health Service was considerable and increasing, these increases were not disproportionate if concurrent rises in wages, prices and national production were taken into account, together with the greater demands made by an increasing population, including higher proportions of old people and young children. Nevertheless, at the end of 1956, by which time the cost of the service had risen again,[3] the Government decided that further measures should be taken both to help to prevent the Exchequer cost from rising still further and to make the public more aware of its responsibility for meeting these costs. Consequently, in December 1956, the shilling charge per prescription, levied since 1952, was raised to a charge of a shilling for each drug supplied, while an Act passed the following spring, the National Health Service (Contributions) Act, 1957, doubled the rate of insurance contributions to the National Health Service. These contributions are now separate from the general National Insurance contributions, but both are paid together for administrative convenience.

[1] Actual expenditure on hospital running costs rose from £241,488,379 in 1952–53 to £337,587,632 in 1957–58; capital expenditure during the same period from £9,747,301 to £17,819,995 (Report of the Ministry of Health, 1958, Part I. Cmnd. 806. Table 3). According to the Guillebaud Committee (Report. Par. 26, p. 12), the hospital service absorbed 52 per cent of the total cost of the Health Service in 1949–50, and 61 per cent. in 1953–54.

[2] Guillebaud Committee Report. Par. 36, p. 19.

[3] The total cost of the Service for the year ending March 1958 was approximately £626m., the net cost to the Exchequer about £480m. (Report of the Ministry of Health, 1958. Part I, p. 1.)

THE NATIONAL HEALTH SERVICE

The National Health Service was the boldest of the ventures made in the period of reconstruction which immediately followed the Second World War. The Act which brought it into being was passed in an atmosphere of controversy, and there has been much criticism of its working since. Nevertheless, it can be said that 'With the general policy of the National Health Service, the whole country is agreed', and 'the remarkable thing is' that, despite the mistakes and miscalculations that have been made, 'the scheme works so well'.[1] Whether or not it proves to be 'a wealth producing as well as a health producing Service', in the sense that it improves the health of the working population sufficiently to offset its cost, may be in doubt; that it has given millions access to the best medical treatment and care available for them without, at the same time, subjecting them to crippling financial anxiety, is certain, and this in itself is no mean achievement.

[1] Sir Henry Lesser, Introduction to *The Health Services. Some of their Practical Problems*, p. 11.

CHAPTER VII

SOCIAL ASPECTS OF HOUSING AND TOWN PLANNING

'Town planning is not mere place-planning, nor even work-planning. If it is to be successful it must be folk-planning.

This means that its task is not to coerce people into new places against their associations, wishes and interests . . . instead its task is to find the right places for each sort of people. To give people, in fact, the same care as we give when transplanting flowers.'—PATRICK GEDDES.

W HEN, in the nineteen-thirties, Political and Economic Planning surveyed the British social services, it excluded the Housing Acts from its purview on the general grounds that, according to its definition, the public social services were those which 'had as their object the enhancement of the personal welfare of individual citizens in the community', and, although it was admitted that housing management and the administration of rent rebate schemes introduced a more personal element, 'slum-clearance and the provision of new houses under these Acts are not, strictly speaking, personal services'.[1] Housing and town planning were listed, along with sanitation and street-lighting, as 'impersonal environmental services', a classification which reflects the current under-estimation of the sociological implications of such housing operations as the removal of families from neighbourhoods where they have many ties and associations to distant neighbourhoods where they have none, or the mixing of families with widely different standards and backgrounds on new housing estates. The enforcement, in the interests of health and decency, of minimum standards of construction and amenity was, in its early days, a primary, and still is an important, objective of housing policy, but we are now increasingly sensitive to social as well as physical needs, and in so far as the objectives of housing policy, both national and local, are broadened so as to embrace provisions to meet these needs, so far can housing claim to be a social as well as an environmental service.

Looking back, it is easy to criticise the Victorian approach to housing in which 'the operative word was drains'[2] and all that

[1] P.E.P., *Report on the British Social Services*, 1937, pp. 10 and 37.
[2] M. P. Fogarty, *Town and Country Planning*, p. 17.

drains symbolise, and the builders and planners who 'did not realise that they had cut off our people from the chiefest natural means of grace', for they 'did not appreciate the curse and cruelty of ugliness'.[1] Conditions in the first half of the century as revealed by such reports as *The Sanitary Condition of the Labouring Population of Great Britain* (1842) and the *Royal Commission on the State of Large Towns and Populous Districts*[2] were such, however, that the obvious need at that time was for legislation which would tackle the threat to health and living standards presented by the squalid courts, the back-to-back houses, and the undrained cellar-dwellings which characterised the poor and congested areas of the growing towns.

When once the need for some measure of governmental interference in the interests of public health was accepted, housing legislation proceeded along two lines. In the first place, it established and enforced minimum standards in the contruction of new houses. Throughout the century and, indeed, until after the First World War, house-building was carried out almost entirely by private enterprise for private gain, but, after the middle of the century, it became increasingly subject to regulations governing structural soundness and sanitary provision. At first this control was sporadic and limited, but the Public Health Act, 1875, empowered the Local Government Board to permit sanitary authorities throughout the country to make building by-laws, and while these 'had many deficiencies which were only gradually removed, and operated very unevenly over the country as a whole' . . . 'nothing else made so much difference to the physical condition and appearance of British towns. Large parts of them were built under this regime and still survive. They seem a grim and depressing legacy, yet they represent a considerable advance on what came immediately before. The streets of this time were monotonous, but the monotony of order was an advance on the earlier monotony of chaos. They were devoid of all inspiration, but at least they were sanitary, exposed adequately to air and moderately to light, and this was a result achieved widely and by deliberate provision, instead of occasionally and more or less by chance.'[3]

By-law houses built in the latter part of the nineteenth century are still found in their thousands in the inner areas of our towns, and many, if not most of them, are likely to continue in use for another twenty-five years or more, 'a short period in the development of a city but spanning all the years of childhood for several generations of schoolchildren; a short time in terms of municipal

[1] Alfred Salter as quoted by Fenner Brockway, *Bermondsey Story*, p. 89.
[2] First Report 1844, Second Report 1845.
[3] William Ashworth, *The Genesis of Modern British Town Planning*, 1954, p. 91.

investment, but long enough to cover the life of a family from the marriage of the parents until the children grow up and leave for homes of their own'.[1] Although reasonably structurally sound they are frequently in a poor state of repair, for repairs are expensive and rent restriction over a number of years has meant that in many cases the level of rents charged has not been sufficient to allow for proper maintenance, and many owners have let their property fall into disrepair. One of the purposes of the Rent Act, 1957, is to help to remedy this situation. This Act decontrols all rented properties with a rateable value of over £40 in London and £30 elsewhere in England and Wales. Houses whose rateable value is less than this remain subject to rent control. Their rents can be raised to twice their gross annual value where the landlord is responsible for all repairs. Should he also be or become responsible for interior decorations this amount can be raised to two-and-one-third times; where the tenant is responsible for both repairs and decoration it is reduced to one-and-one-third times, and if the responsibility is shared the figure may be fixed by agreement, or failing that, by the county court, somewhere between the two. Positive inducements to improve old property are contained in the Housing Repairs and Rent Act, 1954, which provides house owners with financial assistance up to a maximum of £400 towards the improvement (excluding ordinary repairs and maintenance), or conversion of their property, provided that the dwelling so improved will provide satisfactory accommodation for at least fifteen years.

Even when legislation insisting that newly built houses shall conform to the minimum standards acceptable to the generation formulating them has been passed, this still leaves unsolved the problem of dealing with the legacy inherited from its predecessors with lower standards, a legacy likely to include houses no longer regarded as fit for human habitation, but, in fact, inhabited and often densely inhabited, by families unable to find or possibly to afford alternative accommodation. Hence, when once the community had accepted responsibility, however limited, for the conditions in which its members were housed, it was faced with the problem of slum clearance and its corollary the rehousing of the inhabitants of the dwellings now condemned and demolished. It was only slowly and to a limited extent that, during the second half of the nineteenth century, the responsibility for slum clearance was accepted, and even when Parliament passed the requisite legislation, local councils were reluctant to use the powers thus

[1] B. N. Stancliffe and Mary S. Muray, 'Till We Build Again, An Enquiry into Social Conditions in a Selected Area in Salford', *Social Welfare*, Vol. XII, No. 4, October 1948, p. 78.

conferred upon them. Apart from the legal and technical difficulties which had to be solved, the cost of effecting the improvements sanctioned was considerable. Not only had the very difficult question of compensation to the owner of the property and the land on which it stood to be settled, but, as experiments by one or two local authorities showed, the closure of cellar dwellings and the demolition of insanitary courts without making alternative housing provision simply accentuated the evils of overcrowding and bad living conditions in the neighbouring dwellings, and the costs of rehousing, particularly of acquiring land for the purpose, were heavy. As at that time there were no Exchequer subsidies and the costs of demolition, compensation and rehousing all had to be met from the local rates, it is not surprising that local authorities were hesitant in their approach to slum clearance, and, compared with the magnitude of the problem, little was accomplished. Nevertheless, by the end of the century the principle had been accepted that, in the interests of public health and decency, all new houses built must conform to minimum standards, and dwellings so unsound and insanitary as to constitute a serious menace to life and health, could and should be demolished by the local authority, whatever the wishes of their owners, and their inhabitants rehoused.

During this period towns were expanding rapidly, assisted by the developments in public transport which were taking place, developments which were accelerated as the nineteenth century gave place to the twentieth and electric trams and motor buses began to appear on the streets. Hence, despite bad conditions and serious overcrowding in the slum areas, there was, by accepted standards of working and lower middle class housing, no recognised serious overall shortage. The problem of an overall shortage made itself felt at the close of the First World War, when the soldiers who had been promised 'homes fit for heroes to live in', returned to find that, owing to the inevitable slowing-up of building operations during the war, such homes were very difficult to find. Meanwhile, building material was short and costs had risen to such an extent that it was no longer possible for private builders to build houses to the accepted standards and let them at rents which working people could afford to pay. Hence the Government of the day accepted responsibility, not only for enforcing minimum standards of housing construction and encouraging slum clearance, but also for taking action to meet working class housing needs. The newly created Ministry of Health was made responsible for housing, and subsidies were paid to local authorities, and, to a lesser extent, to private builders, to encourage them to build houses of the required standard, which was higher than that of pre-war days,[1] to let to working class people. These subsidies were intended to bridge the gap between the economic rent,[2] and the rent it was reasonable to charge. Meanwhile, insanitary dwellings in slum areas were continuing to present their special and serious problems, and as general living standards improved, slum conditions were less easily tolerated, and so, particularly by the 'Greenwood' Act of 1930, special subsidies were made payable to local authorities undertaking slum clearance and rehousing. After 1933 subsidies for houses built to accommodate members of the general public on local authority housing lists were discontinued, as by that time the overall shortage had abated somewhat. The demand for houses to rent had not been wholly met, however, and there were, and still are, many people living in substandard dwellings in which there was a minimum of comfort and amenity, but which were not sufficiently detrimental to health to be scheduled for clearance. Slum clearance subsidies were continued.

At the end of the Second World War the shortage of housing accommodation was once again acute and widespread. The declared aim of the immediate post-war housing policy was that of meeting housing need wherever it existed irrespective of social class, and hence all references in previous Acts limiting powers and responsibilities of local authorities to the provision of accommodation for the working classes were repealed by the Housing Act, 1949. Already, in 1946, a new general subsidy of £22 a house (£16 10s. from national funds, the remainder provided by the local authority building the house) had been authorised, and, although there were variations in the amount, it remained in operation until the autumn of 1956 when, by the Housing Subsidies Act, all subsidies, except those payable in connection with slum clearance schemes and with the creation of new towns and the other large-scale projects by which congested cities were seeking to disperse their overspill population to distant areas, were first reduced to £10 and then discontinued.

Already, before the passing of the Housing Subsidies Act, general subsidies were being subject to a good deal of criticism. They were paid at a standard rate, and although intended to reduce rents sufficiently to place houses being built within the means

---

[1] In order to qualify for a subsidy under the Housing Acts of 1923 and 1924, as consolidated by the Housing Act, 1925, houses were required to contain a bath in a bathroom, the density must not exceed eight houses to the acre in agricultural districts and twelve houses elsewhere, the floor area had to be between 620 and 950 superficial feet in the case of cottages, and 550 and 880 superficial feet in the case of flats.

[2] The economic rent is the rent which has to be charged if the builder is to receive a return on his capital investment within the life of the house, allowing for repairs and depreciation.

of the majority of those in need of housing accommodation, there was some evidence that, despite the subsidy, families in the lower income groups, especially those with a number of dependent children, were unable to move into the houses being built for them unless they were prepared to make considerable sacrifices in other directions.[1] Moreover, although it was recognised that a policy of mixed development on corporation property might have advantages socially, the justice of subsidising families able to afford the economic rent of the houses they were occupying was open to question, since it created 'a privileged class who are receiving a contribution towards their expenses from people poorer than themselves and living in dwellings of a far lower standard. . . . It is illogical that a family should be unable to afford the rent of a new house, when the rates included in the rent are levied partly to subsidise a neighbour who could do without this assistance.'[2]

A method of dealing with the anomalous situation just described which has found favour in some quarters is that of 'rent rebates' or differential rents. Rent rebate schemes vary in detail but, in general, their aim is to differentiate the rent charged according to family need. Families in the lower income groups are charged rents they can afford, such amounts being calculated either by fixing a minimum subsistence income which should be left after the rent has been paid, or by limiting the rent payable to a fixed proportion of the family income. The money to balance these reductions may be found by an additional contribution from the rates, but this is a measure which has the disadvantage of imposing a further burden on those who are not enjoying, and can never hope to enjoy, the benefits of a subsidised dwelling. An alternative which has sometimes been adopted is that of using a whole or part of the statutory subsidy for this purpose.

Although local authorities have possessed powers to operate differential rent schemes since before the war, little use has been made of them. Objections to these schemes made by authorities not using them include objections in principle, such as the one that rent rebates mean that a municipal tenant obtains a reduction of his rent in times of difficulty and this is unfair to tenants of private landlords who do not share this privilege; dislike of administering a means test; fear that dissatisfaction might be caused by charging dissimilar rents for similar accommodation, and the

[1] P.E.P., *Planning*, No. XVI, No. 212, 24 April 1950. 'A New Policy for Housing Subsidies.'

[2] Ibid., p. 264. Cf. James MacColl, *Policy for Housing*, Fabian Research Series, No. 164, 1954, p. 20. 'The great indictment of the present subsidy is that there is not enough money to help those such as large young families, who most need it because so much is going to the benefit of families who can well afford to pay a bigger rent.'

general difficulty and expense of administering such a scheme.[1]
Social security measures, particularly family allowances and the
payment of rent allowances by the National Assistance Board,
serve to mitigate hardship and these operate uniformly throughout the country whereas local variations are such that it would be
difficult, even if desirable, to achieve a uniform rents rebates
scheme. On the whole the arguments in favour and those against
such schemes are fairly evenly balanced, but in areas where they
do not operate the financial difficulties of a large and poor family
transferred from a low rented house near the centre of the city to a
more spacious and convenient, but also much more expensive,
house on the outskirts, may be very considerable.

As the aims of British housing policy have now been enlarged to
include, not only the maintenance of minimum health requirements and the clearing of the worst of the slums, but also provision
to meet housing need wherever it may exist, it is necessary to consider by what means and according to what standards these needs
can and should be assessed. This assessment must be made
whether we are considering what proportion of the national resources of money, manpower and materials should be allocated to
housing and so have to balance the 'need' for houses against the
'need' for schools, hospitals, prisons, power stations, roads and
other public utilities, or whether we are trying to assess the urgency
of the need for accommodation of a particular family so that it
can be allocated its proper place on the local authority housing
list.

Housing needs are to some extent a reflection of the general
living standards of the time, and it can be argued that the urgency
of the post-war housing problem has been accentuated by the
nation's rising standards and expectations.[2] One assumption,
which is basic to British housing policy, is that each family unit,
that is each married couple together with their dependent children, if any, and such unmarried adult sons and daughters who
wish to remain with them, is entitled to a home of its own, and
should not be compelled to share its dwelling, still less combine as

[1] In 1949 the Society of Housing Managers made an inquiry into the use
made by local authorities of rent rebate schemes. Of the 1,470 housing authorities in the country, 941 replied to the Society's circular asking for information;
78 of these reported that they operated a rent rebate scheme and an additional
72 said that rebates were given in cases of special hardship although no general
scheme was in operation. The objections to such schemes listed in the text are
those made by the local authorities not operating them. Society of Housing
Managers, *Rent Rebates, A Review*, pp. 25 and 26.
[2] 'The causes of the housing problem in Great Britain today are the higher
social standards of the people.' Minister of Health (Mr. Aneurin Bevan),
6 November 1950, 480 H.C. Deb. 5 s., col. 644.

part of the same household[1] with members of the older generation or any other group of persons simply because no suitable alternative accommodation can be found. The latest information about the extent to which dwellings are, in fact, shared between different households, and the composition of these households in terms of family relationship is contained in the 1951 Census Housing Report published in 1956. The census returns showed that in 1951 86 per cent of the private households in England and Wales had a dwelling to themselves, but nearly two million, that is 14 per cent of the total number, were in shared dwellings. Nearly 80 per cent of these sharing households were small, consisting of one, two or three persons. On a 'modest standard of accommodation'[2] about three-quarters of all sharing households, nearly one and a half million in all, were 'not seriously deficient' in numbers of rooms in relation to the households contained in them, and the remaining quarter included 150,000 persons living alone in one room. At the same time, out of the 14½ million private households in Great Britain, nearly two million were 'composite', that is, they contained persons other than those in the primary family unit.[3] Almost half of them contained, apart from the head of the household, a 'family nucleus' composed either of a married couple and their children, if any, or of one parent with one or more children. A further 968,000 households contained a close relative, such as parent, brother or sister of the head of the household or his spouse, in addition to the head, his spouse and children. Among these were 37,000 households which contained both parents of the head of the household or his spouse.[4]

While the information given in the Census Housing Report and summarised in the preceding paragraph gives us some idea of the extent to which dwellings are shared and families combine as households, it does not tell us how many of these families or single persons now living as part of a composite household would live separately if alternate accommodation were available. Personal ties, physical infirmities, financial considerations, any or all of these and other circumstances may affect a person's or a family's decision as to whether or not to break away from a composite

[1] A private household is a housekeeping unit consisting of a single person or group of persons, who may or may not be related, but who share meals.
[2] The standard allowed for a living-room for each household, in addition to a bedroom for each married couple, for each pair of children and for each other person. Census 1951, England and Wales, *Housing Report*, p. cxxvi.
[3] A 'primary family unit' for Census purposes consists of those members of a private household who fall into specified affinity groups, namely the head of the household, his spouse, designated children and near relatives comprising ancestors and unmarried brothers and sisters over 16; together with resident domestic servants. Ibid., pp. 121–122.   [4] Ibid., p. cxxvii.

household or seek a separate dwelling. Among the factors taken into account is likely to be the adequacy of the accommodation of the dwellings shared, however.

Adequacy of accommodation, whether in dwellings occupied by single families or in shared dwellings, is usually measured by means of one or other of the overcrowding standards which have been formulated during the last thirty years. Successive Census Reports have provided density measurements of occupation of dwellings by relating the number of persons in each household to the number of habitable rooms available. On this basis there has been a considerable improvement during the last thirty years. In 1921 households living at a density of more than two persons per room formed 5·69 per cent of all occupations, in 1931 3·88 per cent and in 1951 1·18 per cent, a reduction which the Registrar General attributes to the reduction in the size of families over the same period.[1] But, density of occupation measured in terms of persons per room is not, by itself, an adequate measurement of overcrowding. As the Census Housing Report recognises, 'it may be valid when applied as a statistical average to summarise the general conditions of a large group of householders . . . but it cannot be used to determine whether a particular household is overcrowded'.[2] The 'persons' may be of the same or opposite sex and of differing ages, while the 'rooms' include living as well as bedrooms and may be of differing sizes, and any realistic definition of overcrowding must take these factors into account. The Housing Act, 1936, laid it down that a dwelling house would be deemed to be overcrowded if persons over the age of ten not living together as husband and wife were compelled to sleep in the same room, or if the number of persons living there exceeded the permitted number for the number and floor area of the available rooms.[3] This standard was framed in connection with legislation designed to penalise landlords who permitted overcrowding[4] and cannot be regarded as a really adequate measure of housing need, especially as, like the census density measurement, it does not distinguish between bedrooms and living rooms. The importance of making this distinction was recognised as early as 1920 by the Manchester

[1] *Housing Report*, p. lxv.
[2] Ibid., p. lxiv.
[3] Where a dwelling consisted of one room, the number of occupants permitted by the Act was 2, of two rooms 3, three rooms 5, four rooms 7½, and five rooms 10, with an additional 2 in respect of each room in excess of five. Children under the age of one year are not counted and children under ten count as half a unit. No regard is paid to any room with a floor area of less than 50 square feet and bathrooms, sculleries, etc., are not habitable rooms. Housing Act, 1936, Section 58 and Fifth Schedule.
[4] Housing Act, 1935.

Public Health Committee which in that year formulated an over-crowding standard based on the separation of the sexes over the age of ten and a maximum density of not more than $2\frac{1}{2}$ persons per bedroom. Reporting in 1949, the Housing Management Sub-Committee of the Central Housing Advisory Committee recommended to local authorities that 'overcrowding as a factor of housing need should be measured in terms of bedroom deficiency, that is to say, the number of bedrooms over and above those already occupied that a family would need for adequate sleeping arrangements',[1] but the Committee does not clarify this further except to say that 'the living room should be disregarded, as its use for sleeping worsens substantially the family's living conditions'. While disclaiming any intention to do more than postulate certain hypotheses, the Housing Census Report concludes an elaborate analysis of the extent to which households of differing composition have adequate accommodation as measured by four hypothetical standards, by saying that, 'On the hypothesis that, apart from one person households, the accommodation in a dwelling is inadequate for its inmates unless it contains one habitable room in addition to a bedroom for each married couple, for each pair of children of the head, and for each other person, it is possible to say that, in England and Wales at least 650,000 households had inadequate numbers of rooms in their dwellings in 1951.'[2] Since that time there has been considerable house-building activity, and it has been calculated that the stock of houses in England and Wales rose from 12,538,443 in 1951 to 13,129,436 in 1955.[3] During this period houses were being built faster than the population was growing, and although there is likely to be some slowing down as, in accordance with the present Government policy, local authorities concentrate on slum clearance, some progress towards the abatement of overcrowding and provision of suitable accommodation to enable composite households to split up where this is desired seems likely to continue.

In order to obtain a realistic picture of housing conditions and to estimate the extent to which new dwellings are required, it is necessary to try and assess not only the number of dwellings in which the accommodation fails to meet the requirements of the occupants, but those in which it is in excess of requirements, and the extent to which exchange is possible. 'Under-occupation' is

[1] Central Housing Advisory Committee, *Selection of Tenants and Transfers and Exchanges*, H.M.S.O., 1949, par. 16, p. 7.　　[2] Op. cit., p. cxxvi.
[3] The figures are taken from 'The Census and the Estimation of Housing Need and Housing Progress', C. J. Thomas, *Town Planning Review*, 13 July 1957. See also A. M. Carr-Saunders, D. Caradog Jones and C. A. Mosee: *A Survey of Social Conditions in England and Wales*, 1958 edition, chapter 4.

even more difficult to assess than overcrowding, however, and possibilities of transfer are limited, especially as many of the 'under occupied' dwellings are large family houses in decaying neighbourhoods, owned or tenanted by elderly persons who have been left alone or in couples as a result of the death, marriage or migration of other members of their families. These elderly men and women are reluctant to move away from their old homes with all their associations, and from the neighbourhood with which they are familiar,[1] and, in any case, such houses are not attractive to the younger generation unless they are first sub-divided into flats. One of the arguments put forward in favour of the abolition of rent control when the Rent Act, 1957, was being debated, was that as long as rents were kept low, elderly people occupying houses too big for them were under no financial pressure to move to smaller houses or to let off some of their surplus rooms, and so a good deal of house space was being wasted.[2] But financial pressure cannot rightly be brought to bear on people unless suitable smaller dwellings are available for them to move into, and this is not always the case. Local authorities should, and a number do, include in their housing programmes a sufficient number of small units suitable for elderly persons, and this provision, the importance of which is stressed in a circular issued in 1957 by the Ministry of Housing and Local Government,[3] should also facilitate transfers by elderly persons who are still occupying three-bedroom municipal houses which they had allocated to them when their families were at home and their housing need great.

While the main problems of housing need arise from deficiencies in number and size of dwellings, these are not the only difficulties. A dwelling may be sufficiently large to meet the needs of the family occupying it if it is used to capacity, but the family may not necessarily be willing or able to do this. They may huddle together in two out of the three bedrooms because they are short of beds or bedding or because the third room is damp or cold,[4] children may be denied the opportunity of doing their homework in a quiet room because the need for this is not appreciated and the heating grudged, or a lodger given a room to himself while the family crowds together in the remainder of the dwelling. Nor is it only in connection with space allocation that the use made of a

---

[1] Some evidence bearing on this question is contained in a small survey made in Liverpool in 1952, *Social Contacts in Old Age*. The proportion of elderly people with houses too big for them who were willing to move was comparatively small.
[2] This is discussed by H. R. Parker in *The Rent Act*, Town Planning Review, January 1958, p. 310.   [3] Circular 18/57.
[4] Examples are given in J. M. Mackintosh, *Housing and Family Life*, p. 70, and pp. 77–78.

dwelling may be as important as the dwelling itself, the same applies to the way in which fabric and fittings are treated. Hence, not only must a local authority or housing trust provide dwellings of suitable size and convenience, it must see that they are properly managed, for good management may make a great deal of difference to tenants' attitudes and standards.

The importance and possibilities of good housing management were first realised and demonstrated in practice by Octavia Hill, friend and disciple of Ruskin. In 1864 she undertook the management of three tenement houses in London where conditions were extremely bad, and in time she 'not only converted these dwellings into clean, sanitary houses and brought order into the lives of the tenants, but she also made the venture pay'.[1] This demonstration of the possibility of combining good social work with good business soon attracted attention. More and more property was given into her charge, she began to train other women in her methods, and her ideas spread, not only in this country, but in other parts of the world also, so that housing management is now recognised as an integral part of housing policy.

Housing management, as understood by the Society of Housing Managers, which continues the work begun by Octavia Hill, is based on three principles. The first is that landlord and tenant have a mutual responsibility towards the property and should work together to preserve and enhance its value and usefulness; the second that the business and social aspects of housing management are not independent spheres of activity, but should be combined; while the third is that good relationships must, as far as possible, be maintained between the landlord, or his representatives, and the tenant. The first and third of these three principles are generally accepted but there are differences of opinion about the second. Some local authorities prefer to manage property by means of what has been called the 'specialist system',[2] that is to say, a system whereby, apart from the housing manager and his deputy, the work of the department is divided between a number of persons each exercising his own particular function, be it rent collection, maintenance or welfare, in relation to all or a large number of the houses for which the authority is responsible. As one of these officials, the local authority may appoint a woman welfare worker, responsible for helping the tenants to adjust themselves to their new environment and raise their standards of

[1] Society of Women Housing Managers, *Housing Estate Management*, 1946, p. 2. For an account of how this was done see E. Moberley Bell, *Life of Octavia Hill*.

[2] Peter H. Mann, 'Methods of Municipal Housing Management'. *Case Conference*, July 1957, p. 82.

housing care, but this work is kept quite separate from such business matters as the collection of rents and oversight of repairs.

Each of these methods of housing management has advantages and disadvantages. The chief advantages of the 'Octavia Hill' system of combining the functions of rent collector and social worker are that the collection of rents and oversight of repairs provides a right of entry into every house for a known and accepted business purpose with which the educative and social functions can be combined, and there is no obvious singling out of 'undesirable' or 'problem' families for special visiting. Further, as the worker visits weekly, she gets to know the family when times are normal as well as when trouble or difficulty occurs. On the other hand, it means that a trained and skilled social worker may have to spend a great deal of time and energy on routine work, and even by limiting the length of each visit so that there can be little time for real social work, she cannot undertake to visit more than about 100 tenants a day or at the most between 400 and 500 a week. Hence, on these grounds alone, it is questionable whether a method evolved to deal with small groups of dwellings owned by housing trusts is appropriate for the management of municipal housing estates, or new towns with tens of thousands of tenants. The question has also been raised as to whether 'the methods evolved by Miss Hill to help and protect people too poor and ignorant to help themselves are becoming anachronistic to-day',[1] when municipal tenants are frequently people with high standards of comfort and amenity, with some education and their own canons of behaviour. Even if this be generally true, there are still families who need a great deal of help and teaching before they can benefit from their new environment, however, and whether the exact method adopted is that advocated by the Society of Housing Managers or the alternative of appointing separate welfare workers, it is important that someone whom the tenants know personally and to whom they can turn in times of difficulty, should be available to act as their link with the otherwise impersonal housing authority.

One of the most difficult problems in housing management is the transfer of families from a slum clearance area to their new homes on housing estates or in blocks of flats and helping them to settle there. As has been recognised by the Housing Management Sub-Committee of the Central Housing Advisory Committee, the element of compulsion in the move differentiates rehousing in

[1] M. I. Sharp, 'Management Today: The Part of Tenants' Associations', *Quarterly Bulletin of the Society of Housing Managers*, Vol. II, January 1949, p. 6. This article is criticised by E. Moberley Bell in an article entitled 'Are Octavia Hill's Methods Obsolete?' in the July issue of the same Bulletin.

connection with slum clearance from providing houses for families on the waiting list. To families on the waiting list, municipal housing, whatever its disadvantages, appears to offer more satisfactory conditions of life than those hitherto experienced; families in a clearance area are faced with the prospect of the demolition of their homes and the removal to new ones whether they will or no. This element of compulsion justifies special consideration of the problems which confront the families affected by slum clearance and 'not the least important part of the long process of slum clearance is the careful study of the needs of individual families and the search for ways of meeting them'.[1]

Among the changes brought about by the move from a central urban area to a municipal housing estate or a new town, whether the move is brought about as a direct result of slum clearance or because the family has now reached the head of the waiting list, are changes in the pattern of kinship and neighbourhood relationships, but these have not always been sufficiently appreciated and allowed for by housing committees and administrators. Their extent and importance have been emphasised in all recent surveys of the social effects of housing, however. For example, a survey of family life in Bethnal Green and the effects on it of the removal of the younger generation to housing estates several miles away,[2] revealed that the inhabitants of this area are, for the most part, members of three generation families, bound together in a complex of rights and obligations, the tie between mother and daughter being particularly close, even after marriage. When the daughter, together with her husband and children, migrates to a new housing estate a long journey away, the link between the generations becomes weaker, the reciprocal flow of services is interrupted, and a new pattern of family life, with a closer partnership between husband and wife, now isolated with their dependent children in a strange new world, is gradually built up.

Nor is it only with the kinship group that the break has to be made. However grimy and unattractive the old congested area may be, it is the place to which the family belongs and possibly has belonged for several generations.[3] In such a neighbourhood

[1] Ministry of Housing and Local Government, *Moving from the Slums*, H.M.S.O., 1956, pp. 2 and 3.

[2] Michael Young and Peter Willmot, *Family and Kinship in East London*, a Survey by the Institute of Community Studies, 1957.

[3] A Survey of the Ancoats Clearance Area made just before the war 'confirmed the impression held by most Settlement workers that Ancoats is a community'. 41·2 per cent of the 460 families investigated had been in the same house for more than twenty years, and of the 185 families with a tenancy of less than five years, 117 were Ancoats families in the sense that one or both parents had been born or brought up in the district. Manchester University Settlement, *Ancoats. A Study of a Clearance Area*, Report of a Survey made in 1937–38, p. 13.

kinship forms the doorway to the community, relatives act as intermediaries to friends, and life is neighbourhood centred.[1] Not only
are there close links with relatives, near and distant, and with
neighbours and friends, but the neighbourhood itself, with all its
institutions—its shops, public houses, cinemas, churches and
schools, is a familiar and friendly place, while shopkeepers,
doctors, priests, even health and social workers and officials, are
all well known. Finally the journey to work is not likely to be
the wearisome and expensive business it is to many suburban
families.

It has been suggested that in the face of all this, the 'question for
authorities' is whether 'they should do more than they are at present doing to meet the preference of people who would not willingly
forego these advantages, rather than insisting that more thousands
should migrate beyond the city'?[2] This question involves a further
one, however, namely, 'What would be the cost of such a policy
not only financially but socially?' Earlier in this chapter we considered the extent to which people and families were crowded
together in dwellings, but no less serious is the problem of the
crowding of the dwellings on the ground. 'Sufficient daylight and
some bare ration of sunlight, a little privacy, ease of access and a
small quota of surrounding space are counted to-day among the
bare decencies of social existence,' but it has been reckoned that
these elementary requirements cannot be satisfied at densities of
more than about twenty houses to the acre—less than half the
density of the central areas of many of our larger cities.[3] Hence,
the only way of rehousing the inhabitants of central areas at tolerable standards would seem to be by the extensive use of multi-
storey flats, and this raises the further question as to whether, and
under what conditions, a full and happy life is possible for families
and particularly families with children, in such flats.

There seems to be some consensus of opinion that blocks of flats
are unsuitable for children. 'However desirable, or indeed inevitable, blocks of flats may appear to the town planner, they deny
to children certain vital needs, of which space in which to play and
contact with living and growing things are among the most important.'[4] These needs may be met in part by the provision of a
communal garden and well-equipped play spaces, but even these
amenities do not wholly compensate for space indoors where a
child can make a noise without unduly disturbing the neighbours,
for the possibility of keeping pets or the possession of a garden, or
even a yard, into which the toddler can run at will and still be

[1] Young and Willmot, op. cit., p. 91.
[2] Ibid., p. 165.   [3] Peter Self, *Cities in Flood*, 1957, pp. 39 and 40.
[4] L. E. White, *Tenement Town*.

under his mother's eye, instead of being separated from her by several flights of stairs. After investigating the question, the Flats Sub-Committee of the Central Housing Advisory Committee of the Ministry of Housing and Local Government concluded, 'For one class of family in particular, the family with several children, it is well-nigh impossible to provide a suitable environment in flats. The weight of evidence submitted to us, confirmed by our own impressions formed in visiting large estates of flats, has convinced us that, after all practicable measures have been taken to meet the social needs of families living on such estates, it would still be desirable to provide, even in central areas, the maximum amount of accommodation for families with children in houses and maisonettes rather than in flats'.[1] Such mixed development in connection with slum clearance schemes is encouraged by the Housing Subsidies Act, 1956, as the exchequer subsidy payable under this Act for dwellings provided by a local authority for slum clearance and re-development is payable not only in respect of flats, but in respect of other dwellings also. At the same time, increased subsidies are payable in respect of higher buildings.[2] Even with these extra subsidies, costs of building such flats are high, and it has been estimated that, in blocks of six or more storeys, the average two-bedroom flat costs roughly twice as much to build as an ordinary council house.[3] If, as is likely, the land values are also high, the cost of making provision for additional families in the inner re-development areas instead of further afield is very considerable.[4] It is possible that more might be done than is being done at present to save space on roads and railways, and to house factories and offices in multi-storey buildings,[5] and the re-conditioning of old, but still structurally sound houses in the inner areas, and the prevention of their further decay might be carried further than it has been hitherto. But even allowing for these developments, if the

[1] *Living in Flats*. Report of the Flats Sub-Committee of the Central Housing Advisory Committee, H.M.S.O., 1952, p. 3.
[2] Housing Subsidies Act, 1956. Section 3. Dwellings other than a block of flats of four or more storeys qualify for an annual exchequer subsidy of £22 1s. for sixty years; blocks of flats of four storeys £32, five storeys £38, six or more storeys £50, increased by £1 15s. for each storey by which the block exceeds six storeys.
[3] Peter Self, op. cit., p. 44.
[4] Peter Self quotes estimates made by Mr. N. Borg of the Birmingham Corporation to the effect that if 35,000 of the 100,000 people in Birmingham's development area are housed in three-storey flats and terrace houses in the centre and 65,000 on new estates, the cost will be about £63½m.; if 50,000 re-housed in multi-storey flats in the centre the cost will be £80m. Thus the extra cost of cramming 15,000 more people into the re-development area works out at over £1,000 a head. Ibid., p. 45.
[5] Ibid., p. 42. Cf. Young and Willmot, op. cit., p. 165.

very serious disadvantages under which individuals and families in the congested inner areas of large cities are living is to be overcome, it will be necessary for many families to move elsewhere. Hence local authorities are faced with the land-use problem of deciding what provision shall be made for this 'overspill' population and where, as well as with the social problem of helping the individuals and families who have been moved to make a good adjustment to their new environment with its opportunities as well as its difficulties.

If the congested industrial town was largely the product of the nineteenth century, the suburban sprawl, with its resultant coalescence of separate towns into vast conurbations, has been greatly accentuated during the twentieth, and one of the objectives of post-war planning has been to check this sprawl. This has necessitated increasing public control over land use. The efforts to gain such control go back to the abortive, but significant, Housing and Town Planning Act of 1909,[1] and culminated to the Town and Country Planning Act, 1947. This Act made planning obligatory, and forbade private development of land without the consent of the planning authority. It designated the county councils and county borough councils as the planning authorities for their respective areas, and they were instructed to prepare development plans in connection with it. The plans were to include not only the reconstruction of the devastated and blighted inner areas of the towns and great cities but also measures designed to bring about the planned development areas of their peripheries. It was hoped in this way to preserve the balance between the interests of town and country, prevent the further proliferation of the conurbations, and substitute living communities for featureless housing estates. In this connection, as in connection with the health, education and social security measures passed during the same five years, we believed we were making a new start, and we were determined that the old evils should not be perpetuated, the old mistakes made again.

During the years that have passed since then our achievements have failed to match our hopes. 'We have continued to do things which responsible opinion would agree to be unwise and are making tough problems still harder to solve.' In housing, 'the big cities need houses most, they had the labour and had or soon acquired organisations capable of handling large contracts; and around the edges of these cities there were sites where, in all, some tens of thousands of new houses could be placed without need for costly preliminary or supplementary works'. Further, while it was

[1] The significance of this Act is discussed by W. Ashworth, *The Genesis of Modern British Town Planning*, ch. vii.

'easy for a city to build within or near its boundary, it was almost impossible to build far afield'.[1] The result of all this has been that by far the majority of houses built in England and Wales since the war have been built round the edges of existing towns, especially of large towns, and 'have extended the conurbations and urban sprawl in just the way we had intended to avoid, and which existing massive legislation was intended to prevent'.[2] This is not the whole story. We have, for instance, made a bold and imaginative planning experiment in the creation of new towns, but important as this experiment has been, its scope is limited and for the majority of people rehousing, since the war has meant removal to a suburban housing estate. Thus, in the broad lines of our planning, we have failed to learn the lessons of the past; how far in the detailed planning of housing estates and new towns we are utilising the increased knowledge and fuller understanding of the personal and social, as well as the physical needs of the people moving there which has accumulated during the last decade, remains to be discussed.

One question which is relevant to this discussion is the extent to which the condition of the people moving to the estates has itself changed, so that the problems of a family rehoused by the local authority to-day may be rather different from those of a family making the same move during the inter-war years. One important change which has certainly come about, and which affects rehousing, is the increased prosperity of the working classes largely as the result of higher wages and full employment. A major rehousing problem of inter-war years, which caused much concern, derived from the fact that numbers of those on the housing lists or living in property scheduled for slum clearance were living in acute poverty, either because of low wages or because of prolonged unemployment, which meant that the extra costs of living on a new housing estate might well result in physical deprivation so serious as to counteract the advantages of the move.[3] While, as

[1] H. Myles Wright, 'The First Ten Years', *Town Planning Review*, July 1955, p. 84.
[2] Ibid., pp. 80–81.
[3] The danger of this was brought to the notice of the public by a study, made by Dr. G. C. McGonigle, late Medical Officer of Health of Stockton-on-Tees, of the mortality rates of two groups of people who in 1927 were living in insanitary conditions in a slum area in the centre of the town. Half the population of the area was moved to a well-built housing estate on the outskirts, the rest remained were they were. Contrary to expectation, the death rates, both crude and standardised, of those families which had been moved compared unfavourably with those of the population which had remained in the insanitary area. After considering other explanations, Dr. McGonigle concluded that the families on the housing estate were suffering from dietary deficiencies caused by trying to make their exiguous incomes (most of the heads of families

has already been suggested when discussing subsidies, there are still families for whom the payment of the rents charged for the new local authority houses entails hardship, and there are others who, having become accustomed to a pattern of expenditure in which the rent forms a very small proportion of the total family income, find it difficult to accept the higher commitments which now have to be met, slum clearance to-day, whatever it may have been in the past, is not, in general, a matter of the compulsory transfer of poverty-stricken families from overcrowded and insanitary dwellings to an environment where they will receive 'fresh air at the expense of their food'.[1] For example, even in the notorious slums of Glasgow, 'Many of the miserable decrepit houses still remain, though doubtless relatively less numerous than they were a generation or two ago,' but 'the more striking change is in the people of the slums. Many slum areas are still "tough" spots, but now, to a much greater extent than formerly, many of the inhabitants are hard-working, often skilled or semi-skilled operators in regular employment, earning good and steady wages. Poverty is much less prevalent than it was and is no longer a major factor in driving people into a slum environment, except in the case of a relatively small number of unfortunate old people. Many of the people who have been driven into slum houses since the end of the war have gone that way because of sheer inability to obtain better accommodation for which they were in the great majority of cases willing and able to pay.'[2] The change observed in this particular area appears to have taken place elsewhere also, for it is noted by the Housing Management Sub-Committee of the Central Housing Advisory Committee, who state, 'it is clear from the evidence submitted to us that there is no great difference in level between those now living in clearance areas and those on the general waiting list', and suggest that 'whereas, in the past, economic reasons alone made people less happy in looking forward to the prospect of a new house and less confident in their ability to meet the demands of the move', they can now 'usually face the transition from slum

were unemployed at the time) cover the higher rents of their new homes. G. C. McGonigle and J. Kirby, *Poverty and Public Health*, 1937, ch. vii. The conclusions drawn by Dr. McGonigle have been questioned and some important data, e.g. changes in the age structure of the population moved, are missing, but the survey 'performed a useful service in pointing to the special economic difficulties of rehoused populations'. J. M. Mackintosh, *Housing and Family Life*, 1952, p. 205.

[1] The Medical Officer of Health for Huyton and Roby quoted by N. Williams, *Population Problems of New Housing Estates with, Special Reference to Norris Green*, University of Liverpool Press, 1939.

[2] Thomas Ferguson and Mary G. Pettigrew, 'A Study of 388 Families Living in Old Slum Houses', *Glasgow Medical Journal*, Vol. 35, August 1954.

to new house without anxiety and without the need for material assistance'.[1]

The financial problems associated with rehousing would thus seem to be less serious than they were a generation ago, but this does not mean that they are non-existent. They have changed their character, but have not disappeared. The emphasis now is not so much on the struggle to survive, but on the struggle to live up to the higher material standards imposed by the new house and the neighbourhood,[2] and in attempting to do this many housewives find it difficult to resist the insidious, or even overt, pressure of the representative of the hire purchase firm.[3] The resulting commitments necessitate a reduction of spending in other directions, or, alternatively, the husband may feel obliged to work overtime or the wife go out to work. Either way there is likely to be some financial strain, some personal and social adjustment to be made.

Closely allied to the problem of maintaining standards is that of preserving or establishing status, for on a new estate where all are strangers status is likely to be judged by material possessions. The importance attached to status by the people living on the estates raises the policy issue of the desirability or otherwise of attempting to mix people of differing social backgrounds and standards on the same estate. The inter-war estates, particularly those built in the thirties to house families from slum clearance areas, were often occupied by families all of whom belonged to the same social class, and were characterised by a grey level of poverty, accentuated in some parts of the country by prolonged unemployment. The glaring deficiencies, both of these estates and of the blocks of flats built in the central areas during the same period, with their lack of leadership, low economic and social standards and high proportion of 'problem' families led to a swing of opinion in favour of mixing classes, which, it was thought, would ensure a more balanced community and a more rich and varied social life. Even before the war, however, the reluctance of the classes to mix had become apparent. Evidence of this was given in a survey of the Bristol housing estates made in 1939, which revealed that attempts to introduce families cleared from slum areas among well-established

[1] *Moving from the Slums.* Seventh Report of the Housing Management Sub-Committee of the Central Housing Advisory Committee, 1956, p. 2.

[2] 'The first essential is money for material possessions. When people move to Greenleigh the standard of life, measured by the quality of housing is at once raised. . . . Furniture and carpets have to be bought. . . . Moreover the house is only the beginning. A nice house and shabby clothes, a neat garden and an old box of a pram do not go together.' Young and Willmot, op. cit., p. 130.

[3] The extent of this pressure is discussed in a series of articles in *The Manchester Guardian* entitled 'Credit on the Doorstep', the first of which was published on February 21, 1956.

artisan families led to the withdrawal of the latter,[1] and post-war surveys have confirmed the existence of this status consciousness. For example, investigations into the social relationships of the inhabitants of two housing estates, one in Liverpool and one in Sheffield, showed that they tended to divide themselves into 'roughs' and 'respectables'. The great majority, the 'ordinary working-class folk', as they designated themselves, formed one group, while over against them were the minority with higher standards and aspirations who 'kept themselves to themselves' (sometimes not even allowing their children out of the garden), and eschewed both neighbourly relationships and community activities.[2] However, the Liverpool survey showed that the assumption of superior social status was no more frequent among the skilled than the unskilled workers,[3] although the sprinkling of foremen and other supervisory grades on the estate kept aloof from community activities, and, despite divisions and hostilities, the conclusion of the Sheffield study was that 'On the whole our evidence reinforces the contention that a policy which leads to the segregation of one group is undesirable.' It was admitted that, 'if people with very different standards and habits are forced into close contact conflicts may all too easily occur', but 'the mixture does', it was suggested, 'provide a wider range of visible ideals which can lead to changed aspirations and a different style of living'[4]—a statement which, incidentally, presumes that the change is likely to be a desirable one. The Sheffield investigators appeared to consider that, while people with different social standards do not make good neighbours, this does not necessarily preclude them from forming a satisfactory larger community, such as may be found, for example, in a well-established small town. There is a difference between neighbourliness and community spirit. 'Neighbourliness is mainly a matter of personalities and immediate day-to-day needs. It is a matter chiefly for people in the same social class, living in the same street. The community spirit is on a much larger scale. It need not involve people dropping into each other's houses, or even necessarily knowing one another, and it should be broad enough to embrace people of widely differing backgrounds and social classes. It is the feeling of belonging to a social group with common interests and responsibilities—a group, in fact, with a life of its own.'[5]

The conclusion which can be drawn from this discussion on the

[1] R. Jevons and J. Madge, *Housing Estates, a Study of Bristol Corporation Policy and Practice between the Wars*, p. 69.

[2] *Neighbourhood and Community*, an Inquiry conducted by the Universities of Liverpool and Sheffield, e.g., pp. 121–123, and 135 ff.

[3] Ibid., p. 139.

[4] Ibid., p. 124.

[5] M. P. Fogarty, *Town and Country Planning*, p. 110.

mixing of classes on housing estates would seem to be, then, that difficulties between neighbours can best be avoided if tenants are housed in 'small, though coherent sub-units'[1] of people of similar habits and backgrounds. If, in addition, such units consist of groups of people from the same area (as would be possible in re-housing in connection with slum clearance, but less easy when selecting tenants from the housing lists), the loneliness of the people, and particularly the women living on the housing estate would be mitigated, and the city could be rebuilt 'without squandering the fruits of social cohesion'.[2] Such sub-units should, however, form part of a larger and more varied community. The form which this has been envisaged in most post-war planning has been the rather unfortunately named 'neighbourhood unit'.

In the passage quoted above Professor Fogarty describes the community spirit as 'the feeling of belonging to a social group with common interests and responsibilities', and the 'neighbourhood-unit' planning of the immediate post-war years represents an attempt to build up communities on this basis. Neighbourhood units were designed to house approximately 10,000 people or 2,000 families of differing age, occupation, interest and class. This number was chosen as large enough to justify the provision of institutions and amenities for day-to-day living, such as schools for young children, a sufficient variety of shops, churches, public houses, a branch library and clinic; yet to occupy an area small enough for the inhabitants, even the mothers with their prams and the young children just starting school, to move freely around it, and, in particular, to reach the 'neighbourhood centre' where most of the amenities and activities would be concentrated.

Neighbourhood units were widely accepted as the basis for planning in the years just after the war, but they have been sub-ject to a considerable amount of criticism. One of the major criticisms levelled at neighbourhood unit planning is that it is based on home and leisure time needs and interests, and is not related in any way to the working lives of its inhabitants. 'Neigh-bourhood units' have been described by their advocates as the modern equivalents of the old village communities,[3] but one of the closest bonds uniting the inhabitants of the village was that of

---

[1] Jevons and Madge, op. cit., p. 69. Cf. N. Williams, op. cit., p. 48. 'We have found that neighbourhoods flourish best in small clusters containing between forty and sixty houses, all at the same rent and with the same type of tenant.'

[2] Young and Willmott, op. cit., p. 166.

[3] See, for example, the discussion in the *City of Manchester Plan*, p. 135, where the neighbourhood unit is described as 'a modern urbanised version of the traditional village', the counterpart of the village green being the neighbour-hood centre with its local shops, churches, public house, bank, library and health centre.

similar or related occupations. Now, however, the work-place and the home are often widely separated and the link between them a very tenuous one, so that people living in the same neighbourhood may work in different trades in different parts of the city. Thus it would seem that modern man may have to make a choice between two bonds of association—that of locality and that of common employment. Moreover, the growth of communications combined with almost universal literacy makes it possible for people to lead full and satisfying lives and to pursue many different interests while at the same time having but few contacts with the people of their own neighbourhood, so that the question arises as to whether neighbourhood planning may not be 'a wishful looking backwards to a tradition no longer valid'.[1] There are, however, many people who live very narrow and often lonely lives, and opportunities for forming associations with others having common interests and living in the same area may help them overcome this social isolation. If this can be encouraged by planning, something worth while will have been achieved.[2] Moreover, the feeling that one belongs to a local community, in the life of which one can play a significant part, and for which one develops a sense of responsibility, is surely the foundation of local democracy and good local government.

Another controversial issue which has arisen in connection with 'neighbourhood planning' is the extent to which the separate units should be self-contained. Thus the generally accepted idea of the maximum possible degree of self-maintenance by the provision within the 'neighbourhood' of all the services necessary for everyday living has been criticised as being too rigid. For example, a survey of Middlesbrough revealed a good deal of 'inflow' and 'outflow' in and out of existing neighbourhoods, which varied both with the type and situation of the neighbourhood and the nature of the institutions considered, whether they were, for example, schools and of what kind, shops and of what kind, churches, public houses or other services to meet ordinary needs. It would appear from this investigation that 'the choice of institutions we frequent is not subject to distance alone, but to a variety of additional considerations and characteristics', and the investigators concluded that 'convenient access to institutions is essential, but standards of convenience vary for different groups, and for different types of services. There will inevitably be a good deal of criss-cross movement and residential cells should therefore be closely related to

[1] M. P. Hall, *Community Centres in Manchester*, p. 85.
[2] For further discussion see *Planning*, Vol. XV, No. 296—'Can Communities be Planned?' also the discussion on community centres and associations in Chapter XX.

each other. The pattern of urban areas should express and facilitate the coherence of groups of neighbours, it should not be split up by a number of sub-divisions.'[1] Neighbourhoods are not separate entities, they are parts of a larger whole, the town or city itself, and this should be emphasised. The planning of neighbourhoods is thus incomplete in itself, it must form part of the ordered planning of the whole town.

Although research in this field is going forward, we are still ignorant of many of the factors which encourage that sense of belonging which makes such a difference to the happiness of people living in a particular district and transforms an area which starts as a geographical expression into a local community with its own traditions and values. It may be that the launderette does more to bring the women together than the clinic; the school or public house may be more significant for the development of social contacts than the community centre. One thing would appear to be certain, however, and that is that community development takes time. It is not likely to be accomplished in one or possibly even two generations. This raises a very difficult issue of housing policy, namely, that of the treatment of young couples who have grown up on a local authority housing estate or in the satellite town, and now want to marry and set up house in the neighbourhood to which they feel they belong. If this very natural wish is to be fulfilled they must be given a dwelling in the area, but this may mean giving them priority over families in the central area who have perhaps been living for years in almost intolerable conditions, waiting for their chance of a house, and it also means extending the advantages of the subsidy from one generation to another. Hence, apart from any other considerations, such action may not be acceptable politically, but it seems wasteful to allow young people, who for years have benefited from the healthier conditions which estates undoubtedly provide, to drift back on marriage to the congested areas from which their parents were moved at considerable public expense.

The extent to which families fail to settle in their new surroundings and drift back to the central areas is not easy to ascertain, and, even if ascertained, does not tell us the number of families who would go back if they could find a house to go to. For many families there seems to be a conflict between the advantages which they realise the children are deriving from living on a suburban estate and the loneliness and strangeness which they themselves experience.[2] The

---

[1] Ruth Glass, *The Social Background of a Plan*, p. 43.
[2] Young and Willmott, op. cit., pp. 103–105. Cf. J. M. Mackintosh, op. cit., pp. 209 ff., where the findings of two local inquiries, one in Glasgow and one in Manchester are discussed.

majority of rehoused families appear to settle down in the end, although some do go back to the central areas, and others, more ambitious and prosperous, acquire semi-detached houses of their own on private enterprise estates. There is a further group that does not fit in, however, those tenants who are so unsatisfactory that, after causing much tribulation to the housing authority, they are given notice to quit. Evidence obtained by the Housing Management Sub-Committee of the Central Housing Advisory Committee suggests that in each year these number about 2,500 families, or about 0·19 per cent of the total 2½ million tenancies.[1]

Although comparatively few in number these unsatisfactory tenants are a serious source of worry to local housing authorities, particularly those who not only default with their rent but who are generally incompetent in managing their affairs, are dirty in their habits, neglect the house and annoy or disgust the neighbours. These families must be given patient, persistent and personal attention if they are to be helped to overcome their difficulties and improve their standards, and the Housing Management Sub-Committee, in the Report quoted above, emphasised the need for housing authorities to employ staff trained for this difficult work and allow them sufficient time to carry it out.[2] Should all efforts fail and eviction appear inevitable the outlook for such families is dark. They are seldom able to find alternative accommodation for themselves and either double up with another family, causing or accentuating overcrowding, or drift into 'Part III accommodation', that is accommodation provided by local welfare authorities under Part III of the National Assistance Act, Section 21 of which directs county and county borough councils to provide 'temporary accommodation for persons who are in urgent need thereof, being in circumstances which could not reasonably have been foreseen, or in such other circumstances as the authority may in any particular case determine'. This may well lead to the break-up of the family either temporarily or permanently, since in many areas such accommodation is reserved for mothers and young children, while, even if the whole family is allowed to reside there, conditions may be detrimental to the maintenance of anything in the nature of an ordered and responsible family life. It is thus desirable that efforts should be made to see that families do not remain in this kind of accommodation indefinitely, becoming increasingly apathetic and irresponsible, and experiments in their rehabilitation and resettlement in suitable dwellings have been made in several areas. In some places 'intermediate accommodation' or 'half-way houses' have been provided either by the

---

[1] *Unsatisfactory Tenants.* Sixth Report of the Housing Management Sub-Committee of the Central Housing Advisory Committee, p. 2.   [2] Ibid., p. 6.

authority or by voluntary effort. These are houses where the standards and amenities are not as high as in most local authority houses, and where, to a greater or less degree, help, guidance and supervision from health and social workers is provided with the objective of assisting the family to re-establish itself to re-occupy a normal home of its own. When that stage is reached the family is rehoused by the local authority, possibly in one of its older houses, and the half-way house is again available for another family.[1]

The discussions of the last few pages have centred round the problems of community development on local housing estates, and, as has already been pointed out, the majority of people rehoused since the war have been accommodated on those estates. Apart from rehousing in flats in the central areas, already touched on, there have been two other experiments which are of interest, however. The first of these is the creation of entirely new towns by the New Towns Act, 1946; the second the use of existing small towns at some distance from a city with a surplus population as nuclei for the resettlement of a large number of families from that city. Arrangements of this kind were made possible by the Town Development Act, 1952.

As the name suggests, new towns were intended from the start to be completely independent of any existing cities, and to ensure this independence, they are being managed during their early years by Development Corporations appointed by the Ministry of Housing and Local Government, one for each town, with the intention that these corporations will, in time, be wound up and the towns governed by normal democratic methods. Another feature which distinguishes new towns from local authority housing estates, or even satellite towns such as Wythenshawe (Manchester), Kirkby (Liverpool) or Harold Hill (London County Council), is the way in which they are being peopled. This is being done by first attracting industries to the towns, and then the people to work in them. Thus in the new towns serving the London area[2] incoming firms are allowed to bring as many workers as choose to come, and any additional labour required is recruited from a list of workers with the necessary experience and skills compiled from the housing lists of the London County Council housing authorities. This policy has been generally successful as far as industrial firms are concerned, but offices and business firms

[1] A circular issued jointly by the Ministry of Housing and Local Government and the Ministry of Health (17/59 and 4/59 respectively), *Homeless Families*, reviews existing preventive and rehabilitative measures and the possibilities of their extension.

[2] The position in some of the other new towns is rather different, e.g., Newton Aylcliffe and Peterlee (Co. Durham) were built for families living in scattered and rather derelict mining villages.

have been more reluctant to move in, and it has been suggested that some Government departments might set the example. This provides a means by which the tendency, already noted in some of the new towns, for them to become one-class communities can be avoided. Another is by providing in each town a sufficient number and variety of more expensive houses and thus helping to encourage executives of firms located there to live, like their work-people, in the town where they have come to work.[1]

Although the way of peopling the new towns which has just been described gives the residents a much better start than those of the housing estates, many of the social problems they face are similar. Rents are high, for the Corporations have to pay their way and repay the money spent by Parliament to get the towns going, and, unlike the local authorities, new town corporations have no pool of pre-war houses to help to reduce them. As in other new areas, the inhabitants are mainly young couples with the result that the age balance is distorted, the towns overflow with children,[2] and the local education authorities in counties where they have been sited have been faced with immense problems.[3] Nor is education the only form of community development which has to be planned from the beginning: churches, libraries, clinics, shops, community centres, all have to be provided. As in the 'neighbourhood units' on the housing estates, it was hoped that a 'rich community life' would flower in these favoured surroundings, and, here as elsewhere, there has evidently been some disillusion-ment, partly, perhaps, because the facilities provided have been 'too little and too late'.[4] Nevertheless, by and large, the experi-ment of the new towns seems to have been generally successful. They are proving industrially prosperous and financially solvent, and at the same ttime are providing for their inhabitants a more satisfactory way of life, particularly by bringing work and residence within more easy reach of each other, than is found in most new housing areas.

New towns are one of the most interesting of our post-war

[1] Peter Self, op. cit., p. 88. Two Government Research Departments have already moved to one of the new towns.
[2] Lord Beveridge described Newton Aylcliffe in 1951 as 'a town of toddlers, or those just past the toddling age'. It was a town of few adolescents, and at that time had only three grandmothers to its 1,000 population. Lord Beveridge, *New Towns and the Case for Them.*
[3] In Hertfordshire, where there are four new towns and two L.C.C. housing estates, the school population rose from 60,000 to just over 100,000 in the ten years 1945–55. This increase was due largely but not entirely to the influx of new residents. The problem was two-fold, the 'bulge' and the new housing. H. W. Davies, 'Education in the New Towns', *Town and Country Planning,* Vol. XXIV, January 1956, p. 17.
[4] Wyndham Thomas, 'Inside a New Town', *Town and Country Planning,* January 1956, p. 38. Cf. Peter Self, op. cit., pp. 90–91.

planning experiments, but there are only fifteen of them all told, and, successful as they have been in themselves, the contribution they have made to the relief of the housing and industrial congestion in the conurbations is a tiny one. Another experiment in dispersal is that of selecting a small town some distance from a conurbation and encouraging industries and people to settle there. Such projects are supported by the Town Development Act, 1952, but, although the London County Council, the chief exporting authority, has explored its possibilities with enthusiasm, the results have been meagre.[1] We are still a long way from the solution of the problems posed by the conurbations.

During the years which have elapsed since the Second World War the related problems of housing and town planning have remained among the most serious of our social problems and our efforts at solving them have been by no means uniformly successful. Some progress has been made, however. Slowly overcrowding is declining, slowly the worst of the slums are being cleared, slowly the people in greatest need are being rehoused. But in the course of accomplishing these desirable ends we are repeating many of the mistakes of the past. We are concentrating on housing at the expense of community provisions, failing to stop the ugly sprawl of our towns, paying insufficient attention to social as distinct from physical needs. These mistakes and shortcomings are doubly unfortunate as the housing and planning of to-day not only changes the lives of the families occupying the newly built houses and moving into the new towns and neighbourhoods, it also determines the way of life of their children and grandchildren. There is another side to this question of continuity, moreover. Even if the house and surroundings are well planned, the move to a new home does not necessarily result in improved standards either immediately or even after a relatively short period. A study made in Glasgow of slum families rehoused for upwards of ten years revealed that 'there is still ample evidence of social immaturity, of failure to reflect improved environment, and this is nowhere more disappointing than in relation to adolescent delinquency, for it might have been hoped that the younger generation would have begun to move away now from the tradition of the slums.'[2] As the

---

[1] Peter Self, op. cit., pp. 66–75. Cf. A. Myles Wright, op. cit., pp. 78–79.

[2] Thomas Ferguson and Mary G. Pettigrew, 'A Study of 718 Slum Families Rehoused for Upwards of Ten Years', *Glasgow Medical Journal*, August 1954. Cf. J. H. Baghot, *Juvenile Delinquency*, 1941, pp. 69–71. As the result of a detailed inquiry in Liverpool made immediately before the war, Mr. Baghot concluded, 'It would appear . . . that the effect of moving families from overcrowded areas to new housing estates is to reduce the amount of delinquency among the juveniles concerned. The reduction is not apparent immediately, but is progressive and varies according to the age of the estate.'

authors of this study conclude, 'the eradication of slum sickness does not come with the mere erection of new houses', and it requires more than one generation to accomplish. Hence, not only must we be prepared in setting our standards of building and planning to think of the future as well as the present, we must also be prepared to tolerate the apparent failure of the improved environment we create to affect the quality of living in this generation in the hope that it will have its effect on those still unborn.

PART TWO

INDIVIDUALISING THE SOCIAL SERVICES

'Love does not cling to the *I* in such a way as to have the *Thou* only for its "content", its object; but love is between *I* and *Thou*. . . . In the eyes of him who takes his stand in love, and gazes out of it, men are cut free from their entanglement in bustling activity. Good people and evil, wise and foolish, beautiful and ugly, become successively real to him; that is, set free, they step forth in their singleness, and confront him as Thou. In a wonderful way, from time to time, exclusiveness arises—and so he can be effective, helping, healing, educating, raising up, saving. Love is responsibility of an *I* for a *Thou*.'—MARTIN BUBER.

CHAPTER VIII

SOCIAL WORK IN THE SOCIAL SERVICES

PART ONE of this book consisted, in the main, of a description of the major social services, services provided by statute to meet the basic needs of individuals and families. The needs that those services were provided to meet, income maintenance when earnings are interrupted, medical attention when required, reasonable accommodation for the family, are common to considerable numbers of people, and, in a complex society, can only be adequately met by large-scale planning, and administration designed to promote speed and efficiency. This means that, although these services are provided to further the well-being of the individual citizen, there is a danger lest, despite the care and courtesy of the officials administering them, they may operate in such a way that the citizen feels that he is being treated as something of a cipher, his personal needs, problems and viewpoint overlooked or not fully understood. Moreover, while the majority of people in need use the social services sensibly and with discrimination and overcome their difficulties without further help, there are individuals and families who cannot solve their problems unaided or make constructive use of the services without intensive, individual assistance. Hence, within the administrative setting of the social services, there is need for social work focused on the individual in his uniqueness to complete and make fully efficient services designed for the common good. This is becoming increasingly recognised by planners and administrators in both central government departments and the local authorities and it is resulting in the employment of increasing numbers of social workers in the statutory services.

The recognition of the value of social work and the special contribution which the social worker has to make to individual and social well-being was accorded slowly and late by the framers and administrators of the statutory services, however, and it was within the context of voluntary effort that the skills and disciplines of social work were first developed and put to the test. The main contribution of the Charity Organisation Society (which later significantly changed its name to 'Family Welfare Association') to social service was that, although it did not originate organised charity,[1] it became, in a capital where poverty was endemic and philanthropy widespread but unorganised, 'the centre for friendly and systematic investigation and thoughtful relief.'[2]

In the circumstances of the time it was natural that much of the thought and work of the society should centre round the problem of 'pauperism', the social and moral degradation of those who were not simply poverty stricken but who were living on the charity, whether private or public, of their fellows. The prevalence of this evil was attributed by the founders and supporters of the Charity Organisation Society chiefly to unwise attempts to mitigate poverty by indiscriminate charitable relief which undermined the deterrent effects of the Poor Law and encouraged the careless and undeserving. Underlying this diagnosis of the situation was the belief that in the vast majority of cases personal inadequacy of one kind or another was the main reason for the family's failure to remain independent and self-supporting. Hence, while the Charity Organisation Society campaigned actively for specific projects for social betterment, such as the provision of tuberculosis dispensaries and the care of the feeble-minded, it opposed any form of statutory assistance, such as the provision of school meals, which, it thought, might undermine individual or family responsibility. The Society believed that pauperism could only be eliminated and poverty itself reduced by the restoration of individuals and families to self respect and independence, and the only way to accomplish this was to treat them as units, endeavouring in each case to understand the causes of the applicant's social inadequacy and to find ways to overcome them. In making this diagnosis the Charity Organisation Society underestimated the part played in the causation of poverty by social and economic factors outside the control of the individuals concerned.[3] Nevertheless, the personal factors they stressed were relevant and important in many of the cases they investigated and sought to help, and even if, as a later generation came to believe, society can overcome most of its obvious social evils by policies designed to secure a

[1] If anyone can be said to have done this, the credit should probably go to Dr. Thomas Chalmers, a Presbyterian minister, who between 1819 and 1823 established and maintained in his parish in Glasgow a system of poor relief involving intensive investigation and supervision by the church deacons, each of whom was responsible for a small group of families. An account of this and other nineteenth-century experiments which anticipated C.O.S. methods and approach is given in A. F. Young and E. T. Ashton, *British Social Work in the Nineteenth Century*.

[2] C. L. Mowat, 'Charity and Casework in Late Victorian England', *The Social Service Review*, Vol. XXXI, No. 3, September 1957, p. 269.

[3] This was shown by the findings of Booth and Rowntree described in Chapter II above. See also the criticisms of the Society made by Beatrice Webb, *My Apprenticeship*, chs. iv and v.

'minimum standard of civilised life' for all its members,[1] these personal problems and inadequacies still remain.

The social work principles which were basic to the philosophy and work of the Charity Organisation Society, and which are still valid to-day despite the changes in outlook and in social and economic circumstances which have taken place since, derive ultimately from the belief that men's needs cannot be met by material help alone, and that their wishes must be respected, and co-operation secured in any plans made to deal with the situation which has led them to seek for help. Hence the relationship between the client and the caseworker must be such that he is 'free to be himself, without shame or guilt, to tell the truth, to accept or reject the help offered, and to co-operate in establishing his rights or in following out a jointly determined policy, all of his own free will'.[2] The help given may include some form of material assistance, for example a loan or grant, but such assistance is given, not as an end in itself, but as part of a considered policy of social rehabilitation. Consequently, when given, it must be adequate in amount, adapted in form and method to the needs of the client, and given in such a way as to foster his self respect. But the main contribution which the caseworker has to make to the solution of the client's difficulty is not in giving him material help, however generous and suitable, or even in planning and contriving on his behalf, it is in the relationship she forms with him. His need is 'not alms but a friend', as Octavia Hill put it. The relationship to be achieved is one which will support and strengthen the client, help him to a better understanding of his difficulties, and enable him to make better use of the community services available to him. In the establishment and maintenance of this relationship the outlook and attitudes of the worker are all important. 'In the last resort the social worker has only one piece of equipment to work with, her own personality.'[3]

A client-worker relationship in which the worker is able to put herself alongside the client and make him feel that they are facing a difficult situation together, is essential to good casework, but there is another aspect of the situation which should not be lost sight of. The caseworker is acting in her professional as well as in

[1] The phrase is Beatrice Webb's. 'The sole purpose of the Minority Report', she wrote, 'was to secure a national minimum of civilised life . . . open to all people, of both sexes and all classes . . .' *Our Partnership*, pp. 481–482.

[2] Una A. Cormack, 'Principles of Social Case Work', *Social Work*, Vol. IV, No. 3, July 1947, p. 71. In certain forms of social work, e.g. probation, there are sanctions in the background which may modify this situation. See below, p. 135.

[3] Roger A. Wilson, 'Aims and Methods of a Department of Social Studies', *Social Work*, Vol. VI, No. 4, October 1949, p. 58.

her personal capacity, and represents the agency, public or voluntary, to which, rather than to any individual, the client first came for help. In its turn the agency has responsibilities not only to its clients but to the community which supports it and of whose services it is a part. Hence for the purposes of her work with the client the caseworker must accept the limitations imposed by the policy and functions of her agency and the accepted standards of community care in the society to which they both belong. In her capacity as private citizen she may seek to improve standards and rectify faulty legislation, and one of the civic responsibilities of both casework agencies and professional associations of social workers is to bring to the notice of public and Parliament the deficiencies and anomalies of which they become aware in the course of their work, a responsibility which, in this country, is generally recognised and accepted,[1] but until the public has been convinced and the remedies obtained, both worker and client must work within the situation as it is.

The general principles discussed so far derive from the beliefs and traditions of the men and women who created the Charity Organisation Society in 1869, and during the next thirty years laid the foundations on which social casework has been built, but many changes have taken place since then, and casework to-day differs in many respects from that undertaken in the late nineteenth century.

One of the most important of these changes is that of the social worker's own outlook. This has been profoundly modified during the last half century, especially by insights derived from psychology and psychiatry, both of which are now generally recognised as relevant to the practice of social work. Reliance on psychology and the psychologist, and more especially on 'dynamic' psychology, is more general and has been carried further in the United States than over here, but in this country too, trained social workers have readily incorporated its discoveries and presuppositions into their thinking about their cases. This has had at least two significant effects. Firstly, while it is recognised that the roles of the psychotherapist and the social caseworker are distinct and different,[2] the

---

[1] For example, the Charity Organisation Society provided a good deal of the evidence in connection with the move to reform the law relating to hire purchase which led to the passing of the Hire Purchase Act, 1937. More recently, casework organisations and professional associations have interested themselves in the law relating to adoption and the proposals which are now being considered by the Ingleby Committee for legislation which will make it easier to prevent the break-up of families. For a discussion of this responsibility in the American setting, see Donald S. Howard, 'Social Work and Social Reform', in Cora Kasius (ed.), *New Directions in Social Work*, New York, 1954, pp. 159 ff.

[2] 'In conclusion, the social caseworker's role would appear to be more active and educative than that of the psychotherapist. Her aim is more limited and is

caseworker to-day is much more concerned with attitudes and relationships than her predecessor was a generation or more ago, and is more prepared to use her special 'skills' to influence the client modify them and adjust more easily to his social situation. The emphasis has shifted from social conditions and circumstances, as they affect the client, and how they can be put right, not least by his own efforts, to personal relationships and how they can be adjusted. Nevertheless, economic realities cannot be ignored, and environmental influences, including the traditions and mores of the particular group or culture to which the client belongs, are both influential and important. Thus the social worker must take into account economic and social as well as psychological factors in diagnosing a situation, and incorporate the knowledge gained from economics, sociology and social research into her thinking along with that gained from psychiatry and psychology.[1] As a leading American social worker has reminded us, 'No one can presume to understand a problem of poverty without some knowledge of human behaviour, and no one can treat a problem of human behaviour intelligently without reference to its economic and social framework.'[2]

The second way in which the psychological approach has made itself felt in social work is in relation to moral judgments. In its early annual reports the Charity Organisation Society did not hesitate to record that cases were dismissed as 'undeserving',[3] and although this designation was subsequently abandoned, many, although by no means all,[4] Victorian social workers were somewhat didactic and moralistic in their approach. The social worker to-day is more likely to try to discover and understand the reasons for her client's behaviour than to assess his or her moral responsibility, and will make more allowances for unconscious motivation and the irrationality of human behaviour than was done in the past. Along with this approach goes a strong reluctance to impose one's own standards on those with different traditions and social norms. This attitude is generally associated with a real

---

concerned with changing attitudes rather than with the personality. She sees her client clearly as a member of the community and endeavours to help him function in society again.' A. B. Lloyd-Davies (Senior Psychiatric Social Worker, West Sussex Child Guidance Clinic), in *The Boundaries of Casework*, p. 43.

[1] This point is made by Professor T. S. Simey in the same symposium, pp. 60–69.

[2] Gordon Hamilton, *Theory and Practice of Social Case Work*, New York, 1940, p. 4.

[3] According to the Annual Report for that year, 1,150 applicants were so dismissed in 1871. C. L. Mowat, op. cit., p. 266.

[4] For example, Canon and Mrs. Barnett's reaction against this attitude is described by Mrs. Barnett in her biography of her husband, *Canon Barnett, His Life, Work and Friends*.

respect for human freedom and dignity, but when the client's standards are seriously at variance with those of the community as a whole, the vital distinction between understanding and accepting the client, deviate though he may from accepted norms, and condoning irresponsible and anti-social conduct is not always easy to maintain or explain. The distinction is a real one, however, and its observance is essential if client and community are ultimately to be reconciled.

Changes in attitude, due largely to the acceptance by social workers of the findings of psychology and particularly of psychological medicine to social work practice, have been among the most important of the major twentieth-century developments in social work. A second development has been the adaptation of the principles and methods evolved by the Charity Organisation Society to deal with family problems of all kinds and particularly problems of poverty, to meet the needs of different categories of people in different institutional settings. An example of this is the origin and development of medical social work or almoning, by means of which specially trained social workers co-operate with doctors and other members of the hospital team in helping patients and their families to overcome the social and personal difficulties and stresses which so frequently accompany and follow illness.

The work started in a very modest way in 1895 when Miss Mary Stewart, a social worker trained by the Charity Organisation Society, was established in a 'dingy, dark, unventilated corner' of the out-patient department of the Royal Free Hospital. Her principal duty, as laid down by the Hospital Board, was 'to prevent the abuse of the hospital by persons able to pay for medical treatment', but she herself was imbued by more positive aims and sought to create a constructive social service based on the application of casework principles to the special needs and problems of hospital patients. Thus, from the first, there was some discrepancy between the functions of the almoner as envisaged by hospital boards and committees and those same functions as envisaged by the almoners themselves, a difficulty which was not wholly solved until the National Health Service Act made hospital treatment free to the user. Nevertheless, almoning was gradually established as a recognised branch of social work, and trained almoners were appointed in increasing numbers not only in hospitals, both voluntary and municipal, but, during the inter-war years, by public health authorities, especially for work in clinics for tuberculosis and venereal disease.'[1]

---

[1] A general description of the work of an almoner is given by Jean Snelling in Cherry Morris (ed.), *Social Case Work in Great Britain*, and in two short books by I. F. Beck, *The Almoner* and *Ten Patients and an Almoner*.

SOCIAL WORK IN THE SOCIAL SERVICES

Medical-social work is an important, but not the only example of the successful adaptation of casework principles and methods to meet the needs of a particular category of people and of the ability of the social worker to adapt herself to the traditions and disciplines of a well-established institution, in this case of the hospital. Another example is the probation service, in which casework methods are used in the treatment of delinquency. The means used by the probation officer in carrying out his statutory duty to 'advise, assist and befriend' offenders placed under his supervision by the court, are fundamentally those of all caseworkers, but the relationship between officer and probationer has to be made within the terms of the probation order. This means that the relationship is not entirely voluntary, since, although a person over the age of fourteen has to consent to the making of an order, the alternatives are usually unpleasant, while cases which the probation officer himself believes unsuitable may be placed on probation by the court. Moreover, should the offender fail to be of good behaviour and comply with the conditions of the order, he can be brought back and punished for his offence, a fact known to both parties. There is, thus, in the background an element of direction and compulsion. Despite this, the officer, as a good caseworker, must endeavour to base the relationship on 'trust, encouragement and persuasion',[1] and usually succeeds in doing so, adapting his methods to suit the age, personality, and social and family background of the client.[2]

Almoning and probation were two relatively early experiments in specialised casework, and were later to be followed by others, notably psychiatric social work and child care. These developments not only opened up new fields of work but created a new group of professions, thus emphasising what had already become apparent, that social work was an activity which demanded both knowledge and skill, and that if they were to carry out their work efficiently and effectively social workers must be adequately trained. Hence the third important twentieth-century development in social work has been the development of professional training. The beginnings of formal social work education in this country can be traced back to the closing years of the nineteenth century when the Women's University Settlement, Southwark, the National Union of Women Workers and the Charity Organisation Society set up a Joint Lectures Committee. This was followed by the establishment of a School of Sociology, 'a definite attempt

---

[1] Max Grunhut, *Penal Reform, a Comparative Study*, p. 309.
[2] For further discussion of the work of a probation officer see the chapter by W. G. Minn in Cherry Morris (ed.), op. cit., Elizabeth Glover, *Probation and Re-Education*, and Joan King (ed.), *The Probation Service*.

to induce people *to think* and not to shrink from applying theory to practical work'.[1] Meanwhile, in Liverpool, the joint efforts of Miss Elizabeth MacAdam, the Warden of the Victoria Settlement, and Professor (later Sir Edward) Gonner, Professor of Economics at the University, resulted in both the creation of the first provincial school of social science and the first attempt to bring the training of social workers within the orbit of a university.[2] In 1912 a similar link was forged in London when the hitherto independent School of Sociology was taken over by the London School of Economics and transformed into the present Department of Social Science and Administration. Since then universities have accepted increasing responsibilities not only for the provision of background social science or social studies courses, but also for professional training.[3] This grafting of social work education and training on to the universities with their academic traditions and standards has created its own problems.[4] but it gives the student the stimulus of contacts with university life and thought, encourages him to relate the findings and techniques of social research to social work problems and practice, and makes it easier to emphasise the common elements in professional training.

The fourth major development affecting the scope and practice of social work which has taken place during the last fifty years has been its incorporation into the principal statutory social services, a development which has taken place gradually and late. 'One of the great tragedies of our history,' said Roger Wilson, addressing the British National Conference on Social Work in April 1950,[5] 'is that two such original thinkers as Octavia Hill and Beatrice Webb, representing two converging approaches, should have come together on that great formative influence, the Royal Commission on the Poor Law of 1905–9, and, as far as I can see, should have failed to learn anything from each other.' The failure to incorporate the developing skills and understanding of social work into

---

[1] Quoted by Marjorie J. Smith, *Professional Education for Social Work in Great Britain, an Historical Account.* Author's italics.

[2] The start and subsequent progress of the Liverpool School are described by its present professor, T. S. Simey, 'Fifty Years of Social Work Teaching', *Case Conference*, Vol. I, No. 8, pp. 5–9.

[3] Examples of professional training courses are the courses in Applied Social Studies at L.S.E. and Birmingham, the Diploma in Social Work at Southampton, the Diploma in Social Administration, Liverpool. More specialised courses are Mental Health courses at L.S.E., Manchester, and Edinburgh and the course in Medical Social Work at Edinburgh.

[4] See Marjorie J. Smith, op. cit., p. 31, for an appraisal of this situation by the Director of an American School of Social Work. In the U.S.A. social work training is given in graduate schools.

[5] The address was published as *Social Work in the Changing World.* The words quoted are on p. 4.

the statutory services, which were being created and expanded during the years before and immediately after the First World War, was a real loss both to the services and to the profession, but it was understandable. The emphasis in these growing and developing services, as seen for example in the establishment of labour exchanges and juvenile employment bureaux, the introduction of health and unemployment insurance, and the medical inspection and treatment of schoolchildren, was on helping normal people cope with the normal contingencies of life, and so avoid serious family or social breakdown, and 'social work was peripheral, not central to this scheme of prevention'.[1] Except in specialised fields, such as the treatment of delinquency, it was not until much later, during the Second World War, when she was brought in to deal with family problems attendant on evacuation and the disruption caused by bombing,[2] that the social worker really came into her own as a participant in statutory planning and administration.

Not only were the pre-war social services created largely to help normal people to meet recognised needs, they were governed to a considerable extent by the policy of the break-up of the Poor Law. In effect, this meant substituting for the general destitution authority with its all-purpose 'social worker', the relieving officer, a number of administratively separate departments, and 'the arrangement of social work tasks has tended to follow the administrative arrangement of the social services'.[3] Hence to-day each central government or local authority department has its own officials and workers, the disablement resettlement officer employed by the Ministry of Labour, the National Assistance Board inquiry officer, the local education authority school attendance and welfare officer, for example, and each of these workers undertakes, as a greater or less part of his day-to-day duties, some social work responsibilities, responsibilities for which he may have had little or no specific training.[4] This approach has serious limitations, but specialisation of function is not all loss, as it means that it is possible for the worker to learn and pass on to others the special techniques and attitudes most appropriate for the different categories of persons with whom he deals. By itself this is not enough, however, as the worker's skill is limited and only related to the work of his own department.

[1] Barbara N. Rodgers, 'The Administrative Setting of Social Service: Some Practical Implications', *Case Conference*, Vol. I, No. 3, July 1954, p. 9.

[2] R. M. Titmuss, *Problems of Social Policy*, pp. 289–291 and 384–385.

[3] R. M. Titmuss, 'The Administrative Setting of Social Service: Some Historical Reflections', *Case Conference*, Vol. I, No. 1, May 1954, p. 7.

[4] See Barbara N. Rodgers and Julia Dixon, *Portrait of Social Work*—a study of social services in a northern town.

As each of these services has developed, it has tended not only to recruit its own staff, fitting them into its own administrative hierarchy, but also to provide its own in-training, but the situation is now changing. One or two departments, notably the local authority children's departments which were created after the Second World War, and in which the work is particularly exacting and difficult, rely as far as possible on trained social workers, and it is noticeable that when the hospitals were transferred to his authority in 1948, the Minister of Health issued a circular[1] pointing out that, with the passing of the National Health Service Act, the almoner was freed from assessment duties and could now 'engage fully on the important medical social work for which she had been specially trained'. There were also indications that other departments, for example local authority health and welfare departments, have begun to appreciate the need for, and the special contribution to be made by, trained social workers in dealing with particular problems, especially those of seriously handicapped persons and their families, and of families who present special difficulties. This is an important advance, but is unfortunately meeting an obstacle which is proving very difficult to overcome, the shortage of trained social workers. The number of men and women undertaking professional social work training at the present time is inadequate even to meet the needs of the services where they have already established themselves, so that, for example, hospital vacancies for almoners remain unfilled, and the demand for psychiatric social workers, both for adult work in connection with the hospitals and for child guidance clinic work, far exceeds the supply.[2]

This situation, one in which it is becoming increasingly recognised that the effectiveness and humanity of the administration of the social services depends to a considerable degree on the skill and understanding of those who staff them, while at the same time there is a stultifying shortage of social workers, forms the background to the recommendations of the Report of the Ministry of Health Working Party on Social Workers in the Local Authority Health and Welfare Services, published in 1959. Although restricted by their terms of reference to the consideration of staffing problems in health and welfare departments, the Working Party, under its chairman, Dr. Eileen Younghusband, have in fact made recommendations which, if implemented, are bound to affect the

[1] Ministry of Health Circular, H.M.C. 48 (53) B.G. 48 (57).
[2] These problems are discussed by the Report of the Committee on Medical Auxiliaries (Cmd. 8188) which discusses the supply of almoners, the Report of the Committee on Social Workers in the Mental Health Services (Cmd. 8260) and the Report of the Committee on Maladjusted Children.

whole pattern of social work and training. They start with the assumption that the people whose needs the social services are to meet may be divided into three categories, namely those 'with straightforward and obvious needs who require material help, some simple service or a periodic visit', those with more complex problems who require systematic help from trained social workers and those 'with problems of special difficulty requiring skilled help by professionally trained and experienced social workers', and propose to meet these gradations of need by three types of social worker trained in different ways. These are the 'welfare assistants' who will be expected to undergo 'a short but systematically planned in-service training', the social worker with a general training in social work equivalent to two years' full-time training, and the workers with a full professional training which includes a university degree, diploma or certificate together with a recognised social work qualification. These would act as consultants and advisers to other workers and undertake casework in connection with personal or family problems of special difficulty. University basic and professional courses are already in existence and expanding, especially at the professional level, but hitherto no satisfactory general training has been available for the many less-academic people who, given this, would make valuable 'middle grade' social workers. This, the Younghusband Commitee propose to remedy by means of a new general training outside the universities lasting two years full-time or two to three years part-time and one year full-time and leading to a national qualification (National Certificate in Social Work) of sufficient standing to be recognised by the Local Government Examinations Board and the National Joint Councils as qualifying for appointment, promotion and salary grading on the administrative, professional and technical salary scales. Systematic in-training is recommended for 'welfare assistants'. In order that these and other related proposals can be fully implemented on a national scale the Working Party recommends the setting up of a National Council for Social Work Training and the establishment of a national staff college.

The publication of the Younghusband Report let loose a flood of appreciation, discussion and criticism, and in February 1960 the Earl of Lewisham opened a House of Lords debate on the subject. At the conclusion of a lively discussion Lord St. Oswald, speaking on behalf of the Government, warmly welcomed the report and explained that its recommendations were being considered in the light of the views of government departments, local authorities and the main voluntary bodies.[1] There the matter rests at the time of writing.

[1] House of Lords Official Report, Vol. 221, No. 39, Wednesday, 17th Feburary, 1960.

The growth of statutory organisations and the incorporation of social work in them, important and extensive as this has been, have not done away with the need for voluntary organisations which specialise in such work, however. Some of these, such as the Family Service Units, whose work is described in a subsequent chapter, specialise in work with problem families, others, such as the family casework agencies which are concerned with all families in difficulty and which are found in large units of population in many parts of the country, undertake work of a more general character.

The work of a family casework agency is so varied and the problems brought to it so diverse, that it is difficult to summarise them in a few sentences.[1] To the agency come people in need of material help such as clothing, furniture or bedding; people involved in legal difficulties such as those which arise between landlord and tenant; people with family problems ranging from adoption to matrimonial difficulties; people in doubt about their position with regard to some form of social insurance or assistance, or who are aggrieved because they think they have not obtained their rights, and many others—lonely, stranded, puzzled, unhappy and despairing. Moreover, as the case worker listens to the lengthy and often incoherent stories told to her by her clients, she often finds that the problem brought to her for solution is not the real difficulty. Involved in it may be a number of others, perhaps more fundamental and frequently involving other members of the family, and it may take weeks and months, or even years of skilled and patient work before they can be overcome and the family set on its feet again.

Two main features characterise the work of family casework agencies. First, as the designation implies, they are concerned not only with individuals but with families. The client is regarded not simply as an individual, but as a member of the family group, and in considering the help or advice to be given, the caseworker must keep in mind the effect it might have on family relationships and wellbeing, since it is her aim to preserve the integrity of the family unit as far as possible.

The second distinguishing feature of family casework is the close liaison maintained with the statutory and voluntary bodies concerned with every type of social service. Families coming to the agency for assistance may be found to be in need of help which only a specialist body can give, and if so are referred to the appro-

---

[1] For a clear description which includes useful illustrative material, see ch. iii, in Cherry Morris, op. cit. It is written by Miss D. M. Deed, then Training Secretary, Liverpool Personal Service Society, now Lecturer in the Department of Social Science, Liverpool University.

priate organisation, while, on the other hand, a specialist agency confronted with a problem outside its scope will refer the case to the family agency. Many cases demand the joint efforts of a number of agencies for a solution of their problems, however, and in these circumstances the family caseworker has a special responsibility for keeping in mind the situation as a whole, and for endeavouring to co-ordinate the efforts of the various specialists, so that overlapping and conflicting policies can be avoided as far as possible.[1]

The range of work undertaken by a family casework agency is very wide, and in addition to the intensive personal work with individuals and families which is their central function, some agencies provide citizens' advice bureaux, poor man's lawyer and other kindred services. The majority act as almoners for national benevolent funds, while those recognised for the purpose give practical social work training to students from university social studies departments, the Home Office, and the Institute of Almoners. A good family casework agency thus makes a valuable contribution to the life of the community which it serves. Unfortunately, many such agencies are handicapped by financial difficulties and staff shortages, and are unable to develop their work as intensively or extensively as they would like. The nature of the problems brought to them is changing, but their numbers show no signs of diminishing, and since they are often problems of adjustment and relationship, or relate to problem families who cannot, unaided, take advantage of specialist services, they frequently demand long-term and very skilled work. If family casework agencies are to keep an ever-open door to those in need of advice or assistance, means of overcoming their financial and administrative difficulties must be found.

The difficulty which family casework agencies are finding in recruiting suitable staff is but one aspect of the problem of the recruitment of men and women of the right intellectual and personal calibre to the profession of social work, a problem to which reference has already been made. It is one which is far-reaching in its implications. More than any other profession, except perhaps teaching, social work depends for its success on the quality of its workers, and it can only continue and develop if a sufficient number of men and women will come forward to act as agents of the community in its concern for individuals and families who cannot adjust themselves to the complexities of living without individual support and help.

[1] Liverpool Personal Service Society Inc., Annual Report, 1946–47, p. 4. The question of co-operation between different agencies undertaking casework is discussed below, Chapter XXI.

CHAPTER IX

ADVICE FOR THE CITIZEN

THE principal function of the family casework agency is that of helping people to overcome their serious personal and social problems, but such agencies are also frequently confronted with requests for miscellaneous information and advice of all kinds. Nor are they alone in this; trade union organisers, political party agents, clergymen, teachers and doctors are all consulted by puzzled and ignorant people, uncertain as to their rights or liabilities, or at a loss when faced with the intricacies of an official form. Much general advice is still being sought and given in this way, but many areas now have citizens' advice bureaux which have been set up for the specific purpose of answering the citizen's questions and dealing with his difficulties, and where established, such bureaux have proved to be of great value.[1]

Citizens' advice bureaux were started to deal with difficulties likely to arise as the result of the impact of war on civilian life. When it became clear that the Second World War was imminent, experienced social workers and administrators realised that the dislocation of personal and family life likely to ensue and the inevitable increase in the amount and complexity of government control would necessitate a more systematic advice and information service than existed at the time, particularly in the target areas. Plans were prepared, and on the initiative of the National Council of Social Service, acting in co-operation with local individuals and organisations, citizens' advice bureaux providing 'a free service of advice to every citizen' were started in centres of population throughout the country. Where a case work agency or council of social service existed in the locality the new service might be established under its auspices, but bureaux were needed in many places where no such organisation existed, and in these areas the officials of the National Council of Social Service encouraged the formation of *ad hoc* committees to be responsible for their establishment and maintenance. These committees were made as representative as possible of the varying interests, statutory

---

[1] For much of the information about citizens' advice bureaux contained in this chapter I am indebted to Miss K. M. Oswald, Secretary, The National Citizens' Advice Bureaux Committee.

and voluntary, religious, political and general in the area, for it is a cardinal principle of the citizens' advice bureaux service that 'a citizens' advice bureau should be organised by the community for the community', and should recognise no differences of class, race or creed.

Local committees and bureaux are autonomous, but the National Council of Social Service advises and assists them through the secretariat of the National Citizens' Advice Bureaux Committee. With the help of advisory officers in the north and midlands, its staff are able to advise bureaux secretaries on administrative questions such as finance, publicity, and the best ways of maintaining co-operation with other statutory and voluntary services. They also seek to ensure that the organisation of newly opened bureaux is on a sound footing. Among its other activities, citizens' advice bureaux headquarters maintains a regular and comprehensive information service, and a special department of the National Council of Social Service issues and keeps up to date that mine of information on current legislation, 'Citizens' Advice Notes'. Close touch is maintained with government departments, especially on such matters as the best means of informing the man in the street of the effect of new legislation on his rights and duties.

The citizens' advice bureaux movement was in origin a voluntary one, and while close co-operation has been established with central and local government departments at all levels, it has remained as such, except in certain areas, where the bureau functions within the local authority information centre. Voluntary status is an advantage in many ways. Citizens' advice bureaux set out to give not simply information but advice, and it is considered essential that not only should this advice be disinterested, and as far as humanly possible free from bias of any kind, but that it should be known to be so. This would not be easy if the bureaux were maintained as part of the machinery of government, whether central or local, especially as many inquirers come to the bureaux because they are dissatisfied with the treatment they have received at the hands of a government or local authority department. In these cases the independent status of the bureau is particularly important, since it enables the adviser to see both sides of the question, and balance the demands of the individual, who is inclined to stress his own particular needs to the exclusion of all other considerations, and the decision of the authority, which is based on general considerations of community welfare. The independent status of the bureaux also enables advice to be given about personal problems and in cases 'in which it would be improper for a local authority to advise, since if it did so it would be intervening in issues which lie between the private citizens, and helping one as against the other'.[1]

The voluntary character of bureaux, valuable as it is considered to be, has its disadvantages. In particular it has meant that the work of some bureaux has been hampered by financial and associated difficulties, such as that of obtaining adequate and suitable premises or sufficient equipment, and this has necessitated statutory assistance.

In the early days of the war, official recognition was given to the bureaux service by a dual-purpose grant from the Ministry of Health. This was intended both to help in the establishment of individual bureaux (to whose funds local authorities might also contribute under civil defence powers), and as a contribution towards the cost of central and regional services provided by the National Council of Social Service. Grant-aid for the former purpose was discontinued in 1945 when the Ministry of Health (in Circular 197/45) gave local authorities powers to provide an information service, either directly or through a voluntary agency such as a C.A.B. These powers were subsequently confirmed in the Local Government Act, 1948 (Section 134), and the majority of bureaux are now grant-aided by their local authorities, the grants varying from relatively large amounts, possibly in the region of £2,000 a year in some large towns, to £25–£30 a year in small ones where the bureau staff may be wholly voluntary. Help may also be given in kind, for example, in premises, equipment and personnel. The grant for central services was continued year by year, and together with an allocation from the voluntary funds of the National Council of Social Service, provided a national headquarters organisation, an information service and the salaries of the C.A.B. field officers. In 1948 the grant was substantially increased in view of the increased cost of the service. It was therefore a very serious blow to the National Council to receive, at the end of the first month of the financial year 1950, an intimation of the reduction of that year's grant by 50 per cent and of its discontinuance thereafter. This left the central organisation with considerable financial difficulties. but despite this hindrance the service has continued to develop.

The number and character of the inquiries brought to bureaux have varied and still vary according to place, time and circumstance. Since the service was established to meet the emergencies of war, it was natural that during the war years difficulties arising from war-time conditions should predominate. It quickly became clear, however, that even then many other matters were troubling

[1] N.A.L.G.O. Report on Relations between Local Government and the Community. Quoted in *Advising the Citizen*, p. 36.

citizens sufficiently to bring them to the bureaux. Citizens' advice bureaux workers found themselves confronted with requests for information and advice about hire purchase, old age pensions, social insurance and family problems as well as with queries about evacuation, bomb damage, service pay and allowances, communications with persons in enemy countries and food and clothes rationing. As with other war-time services[1] it soon became evident that a service created primarily to meet an emergency was also meeting a permanent need, and although the number of bureaux decreased after the cessation of hostilities, many of those which were discontinued were small bureaux which had not sufficiently established themselves in the community they set out to serve. The number and variety of inquiries now received annually by bureaux throughout the country, and the confidence placed in them by government departments, are strong indications of the efficiency and usefulness of the service.[2]

In addition to their regular work, citizens' advice bureaux have found opportunities, from time to time, of advising bewildered and unhappy individuals in connection with the personal problems which arise at times of unforeseen emergency or disaster. For example, in 1952, they were called in to help at the time of the floods at Lynmouth, and the experience gained there was put to further use during the more devastating East Coast floods of the following year. In 1956 temporary citizens' advice bureaux were established at the headquarters of the British Council for Aid to Refugees and at the larger reception centres for Hungarian refugees, while experienced workers were appointed to provide C.A.B. services at each of the hostels for British subjects expelled from Egypt as a result of the Suez crisis of 1956.

The confidence of the public in the quality of the counsel given at citizens' advice bureaux on general questions as well as in emergencies, is shown not only by the substantial number of inquiries which are brought to them, but also by the increasing readiness of men and women to ask for advice on serious personal difficulties. It is the general opinion of bureaux workers that the proportion of inquiries in which advice rather than information is sought, and which may involve real casework before they can be solved, is growing.[3] The line between giving advice and under-

---

[1] As, for example, the hostels for evacuated old people described in Chapter XVIII below, and the Family Service Units' work with problem families outlined in the chapter which follows.

[2] Examples of this may be found in the Annual Reports of the National Council of Social Service.

[3] Examples of the various types of enquiries brought to Citizens' Advice Bureaux and the action taken to deal with them are given in Lord Beveridge, *Voluntary Action*, Appendix C, pp. 381–97.

taking casework is, as a matter of fact, sometimes difficult to draw, for 'an apparently simple query when followed up may reveal a complicated family tangle needing wise counsel and positive action'.[1] This raises serious difficulties especially in those towns and country areas where there is no family casework agency to fall back on.

The increased complexity of the inquiries brought to bureaux has resulted in increased emphasis on the importance of recruiting to C.A.B. work men and women of good intelligence and understanding, and of giving them adequate training. The majority of workers are volunteers. In January 1958 the 430 citizens' advice bureaux in the country were staffed by no less than 2,000 voluntary workers of widely differing background and experience. They included older married women, many of whom had been teachers, nurses or social workers before marriage, and retired officers, civil servants and business men. Such experienced men and women are the first to recognise their need for training and refresher courses through which they can keep themselves informed of current social policy and legislation, and which will assist them discover the specific role which bureaux play in relation to other social services. Hence they are quick to take advantage of the short courses organised by the headquarters staff in different parts of the country. In order to maintain the high standard of service which government departments and the general public have come to expect, a scheme for the registration of approved bureaux has been in operation for many years, and new workers are required to undertake a course of training which will help them not only to deal with such difficulties as are within their compass, but also to recognise when it is necessary to ask for the help of a specialist, be he a social worker or a professional worker in another field.

Citizens' advice bureaux maintain close contacts with the social workers in both the statutory and voluntary services in their areas, and in addition are usually able to make arrangements for panels of specialists to be available to give advice in cases where this is needed, and the inquirer is not able to pay the full fees. For example, an old age pensioner, formerly self-employed, in need of help from an accountant in filling in his income tax returns and from a surveyor in estimating the repairs that will be needed to get rid of extensive dry rot in his house would be the kind of person to be assisted in this way. The difficulties encountered by persons of limited means who embark on complicated financial transactions have become so apparent to bureaux workers in recent years that the National Citizens' Advice Bureaux Committee has compiled two booklets designed for the general public, *Buying a*

[1] Liverpool Personal Service Society Annual Report, 1946–7.

House, Do's and Don'ts (N.C.S.S., 1956) and *Hire Purchases and Credit Buying* (N.C.S.S., 1957). These booklets give information which will enable people to avoid getting into those difficulties with which the C.A.B. worker is all too familiar, for instance, those caused by an intending purchaser of a house signing a legally binding document without having first obtained the necessary professional advice on the condition of the property and the terms of the contract. The National Citizens' Advice Bureaux Committee recognises that one of its functions is to examine the causes of, and inform the public about problems which frequently come to the notice of bureaux workers, since all too often they can give help which is only of limited value to the individuals troubled by such problems as their advice has been sought too late.[1]

Among the problems with which citizens' advice bureaux are confronted are those in which legal advice, and possibly even court proceedings, are required if the client is to obtain his rights. If he can afford to consult a solicitor privately the client will be encouraged to do so, but in a large number of cases this is out of the question, and unless free or assisted service is available, the case goes by default. Recognition of the need for a nation-wide legal aid and advice service to meet this need and to replace the rather limited existing voluntary services led to the passing of the Legal Aid and Advice Act, 1949, the object of which was 'to provide assistance in a more effective form in the conduct of civil proceedings, and legal advice for those of slender means, so that no one will be financially unable to prosecute a just and reasonable claim or defend a legal right'.[2] To attain this objective the provision of both legal aid, that is, 'assistance in conducting or defending proceedings in the courts whether by remission of court fees, free legal representation, provision for the payment of witnesses' expenses and otherwise', and legal advice, that is, 'advice in legal matters, the drafting of documents and negotiations apart from litigation',[3] were considered necessary, and the Act includes both.

---

[1] An example of the increased use of C.A.Bx. by all sections of the community is the number of inquiries which have come to them as a result of the Rent Act, 1957. Between July 6th, when the Act became law and August 31st, the forty-two bureaux in the London area dealt with about 25,000 inquiries and provincial bureaux were also inundated with inquiries from both landlords and tenants. Bureaux workers were prepared for this extra work by short training courses which were arranged in conjunction with the Ministry of Housing and Local Government and held throughout the country. 'The personal situations which arise among landlords as well as tenants are so varied that no central information can be a substitute for the local knowledge and skill of Bureau workers'. (National Council of Social Service, Annual Report, 1957, p. 13.)

[2] Legal Aid and Advice Bill, 1948. Summary of the Proposed New Service, Cmd. 7563, H.M.S.O., 1948, p. 3.

[3] Report of the Committee on Legal Aid and Advice in England and Wales, Cmd. 6641, 1945, par. 2.

However, at first only those parts of the Act which provide for legal aid in the High Court or Court of Appeal and proceedings remitted from the High Court to the county courts were implemented. County court cases were included after January 1956,[1] while by the County Courts Act, 1955, county courts had been given jurisdiction to hear and determine any action founded on contract or tort,[2] where the debt, demand or damage did not exceed £400.[3] These changes mean that most litigation involving disputes between landlord and tenant and actions arising out of hire purchase legislation comes within the scope of the legal aid scheme.

The legal aid scheme brought into being as a result of the Act is administered by the professional organisation of the legal profession, that is the Law Society, under the general guidance of the Lord Chancellor. There are obvious objections to a state legal aid service, especially in view of the extent of statutory intervention in all departments of life, and the set-up provided by the Act seems the one best designed to further the interests of justice.

For the purpose of the Act the Law Society established 12 area and 112 local committees, and it is through these area and local committees that the scheme is operated. Applications for legal aid are made to the secretary of the local committee, which has then to decide, subject to the right of appeal to the area committee, if the applicant has reasonable grounds for taking proceedings, and the terms on which a 'civil aid certificate' entitling him to legal aid will be granted.

Since the legal aid is only intended for those whose means are insufficient to enable them to engage solicitors and counsel and pay the necessary court costs themselves, and since even those who are assisted by the scheme are expected to contribute according to their means, applicants for legal aid must submit to an assessment of their resources by the National Assistance Board, which will decide on the amount of the contribution, if any, they should be asked to make. The benefits of the service are available to persons whose 'disposable income', that is income after allowances have been made for rent and rates, income tax, maintenance of dependants and other necessary outgoings which the Board considers reasonable, is limited. In 1960 this limit was raised to £700 a year. Only persons with a disposable income of less than £250 per annum and a disposable capital (that is capital including allowances for such items as the house in which the person resides and his furniture) of less than £125 receive legal aid entirely free.

---

[1] Legal Aid and Advice Act, 1949, commencement, No. 5. Order 1955.
[2] A civil wrong independent of contract.
[3] Under the County Courts Act, 1934, the limit was £200.

148

Other litigants are asked to contribute up to one-third of their disposable income over £250 per annum. Hence litigation, even with legal aid, may still be quite costly in relation to the means of the applicant, and while this may be considered to be desirable in order to discourage vexatious and frivolous suits, the rather rigid limits imposed may mean that prosecuting a just and reasonable claim or defending a legal right will still involve considerable financial sacrifice for people of moderate means.

While a statutory legal aid scheme covering civil cases was brought into being immediately after the passage of the Legal Aid and Advice Act, the provisions of the Act relating to legal advice did not come into operation until March 1959. Provisions are made for both statutory scheme and a voluntary scheme. Under the former the a advice to be given is limited to oral advice from a practising solicitor on the Legal Advice Panel and the fee for each interview has been fixed at 2s. 6d. Applicants in receipt of National Assistance are not normally expected to pay this fee. All applicants must satisfy the solicitor to whom they make their application that they cannot afford to obtain advice in the ordinary way, and an applicant is not eligible to receive advice if his income for the previous week exceeds £4 10s. after making deductions for the maintenance of dependants, income tax, and national insurance contributions. In addition to the statutory scheme there is a voluntary one whereby applicants may obtain oral advice from a solicitor on the Legal Advice Panel or his representative for a fee of £1 for each thirty-minute interview on any one legal question. If this time is inadequate to dispose of the difficulty the applicant will be advised of the approximate cost of any further advice which may be necessary.

While a statutory service providing legal advice at small cost is an innovation, the need for such facilities for people of small or even moderate means has long been evident. For many years a free service operated by public-spirited solicitors and known as the Poor Man's Lawyer service was active in London and some of the larger provincial towns. A wide range of inquiries including disputes between landlord and tenant, accident compensation, matrimonial problems, hire purchase difficulties, neighbours' quarrels and the like were brought to the service. It may be expected that the new service will have to deal with equally diverse problems, and it may be hoped that through it many citizens will be helped to arrive at a satisfactory settlement of their claims without recourse to court action.

Serious matrimonial difficulties are prominent among the personal problems brought to casework agencies, citizens' advice bureaux and legal aid and advice sessions, and in recent years a considerable amount of attention has been given to the possibility of co-ordinating and extending marriage guidance work. Thus the terms of reference of the Committee on Procedure in Matrimonial Causes, appointed in 1946, included consideration as to 'whether any (and if so what) machinery should be available for the purpose of attempting a reconciliation between the parties, either before or after proceedings have been commenced',[1] while the more recent Royal Commission on Marriage and Divorce, although not specifically instructed to do so, was led to consider 'the means by which harmony and union once threatened could be maintained and restored'.[2] Part IV of this report deals with 'Marriage Guidance and Reconciliation'.

As the Morton Commission recognised,[3] much patient and unspectacular help has been, and is being, given to people with matrimonial difficulties by clergymen, doctors, solicitors, family caseworkers and other social workers in the course of their day-to-day work. The work of probation officers is particularly important in this connection as one of their statutory duties is that of interviewing, with a view to their reconciliation, couples who apply to the magistrates' court for separation orders, and even at this late stage reconciliations can be effected. The officers will also advise and assist husbands and wives who approach them for such help, even where an immediate separation is not in question, and a 'very large part'[4] of their conciliation work consists of giving such unofficial help. There are, however, many people who hesitate to approach officials associated in the public mind with the supervision of delinquents and the rather sordid atmosphere of the matrimonial courts, yet who need skilled advice. Hence the need for specialist marriage guidance services not in any way connected with the courts.

One of the best-known organisations established to meet this need is the National Marriage Guidance Council. Its work is based on certain ethical principles, the most important of which are that successful marriage, the foundation of happy family life, is vital to the well-being of society; that marriage should be entered upon as a partnership for life, 'with reverence and a sense of responsibility'; and that the right basis for personal and social life is that sexual intercourse should take place only within marriage. Children should be regarded as the natural fulfilment of marriage, but 'scientific contraception, when used according to conscience within

---

[1] The final report was published in February 1947. Cmd. 7024. The Committee met under the chairmanship of Mr. (now Lord) Justice Denning.

[2] Cmd. 9678, 1956, par. 327, p. 93. The chairman of this Commission was Baron Morton of Henryton.

[3] Par. 333, p. 94.

[4] Ibid., par. 334.

marriage, can contribute to the health and happiness of the whole family'.[1] The Council is undenominational in both work and membership, but the Roman Catholic Church has its own Catholic Marriage Advisory Council, based on its own beliefs and teaching. The work of the National Marriage Guidance Council is both educational and remedial. The Council itself attaches great importance to its educational work, work which aims at making available to young men and women 'such guidance as may promote right relationships in friendship, courtship, marriage and parenthood', and, more specifically, at assisting those about to marry to understand 'the nature, responsibilities and rewards of the married state'. The better known remedial work with couples in difficulty is carried on mainly by the local councils which have been established in many parts of the country and which are associated with the National Council. Much of the work is carried on by 'counsellors', carefully selected men and women, working on a part-time voluntary basis, but these lay people have the support of professional tutors and consultants. The counsellors hold the initial interviews with clients, and may carry the case through, should no problem needing specialist advice present itself. Their method of approach is to listen to the clients' stories in a friendly, unhurried atmosphere, free from blame or criticism, and so help them to face up to their feelings and attitudes, appreciate their partners' needs as well as their own and work their way through to decisions acceptable to themselves. Sometimes practical suggestions are made to meet the immediate situation, but, apart from this, the Council deprecates the giving of specific advice by counsellors, especially in the early stages of the relationship, for it recognises that 'the greatest mistakes are made through trying to solve the difficulty before really understanding the person'.[2] Should it become apparent, during the course of the discussions between client and counsellor, that there are difficulties present which are beyond the latter's competence as a layman, he will refer the case to the appropriate consultant, medical, psychiatric, legal or spiritual. The decision as to when and to whom the case should be referred is not always an easy one, and indeed the whole

[1] General Principles and Aims of the National Marriage Guidance Council as re-worded in 1952.
[2] John H. Wallis, *Marriage Counselling*, p. 25. The above description of the counsellor's approach is based on this booklet which has been issued by the National Marriage Guidance Council as 'Counsellors' Training Booklet, No. 2'. Cf. an article in *The Times*, 7 December 1956, where it is stated, 'The help the counsellors offer is not what is commonly supposed. It is not in the main "giving advice", still less imposing a solution or apportioning blame. Essentially it is an attempt to befriend husband and wife and patiently to help them work their own way through to their own acceptable decisions.'

151

set-up places heavy and exacting responsibilities on the shoulders of the men and women who volunteer for this service. Hence the Council has evolved an elaborate and searching selection procedure for its counsellors[1], and those selected undergo rigorous training. 'There is no other form of voluntary work where such demands are made.'[2]

A marriage welfare service organised on very different lines is the Family Discussion Bureau. This was established in London in 1948, as the result of a request made to the Tavistock Clinic by the London Family Welfare Association. The Family Welfare Association had become concerned about the difficulty its caseworkers were experiencing in dealing with the many serious matrimonial and family problems which were brought to them during the years immediately following the war. New skills and techniques appeared to be needed if these problems were to be dealt with effectively, skills based on a deeper understanding of the part played by irrational attitudes and unconscious motives in bringing about matrimonial disharmony than that possessed by the majority of family caseworkers. It was help in achieving this deeper understanding and fashioning these therapeutic skills that the F.W.A. sought from the analytically trained psychiatrists working at the Tavistock Clinic, and as a result of negotiations between the two organisations, an organisation named 'Family Discussion Bureaux' was established. Its objectives included providing a service for people seeking help with marriage problems, devising techniques appropriate to such a service, evolving a method of training caseworkers, and finding out something about the problems of inter-personal relationships as they reveal themselves in marital difficulties.[3]

At the beginning it was hoped that the Bureau workers would undertake a good deal of preventive work, mainly through the medium of group discussion, and that this would throw some light on the beginnings of marriage breakdown. Some interesting experiments along these lines have been carried out, but they have been more limited in scope than was originally intended. The reasons why this side of the work has not developed on the scale envisaged are, the workers consider, first, that when, as here, resources are limited, the caseworker is under great pressure both

---

[1] In 1957–8, 105 of the 188 candidates who attended the thirteen residential selection conferences organised by the Council were accepted.

[2] John H. Wallis, op. cit., p. 1. See also *Marriage Counselling* by J. H. Wallis and H. S. Booker.

[3] Foreword by B. E. Astbury (formerly General Secretary, F.W.A.) to *Social Casework in Marital Problems*, a report of the work of the Family Discussion Bureau.

from society and from her own feelings, to use them for the relief of existing pain and misery; second, because financial support is more easily obtained for remedial work; and, third, because since 'prevention usually involves changes in institutional or individual outlook and behaviour, it commonly arouses a degree of resistance which in the case of therapy is often overcome by the need to be relieved from active pain and distress'.[1] Bureau workers (including both caseworkers and consultant psychiatrists who work together as a team) have, therefore, concentrated on the task of evolving the special casework skills they felt were required for therapeutic work and applying them to meet the needs of the married couples experiencing serious difficulties referred to them by other case-work organisations and citizens' advice bureaux. While emphasising that the work is experimental and any conclusions which may be drawn at this stage of the experiment can only be tentative, the sponsors of the experiment claim that the experience of the Family Discussion Bureaux indicates that 'a closely integrated team of social workers in continuous association with psycho-analytic consultants has provided a setting in which caseworkers can, without the experience of an individual analysis, gain and use an understanding of unconscious forces, including the dynamics of the client-worker relationship, as the basis for therapeutic case-work'. They further suggest that this method of teamwork in partnership with psycho-analytic consultants might be valuable in other settings in which the personality of the individual is the central problem.[2]

Since all the three principal specialist agencies which have come into existence since the war to undertake marriage guidance work were started on a voluntary basis, they have all been faced by the problem of finding sufficient money to maintain and expand their work. As early as 1947 the Denning Committee recommended that voluntary agencies experimenting in the field of marriage guidance should be grant-aided, since marriage guidance is a form of social service of value to the State though not appropriate for the State to undertake itself.[3] This view was endorsed by the Royal Commission on Marriage and Divorce where it is suggested that 'it would be unwise to attempt to define any formal pattern of conciliation agencies or to set up an official conciliation service. The State's role should rather be to give every encouragement to the existing agencies, statutory and voluntary, engaged in matrimonial conciliation; as well as to other agencies which may be approved in the future. Voluntary agencies which have proved

[1] *Social Casework in Marital Problems*, pp. 153-4.
[2] Ibid., pp. 23-4.
[3] Cmd. 7024, pars. 28 and 29, pp. 12-13.

their worth should receive financial assistance from public funds.
. . . In extending the existing facilities, experiment and diversity of
method and technique should continue to be encouraged,' and 'In
matters involving such intimate and personal problems it is important to maintain as much diversity of pattern as possible, since
it is only through wide experience gained from a variety of sources,
that the best method of approach is likely to emerge.'[1]

The government of the day accepted the recommendation of the
Denning Committee that voluntary organisations undertaking
marriage guidance should be grant-aided, and in 1948 the Secretary of State for the Home Department set up a committee under
the chairmanship of Sir Sidney Harris to review the situation.
This Committee recommended that financial assistance should be
given out of central government funds to the National Marriage
Guidance Council, the Family Welfare Association and the
Catholic Marriage Advisory Council, to help meet the cost of
headquarters administration and to cover the cost of training
counsellors, about which the committee felt particularly concerned.[2] It was suggested that local centres should receive help
from their own local authorities.

Following the above recommendations, annual Exchequer
grants were authorised, while at the same time the Home Secretary
set up a Marriage Guidance Training Board composed of representatives of the three societies together with the Home Office, the
Ministry of Health and the Ministry of Education. This Board was
to plan and supervise selection and training schemes for marriage
guidance counsellors employed by these societies. The Morton
Commission considered that some expansion and improvement of
training facilities was desirable and recommended that 'the relatively modest increase in expenditure which will be called for in
order to provide better training facilities and to meet any additional expenditure at headquarters should be met by an increase
in the Exchequer grants'.[3] They also recommended that local
authority grant aid to local agencies should, if approved by the
appropriate Minister, rank for a specific Exchequer grant to the
extent of not less than 50 per cent. The question of direct grants to
marriage guidance organisations was raised in a House of Lords
debate on October 26, 1956, and several influential speakers urged
that these should be increased, but all the Lord Chancellor would
say in reply was 'I hope that as soon as circumstances become more
propitious it will be possible for greater contributions to be made

[1] Cmd. 9678, par. 341, p. 97.
[2] Report of the Departmental Committee on Grants for the Development of
Marriage Guidance, Cmd. 7566, November 1948.
[3] Cmd. 9678, par. 344, p. 98.

by the State towards this work.'[1] The position with regard to the National Marriage Guidance Council is that an initial Exchequer grant of £5,000 a year for general purposes with an additional sum to be allocated to training was later transformed into a lump sum grant of £10,000. More recently still this has been increased to £15,000. Smaller amounts have been allocated to the other two organisations, and local authorities are encouraged to grant aid the work of local councils.

The advisory or counselling services described in this chapter differ considerably both in range and type of problem handled and method of approach. They have this in common, that in all cases their aim is to provide the informed advice or skilled help required to enable the person concerned to face and overcome the particular difficulty which has brought him to the agency. This involves the establishment of a relationship, however brief or formal, between worker and client, and only if the relationship is a good one based on mutual respect, can it be used constructively, and the interest of the client be served.

[1] *Hansard* (Lords), Seventh Volume of Session 1955–56, col. 1058.

CHAPTER X

PROBLEM FAMILIES

THE mid-Victorian philanthropists who founded the Charity Organisation Society were, as we have seen, moved to take action not so much by the poverty of the people and their material deprivations, as by the moral and social degradation which so often accompanied it, particularly in the slums of the large cities. This they attempted to remedy by measures designed to restore individuals and families to self-respect and independence, hoping by a slow but sure process of personal reclamation to raise the standards of the people as a whole. Their ideals were high and their devotion great, but in general they made little impression on the vast mass of slum dwellers, and the next generation likened them to men standing on the edge of a morass in which their fellows were struggling and dying, pulling out a victim here and a victim there, but making no attempt to drain the swamp. Twentieth-century reformers, reacting from the individualist policy and moralist outlook of their immediate predecessors, attributed the social evils which had so distressed the Victorian philanthropists to environmental causes which could and should be remedied by social and economic planning. Thus they sought to raise the standards of the 'submerged tenth' by such measures as minimum wage legislation, the provision of labour exchanges, social insurance, preventive health services and the like, and believed that when general social conditions were improved the worst features of slum life would disappear. Up to a point their hopes were realised, and on the eve of the last war public officials were able to compare the condition of the people, and particularly of the children, with that at the beginning of the century, and with some justification congratulate themselves on the improvement. It was true that health visitors, sanitary inspectors, school attendance officers and other social and health workers were aware of the existence of families in the slum areas of the big towns, on the new housing estates, and even in the country villages, who remained sunk in squalor and apathy, hardly touched by the social progress around them. It was also true that ten years previously the Wood Committee[1]

---

[1] A joint committee of the Board of Education and the Board of Control set up in 1926 under the chairmanship of A. H. Wood. It reported in 1929.

investigating the problem of mental deficiency, had called attention to the existence within the community of a 'social probblem' group containing a high proportion of mental defectives, paupers, criminals and other social undesirables, but the general public was largely ignorant of and indifferent to the discussions which followed the publication of this report, and, except perhaps in areas where there had been prolonged unemployment, was generally complacent about social conditions.

The evacuation shattered this complacency. For the first time middle- and working-class people living in country and suburb were brought into close contact with the slum dwellers from town and city, and learnt by direct experience that the 'submerged tenth' still existed, 'like a hidden sore', 'poor, dirty and crude in its habits'.[1] Among these 'submerged tenth' were, so it was said, a number of 'problem families', that is families 'always on the edge of pauperism and crime, riddled with mental and physical defects, in and out of the courts for child neglect, a menace to the community of which the gravity is out of all proportion to their numbers'. Since then various attempts have been made to define and describe such families, discover the reasons for their continued existence, and the best methods of dealing with the problem.[2]

A major difficulty which is encountered at the outset of any discussion of 'the problem of the problem family' is the question as to whether or not the families usually subsumed under this heading really form a coherent group with common characteristics. The phrase coined by the Wood Committee and in use before the war, 'social problem group', definitely suggested this, and while some authorities limited its use to denote only groups of families containing mental defectives of the primary amentia type, the term has also been used less precisely to cover families with hereditary deficiencies and abnormalities, with the implication that together they constitute 'a noxious social aggregate'.[3] The postwar term 'problem family' has different implications, however, and the 'problem families' of to-day do not correspond with the social problem group of the years before the War. As used by social workers and administrators, the phrase appears to denote families with multiple problems whose standards of living, and particularly child care, are markedly low, and who seem to be little

---

[1] Women's Group on Public Welfare, *Our Towns, a Close Up*, Introduction, p. xiii. This is a study undertaken as a result of a resolution from the National Federation of Women's Institutes deploring certain conditions of English town life disclosed by evacuation, and asking that remedies should be sought.

[2] For a critical review of the literature concerning the 'problem' family, see A. F. Philp and Noel Timms, *The Problem of 'The Problem Family'*.

[3] C. F. Blacker (ed.), *Problem Families: Five Inquiries*, p. 12 and footnote.

influenced by, or are even resistant to, measures of general social amelioration. Such a characterisation may, of course, conceal both subjective judgments on the part of the administrator or social worker applying it, and wide diversities of outlook and pattern of life as between the families so described. So great may these diversities be, and so difficult may it be to distinguish between 'problem' and 'near problem' families, that many workers in contact with them would be inclined to echo the words of the Medical Officer of Health for Rotherham Rural District Council, 'I never did like the term "problem families" and think that it has the most unfortunate effects upon the staffs of any social services who have the habit of using it. . . . I should be glad if I never heard the term again.'[1] Nevertheless, the very fact that it is so widely used both here and in other countries would appear to suggest that it has some validity and usefulness, that there are families who, however diverse they may be, present certain common characteristics and are in need of special forms of social care, and hence it is necessary to examine the description a little more closely.

One of the characteristics of a problem family so regarded is that it always has multiple social, personal and financial problems, but not every family with a multiplicity of such problems is a problem family. It is their attitude towards their difficulties and towards those who would help them solve them which sets such families apart. 'Their peculiar characteristic', wrote Tom Stephens in his study of sixty-two families in Liverpool and Manchester made in 1945, 'is their inability to make the best of their circumstances and to profit by the facilities and services which are available for them,'[2] and later in the same study he continues, 'The distinctive feature of the life of a family who have become a social problem is their passive acceptance of their conditions. Indeed with every kind of case . . . the collapse of morale and complete abandonment of any effort to recover is the key problem.'[3] This is confirmed by other writers on the subject, such as Professor A. C. Stevenson, who remarks, 'They are not merely disheartened, or have given up trying very hard; it just no longer occurs to them to visualise any improvement in their way of life,'[4] and Dr. Stallybrass, late Deputy Medical Officer of Health for Liverpool, summed them up as 'Families presenting an abnormal amount of subnormal behaviour over long periods with a marked tendency to backsliding.'[5]

[1] Annual Report, 1950. Quoted at the beginning of A. F. Philp and Noel Timms' study, *The Problem of 'The Problem Family'*.

[2] T. Stephens (ed.), *Problem Families*, p. 2.

[3] Ibid., p. 65.   [4] *Recent Advances in Social Medicine*, 1950, p. 143.

[5] Liverpool Council of Social Service, *Problem Families*. Report of a Conference convened on 26 January 1946, p. 7.

It has been pointed out, however, that despite their general inefficiency and apparent indifference to commonly accepted standards problem families are not necessarily without norms and standards of their own. Thus one student of the problem has suggested that 'The more typical problem families do not simply abandon the more normal code of accepted morality, but tend to articulate their own specific type of standard as a component of a particular sub-culture, and by these standards their own low level of performance seems justified.'[1] An attempt made on rather different lines has been to distinguish between 'mediaeval' families who, it is thought, might represent the continued survival in our midst of a more primitive way of life, and are well adjusted to this pattern of behaviour, and 'slum breakdown' families who are falling away from normal patterns and standards and more or less rapidly disintegrating.[2] As yet this suggestion is little more than a hypothesis, interesting as it is, and we are still a long way from being in a position to answer with any precision or certainty the question as to what factors are most important and influential in creating problem family characteristics.

In considering whether it is possible to regard certain conditions which are commonly present in problem families as causative, it is necessary to remember that 'Each problem family presents a unique complex of circumstances, which can only be understood when regarded in its entirety.'[3] Moreover, innate and environmental conditions are usually inextricably blended so that it is extremely difficult to separate cause and effect. For example, ill-health, particularly of the mother, is frequently regarded as a contributory factor in the creation of a problem family, but 'We do not know whether this is cause or effect, i.e. one of the factors producing the problem family or the result of trying to fight against an intolerable situation. . . . Perhaps the psychosomatic nature of this illness should be considered more carefully than has been done hitherto . . . it is possible that much of the minor physical illness which these women suffer should be seen as symptomatic of a more general state of depression or of gross dependency needs which are also responsible for the neglect of their home and children.'[4] Similarly, evidence of poverty is to be found in many problem family homes, but, while in some cases this may be primary

[1] N. Timms, 'Social Standards and the Problem Family', *Case Conference*, January 1956, p. 9. The research on which this observation is based is discussed in W. Baldamus and N. Timms, 'The Problem Family—a Sociological Approach', *British Journal of Sociology*, December 1955, p. 318.
[2] D. H. Stott, *Unsettled Children and Their Families*, pp. 57–58. See also *The People of Ship Street* by Madeline Kerr.
[3] T. Stephens, op. cit., p. 3.
[4] A. F. Philp and Noel Timms, op. cit., p. 15.

poverty due to low wages, invalidity or widowhood, it may also be due to the inability or unwillingness of the breadwinner to hold down a steady job, which in its turn may be due to physical or psychological inadequacies. There is, however, a good deal of agreement that, generally speaking, 'it would take more intelligence and more stability than that possessed by most problem parents to budget on the income provided and to balance successfully long-term and immediate need'.[1]

'Intelligence' and 'stability' are, indeed, conditions most frequently regarded as basic when the reasons for continued existence of problem families are discussed. For instance, one investigator writes, 'Of the five commonly recognised features of problem families, namely mental subnormality, temperamental instability, ineducability, a squalid home and the presence of numerous children, the first two, though less immediately conspicuous than the last three, can best be regarded as having causal status.'[2] But this same writer also points out that 'many mentally subnormal families lead harmonious and socially useful lives',[3] and it has been remarked by another author that a 'problem' mother may be so exhausted and apathetic as the result of her unequal struggle with untoward circumstances and poor physical health that she cannot make proper use of the intelligence she has, and so appears less intelligent than she really is.[4] Such research as has been done into the relationship between subnormal intelligence and the social inefficiency which produces problem families is suggestive, but not conclusive,[5] and it seems that mental subnormality, while important, is but one facet of a complex situation.

We are probably even less sure of our ground when discussing the influence of temperamental instability than when considering that of low intelligence, and although suggestions as to this have been put forward much more research is needed. For example, considerable insight into the often disturbed emotional life of the problem family can be gained by considering the personal relationships problem family parents and children establish with each other and with those outside the family, but as yet little use has been made of this approach.[6] On the whole, although much has been written about problem families in recent years, and some useful local surveys, have been undertaken,[7] there is still room for further

[1] Ibid., p. 11.　　　　　　　　[2] C. P. Blacker, op. cit., p. 27.
[3] Ibid., p. 21.　　　　　　　　[4] D. H. Stott, op. cit., p. 59.
[5] For example, M. D. Sheridan, 'The Intelligence of 100 Neglectful Mothers' in British Medical Journal, 14 January 1956, p. 91.
[6] A. F. Philp and Noel Timms, op. cit., p. 20.
[7] E. G. P. Ford, C. J. Thomas and E. Ashton, Problem Families, Fourth Report of the Southampton Survey, 1952 (out of print); R. C. Wofinden, Problem Families in Bristol, 1950.

research along several different lines. Meanwhile, however limited our knowledge and imperfect our skills, we must do what we can to discover and rehabilitate the problem families in our midst, and this preventive and therapeutic work may well contribute to a better understanding of the problem as a whole.

A characteristic of problem families frequently referred to by administrators and social workers is their failure to respond to the possibilities of improved standards of living and measures of social betterment which for the last half-century have become increasingly available to, and appropriated by, the general population. This failure has been, and still is, a challenge to those concerned to consider what special measures can be devised to help such families, and this challenge has met with widespread response from central government departments, local authorities, and voluntary organisations.[1] There is considerable diversity of approach to the problem, and this may have its advantages, since the families themselves vary so much in their characteristics and needs, provided that diversity of approach is combined with good co-operation, so that the services rendered by different authorities and organisations are complementary rather than competing.

A method of dealing with the situation which appears to be widely favoured by central government departments and local authorities is that which treats the problem primarily as an educational one.[2] As the Report of the Chief Medical Officer of the Ministry of Education for 1954 and 1955 puts it, 'The maintenance of the family as a unit and the education and training of the mother in family care are the primary objectives of all those who are concerned with problem families.'[3] This educative work may be shared by a number of officials and workers but it is regarded by the Ministry as primarily the work of the health visitors (including the school health visitors), who, 'with the support of the public health, school and family doctors, have the difficult but essential duty of being the health teachers in the homes and in the classes'.[4] The Ministry of Health circular, *Health of Children: Prevention of break-up of families*[5] is slightly different in its emphasis, but it, too, stresses the role of the health visitor. It bases its case for

---

[1] The following comment, made by Dr. G. F. Bramley, Principal School Medical Officer, Gloucestershire, and quoted in *The Health of the School Child*, 1954 and 1955, p. 131, illustrates this paragraph: '. . . My opinion is, however, that it is because of the general improvement in the standard of living that the problem families stand out, and they are not increasing. Much is being done for them and better understanding as well as material and physical help will do more.'

[2] Cf. A. F. Philp and N. Timms, op. cit., pp. 24–6.

[3] Op. cit., p. 131. [4] Ibid., p. 132.

[5] Circular 27/54.

local authority intervention on the 'risk of mental illness as such psychological disturbance and retarded mental development' incurred by children in problem families, 'where one or both parents are often handicapped by physical ill-health or are of low intelligence or suffering from mental instability'. This risk enables a local authority to take action under Section 28 of the National Health Service Act, 1946, and in this action the health visitor is expected to play a leading part as, 'by reason of her close contact with families with young children [she is] particularly well placed to recognise early signs of failure in the family which may lead to the disruption of normal home life with consequent risk to the mental health of the children'. It is recognised, however, that, although the health visitor can often 'from her own training and experience offer advice which will enable the family to overcome these difficulties', at other times she may need to call in other local authority workers such as the mental health worker or the home help, or ask for the co-operation of a voluntary organisation. It must be emphasised that only if the health visitor has sufficient sympathy, flexibility and understanding to enable her to reach the families she is seeking to help and advise, and only if she appreciates that, especially where emotional problems are involved in the situation, educational measures are insufficient in themselves, will she be able, by acting in co-operation with other workers, to achieve the improvements in standards of child care she seeks to bring about.

Complementary to the educative approach of the health visitor is that of the social caseworker, and the value of casework as a method of helping problem families overcome their difficulties is now generally accepted. Most family casework agencies have, and always have had, a proportion of problem families on their books, and in many instances are now devoting increasing time and attention to them. During the war a new agency, the Pacifist Service Units, came into being and gave special help to such families. The units originally consisted of conscientious objectors who grouped themselves together to undertake relief work in the target areas, and on Merseyside they were put in charge of a group of unbilletable bombed-out families. As time went on the workers realised that the family problems which they were trying to cope with were not wholly, or even mainly, due to the war, although they had been accentuated by it. They were deep-seated and appeared to be permanent, but the Units believed that they could be tackled by the methods they had first used with the unbilletable evacuees. These were based ultimately on religious and ethical principles which included a deep respect for individual human beings and led to 'friendship without condescension or professional aloofness; not forced or superficial but a relationship of mutual trust as between equals'.[1]

The approach of the Units to the families they were seeking to help, though fundamentally a casework approach, and with the essentially casework aim of helping the family to become self-respecting and independent, differed in some respects from that of the older agencies. This was due in part to the problems with which the Units were faced. Whereas in most casework situations the client approaches the agency because he is conscious of needing the help it has to offer, the families helped by the Units were referred by other agencies, who considered that the intensive help offered by them was needed to deal with the problems presented. Hence the offer of help came from the Unit to the family, and the worker assumed and to some extent retained the initiative. His position was completely unauthoritarian, however, and he could be asked to withdraw at any time. Further, while the basis of most types of casework is the spoken word, the interview between worker and client, the Units relied largely on friendship expressed in action to work the miracle and bring the family's dead or dying self-respect to life. The worker went to the family prepared, if necessary, to clean and distemper, scrub dirty floors, cleanse filthy bedding, wash and toothcomb verminous and obstreperous children and generally to assist the family in every possible way, hoping thus to earn their confidence and give them a new outlook on life. Material help, such as clothes, furniture or bedding, would be provided if need be, often with the co-operation of another agency, since the resources of the Units were limited. Manual work and material help were, however, regarded as of little value unless the worker could use them as means of social rehabilitation. Hence, in the long run, it was the worker's personality that counted most. As one of the leaders of the movement in its early days predicted, 'ultimately it is on the interplay of personality, and on the ability of the worker to give from his own spiritual resources that the value of the work will depend.'[2]

Beginning with families given up as hopeless by other agencies, the work of the Units gradually expanded and won recognition. With the ending of the war the specifically pacifist witness on which they were originally based lost a good deal of its relevance, and in 1948 a new national organisation, Family Service Units, took over the Pacifist Service Units' casework in Liverpool and Manchester and began to establish units in other towns as well. Its first aim was 'to provide a service undertaking intensive and comprehensive welfare work among families unable to maintain

[1] T. Stephens, op. cit., p. 46.
[2] Ibid., p. 66.

INDIVIDUALISING THE SOCIAL SERVICES

proper standards of home and child care without special assistance', but it hoped also to develop a preventive service 'so that disintegration may be averted by timely help', and to conduct a 'comprehensive research project' to study the causes leading to the disintegration of family life. So far, although some research has been undertaken, most of the energies of Family Service Units have been directed to implementing the first of these aims, and to that end the organisation has developed an intensive casework service, employing carefully selected and trained social workers for the purpose. Thus the approach is more professional, and more conscious use is made of casework skills, than in the early days of the Pacifist Service Units, but 'the emphasis is still on the relationship which the caseworker has with his client and on his ability to respond in a wide variety of ways to the many different needs in the family's situation'.[1] Most of the families helped must be given psychological and social support which may involve intensive visiting over long periods, and hence case loads must be kept low. Consequently costs in money and manpower are relatively high compared with the numbers of families helped, and there may appear to be little to show for it.[2] Nevertheless, in so far as families who would otherwise break down are thereby enabled to continue functioning, even if at a relatively low standard of efficiency, the effort is worth while if only for the sake of the children, the parents of the next generation,[3] and quite apart from other considerations we may remind ourselves that 'the attitude that society adopts to its deviants, and especially its poor and politically inarticulate deviants, reflects its ultimate values'.[4]

Family Service Units is a voluntary organisation and much of the casework with problem values is undertaken by voluntary organisations, but of recent years some local authorities have begun to appoint their own caseworkers especially for this work. This is tentatively encouraged by the Ministry of Health Circular, *Prevention of Break-up of Families*, already referred to, which says, 'It may well be that some local health authorities will find there is need to employ a trained social caseworker, who might of course be one already engaged in similar work under other powers, in order that the particular needs of such families may be studied and met in appropriate ways.' Similar work may be undertaken by

[1] A. F. Philp and N. Timms, op. cit., p. 45.
[2] Tom Stephens estimated that out of 62 families visited for a minimum period of six months, 'barely more than one-tenth' responded by a substantial improvements in standards, but much larger numbers were helped to maintain standards somewhat higher than they would otherwise have done and in some cases complete family breakdown was averted.
[3] *The Health of the School Child*, 1954 and 1955, p. 132.
[4] R. M. Titmuss, Foreword to *The Problem of 'The Problem Family'*.

workers appointed by children's committees for 'preventive' work,[1] and one of the unsolved administrative problems of the present time is which is the most appropriate local authority department to assume the major responsibility for dealing with family problems of the kind discussed in this chapter. The position may become clearer when the departmental committee set up in 1956 under the chairmanship of Viscount Ingleby to make recommendations, *inter alia*, as to 'whether local authorities responsible for child care under the Children Act, 1948, in England and Wales should, taking into account action by voluntary organisations and the responsibilities of existing statutory services, be given new powers and duties to prevent or forestall the suffering of children through neglect in their own homes', makes its report.

While opinions may differ as to which, if any, of the existing local authority departments should expand their social work with problem families and along what lines, most people are agreed that if these families are to be helped effectively, close co-ordination between all services dealing with them must be established and maintained. Problem families are more likely to suffer from too much rather than too little attention from administrative and health and social workers, and over-visiting by a number of different officials and social workers is at least as likely to increase apathy and resistance as to overcome it.[2] The need for co-ordination was recognised in a circular, *Children Neglected or Ill-treated in their Own Homes*, issued jointly by the Home Office, the Ministry of Health, and the Ministry of Education in 1950,[3] in which attention is drawn to the necessity for 'considering the needs of the family as a whole' if effective action is to be taken to deal with child neglect. While in some areas, at any rate, useful work appears to have been done by the case committees and conferences established as a result of the recommendations contained in this circular, some of the problems of establishing mutual understanding between workers trained in different disciplines and with different ideas as to what the real needs of problem families really are, do not as yet appear to have been wholly solved. It may be, as has been suggested,[4] that co-ordination is not enough, and a comprehensive family service will one day come into being, with more extensive powers to deal with family problems than now possessed by any single local authority department, but for the present

[1] Discussed in Chapter XIV.

[2] An extreme example of over-visiting is given by D. V. Donnison and Mary Stewart in *The Child and the Social Services*, Fabian Research Series, No. 196.

[3] Home Office Circular 157/50; Ministry of Health, 225/50; Ministry of Education, 31 July 1950. This circular and its implementation is discussed further in Chapters XIV and XXII.

[4] D. V. Donnison and Mary Stewart, op. cit., p. 6.

social workers must achieve what corporate action they can within the framework of the existing services. By such co-operation not only can individual families be helped more effectively, but a better understanding of the characteristics and needs of families in difficulty achieved.

The types of assistance rendered to problem families described so far are given to the family in its own home, and apart from the small-scale experiments made in rehousing evicted families in special rehabilitation houses under supervision, already described in Chapter VII, and the provisions by which neglectful mothers can be sent to recuperation centres with their younger children,[1] no measures have been taken in this country to segregate such families and give them supervision and training in a specially selected environment. Experiments along these lines have, however, been carried out in the Netherlands, for example in Rotterdam, where 'socially weak' families may, after a period in an observation centre, be transferred to a group of dwellings called Zuidplein, which will house about 570 families. Here the families are 're-educated' socially with a view to rehousing among normal families in another part of the town.[2] Experiments along similar lines have been conducted at Utrecht and Amsterdam and special camps established for the 'anti-social'[3] in Drenthe and Hilversum. Families so separated from the normal community are regarded as 'diseased biological units, social deterioration being the chief symptom of the disease'[4] and it is considered proper that for the sake of society in general, such families should be removed to an environment where they are protected against their own inadequacies and there is a chance for the children to develop.[5] At present, the main sanction which can be used to get families 'into care' in one of these projects is that of refusal of housing accommodation elsewhere, for the housing shortage is general, but special legislation has been formulated which would enable the authorities to place 'anti-social' families under supervision, and, should this prove fruitless, in a re-education camp. These are drastic powers and the arguments against any attempt to introduce similar ones in Britain have been forcibly stated by the

---

[1] See Chapter XIV below.
[2] The experiment is described by J. van Mill, Director of the Municipal Welfare Department of Rotterdam in two pamphlets, *The Zuidplein Project* (January 1953), and *The Zuidplein Project, Continuation* (April 1957).
[3] Anti-social families are families unwilling or unable to accept social aid voluntarily, as distinct from the 'socially weak', who show some willingness to co-operate.
[4] A. Querido, op. cit.
[5] I. L. Burgess, 'Homeless Families in the Netherlands', *Case Conference*, Vol. I, No. 7, November 1954, p._22.

Women's Group on Public Welfare. 'Even accepting the existence of this intransigent group and appreciating that special measures must be taken for such problems', they write, 'we are not in favour of any form of compulsory special powers for the following reasons: partly because, since co-operation is the essence of successful rehabilitation we are doubtful whether such results as would be obtained by compulsion would be worth the cost in the loss of human dignity and independence; partly because it is almost impossible to draw the line between "problem" and "near problem"; but chiefly because we dislike the idea of labelling any section of the community to its detriment. . . . To segregate the failures in society is in our view an indignity which no advantage of hygiene and progress can outweigh.'[1]

The arguments of the Women's Group on Public Welfare are politically sound, but the Dutch experiments, however we may criticise them, at least show an awareness of the problem and determination to take active measures to deal with it. If, as we must, we reject measures of compulsory segregation or training except for those whose neglect of their children is sufficiently serious to constitute a criminal offence, we must develop other methods of dealing with the situation. This involves, among other things, a good deal of further research. Fundamental research of the extent and of the kind needed would be expensive and its findings might not be immediately applicable, but if in the long run, it leads to effective preventive and rehabilitative measures it would be of great value not only to the families concerned but to the community as a whole. Problem families are a continual drain on the man- and money-power of social services, for all that they appear to profit so little from them, and their presence in our midst lowers the whole tone of neighbourhood and community life. We are still groping with this problem and our attempts at treatment are hampered by our lack of knowledge and understanding, and hence research and experiment should be encouraged in every possible way.

[1] Women's Group on Public Welfare, *The Neglected Child and His Family*, pp. 106–7.

PART THREE

SOCIAL SERVICES FOR CHILDREN AND YOUNG PEOPLE

'By the present Declaration of the Rights of the Child, commonly known as the Declaration of Geneva, men and women of all nations, recognising that mankind owes to the child the best that it has to give, declare and accept it as their duty that beyond and above all considerations of race, nationality or creed:

1. The child must be given the means requisite for its normal development, both materially and spiritually.

2. The child that is hungry must be fed; the child that is sick must be nursed; the child that is backward must be helped; the delinquent child must be reclaimed; and the orphan and waif must be sheltered and succoured;

3. The child must be the first to receive relief in times of distress;

4. The child must be put in a position to earn a livelihood and must be protected against every form of exploitation.

5. The child must be brought up in the consciousness that its talents must be devoted to the service of its fellow men.'—*Declaration of the Rights of the Child*, adopted by the Assembly of the League of Nations in 1924.

CHAPTER XI

THE WELFARE OF MOTHERS AND
YOUNG CHILDREN

A WIDE variety of welfare services, both public and voluntary, exists to meet the needs of children. Their development was fostered partly by the pity aroused in most people by the suffering of the innocent and helpless, and partly by a desire to improve the future health and fitness of the nation. During the years between the wars this latter incentive was reinforced by the anxiety caused by the decline in the birth-rate. Children were becoming scarcer, and as they became scarcer they became more precious, and the greater were the efforts made to ensure that those that were born received the best possible care, so that they might survive and grow into healthy and well-adjusted men and women able to make their maximum contribution to the nation. Moreover, it is now realised that since parenthood is becoming to a large and increasing extent voluntary, it must be made attractive, and the nation as a whole must take over a large measure of responsibility for the maintenance and upbringing of children, so that parents of large families do not suffer serious economic and social disadvantages compared with the single and childless.[1]

All these considerations have helped to bring about the modern developments in child welfare, but there has been little long-term planning based on a considered policy.[2] Like other social services the child welfare services have grown up piecemeal, partly as the result of the pioneer efforts of individuals, such as Dr. Barnardo or Margaret Beavan of Liverpool, who left behind them vigorous voluntary organisations to carry on their work; partly owing to the initiative of local medical officers of health, such as Dr. Drew Harris of St. Helens who, as already mentioned, started the first milk depot in this country in 1899 and partly to the efforts of such

---

[1] This point is made by the Royal Commission on Population. See particularly Chapters V and XIV.

[2] A plea for a comprehensive family welfare policy based on these considerations is made by the Swedish sociologist, Alva Myrdal, *Nation and Family*, 1945.

enlightened civil servants as Sir James Kay-Shuttleworth,[1] Sir Arthur Newsholme,[2] and Sir George Newman.[3]

A further complicating factor in the development of social services for children has been that, while a policy of providing social services for their benefit has been generally accepted, it has not been without serious misgivings in some quarters, for there were, and still are, those who fear lest such services destroy family responsibility and the underlying values of family life. These fears were strongly expressed during the early years of the century, when the advocates of school feeding and the school medical service had to fight not only apathy and ignorance, but the serious and informed criticism of those who believed so strongly in the importance of maintaining the unity and independence of the family, that they argued that it might be better for a child to remain hungry than for it to be fed in such a way as to destroy the parents' sense of responsibility for its welfare.[4] Similar fears still influence the attitude of some people towards nursery schools and family allowances. In the long run there should be no real conflict between higher standards of community care for children and the maintenance of all that is best in family life. Indeed, the one should strengthen the other, and this has been achieved in certain instances, notably, for example, in the maternity and child welfare services which have done so much to raise the standard of child care. Perhaps the secret of the success of this group of services lies in the fact that they do not take any responsibility for the care of her child from the mother. Instead she is helped through the services of skilled yet sympathetic and understanding people to raise her standards of child care, and to acquire the skill and knowledge which will enable her to come nearer to reaching them.

The maternity and child welfare services are concerned to promote the health of both mother and child so that the mother gives birth to her child with the minimum amount of danger and discomfort, and without serious after-effects on her own health, while the child is born healthy and receives adequate care until he starts school. The legislative framework of these services has already been described in Chapter VI. They provide for the ante-natal and post-natal supervision of the mother, including dental care; skilled attention at the time of the child's birth; and supervision of the health of the infant. With these medical services are associated

[1] First Secretary of the Committee of the Privy Council on Education 1839–49.
[2] Medical Officer of Health to the Local Government Board, 1908–19.
[3] Chief Medical Officer to the Board of Education from the inception of the School Medical Service until his retirement in 1935. From 1919 onwards he combined this with the post of Chief Medical Officer to the Ministry of Health.
[4] F. Le Gros Clarke, *The Social History of the School Meals Service*, p. 7.

measures to ensure that both expectant and nursing mothers and their children have opportunities of procuring the food supplements particularly beneficial to them, while education in the care of children is an important side of the work. This educational work is carried on by lectures, demonstrations and individual advice given at the clinics, and by the health visitors who visit the mothers in their homes and help and guide them in the management and care of their children.

Under the National Health Service Act administrative responsibility for the care of expectant mothers and young children is shared between all three branches of the National Health Service. The provision of maternity and child welfare services, which include both the establishment and maintenance of clinics covering the ante-natal and post-natal care of mothers and the health supervision of young children, and the employment of adequate numbers of domiciliary midwives and health visitors, are among the most important functions of the local health authority. At the same time local executive councils are responsible for the maternity medical services undertaken by general practitioners, while the regional hospital boards have taken over the maternity hospitals and associated consultant services.

These administrative arrangements have been severely criticised, mainly on the grounds that instead of creating a unified maternity service designed to give mother and child continuous care from the time when the pregnant woman notifies her pregnancy to the time when the young child has achieved a successful start in life, responsibility is divided between three independent bodies who may or may not co-operate. The evidence supplied to the Guillebaud Committee showed that there were wide variations between local authority areas in the manner and extent to which co-operation had been achieved. The differences in both practice and opinion were such that the Committee observed that 'the maternity services are in a state of some confusion which must impair their usefulness and which should not be allowed to continue'. Hence they recommended that 'an appropriate body' should be appointed to review the whole of the field, 'to find out precisely what services—medical or educational—are needed for mothers and young children, and how they can best be provided through the framework of the National Health Service.[1] In April 1956 a Committee under the chairmanship of the Earl of Cranbrook was appointed by the Minister of Health for this purpose, and its report was published in 1959.

Among the questions raised by the changes brought about through the National Health Service is that of the role of the local

[1] Cmd. 9663, par. 637, p. 212.

authority clinics. The introduction of the Service was followed by a falling off in attendances at ante-natal and post-natal clinics, a tendency which continued until 1956 since when numbers have risen again. Pregnant women are now entitled to two pre-natal and one post-natal examinations from their general practitioner, or, if he does not undertake this work, from a general practitioner obstetrician, and many prefer this to attendance at a clinic, but relaxation, mothercraft and health education classes are held there, and care is given by the midwife.[1] Women whose confinement takes place in hospital receive ante-natal and post-natal care under its auspices, although this does not preclude the local health authority clinic from being regarded as an outpost of the hospital for this purpose.[2]

Attendances at child welfare clinics have been maintained since 1948, but concern has been expressed because a large number of children attend once or twice only, while the mothers who do bring their babies regularly are usually those from good artisan homes, and 'mothers with a poor standard of care, with large families or with illegitimate infants—those in fact who most need advice and help—are less likely to attend'.[3] An inquiry into clinic attendances in two South-east London boroughs, reported in *The Lancet* in April 1956, revealed that a large number of mothers favoured attendance at child welfare clinics because these provide a means of 'obtaining expert advice, checking progress and relieving anxiety',[4] but many did not think it necessary to visit if the child was making favourable progress while others they felt that the knowledge gained with the first child equipped them to deal adequately with those who followed. Despite the fact that many of the premises were far from satisfactory, criticisms of them were infrequent, but there were considerable differences of opinion between the mothers with regard to the value of the health education given at the clinics and the use of visual aids and group discussion.[5] Health education, according to the Ministry, 'was and remains a chief function of the welfare centre', but, as they point out, the emphasis of the teaching has now changed. 'Whereas in the early days the centre staff were concerned to eliminate gross physical errors in infant feeding and hygiene, and their results were quick and easy to assess, now they have to cope with new

---

[1] Report of the Ministry of Health for the year ended 31 December 1956. Part I, Cmnd. 806, p. 149. Cf. Report of the Maternity Services Committee, pp. 40–3.

[2] Ministry of Health Circular 118/47, par. 14, p. 5.

[3] J. Spence, W. S. Walton, F. J. W. Miller and S. D. M. Court, *A Thousand Families in Newcastle-upon-Tyne*, pp. 163 and 172.

[4] H. D. Chalke, 'Attendances at Child Welfare Centres', *The Lancet*, 28 April 1956, p. 571.   [5] H. D. Chalke, op. cit., p. 573.

and even more subtle problems in growth and development, and the indices of their success have become finer and often manifest themselves only after a long latent period.'[1] This means new ways of approach, the acquirement of new knowledge, and the development of new skills on the part of the clinic staffs especially as 'many patients who once would have been "taught", now seek enlightenment or guidance in order that they may teach themselves'. Whatever changes in emphasis may take place, however, individual consultations with particular members of staff to obtain individual help and guidance remain the basis of the work, and it is still necessary for the work done in the clinic to be supplemented by the home visits which are the special responsibility of the health visitor.

Although the organisation of health visiting by women paid for the work was first undertaken by a voluntary body, the Manchester and Salford Ladies' Sanitary Reform Association, in 1862, the idea was subsequently taken up by local medical officers of health, and since the turn of the century, the health visitor, now specially trained for her exacting work, has been an active and valuable member of the maternity and child welfare team, her speciality being the education of mothers in the health care of their children. This involves visiting mothers and young children in their homes and attending clinic sessions where she both advises mothers individually and gives informal talks or leads group discussions.

The National Health Service Act and the Circulars based on it enlarged the scope of the health visitors' work so that, in intent at any rate, she has become a family health adviser, whose function it is to give advice 'as to the care of young children, persons suffering from illness and expectant and nursing mothers, and as to measures necessary to prevent the spread of infection'.[2] This raises many problems of training, deployment, and the relationship between the work of the health visitor and that of other health and social workers. It was to investigate these and related questions that in September 1953 the Ministry of Health, acting jointly with the Department of Health for Scotland and the Ministry of Education, set up a Working Party to investigate the field of work, training and recruitment of health visitors. The Working Party reported in 1956.[3] At the outset they defined the main functions of health visitors as 'health education and social advice'. This latter phrase is rather ambiguous, and its use raises a number of questions, particularly as to the relationship between health

[1] Report of the Ministry of Health for the year ended 31 December 1956, Part II, 'On the State of Public Health.' Cmnd. 325, p. 143.
[2] Section 24.
[3] Ministry of Health, Department of Health for Scotland, Ministry of Education. 'An Inquiry into Health Visiting.' H.M.S.O. 1956.

visitors and social caseworkers and the extent to which health visitors can and should undertake what may prove to be a very difficult and delicate social work task involving special skill and understanding. The Working Party made it clear that although the social element in health visiting has increased, in their view health visitors go to their clients primarily for health education purposes and not to remedy social difficulties.[1] They point out, however, that 'it would clearly be wrong that an obvious difficulty should be ignored merely because the visitor was not directly concerned', and the visitor 'must also take account of the unit—the family—of which the individual forms a part, and not only of physical but of psychological and social factors'. But her social activities must 'be limited by the necessary functions of others (who will have equal respect for hers), and social action on the part of the health visitor should normally be limited to advice to the client, referral of the case to another worker or a recommendation that a service should be provided'.[2] With her contacts with families of all kinds, the health visitor is in a very good position to detect family strains and problems even while they are still in their early stages, and when these are detected she can and should seek the advice and assistance of the appropriate worker so that measures can be taken to deal with them and prevent them from becoming worse. This means that her training must be so arranged that she appreciates both her own role and its limitations, and the problems faced by other workers and the way in which they deal with them.[3]

The maternity and child welfare services are concerned to raise the standards of health and child care of all mothers and young children. There are, however, two groups which present special problems, and for whom more specialised social provision is needed, namely, the mother who goes out to work and her child, and the unmarried mother and her child.

Before the war women normally gave up outside employment on marriage, except in certain occupations and areas, for example among the cotton weavers of Lancashire and the jute workers of Dundee. During the war the need for women workers in the factories became acute, and although mothers with young children were never directed into industry, they were encouraged to take full or part-time work if at all possible, and special provisions were made to encourage them to do so. The demand for women workers has continued since the war, and it is now generally accepted that a woman continues in employment after her marriage, only giving it up when her first child is well on the way. From then onwards she is likely to remain at home caring for her children for a

[1] Op. cit., p. 100, par. 287.   [2] Ibid. p. 103, par. 293.
[3] Ibid., p. 114, par. 315.

number of years, but there are a minority, who, for one reason or another, return to work while their children are still small.

The numbers of mothers of pre-school children who go out to work is not known precisely. The 1951 Census One per cent Sample Tables showed that 4·5 per cent of the women with children under one year of age were working at that time, but the percentages of mothers of older children are not given. In order to obtain accurate information about the effects of married women's work on the children's development the Institute of Child Health, (University of London), the Society of Medical Officers of Health and the Population Investigation Committee is carrying out a sample survey into the development of 5,386 children born in the first week of March 1946, children drawn from all parts of the country and from every type of home background. The results which have been published to date show that only 3 per cent of the women surveyed started work either full- or part-time before their children were six months old. By the time the children were a year old 4 per cent were working, and this proportion had increased to 15 per cent at the age of four years. Approximately half the mothers were in part-time employment, that is working less than thirty-five hours a week. Many women were employed for short periods only, and in all nearly 26 per cent had at least one job during the first four years of their children's lives.[1]

The unsatisfactory nature of the care given to the child of the woman worker was one of the first evils of the factory system to engage the attention of the social reformers of the first half of the nineteenth century. Investigations revealed that the infant whose mother worked in a factory was usually 'minded' by an old woman or young child, and was kept quiet by frequent doses of mixtures containing opium or laudanum.[2] Rising standards of child care, shorter working hours and other improvements gradually brought

---

[1] J. W. B. Douglas and J. M. Bloomfield, *Children under Five*, p. 118. The authors point out that this data was collected between 1946 and 1950, and 'change in the intervening years has almost certainly been in the direction of more employment rather than less', hence the figures are useful as giving minimum rates for the gainful employment of mothers with children.

[2] For example, the evidence of a druggist from a poor district of Manchester as reported in the Second Report of the Commissioners of Inquiry into the State of Large Towns and Populous Districts, 1845: 'There is scarcely a single family of the really poorer classes in which this custom does not prevail. The mother goes out to her work in the morning leaving her child in charge either of a woman who cannot be troubled with it, or with another child of perhaps ten years old. A dose of "quietness" is given. . . . The child thus drugged sleeps and may waken at dinner-time . . . when . . . the child receives another dose. Well, the father and mother come home at night quite fatigued . . . they must have sleep undisturbed by the child, so it is again drugged, and in this manner young children are often drugged three times in each day.'

the worst abuses of daily minding to an end, but the practice itself persisted in those parts of the country where married women's work remained an accepted part of the social pattern, and it still prevails in these areas. The minder is usually a relative (frequently she is Granny), or a neighbour, who receives a small weekly payment for her trouble. Her standards may or may not be as high as those of the mother who confides the child to her care, but even if they are, the child may suffer as the result of differences of handling, and of the partial separation from his mother.

The alternative to the 'minder' is the day nursery. These were started on a voluntary basis in the nineteenth century, but since the passing of the Maternity and Child Welfare Act, 1918, local authorities have had powers to provide them, and grant aid has been given by the Ministry of Health. On the eve of the last war 104 municipal and voluntary nurseries accommodating 3,700 children were in receipt of grant aid. During the early months of the war a number of residential nurseries were provided in reception areas, but the main drive for increased day nursery accommodation came in 1941, and was occasioned by the need to attract as many women as possible into industry. Special efforts (involving the co-operation of local maternity and child welfare committees and local education authorities with the Ministries of Health and Labour, but financed entirely from central government funds) were made to establish nurseries in those parts of the country where the demand for women's work was great, and the war-time nursery, staffed with the help of the Child Care Reserve, became an established social service.

With the ending of hostilities the need for day nurseries declined and the number of children provided for fell from 47,662 to 41,258 between 1950 and 1958. Nurseries are provided by the local authorities under Section 22 of the National Health Service Act, by voluntary organisations, by factories employing large numbers of women workers, or as private ventures.[1] Factory nurseries have the advantage that the mother has only one journey morning and evening and is not completely cut off from the child during the day.

The Ministry of Health has the overall responsibility of ensuring that the care given to young childen whose mothers go out to work reaches a satisfactory standard, whether these children are placed in a local authority nursery, or in one run by a voluntary

[1] In 1958 local authorities maintained 490 nurseries providing for 23,252 children, voluntary organisations 11 nurseries providing for 424 children. There were 77 factory nurseries providing for 3,116 children, and 467 other private nurseries with places for 10,236 children. Ministry of Health Report, Part I, Cmnd. 806, pp. 154 and 155.

association or a private individual, or are cared for by daily minders. The Nurseries and Child Minders Regulation Act, passed in 1948, seeks to ensure this by providing that all day and short-term residential nurseries and persons other than relatives who receive more than two children under the age of five from different households for reward, either for a substantial part of any one day or for periods not exceeding six days,[1] shall be registered with the local health authority, which is given powers to inspect the nursery or other premises where the children are kept, limit the numbers of children received, and insist that proper standards are maintained. If it is not satisfied, the authority may, subject to the right of appeal by the occupier to a court of summary jurisdiction, cancel the registration. The Act does not give complete protection to children whose mothers leave them in the care of others, however, since it does not include minders taking children singly, nor those who are relatives of the working mother, and there is, too, the administrative difficulty of ensuring that its provisions are known and enforced. Moreover, no special community provisions are made for the school child who, unless there is a play centre in the neighbourhood, or a relative or neighbour to take him in, has to fill in the time between the closing of the school and his mother's return from work either in the streets or in the empty house.

A recent inquiry into the employment of married women outside the home and its social consequences, the findings of which have been published by the Institute of Personnel Management,[2] showed that only $7\frac{1}{2}$ per cent of the working mothers surveyed had made no specific arrangements with relatives or neighbours for the care of their children. From this it may be inferred that the numbers of such 'latch-key' children are comparatively small, but, small though the numbers may be, they accentuate the need for increased provisions in the way of play centres and play spaces particularly in urban areas, which are desirable on other grounds also.[3]

The effects of the mother's absence at work during the whole or part of the day on the physical and psychological development of the child are not easy to ascertain, as so much will depend on circumstance, such as the length of the mother's absence, the alternative care provided and the age and temperament of the child. For the purposes of their survey Dr. Douglas and Mr. Bloomfield matched each child whose mother was working for twelve months or more during the pre-school years with another from the same

[1] Persons receiving children for long periods come within the scope of the child life protection provisions of the Children Act. Nursery schools in respect of which payments are made by the Ministry of Education are also exempted from the provisions of this Act as they are subject to inspection by this Ministry; children's homes and hospitals are also exempt (Section 8).
[2] Viola Klein, *Working Wives*.   [3] See Chapter XVI below.

type of home background whose mother had never worked. It was found that the children of working mothers appeared to have an excess of lower respiratory tract infections, possibly because of the larger number who attended nurseries; hospital admission was also more frequent and the children stayed longer, perhaps because they could not be cared for at home. Nevertheless their growth was apparently not affected, 'nor did they show an excess of bad habits, nightmares, or other signs suggestive of emotional upset', and the general conclusion of the authors was that 'an examination of the record of a national sample of 5,386 children of pre-school age gives no reason for believing that the children of employed women are in any way at a disadvantage'.[1] It is admitted, however, that to reach a final judgment, the children will have to be followed through to adolescence and tested more searchingly than has hitherto been possible. This the authors hope to be able to do.

The health and social problems of the married woman worker with young children are relatively simple compared with those of the unmarried mother or the married woman who has conceived and borne a child who is not her husband's.[2] Between 4 per cent and 5 per cent[3] of the children born each year are illegitimate, with all the disabilities and problems that illegitimacy entails, but this by no means represents the proportion of children conceived outside marriage. Approximately one in five women giving birth to their first baby have been married less than nine months, and these figures are higher in the younger age groups. The extent to which these pre-nuptial conceptions take place came to light with the passing of the Population (Statistics) Act, 1938, and it has been suggested that the large increase in the number of illegitimate births which took place during the war years was due not so much to any loosening of moral restraints, though it is recognised that this did occur, as to the fact that wartime circumstances prevented or hindered the regularisation of irregularly conceived maternities.[4]

---

[1] J. W. B. Douglas and J. M. Bloomfield, 'Maternal Employment and the Welfare of Children: An Account of a Survey in Progress', *The Eugenics Review*, Vol. 149, No. 2, July 1957, p. 71. Cf. *Children under Five*, ch. xvi.

[2] I am indebted to Miss E. M. Steel, Organising Secretary, Church of England Moral Welfare Council, for help, advice and information in connection with this portion of the chapter, but she has no responsibility for the opinions expressed.

[3] The average for the five years 1951–5 was 4·8 per cent. Cf. 5·5 per cent from 1946–50, 6·2 per cent for the war period, 1939–45, and 4·2 per cent for 1935–8.

[4] S. Ferguson and H. Fitzgerald, *Studies in the Social Services*, History of the Second World War, U.K. Civil Series, pp. 90–1. In 1938 the percentage of extra-maritally conceived maternities legitimated by the parents before the birth of the child was 70·2, it dropped to 37·1 in 1945 and rose again to 61·5 in 1955. Registrar General's Statistical Review of England and Wales for the year 1955, Part III, Table IX.

Among mothers under the age of twenty-five, the annual percentage of irregularly conceived maternities was less than in 1938–9; for whatever reason it was among the older women that the rise took place.[1] Since the war the obstacles to marriage for which the war situation was responsible have been removed and the illegitimacy rate has dropped again, but such information as is available suggests that 'pre-nuptial conception cannot be regarded as abnormal', and pre-marital chastity may well be the exception rather than the rule.[2] It is in this setting that the question as to whether, and how far, unmarried mothers can be considered as a homogeneous group presenting special social and psychological characteristics which mark them off from their fellows, must be considered.

One of the difficulties which confronts us when attempting to answer this question is the paucity of the available information. 'Most of the vital pieces of this jig-saw puzzle are missing and only a very few of the available pieces fit together.'[3] For example, much of the information available refers to women who have asked for help from a social work agency, and thus may not be typical of the group as a whole.[4] This is one of the questions which confronts us when considering the significance of the conclusions reached by Dr. Leontine Young, Professor in Casework, School of Social Administration, Ohio State University.[5] Dr. Young's findings are based on the author's own experience with about 350 unmarried mothers and approximately 1,000 further cases from the case material, observations and contributed knowledge of a large number of social workers in American public and private agencies. As the result of her study, Dr. Young could discover no marked economic, social or cultural homogeneity among these girls, except that more of them came from groups showing other signs of social breakdown. There were wide variations in all these conditions. What did impress Dr. Young, however, was the preponderance of certain marked psychological characteristics. She suggests, therefore, that what these girls had in common was that they were all driven to have an out-of-wedlock baby, usually as

[1] Ibid., p. 93.

[2] Cyril Greenwood, 'Unmarried Parenthood: Ecological Aspects', *The Lancet*, 19 January 1957, p. 148.

[3] Ibid., p. 151.

[4] Ibid., pp. 149–50. It is suggested, for example, that the general impression that the unmarried mother is usually younger than her married sister derives from this fact, as it is the younger girls who are most likely to seek help. In fact, apart from mothers under twenty at the time of the birth of the child, one in five of whom is unmarried, and the 25–29 age group, the age distribution of maternities is almost the same for legitimate and illegitimate births.

[5] Leontine Young, *Out of Wedlock*, A Study of the Problems of the Unmarried Mother and her Child.

the result of a short-term casual contact with the father, by an unconscious urge, and this in turn derived from the girl's relations with her parents. The most important factor in this relationship was the domination of the home by one parent, usually the mother, and the majority of girls in the group studied came from homes so patterned, though there were others, for example, girls from broken homes. In most cases the girl's attitude to the dominating parent largely determined her attitude both to the child's father and to the child himself. In so far as the girls in this study are typical, it would appear that the unmarried mother is one who is psychologically sick, and the conception of the baby is an inevitable outcome of a neurosis which is derived from a particular life situation. If this is so, then plans to help the girl and give the child a proper start in life must be made on this assumption.

Dr. Young's conclusions, based on careful study of a particular group of cases, give us valuable insights into the problems and attitudes of many unmarried mothers. There are, however, others whose relationship with their partners appears to be basically different from the brief and apparently casual contacts characteristic of her group. For example, a survey made of 265 mothers in Leicester revealed that the great majority of the putative fathers, other than those living with the mother, were the girls' fiancés or friends; only 19 were casual acquaintances,[1] and the unmarried mothers in this survey may well have included girls who, like so many others, anticipated their wedding day, but in whose case marriage was postponed or cancelled, and girls who had fallen in love with married men and risked the consequences. There is also the quite large group of women who have formed stable partnerships with men, but for some reason the partnership has never been legalised.[2] These co-habitees have quite different characteristics and problems from those unmarried parents whose relationship is less permanent. While many of them present 'problem family' characteristics, others provide their children with a stable home life and good upbringing according to their lights. Although there may be a sense of guilt and fear of discovery in the background which may make the children feel that there is something wrong with the home, it seems that many such families lead 'stable and happy lives'.[3] They may need the help of social workers

[1] C. K. Macdonald, 'Follow up of Illegitimate Children', *The Medical Officer*, 14 December 1956, p. 361.

[2] Greenland, op. cit., p. 150, suggests that, 'it seems reasonable to assume that about one in every three illegitimate births are to women, probably in the older age groups, cohabiting in a more or less permanent relationship'.

[3] This was the conclusion reached as a result of the Newcastle 'Thousand Families' survey. James Spence et al., *A Thousand Families in Newcastle-upon-Tyne*, p. 144.

for various reasons, but it is not primarily for them that social work specifically for unmarried mothers and their children has been developed. Rather is it for those girls and women who must face pregnancy and motherhood without a permanent partner and who are often friendless and alone.

Society's attitude towards the unmarried mother and her child has changed considerably since Victorian days when she was usually regarded as an outcast whose very existence a respectable women was expected to ignore. In such an atmosphere even those who tried to help were often subject to misunderstanding and criticised as condoning immorality, but, inspired by Christian teaching and charity, many women braved public opinion and went to the rescue of their 'fallen' sisters. Their outlook and methods may seem alien to the present generation of social workers, but they laid the foundations on which these have built, and their direct descendants, the moral welfare workers of to-day, play an important part in the social rehabilitation and community care of those in difficulties resulting from irregular sexual relationships.

The National Council for the Unmarried Mother and her Child, an important co-ordinating and propaganda body which has done much to further the reform of legislation affecting unmarried mothers and illegitimate children has had rather a different history. This Council was brought into being in 1918 as a result of the concern aroused when the Registrar General drew attention to the fact that the infant mortality rate among illegitimate children was twice as high as among those born in wedlock. The gap between the two rates has persisted, although it has narrowed with the passing of the years,[1] and it was the existence of this gap, together with the increase in the proportion of illegitimate births during the Second World War which led the Ministry of Health to intervene in 1943. In that year the Ministry issued a circular to local authorities[2] urging them to make special provisions for the care of unmarried mothers and their children. Local authorities responsible for the maternity and child welfare were encouraged to co-operate with and reinforce the work of voluntary moral welfare associations, and to formulate schemes for the purpose. The Ministry considered that in order to further the working of such a scheme a trained worker, experienced in the special problems she

[1] Infant Mortality Rates: Legitimate and Illegitimate Children.

	Legitimate	Illegitimate
1939	49	90
1943	48	71
1955	25	32
1958	22·3	27·8

[2] Circular 2866, *The Care of Illegitimate Children.*

would have to handle, should be appointed wherever possible. Her duties would include co-operation with voluntary associations in advising and assisting the girl with her social and legal problems, finding accommodation for her and the child, and in special cases giving advice about legal adoption.

The response of the local authorities to this circular, and the ways in which co-operation between the authority and the voluntary moral welfare association has been established, have varied from one area to another. In 1955 six county councils and nine county boroughs were using their own social workers, but in the majority of cases this did not preclude grant aid towards the moral welfare work in their areas. Voluntary social work agencies are grant aided in all except six of the county areas and most of the county boroughs where the work is carried on. The value of this co-operation is considerable, but, of course, these are not the only agencies involved. The girl may require financial help from the National Assistance Board; if her need for accommodation is desperate she may be driven to seek it from the social welfare authority; the children's department may become involved in the placement or adoption of the child. Close co-operation between all these agencies is essential if the needs of both mother and child are to be met.

The problems which face the single pregnant women are likely to be multiple—psychological, economic, social and legal. Sooner or later she must tell her parents, and their response to the situation, whether it be by understanding and support, by indifference or by hostility and rejection, may make all the difference to the nature of the problems she will have to face, and how far she is able to tackle them. Her relationship with the putative father must be defined, arrangements made for the confinement, and above all, there is the future of the child to be considered. To help her deal satisfactorily with these problems she needs the support of a wise and understanding friend, who will accept her as a person and help her to plan constructively for herself and her child.[1] This is the role of the social caseworker, whether she be employed by moral welfare association or local authority. In assuming this role the worker employed by a voluntary organisation feels herself freer than does, perhaps, the one attached to a local authority health and welfare department, to take account of the ethical implications of the situation, as well as to deal with the medical and social problems arising from it as they affect both the father and mother of the

---

[1] L. Young, op. cit., p. 170, 'Regardless of her immediate circumstances, every unmarried mother has a vital need for protection and acceptance as a person. When a girl reaches a social agency, her first need is plainly and simply for a good friend.'

child and their families.[1] In either case the important thing is the establishment of a real relationship with the people concerned, for only within such a relationship can the many problems to be faced and decisions to be made be freely discussed. The hardest of these decisions may well be that of the future of the child.

In considering the important question of the future of the child the position and attitude of the putative father and the girl's relationship with him must be taken into account. It is generally recognised that, even if there is no legal bar, marriage is in itself no real solution to the problem unless it is entered into willingly, and not merely because there is a child on the way, for in the latter case it may result in lasting unhappiness to father, mother and child. A number of girls do marry the putative father, whether from choice or social pressure, while others marry another man who is prepared to accept the baby. Sometimes these arrangements do not turn out well, and cause strain and unhappiness, particularly to the child, in others the union proves to be a stable and happy one. A child born out of wedlock whose parents subsequently marry each other may be made legitimate under the terms of the Legitimacy Acts, 1926 and 1959.[2]

In English law the mother is the sole guardian of the illegitimate child, but she may apply to the magistrates' court for an affiliation order, an order which, if granted, will impose a legal liability on the putative father to make weekly contributions to the child's maintenance. Very few unmarried mothers attempt to obtain such orders, however. Corroborative evidence may be hard to obtain, the girl may dread the court appearance and the inevitable questioning, which may have to be very detailed to ensure that justice is done to both parties, or pride may prevent her from seeking redress. Even if an order is obtained it may be difficult to enforce and it is all too easy for the father to evade his responsibilities and leave the girl to carry her burden alone. In Scandinavian countries, on the other hand, the State takes over the duty of establishing paternity and fixing maintenance on the grounds that every child must have a legal as well as a biological father and society has the right to know the fatherhood as well as the mother-

---

[1] At present about 300 outdoor moral welfare workers are employed by organisations affiliated to the Church of England Moral Welfare Council, besides those working in connection with other denominations. A survey made in 1954 showed that apart from eleven dioceses which had failed to make returns, 16,011 illegitimate children were being helped. The Roman Catholic Church and the Salvation Army also undertake a considerable amount of work of this kind.

[2] Under the 1926 Act legitimation was only possible if there were no bar to marriage at the time of the child's birth. This limitation was removed by the 1959 Act.

hood of every child.[1] In addition, the local child welfare committee appoints a welfare guardian for each child, as well as for the children of widows and deserted wives should this be desired. It is the duty of this person, who is often a social worker, to protect and help both mother and child in every possible way. The whole of this legislation is based on the right of the child to the utmost protection and help which society can give.

The crucial issue for a woman with an illegitimate child and no immediate prospect of marriage is whether she will accept continuing responsibility for the child or whether she will surrender him for adoption. Such statistics as are available (which, as already pointed out, mostly relate to mothers who are or have been in contact with social work agencies, that is, in general, to young, single girls having their first illegitimate baby) indicate that only a few such mothers surrender their children for adoption immediately after the birth, although others may do so later.[2] As already mentioned, many young mothers of illegitimate children subsequently marry, and for those who remain single the attitude of the parents is all important. In a large number of cases the girl is able to take the child home to become a member of the family, and the impression left as the result of one survey was that, 'in general, and particularly among the classes in which an illegitimate birth is most likely to occur, we get a picture of tolerance and charity towards both mother and child'.[3] Taking the child home may

---

[1] A more detailed comparison of English and Scandinavian attitudes towards the illegitimate child and the provisions made for him may be found in an article by I. Pinchbeck, 'Social Attitudes to the Problem of Illegitimacy', *British Journal of Sociology*, Vol. V, 1954, pp. 309–22. The Scandinavian provisions are commended in L. Young, op. cit., pp. 124–6. Where there is some doubt as to which of two or three men may be the father, all names are registered, a situation which may harm rather than help the child.

[2] A survey made by the Church of England Moral Welfare Council of the cases helped in 1952 showed that at the end of the year 15·1 per cent of the children had been adopted compared with 38·3 per cent actually in the mother's care and 9·1 per cent in which the mother remained responsible for and had access to the child. *Moral Welfare*, January 1954, pp. 12–18. A follow-up survey made three years later of those cases where the child was not adopted in the first year revealed three subsequent adoptions, but it is suggested that in cases where the mother had a second illegitimate child the second child was adopted, the child in the survey remaining in care of the mother. *Moral Welfare*, January 1957, pp. 14–15. Cf. the placement of the 67 illegitimate children born in Newcastle-on-Tyne in May and June 1947. Nine were received for adoption within a few weeks of birth, three taken from the homes of the maternal grandmother later in the year. Spence, et al., op. cit., p. 144.

[3] Spence et al., op. cit., p. 145. In 17 out of 67 Newcastle cases, the child entered the mother's family. In the Leicester sample, 15 out of the 22 mothers who were single at the child's conception, and who five years later were neither married nor cohabiting and had kept the child, were living with his grandparents. E. K. Macdonald, op. cit., p. 362.

prove an acceptable solution and give the child a stable and secure background, but this is not always the case. Many unmarried mothers come from unhappy and insecure homes and the situation, either physical or psychological, is not likely to be improved by the addition of a child whose presence may result in rivalry or resentment between mother and daughter. In families with high social standards and sensitive to neighbours' opinions and criticisms, the child's relationship with his mother may be concealed, a deception which in the long run may be disastrous, particularly for the child, who is bound to discover the truth sooner or later, and is likely to be profoundly disturbed by his discovery.

Unmarried mothers wishing to keep their children, yet unable to return home with them, are faced with considerable difficulties, as they have to find both work which will enable their support of the child and accommodation in which they can keep him with them, and, if not helped, may easily drift from one unsatisfactory situation or room to another, giving the child an unstable background and poor start in life, and themselves running the risk of further promiscuous relationships. In all, 'an illegitimate infant runs a far greater risk than a legitimate infant of living in a home where the maternal capacity, the family stability and the physical environment and housing conditions are all variable. These, no doubt, are the reasons why illegitimate infants face greater hazards than other children'.[1]

Residential care specifically for unmarried mothers and their children is provided by some local authorities and also by voluntary organisations.[2] It consists of both maternity homes to which the mother can come beforehand and remain for the confinement (a boon for the very young unmarried mother), and afterwards; and mother and baby homes where the mother can stay before and after birth, but not for the confinement itself. If the home is run by a wise and understanding superintendent the girl will not only receive the physical care she needs, but also training in child care and guidance as to her future and that of the child. In this the superintendent of the home will work in close co-operation with the outdoor worker and other social workers concerned with the case. For the sake of both mother and child this co-operation is vitally necessary.

Should it be impossible, or for any reason undesirable, for the mother to retain the responsibility for the child's care and maintenance, adoption is the alternative usually envisaged, and the

[1] Spence et al., op. cit., p. 145.
[2] In 1956 the local authorities provided 27 such homes with 397 beds, voluntary homes known to the Ministry of Health numbered 107 with 1,666 beds.

Curtis Committee considered that 'if successful it is the most completely satisfactory method of providing a substitute home'.[1] But, since it involves the complete surrender of all parental rights, and their assumption by the adoptive parents, it calls for careful thought on the part of all concerned, and strict legal safeguards to protect the interests of the child.

Legal adoption was first made possible by the Adoption Act, 1926. The law governing it was strengthened by the Adoption of Children (Regulations) Act, 1939, and by the Adoption of Children Act, 1949. This legislation was consolidated by the Adoption Act, 1950, but this was modified by the Children Act, 1958, which embodied many recommendations of a committee set up under the chairmanship of Sir Gerald Hurst to consider what changes were desirable in the interests of the welfare of children.[2] A further consolidating Act, the Adoption Act, 1958, repealed earlier statutes and is now the governing Act.

Application for an adoption order may be made either to the High Court, a county court or a juvenile court, but the vast majority of cases are heard in the juvenile courts. Procedure in all courts is governed by the Act mentioned above, and its attendant regulations, and has been carefully devised to safeguard the interests of all three parties concerned—the child, the natural parents, and the adopters. The two last can speak for themselves, but the child is in all cases relatively, and some cases completely, helpless and inarticulate, so the court is bound to appoint a *guardian ad litem*, who, 'with a view to safeguarding the interests of the infant before the court', shall, 'so far as it is reasonably practicable', investigate all circumstances relevant to the proposed adoption and make a confidential report to the court in writing.

As has already been pointed out, the effect of an adoption order is that all the rights, duties, obligations and liabilities of the natural parents are extinguished, and vested instead in the adopter, 'as if the infant were a child born to the adopter in lawful wedlock'.[5] Hence before an order is made, the court must be wholly satisfied both that the adopters are suitable persons to take over the custody of the child, and fully understand the nature and extent of the responsibilities they are assuming, and that the natural parents or

---

[1] Report of the Care of Children Committee, Cmd. 6922, 1946, par. 448, p. 148.

[2] The Committee reported in September 1954. Cmd. 9248.

[3] The word 'infant' here and throughout this discussion is given the legal connotation it is given in the Adoption Act, 1950. It means a person under twenty-one years of age, but does not include a person who is, or has been, married.

[4] Magistrates' Courts Adoption (Juvenile Court) Rules, 1959. S.I. 1959, No. 504 (L5), par. 8. [5] Adoption Act, 1950, Section 10 (1).

guardians have ample time to consider the consequences of their decision to surrender the child.

An applicant for an adoption order who is not related in any way to the infant he or she is proposing to adopt must have attained the age of twenty-five; when two spouses are adopting jointly it is sufficient if one of them has reached this age and the other is over the age of twenty-one. A relative may adopt if he or she has reached the age of twenty-one, and no minimum age is laid down in cases where a parent is adopting his or her own child.[1] All applications must be carefully investigated by the *guardian ad litem* and it is important that the motives, attitudes and relationships of the prospective adopters should be taken into account as well as material conditions, such as the financial circumstances of the adopters and the comfort and cleanliness of the home. It is now specifically stated[2] that in determining whether an adoption order if made will be for the welfare of the child, the court must have regard (among other things) to the health of the applicant, as evidenced in such cases as may be prescribed by a medical certificate.

Although, in the last resort, a great deal depends on the knowledge and insight of the *guardian ad litem*, the relevant legislation goes a long way towards ensuring that only those who really want to bring up another person's child as their own and who are competent to undertake this delicate and difficult task will be given the opportunity of doing so. Care is also taken to see that the adoption order is not made without the full knowledge and considered consent of those who are surrendering the child. An adoption order cannot be made without the consent of the parent or guardian except under special circumstances, such as that the person concerned has abandoned, neglected or persistently ill-treated the infant, that he or she cannot be found, is incapable of giving consent or is unreasonably withholding it or, whether or not satisfied of any of these matters, the court is satisfied that he or she has 'persistently failed without reasonable cause to discharge the obligations of a parent or guardian of the infant'.[3] Where the child is of sufficient age and understanding the court must give due

---

[1] Adoption Act, 1958, S.2. Before the passing of the Legitimacy Act, 1959, parents of an illegitimate child might adopt him after marriage because they could not legitimise him as there was a bar to their marriage at the time of his birth. The mother may marry a man other than the father who is willing to make the child a full member of his family and the spouses may then adopt him jointly. Single mothers sometimes adopt their own children in order to substitute the status of an adopted for that of an illegitimate child. This is not uncommon when a child who has been kept by his mother reaches school age.

[2] Adoption Act, 1958, Section 7 (2).

[3] Ibid., Section 5.

consideration to his wishes in the matter, and it is one of the duties of the *guardian ad litem* in this connection to ascertain as soon as reasonably practicable whether the infant is able to understand the nature of an adoption order. If so he must inform the court of his opinion and ascertain whether the infant wishes to be adopted by the applicant.[1]

Some of the most important additional safeguards introduced into the Adoption Acts of 1949 and 1950 were designed specifically to lessen the possibility of a mother agreeing too readily to the adoption of her child, but afterwards regretting it, and 'snatching back' the infant from the care of the adopters while the proceedings were still going on. Thus, in order that the mother may have time to recover from the physical and psychological strains of childbirth before making so important a decision, her consent is not valid if given before the child is six weeks old.[2] Furthermore, an order cannot be made until the infant has been continuously in the care of the applicant for at least three months, and in calculating this length of time no account is taken of any period during which the child, although already in the care of the prospective adopters, is less than six weeks old. This period gives both adopter and natural parent a chance to discover what adoption will mean. The mother may recover her child, and proceedings be brought to an end during this trial period, but only with the consent of the court, and in considering whether to give or withhold consent, the court must have regard to the welfare of the child.[3] As an additional safeguard for the child during this probationary period the applicant must inform the local authority children's department when he takes the child into his care with a view to adoption, unless the child is over compulsory school age or one of the applicants is his parent.[4] This should mean that a trained and experienced social worker will then be in touch with the case, who will be able to help both the child and his prospective parents over their initial difficulties, and judge if he is likely to settle happily and be well cared for in his new home.

Adoptions may be arranged by the parties directly concerned, or through the medium of a third person or organisation. It was to regulate these 'third party' adoptions that the Adoption of Children (Regulations) Act, 1939, was passed, and its main provisions were subsequently incorporated in the Adoption Act, 1950. Now these matters are dealt with in Parts II and IV of the Adoption Act, 1958. These provisions prohibit any body of persons other than a local authority or a society registered as an adoption

[1] Adoption (Juvenile Court) Rules, 1959, Second Schedule, par. 3.
[2] Adoption Act, 1958, Section 6 (2).
[3] Ibid., Section 34.   [4] Ibid., Section 3.

society by the county council or county borough council within whose area its administrative headquarters are situated, from making arrangements for adoptions, while private persons who assist in any way in the placing of children must notify the appropriate local authority. Only associations recognised by law as 'charitable' may register as adoption societies, and in addition they must show that their affairs are properly managed by a responsible committee, which employs a sufficient number of 'fit and proper' persons to make arrangements for the adoption of children on the society's behalf.[1] Regulations passed in 1943 and amended in 1950[2] prescribe the information which must be given to a parent or guardian who is proposing to place a child with the society for adoption, the information to be obtained in connection with the placing, and the arrangements to be made for the supervision of the children who are in the care of the society pending adoption.

The position in those cases where a private individual acts as intermediary, or the mother makes a direct placement, a position which the Hurst Committee regarded as unsatisfactory,[3] has been improved by the Children Act, 1958, and the Adoption Act, 1958. These Acts replace the existing 'child life protection' provisions affecting the position of children received for reward, and define a new category of 'protected' children, making provision for their supervision. 'Protected' children are children placed with a person other than a parent or guardian or relative and in whose case another person takes part in the arrangement, together with those in the care of persons who have given notice that they intend to apply for an adoption order. In the former cases the intermediaries must give notice in writing to the local authority for the area in which the persons taking the child live not less than two weeks before the child is placed, except in an emergency, when notice may be given up to one week after he is so placed. It is the duty of the local authority to secure that their officers visit 'protected' children in their area from time to time and both satisfy themselves as to the well-being of the children and give such advice as to their care and maintenance as may be needed.[4]

Since except in a minority of 'interim' orders there is no supervision when once an adoption order has been made, contacts can only be maintained on a voluntary basis, and in considering whether or not to maintain such contacts regard must clearly be

[1] Adoption Act, 1958, Section 30.
[2] The Adoption Societies Regulations, 1943 (S.R. & O. 1943, No. 1306). The 1950 Regulations amended Schedule II.
[3] Report of the Departmental Committee on the Adoption of Children, Cmd. 9248, pars. 43–51 and 63.
[4] Adoption Act, 1958, Section 40.

had to the possibility of endangering the emotional security of either child or parent. This is one of the difficulties which arises in connection with proposals to undertake research into the results of adoption, but the Hurst Committee were assured that such research could be undertaken without any ill-effects and were quite definite that it was needed. They said that they were convinced that 'the way to further improvements in practice is through more study of the effects of adoption', and in view of its popularity and finality the need is urgent.[1] Nevertheless, the Committee felt able to record an opinion that, 'in spite of various shortcomings in law and administration and of the fallibility of human judgment, the general result of legalised adoption has been to increase unmeasurably the happiness and well-being of probably over a million members of the community',[2] and it is a view that appears to be widely endorsed.

In considering the long-term effects of adoption we are moving away from the welfare of the young child, for such effects may not manifest themselves until late childhood or adolescence, and in this chapter we have also moved from provisions concerned almost solely with health care to those whose implementation involves dealing with difficult problems of conduct and relationship. Through it all the mother-child relationship and the mother's activities and attitudes have manifested themselves as, in the long run, the determining factors in the welfare of the child. 'Maternal capacity emerged as the chief single factor in the welfare of infants', wrote Dr. Spence and his colleagues in summarising their conclusions about the thousand families in Newcastle-on-Tyne,[3] and it is the objective of the social services for mothers and young children to encourage mothers to develop this capacity, to educate and guide them where it is misdirected or lacking, and to support them if they cannot exercise it without some support. In certain circumstances alternative care may have to be arranged, as when a mother surrenders her child for adoption, but for the most part the services are based on the assumption that 'the primary responsibility for child care will remain with the parents, and that professional institutions will do nothing to diminish that responsibility but will act as aids to parents in what is one of the most necessary and satisfying of all human activities'.[4]

[1] The National Association for Mental Health has since published a study, *A Survey based on Adoption Case Records*, which contains interesting and relevant material.
[2] Op. cit., par. 23, p. 6.   [3] Op. cit., p. 168.   [4] Ibid., p. 176.

CHAPTER XII

THE HEALTH AND WELFARE OF THE SCHOOL CHILD

AT the age of two, if he is one of the fortunate few for whom there are places in nursery schools, at the age of five otherwise, the child passes into the care of the local education authority of the area in which he lives. Henceforth, until the end of the term following his fifteenth birthday at the earliest, the authority will not only see that he is educated according to his age, aptitude and ability, it will also provide midday dinners and midmorning milk for him, it will give him medical examinations, see that he obtains the medical or dental treatment that he requires, arrange special educational treatment should he be physically or mentally handicapped, encourage him to join a youth organisation should this be considered desirable, and finally advise him as to choice of employment. 'One of the features of British education which nationals of other countries usually find some difficulty in understanding is how the public service of education cheerfully accepts responsibility for, and carries so many welfare services, and the extent to which it concerns itself with the whole life of the child and the interaction between home and school.'[1]

This wider conception of education was born with difficulty and grew slowly, however, and the pioneers of school feeding and school medical inspection and treatment, often the teachers and inspectors who knew from first-hand experience how great was the need, had a hard struggle to convince both legislators and the public generally that, in accepting responsibility for the education of its children, the nation had, whether wittingly or not, accepted responsibility for their health and general well-being, since the effective discharge of one responsibility was impossible without undertaking the other. Further, these pioneers had not only to contend with the passive resistance of the indifferent, but also with the active opposition of those who regarded any material help given by the State, unless safeguarded by a deterrent Poor Law, as a threat to family solidarity and responsibility.

The first major victory for the reformers was the Education (Provision of Meals) Act, 1906, which empowered local education

---

[1] G. A. N. Lowndes, *The British Educational System*, p. 119.

authorities to provide milk and meals to elementary school children who were 'unable by reason of lack of food to take full advantage of the education provided for them'. Modest as its provisions were, this Act established two important precedents. In the first place, it is the earliest example of relief from public funds being given to a specific section of the population by an agency other than the Poor Law, and hence it marks the beginning of the break up of that formidable structure, and is the forerunner of the social assistance services of the twentieth century.[1] Secondly, it established the principle that education extends beyond instruction to social care, even if in order to do this it had to state specifically that the social care provided was not an end in itself, but a means to enable the child to take full advantage of the formal education for which the public was paying rates and taxes.[2]

The Act was then important, but it had its limitations. Both it and its successor, passed in August 1914, which made it possible for the Board of Education to make grants in respect of school meals, were permissive, and by 1939 only 151 of the 316 local education authorities in the country were providing solid meals, and 41 authorities did not even provide milk. Meals were limited to children unable otherwise to take advantage of the education provided, and could only be given free when the parents could not afford to pay for them. Hence, strictly speaking, if a child were to receive a free dinner, he had to show both that he was undernourished and that his parents were too poor to feed him properly. The establishment of the school medical service in 1908 provided the machinery by which children could be selected for meals on grounds of malnutrition, but in fact the assessment of nutrition proved a difficult and unsatisfactory business.[3] As time went on some local education authorities dispensed with the medical test altogether and based their selection on family income and needs

---

[1] Notice that it was relief in kind that was given. Non-contributory old age pensions, the first statutory cash grants apart from the Poor Law, were introduced two years later by the Old Age Pensions Act, 1908.

[2] Cf. F. le Gros Clark, *Social History of the School Meals Service*, National Council of Social Service, 1948, p. 9. 'It [i.e. the Education (Provision of Meals) Act] removed the feeding of the children from the shadow of the relieving officer, at all events in intention, and it established the principle that the provision was part of the educational process of the child's life.' This booklet gives an interesting account of the history of the service from its inception to the coming into force of the Education Act, 1944, in April 1945, and forms the basis of a good deal of this and the following paragraph.

[3] Cf. Ministry of Education, *The Health of the School Child*, Report of the Chief Medical Officer of the Ministry of Education for the years 1946 and 1947, pp. 11–13; R. Huws Jones, 'Physical Indices and Clinical Assessments of the Nutrition of Schoolchildren', *Journal of the Royal Statistical Society*, Vol. CL, 1938.

alone, arguing that if a child came from a home where there was acute poverty, malnutrition was almost inevitable, and preventive measures should be taken before the clinical symptoms became apparent.[1] Between 1920 and 1930 the Board of Education acquiesced in this policy, and allowed that a child might be selected for free meals either because of poverty or because of malnutrition; but this was challenged by the May Committee in the economic crises of 1931, and henceforth administrators at the Board were forced to insist that a child could not receive a meal at less than the cost of the food unless he was both necessitous and showed clinical symptoms of undernourishment.

Except in those areas where married women's work was common very few families who could afford to contribute to the cost of the meals took advantage of the service, and in general the acceptance of school meals was regarded as an admission of inability to feed one's child, and hence as something to be avoided at all costs by the self-respecting, many of whom refused to allow their children to partake of dinners although they were entitled to do so. Moreover, in some areas, the quality of the food provided, the standards of cooking, and the conditions under which it was served were unsatisfactory, and this further accentuated the association of the service with poverty and degradation. On the other hand the more enlightened authorities were endeavouring with some success to make the school meals an opportunity for social training and the inculcation of healthier food habits.

In 1934 the Milk Act made it possible for school children to obtain a third of a pint of milk per day for a halfpenny, (free in necessitous cases), and on the eve of the last war about half the children in the country were benefiting from this provision.

The economic and social repercussions of the six years of war brought about developments which completely changed the character and scope of the school meals service.[2] The demand for married women workers in the factories meant that midday meals must be provided for the school children, just as it necessitated the provision of nurseries for their younger brothers and sisters. Moreover, the maintenance of a high level of nutrition amongst the children of the nation, whatever the hardships or deprivations suffered by adults, was a major objective of the government's food policy, and school meals were regarded as a form of differential rationing directed towards this end. Hence in 1940 the Board of Education

---

[1] See also P.E.P., 'Child Health and Nutrition', *Planning*, No. 248, 18 April 1946.

[2] These are described in detail in *The Health of the School Child during Six Years of War*, Report of the Chief Medical Officer of the Ministry of Education, 1939–45.

issued a circular recommending the establishment of communal feeding arrangements, whether free of charge or for payment, for children whose needs were not fully met by the normal provision of food in their own homes,[1] and during the succeeding years efforts were made to extend the service and free it from its old association with poverty and the means test. The 'feeding centre' was gradually transformed into the 'school canteen', and by February 1944 32·8 per cent of the number of pupils present were having dinners, a total of which may be compared with the 4·4 per cent of the public elementary school children receiving dinners in 1938-9.

The Education Act, 1944, and its attendant regulations[2] set the seal on this new conception of the school meals service, by making it a duty of the local education authority to provide milk, meals, and other refreshment for day pupils in attendance at schools and county colleges maintained by them, but, owing to the material and financial shortages of the post-war years, the promised land of free school meals for all children who wish to take advantage of them is still distant.[3] By October 1948 nearly 2,750,000 or 56·6 per cent of the total number of pupils in grant-aided schools were partaking of meals, while during the same year 88 per cent took advantage of the milk in schools scheme.

Started primarily as a means of ensuring that undernourished children from needy families should obtain at least one good meal a day,[4] the aims of the school meals service have broadened to include the provision of opportunities for social training and the inculcation of good food habits, but, if anything worth while is to be done to further these ends, school meals should be properly supervised, served in an orderly manner, preferably with the help of the children themselves, and eaten without haste in a happy atmosphere amid pleasant surroundings. These conditions are not easy to attain, however, and, particularly in the years immediately after the war, shortages of premises, staff and equipment meant that many children ate their dinners in makeshift premises and overcrowded conditions. Efforts have been and are being made to overcome difficulties where they exist, but a sample

[1] Board of Education Circular 1520, July 1940.
[2] Education Act, 1944, Section 49; S.R. and O. 1945, No. 698 and Circulars 34/45, 96/46 and 119/46.
[3] Free meals and milk were promised as a supplement to family allowances when these were introduced, and were taken into account when fixing the rate of the allowance. See Chapter II above. Milk in schools was provided free after the introduction of the family allowances, but payments covering the cost of the food have still to be made for solid meals except in necessitous cases.
[4] 'Indeed, in its early days, "I'm not used to having a Sunday dinner every day" was a remark quite commonly heard in school.' Lowndes, op. cit., p. 131.

inquiry undertaken by the Ministry of Education as late as the second part of 1955 revealed 'a great diversity of conditions within the Service'. The Report concluded, however, that while 'It is inevitable, and perhaps desirable, that attention should be directed to the schools where conditions are badly in need of improvement and there is, therefore, some risk of exaggerating the extent of poor conditions, the results of the inquiry suggest that, despite the restrictions on the development of the Service over the past few years, most children attend schools where the meals arrangements are not open to serious criticism.'[1]

At the time of the inquiry about 48 per cent of the children in the sample were taking school dinners. The geographical situation of the school in relation to the children's homes was of paramount importance in determining whether the dining rate was high or low, and it was pointed out that 'The School Meals Service clearly meets a very real need in country districts, and in very many village schools the school dinner is almost a family affair which enjoys the wholehearted support of teachers, parents and children.'[2] Other circumstances which created a demand for meals were the mother's absence at work,[3] or other calls on her time, but the Ministry recognised that where there was an effective choice between dinner at home and dinner at school the quality of the meal and the character of the dining accommodation would certainly be among the deciding factors.[4] Few head teachers (39 out of 580) thought that many families found it difficult to pay the current charge of ninepence per head (less than half the full cost), though for a large family it might be a considerable item; on the other hand, it appeared to be the general view that most of the families paying ninepence per meal either could not or would not pay an amount covering the full economic cost. 3·8 per cent of the pupils in the sample were receiving free dinners.

One of the precipitating factors which led to the passing of the Education (Provision of Meals) Act was the Report of the Inter-Departmental Committee on Physical Deterioration which was published in 1904. The Committee found that 'on a general survey of the evidence, a large number of children habitually attend school ill-fed'.[5] By comparison, one of the indications of improved national well-being, particularly since the war, is that 'for the

[1] Ministry of Education, Report of an Inquiry into the Working of the School Meals Service, (1955–6), par. 24, p. 6.
[2] Ibid., par. 28, p. 7.
[3] This was quoted 371 times by the head teachers answering the inquiry, compared with 'journey from school too long or difficult' 384 times. The next most frequently quoted reason was 'it suits the mother's convenience', 242 times.
[4] Ibid., par. 29, p. 7.   [5] Cd. 2175, p. 71, par. 358.

overwhelming majority of children, under-nutrition is no longer a problem. Heights and weights continue to increase and there is evidence that children who are nowadays considered to be of poor condition are, in fact, heavier and taller than their predecessors of twenty-five to thirty years ago.'[1] These changes must be attributed to the general improvement in social conditions rather than to any specific welfare service, but the national policy of providing meals and milk for school children has undoubtedly played its part in this general improvement.

Legislative sanction for the medical inspection and treatment of school children soon followed the sanctioning of the meals service, and the initial action taken was even stronger, for, while the Education (Provision of Meals) Act empowered local education authorities to provide meals to necessitous school children, the Education (Administrative Provisions) Act of the following year compelled them to have the children in elementary schools medically examined at least three times during their school career. Unfortunately, the bogy of undermining parental responsibility and the fear of intruding into the sphere of the private doctor, prevented an equally strong line being taken with regard to the provision of facilities for treatment, and this remained optional for a number of years.

The need for medical examination and treatment had long been apparent to those who had eyes to see. Thus, Margaret McMillan, when she became a member of the Bradford School Board in 1894, was horrified by what she saw in the schools. 'Children in every stage of illness, children with adenoids, children with curvature, children in every stage of neglect and dirt and suffering.' The condition of the poorer children was worse than anything described or painted, 'the half timers slept exhausted at their desks, and from courts and alleys children attended school in all states of physical misery'.[2] The findings of the school doctors, when examinations were begun throughout the country twenty years later in 1908, confirmed these impressions. In Liverpool, for example, the early examinations revealed evidence of verminous infestation in over 80 per cent of the girls seen, while 40 per cent of boys and girls were dirty in body and clothing. Very few children appeared to have had any conservative care given to their teeth, and numerous untreated cases of deafness, running ears, defective vision and crippling conditions were discovered.[3] Liverpool's findings were paralleled in populous areas in other parts of the country and some local

[1] *The Health of the School Child*, Report of the Chief Medical Officer of the Ministry of Education for the years 1954 and 1955, p. 6.

[2] Margaret McMillan, *The Life of Rachel McMillan*, pp. 80 and 89.

[3] City of Liverpool, Report of the Education Committee for the municipal year 1947-8, pp. 102-3.

authorities, at least, realised the overriding necessity of providing treatment to deal with such conditions, and went ahead to appoint more school medical officers and establish clinics. Others, influenced by the same fear of pauperising the parents or of offending the practitioners which had precluded mandatory legislation, relied at first on children receiving treatment from their own doctors or through the out-patient departments of the hospitals. They were at length convinced by the long list of untreated cases in their books that action must be taken. Gradually school clinics were established throughout the country and the number and variety of defects treated increased.

The Education Act, 1944, made both medical supervision at appropriate intervals and the provision of free medical treatment for pupils in schools or colleges maintained by them statutory duties of local education authorities.[1] The School Health Service and the Handicapped Pupils Regulations, 1953, prescribed three such inspections unless the local authority obtained permission from the Minister for fewer than three, and a few authorities are limiting their routine inspections to entrants and leavers so that doctors can give more time to individual children who appear to need special attention. On the other hand, some local authorities arrange four, and a few have decided on five routine inspections.[2] These routine inspections are everywhere supplemented by re-inspections or special inspections if the doctor, teacher or anyone else in contact with the child considers it necessary, and the importance of these re-inspections and special inspections may be judged by the fact that in 1957 they numbered 1,109,160 and 924,387 respectively as compared with 2,112,623 routine inspections. In addition to medical inspections, dental and cleanliness inspections are held at intervals and dental treatment offered. The acute shortage of school dentists, which handicapped the service so badly in the years immediately following the war, has abated somewhat, and by the Dentists Act, 1956, ancillary workers, who would work under the close supervision of the dentist, could be used in connection with the service, but in some areas the staff is still insufficient to meet all demands for preventive work[3].

The school health service has a strong educational bias and from its inception it has been regarded as an educational activity, hence it has always been a responsibility of the Board (later the Ministry) of Education and the local education authorities rather than that of the Ministry of Health and local health authorities. The implementation of the National Health Service Act with its

[1] Education Act, 1944, Section 48.

[2] *The Health of the School Child*, 1954 and 1955, p. 14; 1956 and 1957, Chapter VIII.

[3] *The Health of the School Child*, 1956 and 1957, p. 57.

promise of free medical care for all citizens, including school children, necessitated a review of the position, however, especially with regard to treatment, and the administrative arrangements now in force are the result of consultations between the Minister of Education and the Minister of Health. Following these discussions the Minister of Education issued a circular[1] in which it was pointed out that the work of medical inspection and the ascertainment of handicapped pupils was not affected by the establishment of the National Health Service, but consultative and specialist treatment, including out-patient treatment hitherto provided at the request of the local education authority and paid for by them, had now become part of the service provided by the regional hospital boards, and would not be chargeable either to the local education authority or to the patient. Local education authorities and regional hospital boards were encouraged to find the best means of working together on this basis.

Judging by the comments in the biennial reports issued by the Chief Medical Officer of the Ministry of Education since then,[2] there has been some local variation both in the ways in which the school health and the hospital services are supplementing each other and in the degree of co-operation achieved. In some cases the change has meant that the children have had to attend hospital out-patient departments instead of clinics held on local education authority premises, and fears have been expressed that this is detrimental to the child, especially if he has to wait long periods for treatment. This state of affairs is evidently not universal, however, for 'In many cases, regional hospital boards have made no suggestion that specialist clinics should be moved from local authority premises, and even where the transfer has taken place, there have been few complaints by principal school medical officers.'[3] Exchange of information has frequently been and continues to be a source of friction in some areas, but, looking at the situation as a whole, the Ministry evidently felt justified in stating in the *Report on the Health of the School Child* for the years 1954–5 that 'in most cases the link between school health and hospital services is becoming stronger',[4] and gives examples of ways in which this co-operation is being strengthened. Thus, in some areas hospitals appoint school doctors as clinical assistants or arrange for them, and sometimes also for health visitors and school nurses, to visit wards and out-patients' departments. Where introduced, such schemes seem to be working well.

[1] Circular 179, August 1948.
[2] *The Health of the School Child*, 1950 and 1951, 1952 and 1953, and 1954 and 1955.
[3] Ibid., Years 1952 and 1953, p. 117.   [4] Ibid., 1954 and 1955, p. 19.

THE HEALTH AND WELFARE OF THE SCHOOL CHILD

Just as they are entitled to benefit from the hospital and specialist services, so children can obtain free treatment from personal practitioners, but the Ministry considers that this has had little effect on the school health services. It has not noticeably affected clinic attendances. As with the hospital and specialist services, there have been difficulties, particularly with regard to the transfer of information and the furnishing of reports, but, by 1955, the Ministry could state, 'There is not the slightest doubt that co-operation between family and school doctors is increasing, even though there is still scope for improvement in some areas.'[1]

Important as it is to develop good co-operation between the school health service and the hospital and general practitioner services, it is even more important for the service to obtain the co-operation of the child's parents, particularly in cases where some form of treatment is required. Perhaps the most important agent in bringing about this co-operation is the school nurse, or school health visitor, as she is now more appropriately termed, for her duties are more akin to those of the general health visitor than to those of a nurse, and she is now expected to have obtained health visitor training in addition to her nursing qualification.[2] In addition to this home visiting, which is recognised by the Ministry as 'the most important duty of the school nurse',[3] she undertakes various other duties including preparation of children for medical examination, attendance at clinic sessions with the school doctor, cleanliness inspections, visits to nursery schools, and health education, particularly with senior girls. It has been suggested from time to time,[4] that some, at any rate, of this work might be undertaken by less highly trained personnel, leaving the nurse with health visitor training to concentrate on educational and advisory work. In reviewing the work in connection with the schools, the Working Party on Health Visiting goes so far as to suggest that 'It may well be true that in some areas what is wanted at the present time is not more qualified health visitors but more staff with lesser qualifications . . . it is apparent that health visitors are frequently employed on work that offers little or no opportunity for either health education or social advice, and that

[1] Ibid., 1954 and 1955, p. 17.
[2] Cf. Ministry of Health, *An Inquiry into Health Visiting*, par. 297, p. 105. 'Although a large number of parents attend when their children are medically examined and can then consult the doctor and health visitor, we think a closer link with the home will often be as essential to the care of school children as to the care of mothers and children. The home visit is the essential link and the qualified health visitor the right person to make it; in most cases the link is weak and should be strengthened.'
[3] *The Health of the School Child*, 1950 and 1951, p. 34.
[4] Ibid., p. 30.

others could do as well.'[1] In some areas assistants of the kind suggested are already employed, and give the health visitor the opportunity of extending her work in other directions. The Ministry hopes that this will include not only the care of handicapped children, but a share in the task of preventing family breakdown and childhood maladjustment.[2]

As is the case with the health visitor employed in connection with the maternity and child welfare services, so with the school health visitor, the emphasis is shifting from the individual child to the family of which he is a member. This being so, it would seem logical to combine the duties of school nurse and maternity and child welfare visitor, and this was recognised in the Chief Medical Officer's Report for the years 1951 and 1952. 'For many years to come,' he wrote, 'there will still be nurses engaged whole-time on the school health service, but, as time passes the number of nurses working at the same time in other local authority health services will increase. The future is with the family health visitor'.[3] This view is endorsed by the Working Party on Health Visiting which emphasises the need for continuity in the relationship between the mother and the health visitor, a continuity which will be broken when the child makes the critical transition from home to school, should the school health visiting be a separate service. There is also the possibility of overlapping if the family includes children of both school age and under, and the services remain separate. Where there is this separation the closest co-operation between the school health visitors and the health visitors employed by the local authority under the National Health Service Act for child welfare work is clearly essential.

While throughout the greater part of the country the responsibility of following up medical inspections and making home visits in connection with treatment rest with the school nurse, who is the recognised link between the school health service and the home, the London County Council has also a 'care committee' attached to each school or group of schools. Each committee consists of a group of voluntary helpers working under the guidance of a trained social worker who is employed by the Council. The scheme is thus interesting and significant not only as an experiment in a particular form of child care, but as 'an attempt to utilise the spirit of social service in the private citizen in a sphere in which full public responsibility has been accepted'.[4] It arose shortly after the inception of the school meals service and school medical inspection, as a means of maintaining effective contact with the

---

[1] Op. cit., p. 105, par. 297.
[2] '*The Health of the School Child*, 1954 and 1955, p. 137.   [3] Op. cit., p. 35.
[4] Hilda Jennings, *The Private Citizen in Public Social Work*, 1930, p. 19.

homes of children receiving meals or found at medical inspections to be in need of special care, and was designed in the first place to ensure that the children derived the maximum benefit from these publicly provided services. However, it is claimed that it has now become a form of social case work, centring on the school child, but through him impinging on the life of the family as a whole. In the true casework tradition the child is regarded not as an isolated individual, but as a member of a family whose total needs must be considered in relation to him,[1] and thus the outlook of the care committee organiser is social rather than medical, and the scheme more nearly approaches a general welfare service for children than anything in the provinces. At the same time it suffers from the difficulties and shortcomings apparently inseparable from reliance on voluntary workers, the most serious of which is a chronic shortage of suitable volunteers. 'There never has been a sufficiency of volunteers either in quantity or quality to make possible the adequate staffing of every school care committee in the London County Council area,' writes Dr. Eileen Younghusband.[2] Nevertheless she concludes that 'this method of linking school and home is a considerable advance on the usual system of entrusting the follow-up of school medical inspection to the school nurse and providing no general welfare service between school and home'.

Although this care committee system appears to have justified its existence in the London area, it has never established itself in the provinces, and over the country generally there is no recognised form of social service reaching out from the school to the family and dealing with family needs and problems as they affect the school child. There is a claimant for this position, however, namely the 'education welfare' or, as it used to be known, the 'school attendance' service.[3]

The introduction of compulsory education in the 1870's was far from popular, and local school boards soon found it necessary to use the powers that they had been given by the Elementary Education Act, 1870, to appoint special officers for the purpose of enforcing it. The job of these officers was to get the reluctant child to school, and it was rendered more difficult by the fact that not only were parents frequently indifferent or hostile, but farmers, land-

[1] Cf. 'Three Aspects of School Care Work, a Changing Emphasis', *Social Work*, Vol. III, No. 7, July 1945.
[2] *Report on the Employment and Training of Social Workers*, Carnegie U.K. Trust, 1946, p. 82.
[3] I am indebted to Miss Julia Dixon, M.A., for permission to read her unpublished thesis, 'School Attendance Officers: A Survey of their present Functions and of the Development of their Work', and to the Economics Research Section, Manchester University, for the loan of the same. Much of the information which follows has been obtained from this thesis.

owners and other employers who had been deprived of cheap labour by the Act, were reluctant to use their powers as magistrates to enforce it. The task of the school attendance officer was thus often a thankless one, his work was limited in scope and character, and the officers, who were drawn from a variety of occupations, were usually completely untrained. Most of them, however, became really concerned about the welfare of the children in their areas and their work carried them into the homes of the people, particularly those where the poorest and most neglected children were to be found, and thus they obtained a wide knowledge of social conditions and habits, more especially those of the inhabitants of the slum areas of the big cities. It was the information gained in this way that Charles Booth used in his 'poverty' surveys.

As time went on and compulsory education came to be accepted, the school attendance officers came more and more to regard their work as that of helping and encouraging parents who were experiencing genuine difficulties which prevented their children from attending school regularly, and of detecting and preventing neglect, and the value of their work in this connection was recognised in some quarters at least.[1] Nevertheless, despite the persistent attempts of the officers' association to push their claims, developments in the child care services have tended to pass the school attendance officer by so that 'education welfare' appears to be the Cinderella of both education and the social services. This situation is not acceptable to or accepted by the officers themselves, however, for they believe that the education welfare officer has an important and honourable part to play as 'the liaison officer between home, school and the local education authority and all those specialist activities which he will call in to deal with the problems arising in any one case'.[2] Such an undertaking demands that the officers must possess the skill to assess the family situation sympathetically, knowledgeably and intelligently, a good knowledge of the social services and their workings, and the ability to establish good co-operation with other workers, both statutory and voluntary. In this situation the education welfare officer is, and feels himself to be, handicapped by the lack of any recognised training and qualification, and the association has been pressing for this for some time. In this matter of training they are in a similar dilemma to that of 'welfare' workers in other departments, such as mental health workers who have not had psychiatric social work training, and although by their terms of reference the

---

[1] E.g. in the Minority Report of the Royal Commission in the Poor Laws, 1909.

[2] Memorandum submitted by the Education Welfare Officers' National Association to the Ministry of Health Working Party on the Recruitment and Training of Social Workers.

recommendations of the Younghusband Committee were directed towards the training of workers in health and welfare departments, their recommendations were such as to make some form of co-ordinated training for all 'welfare' workers more possible.

Lack of recognised training is not the only matter to be considered in connection with the possible developments in the education welfare services, however. The 'welfare' functions which the officers are stressing must be considered alongside the claims of their routine school attendance work which takes up the greater part of their time and which, despite the changes which have taken place since the service was inaugurated, is still important, not least because it provides the means of discovering those families with previously undetected difficulties and observing early signs of delinquency and neglect. Moreover, the extent to which local education authorities attach importance to and are prepared to develop their welfare services also differs from one area to another. For example, while some authorities actively exercise their powers under Part I of the Children and Young Persons Act, 1933, which deals with the prevention of cruelty and moral and physical danger,[1] and have appointed special officers for this work, in other parts of the country it is left to the National Society for the Prevention of Cruelty to Children.

In general the position is a complex one, and since 1948 has been further complicated by the fact that although the Children Act of that year does not expressedly authorise children's departments to undertake preventive work, it provides them with opportunities for doing so, and, while some departments have used these opportunities to the full, others have been more cautious. Further discussions of the problems of co-operation and co-ordination which arise in connection with the promotion of health and welfare of children and the prevention of cruelty, neglect, delinquency and deprivation must be postponed until the powers and duties of children's departments have been considered in more detail. Meanwhile, it can be said that both school health visitors and education welfare officers can accomplish much valuable social welfare work by the discovery of individuals and families needing social care and preparing the way for the specialist service required by the help and support they give.[2] It is towards the exercise of these functions that such social work training as they receive should be directed.

---

[1] This legislation is described in more detail in Chapter XIV.

[2] For example, a child may have to wait some time for treatment at a child guidance clinic. During this waiting period the school welfare officer or school nurse can encourage and support both parents and child and thus help ensure good co-operation when the time for treatment comes.

CHAPTER XIII

PROVISIONS FOR THE TREATMENT OF HANDICAPPED CHILDREN

AMONG the problems which were brought to light by the introduction of compulsory education was that of the education and care of the physically or mentally handicapped child. It is a medical and social as well as an educational problem, and during the last fifty years progress has been made in all these respects, so that the outlook for the handicapped child to-day is far brighter than that of his counterpart of three generations ago. Advances in medical science, improvements in standards of living, and the higher standards of child care which have resulted from the patient educational work of the health visitors and others associated with the maternity and child welfare and the school health services, have combined to reduce considerably the extent and severity of many of the physical handicaps afflicting children. Great as these advances have been, there are, however, still many children suffering from physical or mental handicaps which may be both severe and permanent. For these children special educational treatment and, in many cases, social care are needed if they are to make the most of the abilities they have, and grow into well-adjusted adults with the maximum degree of economic and social self-reliance permitted by their particular disabilities.

In the early days of compulsory education little or no attempt was made to provide special educational treatment for physically or mentally handicapped children. If they could manage to get to school at all they languished alongside their more fortunate fellows, adding to the burdens of the already overburdened teacher. This was demonstrated by a headmistress who told the Cross Commission in 1887 that during the previous year she had had in a single standard two children paralysed, one an idiot unable to walk but kept at school to enable an older sister to attend, one obviously 'dull', and eight so delicate that they were in constant attendance at hospital.[1] Those who were too infirm to manage the journey to school remained at home, neglected and uneducated, with no prospect other than the workhouse when they grew up and their parents or other relatives were no longer able to care for them. In

---

[1] Quoted by G. A. N. Lowndes, *The Silent Social Revolution*, p. 164.

THE TREATMENT OF HANDICAPPED CHILDREN

some areas voluntary organisations were already at work, making what provision they could for the education and care of the obviously handicapped such as the blind,[1] but the problem was too vast a one to be left to voluntary effort, and by the end of the century it was clear that the State must take action.

The first Act making specific provisions for handicapped children was the Elementary Education (Blind and Deaf Children) Act, 1893, which empowered school authorities[2] to pay for the education and maintenance of blind or deaf children in residential schools. This Act recognised that children so handicapped needed a special type of education, and provided that schools for them should operate under a special code. Furthermore, in order that they should have a longer period of education to help compensate them for their handicap, it raised their school-leaving age two years beyond that of their contemporaries who could both see and hear.

The need of special educational treatment for blind and deaf children was so obvious that it is not surprising that these were the first to be singled out for special care, but by the end of the century the necessity for making provision for the mentally defective and epileptic had been officially recognised by the Education (Defective and Epileptic Children) Act, 1899,[3] and the Passmore Edwards Settlement in London had started the first school for cripples.

The Education Act, 1921, contained a special part, Part V, in which provisions were made for dealing with 'Blind, Deaf, Defective and Epileptic Children'. These provisions covered both ascertainment and special educational treatment, but the procedures laid down, particularly the requirement that the child be certified as mentally or physically defective before education in a special school could be given, tended to stigmatise handicapped children and set them apart from their fellows. In the Education Act, 1944, the duty of securing that provision is made 'for pupils who suffer from any disability of mind or body' is included as part of the general duty of a local authority to provide educational opportunities, according to the age, aptitude and ability, for all children

[1] The first school for blind children was established in Liverpool in 1792.
[2] Until the implementation of the Education Act of 1902 the school boards, afterwards the local education authorities.
[3] Voluntary institutions for the care and training of educable mentally defective children were started in the mid-nineteenth century. The Royal Commission on the Blind, Deaf, and Dumb (1889) recommended special instruction for mentally defective children, and the Leicester and London School Boards established special day schools in 1892. By 1889 about forty centres for defectives and epileptics had been opened in different parts of the country. Report of the Mental Deficiency Committee, 1926, Part II, pp. 52-3.

in its area,[1] a change of emphasis which the Ministry considers has 'helped to effect a revolutionary change in the approach to the education of the handicapped. Special educational treatment is no longer a matter of segregating seriously handicapped children from their fellows, but of providing in each case the special help or modifications in regime or education suited to the needs of the individual child.'[2] This special provision is made for handicapped children because the objective of equality of educational opportunity applies to them as well as to normal children, and this implies diversity of educational opportunity. 'To meet the complex needs of handicapped children we require an education that is diverse in content, method and organisation. Only such education can provide equality of opportunity.'[3]

It is significant that in the relevant sections of the Act the children to be dealt with are always described as 'pupils requiring special educational treatment', that is to say the classification is fundamentally an educational one. Only in cases where the handicap is of such a nature and degree as to prevent a child from benefiting from primary or secondary education alongside normal children, is he to be given special treatment; the criterion is not the severity of the clinical condition, it is the child's ability or otherwise to profit from an ordinary education given in the ordinary way.[4] The School Health Service and Handicapped Pupils Regulations, 1953, recognise pupils who are blind, partially sighted, deaf, partially deaf, educationally sub-normal, epileptic, maladjusted, physically handicapped, delicate and suffering from speech defects as requiring special educational treatment.

Each of these categories of handicapped children needs a special and different adjustment of the educational system, and within each category there are wide differences between individual children. Special educational treatment is, in consequence, a branch of the education service making heavy demands on the skill, understanding, and patience of those teachers and administrators who undertake this responsibility.

The first task is that of discovering or 'ascertaining' those chil-

[1] Education Act, 1944, Section 8 (2) c.

[2] 'Education in 1955', Cmd. 9785, p. 18. The portion of this Report dealing with handicapped pupils has been substantially reprinted in a separate pamphlet, *Education of the Handicapped Pupil, 1945-55*, H.M.S.O., 1956.

[3] Scottish Education Department, 'Pupils with Mental or Educational Disabilities', Edinburgh, H.M.S.O., 1951, Cmd. 8401, p. 7.

[4] Education Act, 1944, Sections 33 and 44. *The Health of the School Child*, Report of the Chief Medical Officer of the Ministry of Education for the years 1939-45, H.M.S.O., 1947, p. 98. Cf. the definition of a disabled person given in the Disabled Persons (Employment) Act, 1944, where disablement is defined in relation to ability to obtain and hold employment in competition with normal persons. This definition is discussed in Chapter XIX.

dren in need of special treatment, and the Education Act, 1944, makes this a statutory duty of local education authorities.[1] A child may be brought to the notice of the authority as possibly in need of such treatment by his parents, who have the right to have him examined if he is over the age of two, even if at the time of the examination he is not attending school,[2] his teacher, the school medical officer, the school welfare officer, or a representative of an outside statutory or voluntary organisation interested in his welfare, such as a hospital almoner.[3] On receipt of this information the authority will arrange for the child to have a medical examination. They must inform the parents of the time and place at which it is to be held, and, if necessary, serve them with a legal notice requiring them to submit the child for examination.[4] When he has examined the child the medical officer advises the parents and the local education authority as to whether or not he considers the child is suffering from any disability of mind or body, and if so, the extent and nature of this disability, and the category of pupils requiring special educational treatment to which he belongs.[5] There the doctor's responsibility ends. Responsibility for determining the child's educational future rests with the local education authority. In making its decision the authority gives due weight to the result of the medical examination, but may also take into account any information that it obtains from other sources, such as the child's teacher or an educational psychologist.[6] It must also consider the wishes of the child's parents, and if the parents are dissatisfied with the decision of the authority they may appeal to the Minister of Education, either denying that the child is suffering from a disability which makes special educational treatment desirable, or, while admitting that the child is suffering

---

[1] Education Act, 1944, Section 34 (1).   [2] Ibid., Section 34 (2).

[3] 'Authorities should invite the co-operation of all such bodies in assisting them to make their ascertainment complete.' *The Health of the School Child, 1939–45*, p. 99.

[4] Ibid., Section 34 (1).

[5] If so required by the parent or the authority the medical officer must issue a certificate in a prescribed form showing whether or not the child is suffering from a disability and, if so, its nature and extent. The authority can only require a certificate if in its view it is necessary to secure the child's attendance at the appropriate school. If the parent makes no difficulty about it then no certificate should be made out.

[6] *The Health of the School Child, 1939–45*, p. 99. This is one of the differences between procedure under the 1944 Act and that under the 1921 Act. Under the latter Act, if the medical officer signed a certificate of defect as a result of his medical examination, it was the duty of the local education authority to find the child a place in a special school, i.e. the doctor settled the nature of the child's education. The realisation of the inappropriateness of giving this educational responsibility to a medical man led to the procedure being changed to that described above.

from a disability, denying the need for education in a special school.[1]

The special educational treatment the child requires may be given at a residential or day special school, or by making special arrangements appropriate to his disability in an ordinary school. If he is blind or deaf, it must be given in a special school unless the Minister approves otherwise, in all other cases in a special school or an ordinary school 'as may be appropriate in his case'.[2] The policy of the Ministry is to encourage provision and treatment inside ordinary schools wherever possible, so that no child who can be satisfactorily educated in this way shall be sent to a special school.[3] The object of special educational treatment is to help handicapped children to take their place in the normal community when they grow up, and policy with regard to special educational treatment is based on the belief that 'The extent to which they will be able to do so must vary, but the more normal their environment during the vital years of development, the greater is their chance of taking a place of worth within the community.'[4] Nevertheless, it is recognised that the decision as to whether the welfare of a particular child will best be served by attendance at an ordinary school or by transfer to a special one may be difficult. The assessment must always be an individual one, calling for wise judgment and a recognition of the fact that it is not always the degree of disability which is the major consideration.[5] The nature of the handicap is obviously of paramount importance, so also is the child's reaction to it, for having to mix with his fellows not so handicapped may, for some children, result in a tormenting sense of inferiority. There are other factors to be taken into account moreover, such as the competence and understanding of the teacher, the suitability of the building and, not least, the extent to which the individual attention that it may be necessary to give to the handicapped child is likely to prejudice the education of the other children in the class. 'A situation should not be allowed to develop in which a handicapped child receives an education in an ordinary school at the expense of other children, even if for other reasons his retention there may appear advantageous for him.'[6] 'Living in times that are becoming kindly to the less competent we must remind ourselves that the able must not be neglected.'[7]

[1] Education Act, 1944, Sections 34 (6) and 37 (3), See also *The Health of the School Child, 1939–45*, p. 101, 'Appeals to the Minister'.
[2] Education, England and Wales. The School Health Service and Handicapped Pupils Regulations, 1953, S.I. No. 1156, Regulations 15 and 16.
[3] Education in 1955, Cmd. 9785, p. 20.
[4] *The Health of the School Child*, Report of the Chief Medical Officer of the Ministry of Education for the years 1952 and 1953. H.M.S.O., 1954, p. 69.
[5] Ibid., p. 68.   [6] Ibid., p. 69.   [7] Scottish Education Department, op. cit., p. 6.

THE TREATMENT OF HANDICAPPED CHILDREN

Despite the emphasis on the value of education in ordinary primary or secondary schools wherever possible, places in special schools are still needed, and at no time since the 1939–45 War has the demand caught up with the supply. The serious shortage of the years immediately after the war has been to some extent overcome, partly by the provision of new places,[1] and partly by a significant fall in the demand by local education authorities for places for several categories of handicapped pupils, notably the deaf, partially deaf, delicate, physically handicapped and epileptic.[2] Children in other categories may still have to wait for placement, however, and in one category, the educationally sub-normal, the number of children awaiting special school places at the end of 1957 was still more than 13,000, having varied scarcely at all since 1949, despite the fact that there had been a large increase in the number of children in special schools in the intervening years. This may be due in part to the fact that during the years immediately after the war less serious cases were not put on the list as there was so little hope of placing them.[3]

Educationally sub-normal children constitute the largest, and in some ways the most difficult, group of children requiring special educational treatment. They are defined by the Ministry as 'pupils who, by reason of limited ability or some other condition resulting in educational retardation require some specialised form of education wholly or partly in substitution for the education normally given in ordinary schools'.[4] This definition is a comprehensive one and brings together those children whose retardation is due to innate mental subnormality, and those who are backward as a result of some other cause such as long illness, disharmony in the home with its attendant emotional disturbance, or some quite simple condition such as insufficient sleep. The Ministry recognises the importance of ascertaining the cause or combination of causes leading to the child's retardation as soon as possible, since this will influence the kind of educational treatment given, but it is no longer necessary, as it was before the passing of the 1944 Act, to await decision on this issue before commencing special educational treatment. Indeed, the treatment given and the child's response to it may throw light on the cause of the trouble.

The Ministry estimates that children needing special help owing to educational retardation number between 5 per cent and 10 per

[1] 'Between January 1946 and January 1955 the number of special schools increased from 528 to 743, the number of pupils in them from 38,499 to 58,034, and the number of full-time teachers from 2,434 to 4,381, increases of 41, 51 and 80 per cent respectively.' *Education in 1955*, p. 20.
[2] *The Health of the School Child*, 1956 and 1957, p. 133.   [3] Ibid., p. 30.
[4] School Health Service and Handicapped Pupils Regulations, 1953.

cent of the school population, but considers that the majority of these can and should be given the assistance they need inside ordinary schools. Those whose ability is seriously limited need education in special schools, however, and residential treatment may also be needed to help children who, in addition to being mentally handicapped are either emotionally unstable, present serious behaviour problems, or come from unhappy or unsuitable homes. For several years after the war provision for such boys and girls, many of whom were court cases, was quite inadequate to meet the need, and its inadequacy constituted a serious social problem. The difficulty of placing these particular children has lessened somewhat with the increase of special school places, but still constitutes a problem.

In addition to subnormal children who, although unable to gain much from ordinary primary or secondary education, will benefit from schooling specially adapted to their needs, there are those whose subnormality is so severe that they cannot appropriately be catered for within the educational system. The Education Act, 1944,[1] made provision for such 'ineducable' children, as they were then termed, to be medically examined with a view to their referral to the local health authority for supervision and training. These provisions, and the terminology used, were criticised by the Royal Commission on the Law Relating to Mental Illness and Mental Deficiency[2] as likely to cause unnecessary distress to the child's parents. In particular, they thought that no child should be labelled 'ineducable'. Their recommendations were accepted and have been incorporated into the Mental Health Act, 1959. It is[3] now the duty of every local education authority to ascertain what children in their area are suffering from a disability of mind of such a nature or extent as to make them 'unsuitable for education at school'. They must arrange for their medical examination, and if, after considering the advice of the medical officer who has made the examination and such information as they are able to obtain from teachers or other persons with respect to the ability and aptitude of the child, they do decide that he is suffering from such a disability of mind, they must cause the decision to be recorded and furnish the local health authority with a report of the decision and a copy of any written advice, report or information which was taken into account. Before recording their decision the local education authority must give the parents twenty-one days' notice, so that if they wish they may appeal to the Minister. When once a child has been referred to the local health authority in this

[1] Section 57.
[2] Cmnd. 169, pars. 637–49, pp. 218–21.
[3] Sections 11–13 and Second Schedule.

way it becomes the duty of this authority to provide appropriate training for him as long as they consider necessary, but at any time after the expiration of twelve months after recording the decision the child's parents may ask the local education authority to review it, and should the authority again decide that the child is unsuitable to receive education at school, the parents have the right of appeal to the Minister.

The training given to children referred to the local health authority is given in what were formerly called 'occupation' but have now been re-named 'training' centres, and children of school age may be required to attend or even reside at such a centre. These centres give simple habit and social training designed to develop the children's minds and bodies within the limits of their defect, and to help them to learn to live happily in association with others both at the centre, and, even more important, in their own homes. Occupation centres thus provide valuable help for both defective children and their families, but, as in the case of so many desirable and useful institutions, there are far too few of them to meet the need, and in spite of improvements in recent years, there are still areas where there are no centres or not as many as are needed. The problems of providing seriously sub-normal children with suitable training and supervision in their own homes, is moreover, complicated by the longstanding and continued shortage of places in mental deficiency hospitals, which means that many children who can only be helped adequately by residential treatment must remain at home, adding to the res-ponsibility of the local health authorities and causing distress and anxiety to their parents and other members of their families. With the present restrictions on capital development and the difficulties experienced by the hospital authorities in recruiting suitable staff for such institutions, there is no immediate prospect of substantial improvement, although the need for more extensive residential provision is generally acknowledged and attempts are being made to improve the position where the shortage is most acute. Short stay holiday homes, one or two of which have been started by voluntary organisations, help to ease the strain which the care of a seriously defective child imposes on his parents and other members of his family.

Among the children now listed in the School Health Service and Handicapped Pupils Regulations as requiring special educational treatment are those who are maladjusted and, of recent years the needs of this group of children have been receiving considerable attention. The Ministry of Education's recognition of the im-portance of preventing and treating this condition and of the

[1] Mental Health Act, 1959, Section 12.

difficulties which this involves, was shown by the appointment, in 1950, of a Committee to 'enquire into and report upon the medical, educational and social problems relating to maladjusted children, with reference to their treatment within the educational system'. The Committee reported in October 1955. Considerable progress had been made since the London County Council had appointed their first psychologist, Mr. (now Sir) Cyril Burt in 1913, 'to investigate cases of individual children who present problems of special difficulty . . . and to carry out, or make recommendations for suitable treatment or training of such children',[1] and the Jewish Health Organisation opened the East London Child Guidance Clinic in 1927. Nevertheless, the Committee was concerned because it was clear 'that the rate of discovery of maladjustment is very uneven in different areas and that, over the country as a whole, the existing provision is inadequate'.[2] Not only is the provision for diagnosis and treatment unevenly distributed geographically, it is also far from being properly co-ordinated administratively, and we are a long way from the Committee's ideal of 'a comprehensive child guidance service available for the area of every local education authority, involving a school psychological service, the school health service and child guidance clinics, all of which should work in close co-operation'.[3]

While other provisions such as the school psychological service play their part in the prevention and treatment of maladjustment in children, it is in the child guidance clinic that patterns of organisation and procedure have been most specifically evolved to deal with this problem. The first clinic was started in Chicago in 1909 as an attempt to deal with delinquency in childhood, and was associated with the Chicago juvenile court. As time went on it was realised that the methods used in connection with young delinquents could also be applied to other difficult or disturbed children, and clinics dealing with all forms of emotional disturbance in childhood were established, first in the United States and later in this country.

From their early days a characteristic feature of child guidance clinics has been their teamwork. In a clinic run on classical lines, the team consists of a psychiatrist, an educational psychologist, and a psychiatric social worker. The psychiatrist seeks to discover and understand the child's emotional difficulties and conflicts, and helps him to deal with them, the psychologist tests his intellectual

---

[1] Ministry of Education, Report of the Committee on Maladjusted Children.

[2] Op. cit., Chapter I. The Report discussed the 'Nature, Symptoms and Causes of Maladjustment' in some detail, but I have not attempted a summary of this discussion here.

[3] Report. Summary of Recommendations, I.

capacity and educational attainments, and where necessary and possible helps him to overcome any special scholastic difficulties and deficiencies, while the psychiatric social worker is primarily concerned to assess and, if necessary, modify the social factors in his environment which affect his behaviour. In particular she helps the parents to a better understanding of the child's difficulties and of their own relationships with him.

This pattern has now been modified in many clinics, however, and the whole approach appears to be more flexible. New methods of treatment, for example group therapy, are also being used, and new kinds of workers, such as child therapists, are coming in, but whatever the modifications made the work is still essentially team work. Meanwhile the value of the clinics' work has become increasingly widely recognised by other health and social workers as they have achieved more knowledge and understanding of its nature and of the problems involved. This has led to an increased demand for clinic services and the number of clinics has increased from about 50 in 1939 to about 300 in 1956.[1]

Pioneer work in the establishment of child guidance clinics in this country was undertaken by voluntary organisations, but as the value of their work became more widely recognised, some local education authorities established clinics of their own, while others grant-aided those run by voluntary organisations, and, by 1945, local education authorities were wholly responsible for 57 and partly responsible for 6 out of the 79 clinics in the country. Meanwhile, informed medical opinion was becoming increasingly conscious of the need for provisions to safeguard the mental as well as the physical health of the people. This is recognised in the National Health Service Act, and after the passing of the Act in 1946 it became possible for child guidance clinics to be set up by hospital or local health authorities as part of the National Health Service.[2]

Since both local education authorities and regional hospital boards may now be concerned with the establishment of a child guidance service, the situation is rather complex administratively and there are variations from area to area. The method of co-operation between hospital authority and education authority most favoured by the Committee on Maladjusted Children is that

[1] These figures are given in *Child Guidance—the Changing Scene* (Being the proceedings of the 13th Inter-Clinic Conference), N.A.M.H., 1957. This Report describes the changes taking place in clinic procedure and the information given above has been taken from it.

[2] The Sections of the Act under which this is possible are, according to the Committee on Maladjusted Children, Sections 3, 12 and 79 (1) (provision in connection with hospitals) and Sections 22 (1) and 28 (powers of local health authorities). Report, p. 40.

whereby local education authorities would provide the clinic and employ the psychologist (who would also work in the school psychological service) and psychiatric social workers, while the regional hospital board would provide and pay for the psychiatrist. Whatever the exact division of responsibility between local education authority and regional hospital board, there should be constant consultation and co-operation, and 'all child guidance clinics, whether provided by local education authority or by regional hospital boards, should normally be open to all boys and girls in the area up to the age of eighteen, whether they be at school or not. The law should also, if necessary, be amended to allow direct access to clinics for children attending schools not maintained by the local education authority.'[1]

Thorough diagnosis and treatment at a child guidance clinic is a long, elaborate and expensive process, which, with the present shortage of both clinics and the workers to staff them, can only be given to a limited number of children. Consequently in many cases the help given by the clinic is restricted to diagnosis and simple advice as to how to deal with the trouble, advice which may be given either to parents or to the health or social worker referring the case. This state of affairs accentuates the need for a deeper understanding of the causes and symptoms of maladjustment in childhood on the part of educationalists and health and social workers.[2] Probably many of the children brought to the child guidance clinics might never have become sufficiently disturbed as to need psychiatric treatment had their parents and teachers understood how to help them make better adjustments at different stages of growth, and been better able to satisfy their emotional as well as their physical needs. One of the most important functions of the child guidance service is to help parents and others in contact with children to achieve this understanding, and much may, and in some cases already is being done through discussions at child welfare centres, in connection with the school health service, and parent-teacher associations, and through contact with other organisations.

The Committee on Maladjusted Children is quite explicit that 'the aim of these (social and health) services, including the child guidance service, should be to help parents to understand and

---

[1] Report, p. 51. Recommendation 6.

[2] 'The orthodox child guidance team is an expensive instrument which must be used to the best advantage. . . . Methods should gradually be evolved whereby the clinic could safely act as a consultant agency to probation officers, teachers, doctors, health visitors, parents, etc., who might in time be regarded as the general practitioners in the field of mental hygiene.' Professor McCalman, Department of Psychology, University of Leeds, Eight Inter-Clinic Child Guidance Conference, December 1949.

handle their own children, not to relieve them of their normal responsibilities,[1] and one of the prime objectives of child guidance treatment is to repair the impaired relationships which frequently exist between the disturbed child and his family. To achieve this purpose it may, however, be necessary for the child to go away, at least for a time, and the provision of a sufficient number of hostels and special schools is essential if the child guidance service is to function efficiently. In such institutions the ratio of staff to children is necessarily large and their expansion is as dependent on recruitment of staff as on provision of premises.

The child guidance service is a growing and developing one, but its expansion is seriously retarded by staff shortages of all kinds, and particularly shortages of professionally trained workers. Psychiatrists, educational psychologists and psychiatric social workers are all in short supply, and until more men and women with the necessary intellectual and personal qualities can be recruited and trained for this exacting yet interesting work of assisting in the adjustment of disturbed, unhappy and difficult children, progress will continue to be slow.

So far in this and the preceding chapter we have been mainly concerned with the development of statutory provisions to further the health and well-being of the children of the nation, but this is a field in which voluntary effort has also played a prominent part. Voluntary organisations have pioneered in all the forms of child care discussed, from child guidance clinics to school meals. One of the services which has continued to the present day is social case work with crippled or invalid children. This still forms the basis of the work of the Invalid Children's Aid Association which was founded in 1888 by a C.O.S. worker (Mr. Allen Graham), who was moved by the unhappy and restricted lives of crippled children living in poverty-stricken and overcrowded homes at the mercy of ignorant, even if well-meaning and affectionate parents, to devise plans for providing companionship for the children and advice to the parents. The association was an offshoot of the Charity Organisation Society, and strongly imbued with C.O.S. ideas, but it was soon realised that friendly visiting and casework on C.O.S. lines were by themselves totally inadequate to meet the needs of the invalid child. Unable to content itself with visitation 'where the conditions of the home are such that a legion of visitors would be powerless to effect substantial good"[2] the association launched out into big schemes of child welfare work, including hospital and convalescent care, and the provision of milk, tonics, and orthopaedic apparatus. The more efficient of the provincial associations

[1] Report, p. 133.
[2] Extract from an early Annual Report.

founded on the same lines were similarly enterprising,[1] often working in close co-operation with the developing statutory services, by whom they were grant-aided. The greater powers conferred on statutory authorities by the Education Act, 1944, and the National Health Service Act, 1946, have curtailed the activities of these voluntary associations in some directions. For example, local authorities or regional hospital boards have now taken over children's hospitals and residential special schools formerly maintained by voluntary associations. However, certain forms of child care, such as short-term or preventive convalescent treatment, and hospital after-care, where the supervision required is social rather than medical, still remain in their hands, and there is still pioneer work outside the scope of the authorities to be done, as, for example, the provision of convalescent holidays for mothers and young children. At the same time such organisations can only survive if they maintain close co-operation with the statutory authorities and can show that they have a real contribution to make to the welfare of the child which cannot equally well be made by one of the health or education services.

[1] As, for example, the Liverpool Invalid Children's Aid Association, which owing largely to the energy and initiative of Margaret Beavan grew into one of the largest and most progressive associations in the country. In 1918 it changed its name to the Liverpool Child Welfare Association to express the idea that it was concerned with healthy as well as with invalid children, with prevention as well as treatment. Ivy A. Ireland, *Margaret Beavan of Liverpool*, p. 90.

CHAPTER XIV

THE CHILD DEPRIVED OF HOME CARE

'Without affection, life has little meaning for most people and none at all for children'.—RICHARD M. TITMUSS. |

PSYCHOLOGISTS tell us that a happy family life in which the child both gives and receives affection, feels secure, and has his own accepted status and significance, is the most important of his needs, more important even than a high standard of physical care, and studies of delinquency and deprivation among young people have emphasised the serious effects which separation from his family, real or believed rejection by it, or embittered relations within it, may have on his mental and emotional development.[1] Consequently the community has a special responsibility for seeing that those children who have no homes, or who, for some reason cannot be allowed to remain in their own homes, receive imaginative and loving alternative care, and that the numbers of such children are kept as low as possible.

Children deprived of home care may be divided into four groups. In the first place there are those whose deprivation is only temporary, resulting from some such cause as the mother's illness; secondly, those who have no homes, the orphans, deserted and destitute; thirdly those who are removed from their homes either because of their own misbehaviour or because home conditions are so detrimental to their moral and physical development that they cannot remain in it; and fourthly there are those children who are suffering from a mental or physical handicap which necessitates institutional care. Many children are deprived of home care by circumstances beyond human control, and all that can be done is to help them to build their lives afresh in as homelike surroundings as possible. There are others, however, particularly among those taken from their homes because of neglect, ill-treatment, lack of control or moral danger, whose deprivation might perhaps have been prevented, and the community's responsibility for taking

[1] E.g. D. H. Stott, *Delinquency and Human Nature*, Carnegie U.K. Trust, 1950. J. M. Bowlby, *Maternal Care and Mental Health*, a report prepared on behalf of the World Health Organisation, Geneva, 1952.

steps to prevent the deterioration of family life which ends in this deprivation is being increasingly realised.[1]

If this problem is to be tackled effectively further research into the social and psychological conditions underlying the neglect or ill-treatment of children by their parents as well as administrative action is needed. A pioneer study of this nature was undertaken in 1946–7 by the Women's Group on Public Welfare, and its results were published under the title of *The Neglected Child and his Family*. This has since been followed by others such as that undertaken by Mr. D. V. Donnison in Manchester and Salford, *The Neglected Child and the Social Services*, and the Report of the Joint Committee of the British Medical Association and the Magistrates' Associations, *Cruelty to and Neglect of Children*.

It would appear from the available evidence that cruelty or deliberate physical ill-treatment forms only a small part of the problem[2] and would seem to be mainly the outcome of psychological abnormality, but that neglect or failure to make adequate provision for the physical, emotional and intellectual needs of the child, is much more frequent and has wider social implications. It cannot be ascribed to any one cause, but like other social problems it arises from the interplay of a great number of factors, physical, psychological and economic, which, together, bring about a strain too great to be borne. 'Poverty, ignorance, bad housing, marital disharmony, excessive child-bearing, all these play a part,' and 'We are left with the impression not of wilful, cruel, reprehensible mothers (though these do exist), but of women struggling with inadequate equipment, mental and material, to deal with problems which would tax even those highly endowed'. 'In many cases, had the mother been of higher mentality, she might have surmounted the difficulties. Had the difficulties not been so complex her mental inadequacy would not have had such disastrous effects. The cycle is difficult to break; mismanagement—poverty—malnutrition—ill-health—apathy.'[3] This was the verdict of the

---

[1] The Report of the Care of Children Committee, 1946, emphasises this point in paragraph 7, which reads, 'The consideration of the welfare of children deprived of home life inevitably raised in our minds and those of many of our witnesses the question whether this deprivation might not have been prevented. This is a question we regard as of the utmost importance and we hope that serious consideration will be given to it. . . .'

[2] A study group set up by the National Association for Maternity and Child Welfare estimated the proportions as approximately 90 per cent neglected to 10 per cent ill-treated, but this can only be regarded as tentative as some organisations approached pointed out that it is not always easy to say where one ends and the other begins, while the two may go together, *Child Neglect and the Social Services*, pp. 8–9. Compare this estimate with figures published by the N.S.P.C.C. in their annual reports.

[3] *The Neglected Child and His Family*, pp. 71 and 73.

Women's Group on Public Welfare in 1947, and the description given by the Governor of Holloway Prison of women serving sentences for child neglect is very similar.[1] Later studies emphasise the same characteristics and conditions which correspond closely with the accounts given by social workers and investigators of the factors contributing to the creation of problem families and the two problems are closely associated, although not coincident. Child neglect is frequently found in 'problem' families and is both a symptom and a result of their general collapse of morale and social inefficiency, and in these cases it cannot be treated as an isolated phenomenon. Instead an effort must be made to rehabilitate the family as a whole, as may be necessary in other cases also.

This need is recognised in a circular *Children Neglected or Ill-treated in Their Own Homes*, issued jointly by the Home Office, Ministry of Health and Ministry of Education in 1950.[2] The circular, which is based on the recommendations of a Working Party composed of officials of the three departments, states explicitly that 'the Ministers are convinced that it is by means of improved co-ordination that this complex problem can best be dealt with', and the circular suggests to the councils of counties and county boroughs that co-operation might be achieved by designating an officer who will be responsible for 'enlisting the interest of those concerned and devising arrangements to secure full co-operation among all the local services, statutory and voluntary, which are concerned with the welfare of children in their own homes'. This officer is expected to hold regular meetings of statutory officials and representatives of voluntary organisations, and to arrange for 'significant cases of child neglect and all cases of ill-treatment' coming to the notice of any statutory or voluntary service in the area to be reported to him with a view to its discussion at one of these meetings 'so that, *after considering the needs of the family as a whole*[3] agreement might be reached as to how the local services could best be applied to meet these needs'.

These recommendations are significant, first because they indicate definite acceptance by the State of its responsibility for

[1] Report of the Commissioners of Prisons for the year 1949, Appendix No. 1 (B). 'In conclusion it appears that neglect of their children is only part of a general social failure on the part of these women. Their failure is often due to low intelligence, poor social environment in their early years and a lack of a sense of responsibility. . . . For some reason they cannot cope with an ordinary social and domestic life, and so they fail to do something essential, and neglect results. It is of great importance that in nearly every case of neglect or cruelty the act complained of is an act of omission and not of commission. . . . In almost every case the woman loved her children, even if she found them a nuisance.'

[2] Circular 157/50 Home Officeo 78/50 Ministry of Health; 225/50 Ministry of Education, 31 July 1950. [3] Italics mine.

tackling child neglect in its early stages, and by means other than by the use of its coercive powers, secondly, because they are directed towards the rehabilitation of the family as a whole, and not simply to the protection of the neglected child, and thirdly, because they provide the means whereby local authorities may take the initiative in promoting co-operation between the different organisations, statutory and voluntary, concerned in their different ways to further the well-being of individuals and families in their areas. They have, therefore, considerable possibilities, not least because they are widely drawn and leave the local authorities implementing them scope for experiment and variation.

By 1957 54 of the 62 county councils and 69 of the 83 county boroughs were operating the scheme. Fifty-eight authorities had appointed the children's officer as designated officer, 37 the medical officer of health and 23 the clerk to the council. In four areas the chief education officer had been appointed, and in one a lay member of the county council.[1] These differences in the official designated are accompanied by variations in the size, constitution and working of committees in the different local authority areas.[2] In some they consist of meetings of senior officials, in others they are case conferences at which the field workers in direct contact with the cases under discussion are invited to attend, while a few areas have both meetings and case conferences and reports are given from one to the other. The effectiveness of the committee seems to depend on a number of factors, among the most important of which are the personality and ability of the chairman, together with the degree to which social workers with very different preconceptions and approach are prepared to tolerate these differences, exchange information, learn from one another and possibly even give place to one another in the handling of a case.[3] The estimate of the Home Office is that 'Experience during the past five years has shown that, with an interested designated officer supported by active representatives of the services concerned, much good work can be done through co-ordinating machinery. Regular personal contact between the officials leads to greater understanding of each others' work and increases the will to co-operate. The various services have opportunity to pool their

[1] These figures are taken from an article by Gordon Rose, 'Co-ordinating Committees, I. Organisation', *Case Conference*, June 1957, p. 43. They were supplied to the author by the Home Office.

[2] National Association for Maternity and Child Welfare, op. cit., pp. 4–8. Gordon Rose, op. cit., p. 45. D. V. Donnison, *The Neglected Child and the Social Services*, Appendix II, B.M.A. and Magistrates' Association, op. cit., Appendix IV. Younghusband Committee Report, Chapter 12.

[3] This is brought out in Gordon Rose's three articles on Co-ordinating Committees. *Case Conference*, May, July and September 1957, and in the Younghusband Committee Report.

information, and to make an agreed plan to meet the needs of particular cases.'[1]

Valuable as the work of co-ordinating committees has been in many areas, they have their limitations. They have no money of their own, the cost of any measures taken to deal with a particular case remains with the service undertaking them. This limitation is particularly serious, as apart from the National Assistance Board which can only help in certain cases, none of the statutory authorities have power to spend money on material goods such as beds and bedding which may be essential if a family is to be encouraged to maintain and raise its standards or to start afresh after a major disaster such as eviction or the parents' imprisonment. The present position of children's departments in this connection is an anomalous and difficult one. There is no specific provision in the Children Act, 1948, which authorises them to undertake 'preventive' work in the wider sense of tackling the underlying causes of neglect and family breakdown, and although several children's departments are undertaking work of this kind, and have even appointed special officers for the purpose, the financial position remains obscure. As has already been pointed out,[2] one of the questions which the Ingleby Committee is considering is whether children's departments should be 'given new powers and duties to prevent or forestall the suffering of children through neglect in their own homes', and their report, when issued, may well form the basis of new legislation which will overcome these difficulties.

While measures aimed at the prevention or remedy of child neglect should be directed towards the family as a whole, yet the key to the situation is likely to be held by the mother. 'The father may be the head of the family but the mother is its heart, and where families have broken down it is largely because of the failure of the mother.'[3] As we have seen, such failure is generally the outcome of the interaction of a number of causes among which ill-health, poor mental endowment, ignorance and the influence of an unsatisfactory physical environment are usually prominent, and it has been found that many mothers are likely to benefit greatly, and may even find sufficient strength and courage to tackle their difficulties instead of succumbing to them, if they can get away from their homes for a period of refreshment and rehabilitation at a well-run recuperation centre. It is important, however, that the mother should take her youngest child or children with her, partly because she is likely to settle down better if they are there also,

---

[1] Seventh Report of the Work of the Children's Department, November 1955, p. 25, par. 116.   [2] Chapter XII above.

[3] Alison Pope, 'Investigation into the Problem of the Tired Mother', *Social Welfare*, Vol. VII, No. 6, April 1949, p. 139.

partly because it should never be suggested to her that her children are a drawback to her happiness, and, thirdly, because the aim of such recuperation is not simply to restore the mother to health, but to help and encourage her to become a more efficient mother. Education in child care is thus an important part of the work of a centre.[1]

Recuperation centres for mothers and young children are unfortunately few and far between. The three best known ones are 'Brentwood', Marple, Cheshire, run by the Community Council of Lancashire; 'Mayflower', at Plymouth, run by the Salvation Army, and a centre managed by the Elizabeth Fry Memorial Trust, which was started at Spofforth Hall near Harrogate and has now moved to York.[2] The first to start was 'Brentwood', Marple, Cheshire, a centre where mothers recommended by local authorities or voluntary organisations as in need of rest and recuperation because their health has suffered by too frequent pregnancies, illness, poverty, or other hardships, may go with their children under seven. While not primarily intended for 'problem' mothers, it has proved particularly successful with them, and it has been found that they benefit from mixing with others, who faced with equal, if not greater difficulties, have maintained their self-respect and morale. This learning from their fellows is but one of the means by which the 'problem' mothers are helped to discover and apply higher standards of home and child care. They also help in the house, assist in preparing the meals, attend simple cookery and needlework demonstrations, observe the methods used by the helper in charge of the nursery where their toddlers are cared for during the day, and attend the local clinic—for all these activities form part of the accepted manner of life at the centre—and, without realising it, they are slowly being taught the skills essential to the maintenance of a happy and well-ordered home life. Meanwhile, good food, adequate rest and country air are helping to build them up physically, and social activities not only encourage them to take pride in their personal appearance (perhaps the first sign of a dawning self-respect), but help to give them something of the joy in life of which so many have been robbed by monotonous years in drab and squalid surroundings.

The majority of women who go to 'Brentwood' are referred there by voluntary organisations or the local health authorities, and they go there of their own free will, but there appears to be no essential difference between many of these mothers and those who have been brought before the courts and convicted of neglect.[3] Despite

[1] Pope, op. cit., p. 145.

[2] In 1956 Crowley House, Birmingham, was opened. Here fathers are invited to stay at the week-end.

[3] The twelve case studies analysed in *The Neglected Child and His Family*, pp. 24–32, illustrate this point.

the training courses which have been started at Birmingham prison for mothers convicted of neglect, imprisonment is an unconstructive way of dealing with such cases, and may cause intense suffering not only to the neglectful mother but also to her young children, since, in spite of all appearances to the contrary, mothers and children in such cases are often genuinely fond of each other. Re-education at a home run on the lines of 'Brentwood' would seem to be much more hopeful as well as a more humane method of treating such neglectful mothers. A small experimental home for mothers convicted of child neglect, which has accommodation for nine mothers and eighteen children, was opened at Plymouth under the auspices of the Salvation Army in 1948, and neglectful mothers can be put on probation with a condition attached that they reside at the home for four months with their children under five, as an alternative to being sent to prison. The Probation Branch of the Home Office pays the Army on a *per capita* basis for the mothers, while the expenses of the children are met by the local authorities, who would probably have had to maintain them in their own homes if the alternative sentence of imprisonment had been imposed.[1] Similar cases are taken at the centre sponsored by the Elizabeth Fry Memorial Trust.

Residential treatment of the kind described is a very valuable means of helping mothers who, finding their burdens too heavy, refuse to shoulder them, but it has its limitations. Unless a casework organisation such as Family Service Units has been tackling the home situation in her absence, the mother is likely to come back to conditions as bad as, if not worse than those she left when she went away. Further, unless she is given continued active support and encouragement at this stage, her new-found courage and energy may give way under the renewed strain, her good resolutions and newly acquired skills be forgotten, and she may all too easily slip back into her old slovenliness and apathy. Thus, if it is to be effective, residential treatment should not be regarded as a complete answer to the problem of the neglectful mother, but as the more intensive and central part of a much more prolonged process, beginning with the thorough understanding of the case by the social worker, and ending with a long period of after-care, during which improvements begun while the mother was away can be consolidated.[2] The point has also been made[3] that in this concern with rehabilitating neglectful mothers, insufficient attention has been paid to the father of the family, and, for this reason alone,

[1] By April 1955 120 mothers had completed the four months' stay at 'Mayflower' and all but 17 were judged to have benefited in greater or lesser degree from the training given. Recuperative centres are discussed in the Report of the Ministry of Health, 1958, Part II, Cmnd. 871, pp. 152–3.

[2] Alison Pope, op. cit., p. 146.

[3] A. F. Philp and Noel Timms, *The Problem of the 'Problem Family'*, p. 56.

experiments such as the 'rehabilitation' houses and flats started in one or two of the larger cities for evicted families, have considerable advantages for this type of case.

If all attempts to rehabilitate the family fail, and the situation deteriorates to such an extent that the children are suffering serious harm, physically or psychologically, because of their parents' indifference, neglect or active ill-will, then the State must step in to protect them, even if this means removing them from home. The State won its powers to do this with considerable difficulty, for they constitute a direct limitation of parental rights. What was at stake in the struggle was the child's claim to be regarded as a person with rights of his own, which even his parents could not override, and which the community would defend if necessary. Only after a long struggle was such a claim established. 'If it had been a dog I could help you, but it is only a child,' said one magistrate about a case brought before him in the early days of the National Society for the Prevention of Cruelty to Children[1] and during the years that followed Dr. Barnardo, Benjamin Waugh, the founder of this society, and other pioneers, had to devote much of their energy to bringing about changes in the law so that 'the doctrine of parental rights should not be allowed any longer to be the doctrine of children's wrongs'.[2]

Two major landmarks in the history of child protection were the Children Act, 1908, and the Children and Young Persons Act, 1933. The latter Act which, as amended in 1952, is operative at the present day, not only contains provisions for the prosecution and sentence of those who have the custody of children and wilfully neglect or cruelly treat them, or commit specific offences against them,[3] but also empowers juvenile court magistrates to remove children or young persons 'in need of care or protection' from the custody of their parents or guardians and make alternative arrangements for them.[4] A child or young person 'in need of care or protection' was defined in the 1933 Act as one who 'having no parent or guardian, or a parent or guardian unfit to exercise care or guardianship, or not exercising proper care or guardianship' was 'either falling into bad associations or exposed to moral

[1] Quoted in *The Life of Benjamin Waugh*, by Rosa Waugh, p. 146.
[2] National Children's Home and Orphanage Annual Report for 1884. Quoted R. M. Wrong, 'The Welfare of Children', ch. iii in Bourdillon, *Voluntary Social Services in the Modern State*, p. 38.
[3] Children and Young Persons Act, 1933, Part I, 'Prevention of Cruelty and Exposure to Moral and Physical Danger'. A child within the meaning of the Act is a person under the age of fourteen years, a 'young person' is a person who has attained the age of fourteen years and is under the age of seventeen years, but Part I applies only to persons under sixteen.
[4] Ibid., Sections 61 and 62.

danger or beyond control'. Children against whom offences under Part I of the Act had been committed, or who were members of the same household as either the offender or the victim,[1] were included, as were children of vagrants who were prevented from receiving a proper education. Far-reaching as these provisions were, compared with earlier legislation, they were still open to criticism as being ambiguous or inadequate. One source of difficulty was that to be punishable the cruelty or neglect must have been 'wilful', that is intentional, and, while it is easy to see the legal principle underlying the insertion of this word, its presence made it difficult for a court to remove a child from the custody of his parents even when it was obviously in his interests, particularly if he was not in 'moral danger', and hence it was held that an offence under Section 1 of the Act must be proved before such action could be taken. The Children and Young Persons (Amendment) Act which came into operation in 1952 has enlarged the definition of a child or young person in need of care or protection to include one who has no parent or guardian or a parent or guardian not exercising proper care or guardianship and who is 'ill-treated or neglected in a manner likely to cause him unnecessary suffering or injury to health'.[2] It is no longer necessary to prove the offence of 'wilful' neglect or ill-treatment, it is sufficient to show that the condition exists.

Under the Act responsibility for bringing cases to court is divided between the N.S.P.C.C., the various departments of the local authority and the police. Prosecutions for neglect are commonly instituted by the N.S.P.C.C., although in some areas the local education authority may be responsible for such action through its school attendance and welfare department. Since the implementation of the Children Act, 1948, children's departments have commonly dealt with 'care or protection' cases, and under Section 62 (2) of the Children and Young Persons Act they have a duty to bring before a juvenile court any child or young person appearing to them to be in need of care or protection unless they are satisfied that the taking of proceedings is unnecessary or that proceedings are about to be taken by some other person. Section 2 of the 1952 Act makes it their duty to cause inquiries to be made should they receive information suggesting that a child or young person may be in need of care or protection unless they are satisfied that such inquiries are unnecessary. The section has been drafted so as not to disturb existing arrangements for investigation,[3] but it does mean that final responsibility for investigation,

[1] Section 61 (1) 3.
[2] *Children and Young Persons (Amendment) Act*, 1952, Section 1.
[3] Home Office Circular, 208/1952.

should there be any suspicion or rumour of neglect, rests with the children's department.

Various measures may be taken by the juvenile court for dealing with children or young persons found to be 'in need of care or protection'. If it is decided to go on trying to preserve the unity of the family, and keep the child at home, the parents may be ordered to enter into a recognisance to exercise proper care, or the child may be placed under the supervision of a probation officer, but in many cases the time for such preventive measures is found to be past, and the child is taken away from the custody of his parents and either committed to the care of a 'fit person' or sent to an approved school. In such cases he becomes a 'child deprived of home care' in the strict sense of the term, one of the 62,000 of all categories for whom the community is responsible.[1]

For many years after the death of Dr. Barnardo and other nineteenth-century pioneers the general public was not particularly concerned about the quality of care given to deprived children, assuming that they were being properly looked after by the public authorities or voluntary agencies responsible. In 1944, however, attention was drawn to the unsatisfactory conditions existing in many children's homes by Lady Allen of Hurtwood, who wrote a strong letter to *The Times* on the subject and followed it up by a pamphlet *Whose Children?* which gave examples of harsh unimaginative treatment, amounting in some cases to cruelty, mental if not physical. The following year the death of a child boarded out by a local authority, as a result of neglect and ill-treatment, which could have been prevented had there been proper selection and supervision of the foster home,[2] aroused the public from its complacency. In March 1945 an Inter-departmental Committee was appointed under the chairmanship of Miss (now Dame) Myra Curtis, 'to inquire into existing methods of providing for children who, through loss of parents or from any other cause whatever, are deprived of a normal home life with their own parents or relatives, and to consider what further measures should be taken to ensure that these children are brought up under conditions best calculated to compensate them for the lack of parental care'. The Committee issued its report in September 1946.[3] As the result of a comprehensive survey covering all types of care of the deprived child in different parts of England and Wales[4] it concluded that 'while

[1] In March 1957 the number of children in the care of local authorities under the Children Act was 62,033.

[2] Dennis O'Neill. Report by Sir Walter Monckton, K.C.M.G., K.C.V.O., M.C., K.C., Cmd. 6636, 1945.

[3] Report of the Care of Children Committee, H.M.S.O., Cmd. 6922.

[4] A separate inquiry was conducted and report issued by a Committee appointed by the Scottish Home Department, *Report of the Committee on Homeless*

much good work is being done the standard is so variable and at the lower levels so poor that a determined effort must be made to lift the whole treatment of the child without a home to a new, more even and higher level'.[1]

Two major changes were required to bring about this improvement. In the first place the administrative machinery needed a thorough overhaul. Responsibility was divided between a number of central government departments and local authority committees, not to speak of the numerous voluntary organisations, and this resulted in confusion, overlapping and inconsistency of treatment. In order to obviate this the Committee recommended that responsibility for the care of all deprived children should be concentrated, both centrally and locally. One government department should be made responsible for the oversight of all forms of care of the deprived child, its function being to 'define and maintain standards by inspection, advice and direction',[2] while, at the local authority level, county and county borough councils should appoint *ad hoc* committees which would be responsible for the provision and maintenance of children's homes, for boarding out, for child life protection, for the local authorities' function with regard to adoption and for the keeping of records of all deprived children in their respective areas including those in voluntary homes. In order to carry out this work effectively each children's committee should appoint 'an executive officer of high standing and qualifications who would be a specialist in child care'.

These administrative recommendations were accepted by the Government and given legislative sanction by the Children Act, 1948. The Home Office was chosen as the central government department responsible for the care of deprived children and Advisory Councils in Child Care, one for England and Wales and one for Scotland, were appointed to advise the Secretary of State on his duties in this regard. Each county council and county borough council was required to appoint a children's committee unless the Secretary of State was satisfied that owing to special circumstances the authority could best discharge its functions otherwise,[3] and each children's committee must appoint a children's officer, the appointment being subject to the approval of the Secretary of State.[4]

In addition to bringing at least a semblance of order out of

Children, Cmd. 6911. The Chairman was Mr. J. L. Clyde, K.C. The findings and recommendations of the two committees are strikingly similar.

[1] Op. cit., par. 428.   [2] Summary of Recommendations, par. 5, p. 178.

[3] Local Authorities may also combine to form Joint Committees for the purposes of this Act, Section 39 (4).

[4] Children Act, 1948, Sections 38, 39 and 40.

administrative chaos the Act deals with various other legal and technical questions. It defines the responsibilities of the local authority, making it a duty for them to receive into their care orphans, deserted children and children whose parents or guardians are temporarily or permanently prevented from providing for their proper accommodation, maintenance and upbringing, provided such intervention is necessary in the interests of the child.[1] It also makes the children's committee and officer responsible for the supervision of children under eighteen maintained apart from their parents for reward,[2] and further makes it a duty of local authorities to undertake the care of children committed to them by juvenile courts in accordance with the terms of Section 76 (1) of the Children and Young Persons Act. This section provides that children or young persons in need of care or protection, or young delinquents, may be committed by the court to the care of 'fit persons' who then become responsible for their welfare. Hitherto local authorities had not been forced to take on 'fit person' responsibility against their wish, but now they are unable to evade it.

Those sections of the Act which deal with the responsibility of the local authorities for receiving children into care by arrangement with the parents are carefully drafted so as to safeguard parental rights and responsibilities and to ensure that no change in the child's religious persuasion results from his being received into care. Before the child is so received care is taken to investigate the circumstances which have led to the request being made and to encourage parents to make their own arrangements where this is possible. Moreover, Section 1 (3) of the Act makes it clear that the local authority cannot retain the child against the parents' wishes and explicitly instructs the authority to endeavour to secure that he is taken back by his parents, relatives, or friends as soon as possible, provided that this is consistent with his welfare. If the child's parents are dead, or have deserted or abandoned him, or are incapable through permanent disability or unfit through habits and mode of life, to care for him, and the local authority are satisfied that their action is consistent with his welfare, they can, by resolution of the council, assume parental rights over him, but this is subject to appeal by the parents and final decision by the court.[3] Throughout the Act the welfare of the child and the

---

[1] Ibid., Part I, Section 1.
[2] This is generally known as child life protection. The duties of local authorities with regard to this have been restated and to some extent modified by the Children Act, 1958.
[3] This is laid down in Section 2. Note that the provisions of this section only apply to children already in care under Section 1.

rights and responsibilities of parents are both taken into account, but the paramount consideration is the welfare of the child.

The provisions of the Children Act established an administrative framework within which a comprehensive service for the care of children who have not the benefit of a normal home life could be developed, but administrative efficiency, essential as it is, does not in itself ensure the well-being of the child. Much more is needed, especially sensitiveness to the child's emotional needs, and the wisdom and loving kindness which alone can help heal the wounds caused by the loss of his home and family, perhaps under circumstances likely to cause the maximum damage to his personality. This is the crux of the matter, and this is where the Curtis Committee felt that the child care organisations were so often failing. It paid tribute to the physical care·given to the children in the institutions visited, and recognised that this often reached a higher standard than the child would receive in his own home, but it noted that, even where the institution was well managed, there was frequently 'a lack of interest in the child as an individual and too remote and impersonal relations'.[1] The second major improvement required was then to bring about as high standards as possible in the personal and psychological as well as the physical care of deprived children. This is recognised in the Children Act which lays it down that the local authority in whose care the child is must 'exercise their powers with respect to him so as to further his best interests, and to afford him opportunity for the proper development of his character and abilities.'[2] Moreover, in providing for the deprived child full use should be made of the facilities available for all children,[3] so that, although he is deprived of normal home life with his own parents, this does not mean separation from the world of normal children; instead he should be enabled to lead a life as near that of a normal child as possible. It was the intention of the framers of the Act that 'every child in care should have the opportunities available to a child brought up by good parents and under conditions which put him as nearly as possible in the position of a child living in his own home.'[4]

In determining the kind of care to be given in any particular case it is necessary not only to apply general principles outlined above, but to discover, and as far as possible meet the needs of the individual child concerned. It was the recognition of the importance of making individual assessments before final placement

---

[1] Report of the Care of Children Committee, par. 477, p. 160. But compare G. V. Holmes' tribute to the loving, personal care given her by her cottage 'mother' in Dr. Barnardo's Girls' Village Home, *The Likes of Us*, 1948.
[2] Section 12 (1).   [3] Section 12 (2).
[4] Home Office, Sixth Report on the Work of the Children's Department, par. 28, p. 9.

which led the Curtis Committee to recommend that local authorities should provide special facilities for the initial reception and observation of children coming into care for long periods and this has become a duty of local authorities under the Act.[1] By 1954 over sixty centres were in operation and it had been found in practice that reception centre facilities are not only valuable as means of assessment, but also help children who are disturbed and unstable on coming into care to settle down, and these children often remain longer than the four weeks originally proposed as the maximum length of stay.[2] Reception centres have not been without their critics, however. It has been argued that admission to such a centre is not called for, since the information required can be obtained by using child guidance clinics or similar facilities and that a stay in a centre can be disturbing and harmful to the child. After examining these criticisms, Dr. Hilda Lewis, for three years psychiatrist to the Kent County Council Reception Centre at Mersham, concluded that reception centres, though not ideal, are indispensable for dealing with a large proportion of deprived children, and the dangers which may arise from their use can be avoided by sound organisation and careful selection of personnel.[3]

The two main forms of permanent care available for the deprived child are boarding out and institutional care. The former is generally preferred as it means that the child enjoys something more nearly approaching a normal home, and the Children Act lays it down that this should be the form of care given the child unless this is not practical or desirable for the time being.[4] It may not be suitable in all cases, however. Handicapped children needing special medical care and educational training may have to be catered for in institutions especially adapted to their needs, and the young delinquent may require the discipline of an approved school, while the child who is seriously maladjusted as the result of his early experiences may need skilled treatment in a special hostel before he is boarded out. As Miss D. M. Dyson writes as the result of long experience: 'Neither form of care [i.e. in an institution or with foster parents] is in itself better or worse than the other, though either may be better or worse for the individual

---

[1] Report of the Care of Children Committee, pars. 482 and 483, pp. 161–2. Children Act, 1948, Section 15 (2).

[2] Home Office. Seventh Report on the Work of the Children's Department, par. 17, p. 5.

[3] Hilda Lewis, *Deprived Children, a Social and Clinical Study*, pp. 128–34.

[4] Section 13 (1). On 13 November 1949 the number of children in the care of local authorities who were boarded out was 19,271, representing 35 per cent of the children in care. Sixth Report of the Children's Department of the Home Office, p. 12. Cf. the figures for 1957 on the next page.

child. . . . The touchstone is not the excellence of the Home care over Foster Home care or vice versa, but in the choice for each of that form of care which will best suit him.'[1] Nevertheless, the tendency over the last few years has been to emphasise the value of boarding out, and extend its use as far as possible. This policy received the blessing of the Select Committee on Estimates for the Session 1951, which made the gratifying discovery that 'what is generally agreed to be the best method of providing for children in the care of local authorities is also the cheapest,[2] and it is encouraged by the Home Office though with the caveat that, 'it is not overlooked that the quality of boarding out is of first importance and that the percentage of children boarded out is only one indication of the standard of child care'.[3] There are in fact considerable differences between local authorities in the percentages of children boarded out, differences due to some extent to differences in economic and social circumstances which make it difficult to find a sufficient number of suitable foster parents in some areas.[4] Some authorities, in addition to encouraging the boarding out of normal children who are in care for long periods, have been making interesting experiments with the boarding out of children who have hitherto generally received institutional care, for example, babies, handicapped children and children in temporary care, and in many cases these experiments are proving themselves worth while. In institutional care the tendency has been away from the larger homes to what are called 'family group' homes, that is local authorities are housing small groups of children in the care of a married couple or housemother in ordinary houses adapted for

[1] D. M. Dyson, *The Foster Home*, p. 13. Cf. Hilda Lewis, op. cit., p. 126. 'There is today a strong move towards using foster homes on a large scale for deprived children. However much this course is urged on the grounds of economy or psychological advantage, it would be unwise to extend it wholesale (if this were practicable) to older children who still look to their natural parents for company or to children who make exceptional demands because they are unresponsive and need more than average understanding and unremitting patience. . . . For some such children a children's home or boarding school is preferable.'

[2] Sixth Report from the Select Committee on Estimates, Session 1951–2. Child Care, p. xv. The figures they give are a little misleading owing to the higher administrative costs of boarding out which are not taken into account.

[3] Seventh Report, par. 25, p. 6.

[4] E.g. the extent to which opportunities exist for women to obtain work outside their homes or the proportion of children who are specially difficult to place, such as coloured children. The average percentages of children boarded out for March 1957 were 45 per cent for county borough councils, 47 per cent for county councils, but ranged from 20 per cent (Worcester) and 15 per cent (Middlesbrough) to 70 per cent and over in some of the county areas. Home Office, *Children in the Care of Local Authorities in England and Wales, March 1957*, Cmnd. 411.

the purpose. Where married couples are in charge the husband, though acting as father to the family, will go out to work in the ordinary way. Such homes are particularly valuable for the accommodation of brothers and sisters who, if boarded out, would be separated, often an undesirable proceeding.

Most vital of all requirements of the child care service is that of recruiting and training the right kind of people to staff the homes and hostels and act as children's officers and their assistants. As Miss Clement Brown[1] put it, 'In the last resort there can be no guarantee of a child's welfare, except in the quality of the human beings who care for him,' and the Curtis Committee attached so much importance to the recruitment and training of the resident staff—the people who have the day-to-day care of the children— that they issued an interim report on it.[2] The training of the administrative staff is dealt with in Appendix I of the main report. In accordance with its recommendation a Central Training Council in Child Care has now been established, social science departments in selected universities are conducting 'child care' courses[3] intended more especially for the training of boarding-out officers and administrative staff, while courses for house-mothers and others in kindred positions have been organised by local authorities and voluntary organisations. In spite of these efforts there is still a grave shortage of trained staff, particularly for residental posts, and much more should be done to raise the status of this kind of work in the eyes of the public, and attract the right type of people to it.

Lastly, there is the question of the care of the older boy or girl. The responsibility of the local authority or voluntary organisation does not cease when the child starts to earn his own living; indeed there may be as great or greater need for understanding and guidance during the difficult years of adolescence, when the youngster is trying to find his feet in the adult world without the support of a family background, than when the child is still sheltered in a home or foster home. This is recognised by the fact that, although no child can be received into care after the age of seventeen, children already in care remain as such until their

---

[1] Training Adviser, Central Training Council on Child Care. Cf. Report of the Scottish Committee on Homeless Children. Cmd. 6911, 1946, par. 112: 'No amount of legislation and no multiplication of regulations will solve the problem of compensating a deprived child for the loss of his home. It is essentially an individual problem depending for its solution in each case on the insight and experience of those actually dealing with the children.'

[2] *Training in Child Care*. Interim Report of the Care of Children Committee, Cmd. 6760.

[3] In some universities these are combined with other forms of casework training.

eighteenth birthday, and boys and girls whose education is continued after this age may receive financial support until it is complete. The Curtis Committee, stressed that after-care should be a matter of deep concern, and, after commending the schemes developed by some voluntary organisations, recommended that young people going out into the world should be encouraged to keep in touch with the children's officer and to feel that they could turn to him for advice and help in any difficulty.[1] One of the major problems young people encounter is that of finding suitable accommodation within easy reach of their work, and the Children Act empowers local authorities to provide hostels for young people under the age of twenty-one. These hostels are to be available not only for young people under the care of the authority, but for other young workers in the area. This is a valuable provision, as it enables young people hitherto isolated from their contemporaries to mix freely with those who come from ordinary homes and gives them a better chance of growing up into normal members of the community, which is the aim of all forms of care of deprived children.

[1] Op. cit., par. 504.

CHAPTER XV

THE YOUTH EMPLOYMENT SERVICE

A MAJOR question, frequently raised when the aims of education are discussed, is that of the extent to which it should take cognisance of the type of work that boys and girls are likely to go in for when they leave school and prepare them for it. Opinions differ on this issue,[1] but it has long been recognised that the adolescent leaving school for work cannot be left to find his own way in the unfamiliar world of industry and employment, but should be assisted to find the niche in it for which he is best suited by aptitude and ability, and when he has found it be protected from exploitation and injury. Thus, the early years of the century, which, as we have seen, witnessed the gradual realisation by local education authorities that their responsibilities extended beyond instruction to providing for the physical and social needs of the children in their care, also saw the beginnings of the youth employment service. Local education authorities began to advise school leavers as to choice of employment, setting up juvenile employment bureaux for the purpose, and in 1910 this work was officially recognised by the Education (Choice of Employment) Act, which empowered them to advise boys and girls under seventeen[2] as to the choice of a career.

Meanwhile, the passing of the Labour Exchanges Act, 1909, resulted in the establishment by the Board of Trade of employment exchanges, primarily for adults, but often including juvenile departments. Not surprisingly these parallel developments by local education authorities and the Board of Trade resulted in confusion and overlapping, and this was increased by the extension of unemployment insurance to cover boys and girls over the age of sixteen by the Unemployment Insurance Act, 1920. In 1923, as the result of an inquiry into the whole question, local education authorities were allowed to choose between administering the

---

[1] One of the recommendations of Working Party 'B' of the study undertaken by King George's Jubilee Trust into the influences affecting the upbringing of young people was that 'More emphasis should be placed at home and in the school on preparation for work and the production of a positive attitude to work.' *Citizens of To-morrow*, p. 59, Recommendation 1.

[2] The youth employment service now caters for young people up to the age of eighteen years or until they leave school, whichever is later.

236

whole juvenile employment service, including unemployment insurance, in their respective areas, or leaving it entirely alone, in which case the Ministry of Labour, which by now had taken over the employment functions of the Board of Trade, would take full responsibility. Central government control remained divided between the Board of Education and the Ministry of Labour until 1927, when the Minister of Labour was put in charge and made responsible for supervising and paying grants to those local education authorities (104 out of a possible 315) who had decided to exercise juvenile employment powers.

The dual system of local administration thus established continued without any further administrative changes until towards the end of the Second World War, when Mr. Ernest Bevin, who was then Minister of Labour, set up a Committee under the chairmanship of Sir Godfrey H. Ince 'to consider the measures necessary to establish a comprehensive Juvenile Employment Service ... and to make suggestions for a practicable scheme'. The committee issued its Report in September 1945[1] and the changes in the administration of the service which it recommended were embodied in the Employment and Training Act, 1948.

These changes, although important, were not fundamental, since the Committee, while it was unanimous in its view that an administratively unified service was desirable, found itself unable to agree as to which of the two alternative methods of administration developed during the previous thirty-five years was in fact the more desirable on grounds of principle or expediency. This divergence of opinion was perhaps to be expected from the very nature of the service itself, since it has both educational and industrial aspects. It guides and sustains the adolescent in his passage from school to work, and hence, of necessity, belongs in some measure to each of these different worlds. The dual nature of the service has been emphasised as our knowledge of the scope and character of vocational guidance has increased, for it is now recognised that this is more than a series of tests and interviews taking place during the child's last term, or even his last year, at school, but a continuous process, possibly lasting several years, starting when his interest is first aroused in the question of his future work, and not complete until he is settled in congenial employment, with appropriate prospects of advancement.[2]

Consideration of these matters brings home the difficulty of devising machinery which will do justice to all aspects, educational

[1] Ministry of Labour and National Service, Report of the Committee on the Juvenile Employment Service, H.M.S.O., 1945.
[2] J. W. Reeves and V. W. Wilson, *Vocational Guidance in Warrington*. First published as an article in *Occupational Psychology*, Vol. XXIII, No. 2, April 1949.

and industrial, of youth employment work. In the event, the solution adopted was, as far as central government machinery was concerned, the creation of the Central Youth Employment Executive[1] staffed by officers of the Ministry of Labour, and the Education Departments of England and Wales and Scotland, and the Minister of Labour, who remains the responsible Minister, may delegate his youth employment functions to this body.[2] The committee is supported by a National Youth Employment Council, which consists of representatives of interested bodies such as local authorities, teachers, employers and employees, and its function is to advise the Minister on all questions affecting the service.[3]

Unification has thus been brought about centrally, but the dual system remains in the areas. After the passing of the Act each local education authority had to decide afresh whether or not it wished to provide a youth employment service. If it did so decide, the scheme it operated had to be approved by the Minister and cover the whole of its area. Of the 181 local education authorities in Great Britain, 128 are at present operating the service.[4] In the remaining areas the service is administered by the Ministry of Labour through the local employment exchanges. Evidence given by witnesses from both the Ministry of Labour and the Ministry of Education to the Select Committee on Estimates in 1957 indicated that although this set-up is rather illogical, it works reasonably well. Relationships between the parties concerned are generally good and there appears to be no essential difference between the parts of the service run by the Ministry of Labour and the parts run by the local education authorities.[5] Local offices are inspected by inspectors appointed by the Central Youth Employment Executive helped by H.M. Inspectors of Schools and the work of

[1] Until the passing of the Employment and Training Act the service was known as the Juvenile Employment Service, and the word 'juvenile' always used in connection with it. The Act substituted the word 'youth'.

[2] Employment and Training Act, Section 7 (1).

[3] Section 8 and First Schedule. A National Juvenile Employment Council with Advisory Committees for Scotland and Wales was appointed in 1947, in accordance with the recommendations of the Ince Committee. The Youth Employment Council established under the terms of the Employment and Training Act, 1948, had a constitution similar to that of the existing council and consequently membership was continued. It issues triennial reports which outline the developments taking place in the service from year to year.

[4] The number of local education authorities entitled to administer the service was reduced from 315 to 181 by the administrative changes brought about by the Education Act, 1944, which eliminated the old 'Part III' Authorities (i.e. the larger municipal boroughs and urban district councils) which had hitherto been recognised for juvenile employment purposes, and concentrated all the education services in the hands of the county councils and county borough councils. In England and Wales 43 out of the 63 county councils and 73 out of 83 county boroughs operate the service, in Scotland 9 out of 31 county councils

this inspectorate 'has proved particularly valuable in developing and unifying the service through the country', for in this way the Central Executive 'has been able not only to supplement the guidance on policy and procedure which has been issued centrally, but also to spread more widely new ideas and methods which have been successfully tried out elsewhere.[1]

Whether the youth employment service be administered locally by the education authority or as part of the work of the employment exchange, its objects remain the same. They are to assist the adolescent first to choose, and then to find the type of employment best suited to his aptitudes and abilities, and see him happily settled in it. This involves as complete an assessment as possible of the young person's physical, mental and personality traits, and a comparable analysis of the aptitudes required by different occupations. While much of this work is in the experimental stage a good deal of progress has been made in both types of investigation, and vocational guidance procedure is becoming increasingly scientific and accurate.

One of the earliest authorities to explore the possibilities of scientific vocational guidance was the city of Birmingham where experimentation in co-operation with the National Institute of Industrial Psychology began as long ago as 1924. Both children given vocational guidance based on scientific tests and a control group of children advised without the aid of such tests were followed up for some years after leaving school, and their employment records provided definite evidence that 'the adoption of scientific methods in vocational guidance improves very considerably the advice that can be given to children leaving school. Children given vocational guidance by these methods and who follow the advice are much more happily placed in employment, are more permanently settled, and are of greater value to their employers than children who are specially guided but do not follow the advice, and also than children who are given vocational guidance in the usual way'[2]—that is without specific scientific tests. Other authorities have experimented along similar lines. For

and 3 out of 4 town councils. Memorandum submitted on behalf of the Minister of Labour to the Select Committee on Estimates, January 1957.

[5] Mr. A. A. Part, Under-Secretary, Further Education Branch, Ministry of Education, Minutes of Evidence, Seventh Report Select Committee on Estimates, Session 1956–7. *Youth Employment Service and Youth Service Grants.* Q.239. Cf. replies by the witnesses from the Ministry of Labour to Qs. 90 and 119–23, in which the same points are made.

[1] *The Work of the Youth Employment Service, 1953–1956.* A Report by the National Youth Employment Council, p. 3.

[2] Percival Smith, 'Twenty-five Years of Research in Vocational Guidance', *Occupational Psychology*, Vol. XXV, No. 1, January 1951, p. 39.

example, the County Borough of Warrington (Lancashire) sought the advice of the National Institute of Industrial Psychology in framing its youth employment scheme, and the Institute worked out a procedure which included the appointment in each school of a 'careers teacher' who gets to know each boy and girl individually over a period of years, and helps them to participate intelligently in the planning of his own future, regular visits to the school by the youth employment officer for the purpose of interviewing leavers, and school conferences attended by the head teacher, the careers teacher, the youth employment officer and the child's parents, at which the information obtained about the child is reviewed and a decision reached on the vocational advice to be given.[1]

The schemes evolved at Birmingham and Warrington are but two examples of the work that is being done throughout the country to improve the quality of advice as to employment given to school leavers. The Employment and Training Act laid it down that those authorities who elected to operate a youth employment service in their areas must do so in accordance with a scheme approved by the Minister, and he has decided that such schemes must include vocational guidance to school leavers on lines similar to those laid down in a Model Scheme prepared after consultation with the National Youth Employment Council.[2] The requirements of this scheme include the enlargement of the pupil's knowledge of different kinds of work available by means of careers talks given by the youth employment officer and by workers in particular occupations, which may be supplemented by films or factory visits; the recording and collation of information about the health, abilities, aptitudes and educational attainments of the pupil; and a personal interview between the youth employment officer and the school leaver.

The framers of the Model Scheme regard the child's interview with the youth employment officer as 'the most important stage in vocational guidance'.[3] It usually takes place in the youngster's last term at school. His parents are invited to attend and the head teacher or some other member of the school staff is frequently present. It provides an opportunity for the officer to meet the child

---

[1] J. W. Reeves and V. W. Wilson, *Vocational Guidance in Warrington*, N.I.I.P., 1949, p. 8.

[2] Ministry of Labour and National Service, Central Youth Employment Executive, *Youth Employment Service*, Memorandum on the Exercise by Local Education Authorities in England and Wales and Education Authorities in Scotland of their powers under Section 10 of the Employment and Training Act, 1948, H.M.S.O., 1948.

[3] Ministry of Labour and Central Youth Employment Executive, op. cit., p. 5.

and make his own assessment of him, while the latter gets to know an official of the youth employment bureau on his own ground before meeting him in an unfamiliar setting. When, after leaving school, the child visits the bureau the youth employment officer, thanks to his previous contacts and to the information provided by the school, is in a position to recommend the type of employment best suited to that particular child, and to make concrete suggestions to him.

As is the case in so many of the social services, the success of the youth employment service depends not only on the efficiency of its procedure or on the comprehensiveness of its schemes, but on the calibre of its staff. The key position in the service is held by the youth employment officer who, if he is to succeed in his work, must be able to win the confidence, not only of teachers, medical officers and others connected with the schools, but also of the representatives of industry, commerce and the professions. He must also know, not merely in theory but in fact, both what kind of an education the child receives at school, and what goes on in industrial establishments and other places of employment. Last, but not least, he must be accepted by the boys and girls and their parents, so that he will not only be able to formulate advice, but will gain acceptance for it.[1] He must thus be a man of many parts, and the recruitment and training of an adequate number of persons competent to undertake this work is essential if the service is to function effectively. In 1951 the Minister of Labour, acting in consultation with the Minister of Education and the Secretary of State for Scotland set up a committee under the chairmanship of Lord Piercy, then chairman of the National Youth Employment Council, to consider these questions of recruitment and training, and the committee recommended the establishment of a full-time training course, lasting a year, for prospective youth employment officers.[2] This recommendation was accepted in principle by the Minister of Labour, but, for reasons of economy has never been put into effect. Meanwhile the Kent Education Authority has continued the year's residential course at Lamorbey Park, which started in 1948, was intended originally for its own officers, but has been extended to include applicants from all over the country. In 1957 twenty-five students were taking this course.[3] A much shorter course, lasting only four weeks, is run by the Ministry of

[1] 'The ultimate aim of the vocational adviser is to formulate advice and gain acceptance for it.' Report of the National Youth Employment Council on the Work of the Youth Employment Service, 1947–50, p. 13.

[2] Report of the Committee on Recruitment and Training for the Youth Employment Service. H.M.S.O., 1951.

[3] Seventh Report from the Select Committee on Estimates, Q.157, p. 25, Ministry of Labour and National Service.

Labour jointly with the Youth Employment Executive at Birk-beck College, London, for newly appointed officers, and the National Association of Youth Employment Officers organises its own diploma course for existing officers. These courses only cover a minority of the men and women engaged in this work, however. There is no generally accepted training requirement and the great majority learn on the job. As pointed out by one of the witnesses to the Select Committee on Estimates,[1] this is a state of affairs which serves well enough as long as the objective of the service is limited to 'placing' boys and girls in employment, but it militates against the development of a real vocational guidance service. This is unfortunate as the true value of the service lies not simply in placement but in making the best use of the child's talents and abilities, and it should be judged by its success or failure in doing this.[2]

The recruitment and training of suitable officers is one of the difficulties which besets the youth employment service. Another problem is that of ensuring that it is used to the full both by potential employers and young people seeking work. Employers are under no obligation to notify vacancies, nor are young people compelled to make use of the service in finding work. This means that the officials of a youth employment bureau are not always fully conversant with the vacancies in their area, nor are they in touch with all young people who might be capable of filling them. The Ince Committee regarded this as 'a basic weakness of the system and the prime cause for it not being as effective as it might be',[3] and considered various means, including the possibility of compelling employers to notify all vacancies and all juveniles to report, of overcoming it. After careful consideration it rejected such drastic measures, however, and the only hint of compulsion contained in the Employment and Training Act is the clause[4] which empowers the Minister to make regulations obliging schools to furnish the service with particulars about their leavers and other pupils reaching a prescribed age. These Regulations[5] became operative at the beginning of 1950, but for the present apply only to pupils who are within six months of the date on which they will attain the upper limit of compulsory school age and are likely to leave school on attaining this limit. They do not apply to schools

[1] Dr. W. P. Alexander, Secretary of the Association of Education Committees. Op. cit., Q.650, pp. 75–6.
[2] Report, p. v.
[3] Report of the Committee on the Juvenile Employment Service, p, 10, par. 32.
[4] Section 13.
[5] The Youth Employment Service (Particulars) Regulations, 1949, S.I. 1949, No. 118.

maintained by the local education authority in areas where it operates the youth employment service, but the Minister expects that the information passed on to the youth employment bureau from maintained schools will include particulars similar to those required from other schools by the Regulations.[1] The obligation laid on schools to furnish particulars about their leavers means that youth employment officers now know the numbers of young people entering the labour market in their area each half-year and their potentialities, but not all of them will make use of the youth employment bureau. The extent to which both employers and leavers do this is to a large extent a measure of the efficiency with which its officials fit the young worker into the right job, and of the understanding and sympathy with which they carry out their task, but is also affected by such factors as local traditions and employment opportunities.[2]

A difficulty which faces youth employment officers in some parts of the country, for example in mining and rural areas, is that the variety of the occupations available for young people is very limited. In other parts of the country there is a shortage of openings in skilled trades. Facilities exist for the transfer of young people who wish to train for skilled trades to areas where there are wider opportunities, and financial assistance is available for those who are willing to take advantage of such schemes, but in practice, it is found only too often that boys and girls (or their parents) are unwilling to face the prospect of separation from home. Thus an officer who has had long experience in an area where even now there is considerable adult unemployment, and a serious shortage of openings in skilled and semi-skilled occupations for boys, gives it as his opinion that: 'The extent to which boys and girls, now more mature, more thoughtful, and indeed more critical as to employment, are being able to embark upon the careers for which they have been prepared in schools, must inevitably be determined to a very large extent by the opportunities available in the immediate neighbourhood. Experience shows that only a few parents are willing to allow their children to transfer to other districts where skilled openings occur, although the machinery exists to assist them in meeting their financial obligations.'[3] The majority of young people, whatever their aptitudes, are condemned to remain in their own area, restless and frustrated, either without

[1] *Youth Employment Service*, Memorandum to Local Education Authorities, 1948.
[2] For evidence as to the use made of the youth employment service by adolescent boys see the Memorandum submitted to the Select Committee on Estimates by the National Association of Boys Clubs. Report, pp. 114–119.
[3] City of Liverpool Education Committee, Report of the Youth Employment Service for the year ended 31 July 1949, p. 14.

work, or in jobs in which their capacities are not used to the full.

Shortage of suitable openings for the more able of his applicants may thus be one of the problems of the youth employment officer, at least in some areas; a difficulty which is likely to confront him wherever he works is that of placing mentally or physically handicapped children. The number of these may be comparatively small, but each applicant presents his or her individual problems, and satisfactory placement may require a great deal of care and thought. The youth employment officer dealing with the case must understand not only the general physical and psychological consequences of the young person's handicap, whatever it may be, but also its effect on that particular adolescent, and in many cases should make contact with the home so that he knows something about the child's home background and the attitude of the parents to the disability. It is also necessary to help employers to achieve a better understanding of the types of work most suitable for disabled boys or girls, and the ways in which they can be assisted to make good. Thus, for example, there is still a great deal of prejudice to overcome about the employment of educationally sub-normal children. The officer quoted above comments, 'It is frequently overlooked that the boy or girl who is officially classified as "educationally sub-normal" may have as stable a temperament and as pleasing a disposition as his more intelligent brothers and sisters, and may prove as loyal and hard-working an employee on routine duties within his capacity. . . . While they may be slow at learning new operations and require extra patience on the part of the employer in the early stages . . . it has been found in many instances that this patience has been amply repaid, for they develop a loyalty to the employer, and an intense sense of individual responsibility for the piece of work on which they are engaged.'[1]

The special needs of handicapped children and the employment problems they present[2] have been recognised by the Central Youth Employment Executive, which has given a good deal of consideration to the ways in which the youth employment service can help such young people, and has issued a memorandum of advice to local youth employment committees and officers on the subject. In large areas it is possible for specially appointed officers, particularly interested in and with the necessary aptitudes for work with handicapped young people, to devote their full time to

---

[1] City of Liverpool Education Committee, Report of the Youth Employment Service for the year ended 31 July 1949, pp. 15–16.

[2] These problems are discussed in detail in a study made in Glasgow by T. Ferguson, A. N. MacPhail and Margaret I. McVean, *Employment Problems of Disabled Youth in Glasgow*. Medical Research Council, 1952.

it, but for the most part no such special provision is possible and youth employment officers deal with the problems of the handicapped as part of their general duties. This lack of specialisation over the greater part of the service underlines the need for youth employment officers, giving vocational guidance to, or seeking to place handicapped children, to co-operate with all agencies, both statutory and voluntary, operating in this and related fields, and to utilise whatever specialist knowledge and experience is available. 'The interests of the child demand the mobilising of all available resources and no one, however experienced in work of this kind, can afford to dispense with the specialist assistance of others.'[1] In their report for 1955–6 the Youth Employment Council comments on the great trouble taken by officers to advise and place handicapped young people satisfactorily, and also on 'the sympathy and co-operation extended to them by numerous employers in this exacting but most rewarding work.[2] They point out, however, that difficulties of placement may increase with the rise of the school-leaving population, so that it is important that no effort should be spared to develop to the utmost the facilities available in this field, and to continue fundamental research into its problems.

An interesting development which has taken place since the inception of the youth employment service, is its expansion and adaptation to meet the needs of grammar school pupils, for example, by careers conventions and conferences. These schools are making increasing use of it, and, while the service as a whole is not yet fully competent in all areas to deal with such pupils adequately, progress is being made and more attention being paid to the older school leaver. Some of the larger cities have had specialist sections for this group of boys and girls for many years, and also make special provision for young people from the technical and commercial schools.

Vocational guidance does not end when the school leaver is placed in what appears to be suitable employment, and the youth employment service in most areas includes measures for keeping in contact with young people placed by bureaux during the early years of their employment. The procedure most generally used for this purpose is that of holding 'Open Evenings' which the young worker is invited to attend, and is given an opportunity of discussing his work and prospects with the youth employment officers or members of the local after-care Committee. During the three years 1953–6 789,886 of the 1,807,285 boys and girls in Great

---

[1] Report of the National Youth Employment Council on the Work of the Youth Employment Service, 1950–1953, p. 9. The whole of ch. 3 of this report is concerned with handicapped children.

[2] Report for 1955–6, p. 18.

Britain, invited to attend 'open evenings' replied in person or writing, but it is the opinion of a number of youth employment officers that it is often those young people most in need of help who fail to respond, and other means of follow-up must be utilised in these cases, for example, home visits or contacts through employers or youth workers.[1] By these and similar means the young worker is encouraged to look on the youth employment officers as experienced and understanding friends to whom he can turn for counsel and guidance about his employment, who will encourage and advise him if he wishes to better himself, or, if he is unhappy or unsuccessful in his first choice, will give him further help and guidance until he is suitably placed, and can make his own way in the world.[2]

[1] Report by the National Youth Employment Council 1953–56, Table A, p. 23.
[2] Ibid., pp. 9-10.

CHAPTER XVI

THE YOUNG WORKER

THE youth employment officer advises the school leaver as to his choice of employment, and is available to help again if called upon, but once inside the factory, shop or office where he has obtained work the young worker must make his own way, and he may find adjustment to the new life and conditions difficult. However little he may have recognised it, the school as an institution existed for his benefit, and all that went on there was designed and adapted to foster his growth and development. The purposes of industry are different, however; the younger worker is no longer an end in himself, but has become an instrument in the production, distribution and sale of a given article, and while at work, his own interests must be subordinate to those of his employers, be they public corporation or private firm.[1] He must also become accustomed to longer hours, shorter holidays and more monotonous, yet more exacting, tasks than he had at school.

In the larger and more progressive firms the staffs of the personnel management department will watch over him and assist him through the initial period of adjustment, but the Working Party appointed by King George's Jubilee Trust to study influences of employment on young people concluded that 'perhaps only one young person in ten goes into employment where there is a specialist staff to receive, train and generally look after his interests. . . . In nine cases out of ten, therefore, responsibility for training the boy or girl at work falls directly on the immediate superior in the line of control.'[2] This emphasises the need not only for employers and managers, but also for foremen and supervisors at all levels, together with the trade unions, to take an active

---

[1] Cf. Ministry of Education, Central Advisory Council for Education (England), *School and Life*, H.M.S.O., 1947, p. 52: 'The object of employment is the product; in education it is the process which matters. In industry the worker is part of a process ending in goods, in education he is an end in himself.'

[2] King George's Jubilee Trust, *Citizens of Tomorrow*, a Study of the influences affecting the upbringing of young people, p. 78. Cf. M. E. Herford, *Youth at Work*, a five-year study by an appointed factory doctor, p. 79. 'The foreman or chargehand to them represents the firm, the employer; unless these officials know how to lead, the youngster will not stay.'

interest in the training and welfare of young people in their first year or two in industry and employment when work habits and attitudes are being formed.

Increasing attention is now being given to the question of the best methods of induction and training of young workers both skilled and unskilled,[1] although there is still room for improvement, especially for the majority of boys and girls who are neither apprenticed nor in work leading to a recognised profession and therefore not undergoing the training and discipline associated with the mastery of a skilled craft. One encouraging feature in the total situation is that, although the provisions of the Education Act, 1944, establishing county colleges and enforcing the attendance thereat of young workers between fourteen and eighteen have not been fully implemented, day release schemes in connection with either technical schools or colleges for further education are becoming more widespread.[2]

Thus, from the time when he enters his first job the young worker's progress and well-being will depend in large measure on the attitudes of his employers and fellow-workers towards him, and these are matters which cannot be ordered by legislation. What the State does is to insist that his physical environment is safe and healthy, which means regulating conditions in all occupations, and prohibiting his employment altogether in those which are known to be harmful,[3] also to regulate his hours of employment, and to set up wage-fixing machinery in certain trades where ordinary methods of negotiation are exceptionally difficult or impossible.

It took years of endeavour on the part of humanitarians to induce the rulers of the nation to accept the principle that society, acting through the State, must intervene in industry to protect young people from being worked beyond the limits of human endurance in the interests of greater production. Child labour was prevalent before the Industrial Revolution, and the wrongs of one category of such children, the climbing boys, roused philanthropists to seek redress by Act of Parliament as early as 1788.[4] The

---

[1] See, for example, *Bacie Journal*, Vol. XI, No. 4, December 1957, which is mainly devoted to reports on two conferences held in 1957 on 'Industry's Opportunity: the Challenge of the "Bulge".' 'Bacie' stands for British Association for Commercial and Industrial Education.

[2] In 1954–5 the number of part-time day release students was approximately 355,000 compared with approximately 167,400 in 1946–7, and 41,500 in 1937–8. *Education in 1955*, p. 49. Cf. Ministry of Education, *15 to 18*, 1959 (the 'Crowther Report') Part IV.

[3] Prohibitions of this nature are contained in the Lead Paint (Protection against Poisoning) Act, 1926; Cellulose Solutions Regulations, Chromium Plating Regulations, Pottery Regulations and others.

[4] The Act was unfortunately completely ineffective. It was not until nearly a century later that this particular form of cruelty to children was finally brought to an end.

transference of industry from home to factory simply emphasised the inhumanity of the treatment of children of the labouring classes and drew attention to it. The first attempt at restraining mill-owners from overworking the children they employed was the 'Act for the Better Protection of the Health and Morals of Apprentices and others Employed in Cotton and Other Mills and Cotton and Other Manufactures', passed in 1802, but in spite of its lengthy and comprehensive citation most of its clauses applied only to apprentices, that is, to the pauper children sent in wagon-loads from the parish workhouses of London and other large towns, and bound over to their masters until the age of twenty-one. These pauper apprentices were employed in large numbers during the early years of the Industrial Revolution, when the cotton and woollen mills were run by water-power, and situated high up the Pennine valleys away from centres of population. When steam replaced water as a source of power the place of the paupers was largely taken by 'free' children, that is the children of the hand-loom weavers and other badly paid or unemployed workers, who were obliged to send them to the mills to keep the family from starvation.[1] The next effort to protect the children, namely the Cotton Factories Regulation Act, 1819, applied to them. In fact, neither of these Acts accomplished much, as enforcement was left in the hands of the justices of the peace, and it was not until 1833 that factory legislation became effective, owing largely to the inclusion of a clause in the otherwise somewhat emasculated Act passed that year,[2] which authorised the appointment by the Crown, of inspectors armed with judicial and executive powers. From then onwards H.M. Inspectors of Factories played an increasingly important part in both seeing that successive enactments of Parliament were obeyed, however unpopular they might be, and, through their Annual Reports, drawing attention to ways in which the law could be improved and strengthened.

By 1833 the idea of State protection for children who worked in

[1] The conditions under which the children worked and the cruelties they suffered are described in the standard social and economic histories of the period, e.g. J. L. and B. Hammond, *The Town Labourer*, ch. viii.

[2] An Act to Regulate the Labour of Children and Young Persons in the Mills and Factories of the United Kingdom, 1833. It applied only to cotton and other textile mills, and decreed that no child under the age of nine was to be employed at all, children under the age of thirteen were not to work more than nine hours a day, and young people between thirteen and eighteen not more than twelve a day. Apart from the appointment of inspectors discussed above, the Act was noteworthy in that it contained a clause obliging children between the ages of nine and thirteen who worked in factories to attend school for two hours on six days a week. The clause was extremely difficult to enforce, and in some areas was almost a dead letter, but it was the first attempt to introduce compulsory education.

factories was becoming generally accepted, but the struggles of Shaftesbury, Fielden and their supporters to get the Ten Hours Bill passed show how reluctant and how limited this acceptance was. Slowly, however, the scope of factory legislation was enlarged, and by the end of the century it included extensive and detailed provisions limiting hours of work and ensuring a measure of health and safety in factories and workshops of all kinds.[1] This legislation was consolidated in 1901, and the Act then passed proved an effective instrument for ensuring reasonably good conditions in factories. But, as standards gradually improved and new processes, involving new risks, were introduced, the need for new legislation became apparent. This was met by the Factories Act, 1937, which is now the principal Act protecting factory workers. Its provisions were extended, and in some respects amended, by the Factories Act, 1948 and 1959.

In considering the provisions of the Factories Acts it is important to bear in mind that such legislation lays down minimum and not optimum standards.[2] They are, and must be, standards which even the smallest firm should carry out, and can justifiably be prosecuted for failure to do so, but, from the first, the inspectors administering the Acts have regarded it as their duty not only to insist on the maintenance of the standards laid down by law, but to interest themselves in the experiments of those progressive firms who achieve something better, and encourage others to follow their example. Further, factory inspectors, even when insisting that the letter of the law is to be carried out, seek to ensure that both occupiers and workers understand the reasons for its provisions, and try to obtain their willing co-operation in guaranteeing the safety, health and welfare of the workers.

The scope of the Factories Act, 1937, is wider than that of its predecessors. Its provisions cover not only factories and workshops as generally understood, but shipbuilding yards, docks, building sites, film studios, laundries, whether commercial or run in connection with hospitals or charitable or reformatory institutions, in fact any premises where persons are employed in manual labour on any process incidental to the making, altering, repairing, demolition or adaptation for sale of any article.[3] Moreover, young persons employed running errands or working as van boys in connection with a factory are also protected.

[1] These developments are summarised in the Annual Report of the Chief Inspector of Factories and Workshops for the year 1932, Cmd. 4377. This Report included an historical summary of the developments which had taken place since the appointment of the first H.M. Inspectors in 1833.
[2] Cf. the overcrowding standards laid down in the Housing Acts of 1935 and 1936 discussed above, Chapter VII.
[3] Factories Act, 1937, Section 151, which elaborates this definition further.

THE YOUNG WORKER

The Act and its successors are designed in the first place to safeguard the health and safety of workers, and include detailed provisions for securing adequate standards of cleanliness, space, temperature, lighting, ventilation and sanitation, the fencing of machinery, the safe working of the plant, and provisions in case of fire.[1] Statistics over a number of years having shown that young people were more liable to accidents than their elders,[2] the 1937 Act contains a clause[3] prohibiting young people (that is, persons under eighteen years of age) from operating specified machines of a dangerous nature[4] unless they have been fully instructed as to their dangers and the precautions to be observed, and either have received sufficient training in working the machine or are under the adequate supervision of a person who has a thorough knowledge of it. In spite of this provision the special difficulties and strains of the war years were accompanied by an increased accident rate among young as well as adult workers, but there has been a marked diminution since. This, while doubtless in part due to the raising of the school-leaving age, is also attributed by the Factory Department to the increased attention paid by many managements to the training of young workers. Particular emphasis is now being placed on the importance of their proper supervision and on teaching them the elements of safe working.[5] Nevertheless, there is still room for improvement, for accidents due to lack of supervision still occur, and it is sometimes found that the instructor has not realised, or paid sufficient attention to, the limitations of the young person he is instructing. Patient educational work on the part of both inspectorate and all grades of management is still essential to reduce the number of avoidable but sometimes, unfortunately, permanently disabling, accidents.[6]

The establishment of minimum standards of health and safety was early recognised as being within the scope of factory legis-

[1] The 1959 Act strengthens existing safety provisions in a number of ways.

[2] The reasons for this are discussed in the Annual Report of the Chief Inspector of Factories and Workshops for the year 1936, Cmd. 5514, ch. iii.

[3] Section 21.

[4] These machines are specified under the Dangerous Machines (Training of Young Persons) Order, 1954. S.I., No. 921, 1954.

[5] Annual Report of the Chief Inspector of Factories for the year 1946, Cmd. 7299, p. 11.

[6] Annual Report for the year 1949. Cmd. 7839, p. 45. Cf. Annual Report, 1955, p. 50: 'I have emphasised repeatedly in these Reports . . . that however good the general factory conditions may be, there is no substitute for proper instructional training and supervision. If young persons are to be transplanted from a relatively sheltered existence into industrial employment without proper precautions being taken against their inexperience, inquisitiveness, and possible propensities for mischief, accidents must inevitably happen for which their seniors are morally and possibly legally responsible.'

lation, but in the development of more varied and extensive services to enhance the general well-being of the worker the lead has usually been given by enlightened employers, the Factories Inspectorate limiting themselves in the main to encouragement and advice. The importance of paying attention to the well-being of the workers, and establishing good relations between management and men, is now more widely recognised than ever before, but the provision of welfare services by individual firms is no new thing. The day nurseries, schools, community centres, model villages and medical services on which many of our modern industrialists pride themselves are but the twentieth-century equivalents of Robert Owen's Institution for the Formation of Character opened at New Lanark in January 1816, the model village Titus Salt built round his woollen mills outside Bradford in 1854, and the surgery fitted up in the factory of a Lancashire firm, which as long ago as 1845 was employing a works doctor. Even works outings and savings banks had their early nineteenth-century forerunners. These were sporadic experiments, but after the turn of the century more and more firms began to make provisions for their workers over and above the health and safety requirements of the Factory Acts, and some even went so far as to appoint welfare workers to be responsible for their general well-being. The 1914–18 war accelerated these developments, and during the succeeding years 'welfare', which had hitherto centred round the material needs of the worker, gradually developed and merged into the much wider conception of personnel management, with its emphasis on human relations, and its concern with such matters as the engagement and training of the worker, wages, and joint consultation, as well as with health, safety, and the provision of amenities.[1] These developments were watched with interest by the Factory Department, but here, as in other directions, legislation could only insist on minimum standards of material well-being, and the welfare clauses of the Factories Act, 1937, were confined to such elementary requirements as drinking and washing facilities, cloakroom accommodation, seating and first-aid. However, the Secretary of State was em-

---

[1] 'The term personnel includes and embodies all the other titles found in the six divisions into which the function is split: Employment, Wages, Joint Consultation, Health and Safety, Welfare, Education and Training. Conversely, to take one example, the term "Welfare" is not used synonymously with personnel. Welfare is used here to denote one of the divisions included in the function of personnel management.' G. R. Moxon, *Functions of a Personnel Department*, Institute of Personnel Management, 1946, p. 3. Later the author continues: '(Welfare) . . . represents the practical expression of what the heads of a business feel to be the right and proper services which fellow human beings should enjoy. . . . Welfare is an integral part of personnel management and cannot be separated from it.' Ibid., pp. 22–3.

powered to make regulations on other matters affecting the welfare of employed persons or any class of them,[1] and during the Second World War the Department, now transferred from the Home Office to the Ministry of Labour, did much in the face of considerable difficulties, to encourage and, where necessary, enforce, higher standards of well-being for the work-people thronging into the factories and workshops in response to the call for increased production,[2] Moreover, sensitive to the personal problems the war was accentuating, and realising the contribution personnel management could make towards their solution, the Department created its own Personnel Management Branch, staffed by trained advisers whose function it was to assist firms to establish their own personnel organisation, and advise those smaller firms who could not be expected to achieve this.

General interest in the human problems of industry and the contributions management, labour and the State can make to their solution has continued, and, if anything, deepened since the war, and personnel departments are extending their scope and increasing their responsibilities. Some of these extended facilities such as selection and training directly affect the welfare of the young worker, but even those aspects of personnel management which may be of little interest to him, such as schemes for joint consultation, are in reality of great importance, because of their effect on the morale of the factory as a whole. This not only makes a great difference to his present happiness, but may influence his whole future attitude towards industrial relations.

Conditions inside the factory do much to influence the moral and physical development of the young workers, but equally important are leisure-time opportunities for healthy recreation and further education.[3] This is but one of the reasons why the hours of young persons are limited by law, although, with certain exceptions, the State does not attempt to fix the hours of adult male workers. Women, like young people, are regarded as 'protected persons', and like them may not, as a general rule, work more than nine hours a day or forty-eight hours a week. This maximum is reduced to forty-four hours in the case of boys and girls under sixteen, but a limited amount of overtime is permitted to young people between sixteen and eighteen, and to women. In addition to limiting the length of time actually worked, the Factories Act seeks to prevent undesirable 'spread-over' by limiting the length of the working day, inclusive of meals and rest breaks, to eleven

---

[1] Op. cit., Section 46.

[2] For example by making an order insisting on the provision of canteens in larger factories.

[3] These are described in the chapter which follows.

hours.[1] In general, young persons may not start work before 7 a.m.[2] or finish later than 8 p.m., or, in the case of young people under sixteen, 6 p.m. The Act also prohibits women and young persons from working more than $4\frac{1}{2}$ hours without a break of at least half an hour unless there has been a ten minute rest-pause, in which case the period of continuous employment may last for five hours.[3] On Saturdays work must cease at 1 p.m. Since this legislation became operative, the school-leaving age has been raised, and the hours worked by adults as well as juveniles have been shortened in many industries, and it may be that the time is coming when these provisions should be modified. This is an issue which affects all classes of young workers, not only those working in factories.

A useful provision for safeguarding the health of young workers is contained in Section 56 of the 1937 Act which prohibits them from being employed to lift, carry or move any load so heavy as to be likely to be injurious.[4]

One of the most difficult tasks confronting the four intrepid men who in 1833 set out to enforce the factory legislation was to ascertain the correct age of the children employed. Registration of births was not made compulsory until 1837, and for some years inspectors were forced to depend on certificates of age issued by surgeons, many of whom took this duty lightly, while some even faked certificates deliberately.[5] Consequently, in 1844 Inspectors were empowered to appoint 'certifying surgeons' whose duty it was to examine young people entering factory employment, and certify that they were satisfied that the child was of age to be employed, and that he was not incapacitated by disease. As time went on, and it became possible for the child to procure a birth certificate, it was no longer necessary to insist on a medical examination to determine his age, but such examinations were retained as tests of fitness for factory employment, and by the Act of 1901 the certifying surgeons were empowered to attach conditions to the certificates they issued. This was an advance, but in many cases the examination remained perfunctory and a Departmental Com-

[1] Factories operating a five-day week may extend the hours worked in any one day to ten, and the period of employment to twelve.

[2] Section 83 of the Act permits the Secretary of State (now the power rests with the Minister of Labour), by Regulations or by Order, to allow women or young persons to begin at 6 a.m. The only such exceptions made to date are the Bread, Flour, Confectionery and Sausage Manufacture (Commencement of Employment) Regulations, 1939, which allow women and young persons to start at 6 a.m. in such factories.

[3] Under Section 87 of the Act boys over 16 who are employed with men and whose continuous employment is necessary to enable men to carry on their work, may be employed for a five-hour spell without a ten-minute break.

[4] By the 1959 Act this provision is extended to all persons.

[5] Report of the Chief Inspector of Factories, 1932, p. 12.

mittee which considered the question in 1924 condemned the system as unsatisfactory. The Factories Act, 1937, led to some improvement, as it empowered the 'examining surgeon', as he then became,[1] to issue a temporary or modified certificate, and to ask the local education authority for the young person's school medical record, if he thought it would help him decide as to his fitness.[2]

There was still no statutory medical supervision after entry, however, unless the doctor asked for re-examination in connection with the issue of a temporary certificate, and the initial medical examination was only required for boys and girls under the age of sixteen. The Factories Act, 1948, has improved matters by extending this age limit so that young persons under the age of eighteen are now subject to medical examination not only on entry, but annually thereafter. The later Act also brought certain employments, which, although hitherto subject to other provisions of the principal Act, were not covered by the sections relating to the medical examination of young workers, within the scope of these rules.[3] This means that certificates of fitness are now required for young people employed in the loading, unloading and coaling of ships and certain other work on ships in harbour or wet dock, building operations and engineering construction as well as for those employed in factories.

The changes made in the Factories Acts, 1937, 1948 and 1959, thus mark a definite advance towards the goal of the proper supervision of the health of the young worker, but there is still room for improvement. In the first place, there is no real link between these examinations and the other health and medical services, and secondly they are confined to young people in employments covered by the Factories Acts, and there appears to be nothing to prevent a boy or girl rejected by the appointed factory doctor from obtaining equally strenuous or otherwise unsuitable work in connection with a shop or warehouse, outside the scope of factory law, where he will be without medical supervision. In the long run, if and when these sections of the Education Act, 1944, relating to the continued part-time education of boys and girls are fully implemented, these difficulties and limitations should disappear as the young people at work will then remain within the scope of the school health service. Meanwhile, and it may be for many years to come, the problem remains. There are, however, measures which could be taken to increase the coverage and efficiency of the service while awaiting this radical reform. A number of these are set

[1] The Factories Act, 1948, changed his title to that of 'appointed factory doctor'.   [2] Factories Act, 1937, Section 99.
[3] Factories Act, 1948, Section 2. Young Persons (Certificate of Fitness) Rules, 1948, S.I. 1948, No. 2162.

out by Dr. M. E. Herford, an appointed factory doctor, in his book, *Youth at Work*. He believes that the appointed factory doctor has exceptional opportunities for observing and furthering the health and wellbeing of young workers, since 'During the strain of adolescence he alone sees them on entry into industry, every time they change jobs, and once a year up to the age of eighteen if they remain in the same employment,' and 'it is his duty to see that they are fit for work and that the conditions in which they work are satisfactory'.[1] Not only can he advise the young people themselves on all their health problems, but, as an independent observer, he is in a position to exert his influence to improve conditions in the factory as they affect the young worker, and in this respect he is at an advantage compared with the doctor employed by the firm. But his work will be superficial and his influence nullified unless he has ample time for his examinations and is able to work in close co-operation with practitioners in related services, in particular the school medical service and the general practitioner.

At present liaison with these services is far from perfect, and Dr. Herford suggests that the best means of securing continuous supervision of young people from childhood to maturity would be for the appointed factory doctor in a particular area to be appointed by the local authority as part-time assistant school medical officer. Short of this, more might be done to ensure that good use is made of the school medical records. As we have seen, the appointed factory doctor has power under the Factories Act to request the local education authority to furnish him with such particulars as to the school medical record and other information as they possess regarding the medical history of the young person as he may require to carry out his duties effectively, and if so requested the local education authority must furnish this information, but this power is little used. Even when the record cards are obtained they may be found to be incomplete or unsatisfactory in other ways.[2] Similarly, it is essential for the doctor to develop close co-operation with the general practitioners to whom the young people go for treatment, sometimes on the recommendation of the appointed factory doctor, especially as many of these know little or nothing about factory employment. Perhaps the most urgently needed reform is, however, the extension of provisions made for the regular medical examination of young people in industry to those in shops, offices and other non-industrial employments. Since, if Dr. Herford's experience is typical, it is difficult to ensure the

[1] Op. cit., p. 119.
[2] At various times during the years 1952–3, Dr. Herford asked for the school medical records of 402 cases. In 75 of these the report was not received or not available, and in several cases defects which he discovered on examination had not been noted or recorded. *Youth at Work*, pp. 125–9.

examination, and particularly the annual re-examination, of boys and girls employed in small industrial firms, the organisation of a service to cover young people in the wide and varied range of non-industrial employment would be far from easy and might even entail the compulsory registration of all changes of job at the youth employment bureau. Nevertheless, more adequate provision for the medical supervision of these young workers is essential if the health of young people at work is to be adequately safeguarded.

The absence of any requirement about fitness for employment or for continued medical supervision, is but one illustration of the fact that legislation to safeguard the health and welfare of young people in non-industrial employments is less comprehensive than that covering young people in factories. The Shops Act, 1934, included clauses which are designed to establish minimum standards of health and comfort for people employed in shops, and restricted the hours of young persons, while as the result of the findings of a Departmental Committee set up in 1937,[1] the Young Persons (Employment) Act, which restricted the hours of boys and girls employed in certain categories of work outside the scope of the Factories and Shops Acts, was passed in 1938. As a result of the passing of these two Acts, and their consolidation by the Shops Act, 1950, the hours of work for boys and girls in employments covered by them are limited to forty-eight hours for juveniles over sixteen, forty-four for those under this age. Like the Factories Act they also include clauses fixing the maximum length of continuous spells of employment, limiting the daily spread-over and providing for a weekly half-holiday. Their enforcement was entrusted to the local authorities, and there appears to be some reason to believe that their control has not always been as effective as the central government's supervision of factories. In other ways, too, the position with regard to these young workers is not wholly satisfactory, and in 1946 a Committee was set up by the Home Office and the Scottish Home Department, under the chairmanship of Sir Ernest Gowers, to investigate and make recommendations concerning those provisions of the Shops Act which relate to times of closing; the statutory provisions relating to the health, safety and welfare of persons not protected by the Factories, Mines and Quarries Acts; and the statutory legislation of the hours of employment for young persons.[2]

The Committee issued their Final Report in March 1949. After a careful review of existing provisions they make various

[1] Departmental Committee on the Hours of Employment of Young Persons in Certain Unregulated Occupations, March 1937.

[2] Home Office, Scottish Home Department, *Health, Welfare and Safety in Non-Industrial Employments, Hours of Employment of Juveniles*, Report by a Committee of Inquiry, H.M.S.O., 1949, Cmd. 7664.

recommendations. While these are more limited than many would have liked and make no fundamental changes in existing legislation, they would, if they became law, materially improve the position of many young workers, bringing their hours and conditions of work more in line with those enjoyed by the employees in progressive firms. The Committee recommended the extension of protective legislation to cover juveniles in certain employments, such as office work, rail and road transport and various miscellaneous employments not within its scope, but practical considerations led them to exclude agriculture, forestry, fishing, shipping, and private domestic service from any restrictions. In view of the raising of the school-leaving age to fifteen, and the expressed intention of the Education Act that this shall become sixteen as soon as possible, they proposed that the distinction between juveniles under and those over sixteen be abolished, and suggested that the maximum weekly working hours for all young people under eighteen, whether working in factory, shop or occupation other than those listed above, should, with certain specified exceptions, be limited to forty-five hours a week. Modifications in the existing law affecting overtime, continuous spells of work, spread-over, night intervals, half-holidays, and weekly rest-days, were also recommended.[1] Since these proposals would involve a slight increase in the maximum permitted hours for young people under sixteen, they may be regarded by some as inadequate, or even slightly retrograde. In making them the Committee had clearly been influenced both by the need for avoiding any serious dislocation in industry or commerce which might arise if the hours of young people were very different from those of adults, and any possibility that their recommendations might have the effect of reducing output. Similar practical considerations have led them to reject the idea of a comprehensive code governing conditions of employment for all young workers, desirable as this might be. Although more than ten years have passed since this Committee reported, their recommendations have not yet been made law.

The Report and Recommendations of the 'Gowers' Committee on Health, Welfare and Safety in Non-industrial Employments, illustrates the possibilities and limitations of state action in securing good conditions for the young worker. In the main it is restrictive rather than creative, but it constitutes a constant reminder that although the ends of industry and commerce may be the production and distribution of goods, and the young worker is a means to these ends, he is also an immature person whose healthy all-round development must be safeguarded, and the State has a special responsibility for seeing that this is done.

[1] These recommendations are set out in tabular form in Appendix C of the Report.

CHAPTER XVII

THE SERVICE OF YOUTH

THE 'Service of Youth' is the rather ambiguous official title given to the efforts made by statutory authorities and voluntary organisations to provide young people with opportunities for informal education, social intercourse and the creative use of leisure through membership of a group. It is centred round, although not confined to, the fourteen–eighteen age range, and is, in the main, concerned to meet the needs of the young worker, but many organisations accept both younger and older members, and there is a tendency to widen its scope.

The organisations which go to make up the youth movement may be attached to parent organisations such as churches, political parties or settlements, or they may be completely independent, but to a greater or lesser degree they are self-contained, with their own membership, activities, standards and leadership. The movement as a whole is based on the assumption that the adolescent gains from membership a community of his own, which forms an alternative to the compulsory groups of home, school and work which otherwise make up his world. This community should provide boys and girls with opportunities for developing friendships, the stimulus of group activity, scope to work out their own plans, and training in the management of the affairs of their own society under the leadership of mature people.[1] It thus provides experience of a small community which stands or falls by the young people's own efforts.[2]

This underlying assumption, that membership of a small, independent group fosters the development of the adolescent's personality, has not passed unchallenged. It has been argued that youth clubs, as they are organised to-day, contribute towards the disintegration of family life and isolate boys and girls at a critical stage of their development, keeping them in an atmosphere of artificial immaturity and hindering the natural transition from childhood to the adult community.[3] The founders of the Peckham Health Centre went so far as to say that 'Perhaps the segregation of adolescents all at the same stage of development, when they should

---

[1] Central Advisory Council for Education (England), *School and Life*, p. 69.
[2] Planning, Vol. XIV, No. 280, *The Service of Youth To-day*, p. 285.
[3] This criticism is discussed in *The Service of Youth To-day*, p. 298.

be freely learning from every possible degree of maturity, is one of the worst crimes committed against growing boys and girls.'[1] These are two apparently divergent points of view, but it seems that both close association with the adult community and opportunities for withdrawal from it into a group of his own are desired and needed by the adolescent as his development proceeds. As the Rev. Bryan H. Reed puts it, 'The dilemma in which we are caught up arises from the difficulty of creating a social setting for youth work which will give full recognition to two conflicting facts—the fact that much can be given to adolescents through their association with children and with adults, and the fact that the younger adolescents desperately need a society of their own where away from parental influence they can make their first explorations of a wider world.'[2] If they cannot find an organised group which satisfies their need for companionship, activity and adventure, they will form their own cliques and gangs and seek excitement how and when they can. In overcrowded urban areas at any rate, the alternative to the youth club is not the home but the street, the dance-hall, the pin-table saloon or the cinema. The activities young people enjoy in these places may be harmless, even if they are 'somewhat uncreative and lacking in imagination', but temptations to destructiveness, delinquency and immorality are frequently present and not easily resisted.[3] In such areas a young people's club which makes and maintains contacts with the parents of the members may well strengthen rather than weaken family ties, and encourage the parents' responsibility and concern for their children. The social workers in this situation are acting as parent supplements, and not as parent substitutes.[4]

From the administrative standpoint the 'service of youth' is a

[1] Innes H. Pearce and L. H. Crocker, *The Peckham Experiment*, p. 223.

[2] *Eighty Thousand Adolescents*, 1950, p. 158.

[3] The phrase in inverted commas is taken from J. B. Mays, *Growing up in the City*, p. 73. See also p. 91, in the same book: 'The older children live their own lives in the company of their contemporaries. . . . Over the age of twelve, boys do not seem to spend much time in the home except when they are sick . . . partly because of feelings of restlessness, partly because the amenities of the house are not very attractive, and partly as a result of social tradition.' Cf. G. W. Jordan and E. M. Fisher, *Self Portrait of Youth*, p. 3. 'Despite this differentiation in ancestry, religion and early environment . . . these children had a number of common tastes and habits. One was that they never stayed at home in the evening. . . . Had there been, in our area, no elementary form of further education, these youngsters would have roamed the streets or gone to the pictures every evening.' See also J. McAlister Brew, *Youth and Youth Groups*, ch. 2, 'The Adolescent at Large'.

[4] An experimental club in which close contacts with the parents are an essential part of the work is described by J. B. Mays in a study of group-work with problem boys, which he has called *On the Threshold of Delinquency*, and which was published by the Liverpool University Press in 1959.

partnership between statutory and voluntary organisations, a partnership which has evolved to meet the changing needs and ideas of successive generations. Until the First World War the provision of recreational facilities for young people was in the hands of the voluntary organisations. The State interested itself in the vocational education of those who wished to improve their chances in life, or increase their skill in technical college or evening institutes, but voluntary organisations, such as the Y.M.C.A., Y.W.C.A., brigades, scouts, guides, and clubs which sought to provide opportunities for healthy recreation for young workers were left to carry on without assistance or interference. Much good work was done, but only a minority of young people were reached, and then, as now, the orthodox organisations often failed to attract the young people whose needs they particularly wanted to meet— those from poor homes who wandered about the streets in their leisure hours, liable to drift into immorality and crime. The increase in juvenile delinquency during the 1914–18 war led the State to take action[1] by encouraging the setting up throughout the country of juvenile organisation committees, made up of representatives of the local education authorities, voluntary organisations, and persons particularly interested in youth work. In most areas this experiment was only half-heartedly carried out, however, and throughout the inter-war years the initiative remained with the voluntary organisations. They were, however, able to obtain some assistance from their local education authorities by invoking Section 86 of the Education Act, 1921, which empowered these authorities to provide for the social and recreational needs of young persons under the age of eighteen, whether attached to schools or evening institutes or not.

The Second World War, like the First, resulted in major developments in youth work. This time the Board of Education acted immediately, for it feared that 'the strain of war and the disorganisation of family life would create conditions constituting a serious menace to youth'.[2] Hence, as early as September 1939 it established the National Youth Committee, later replaced by the Youth Advisory Council, and in November of the same year issued Circular 1486, *In the Service of Youth*, which laid down the lines along which it hoped the Service would develop. Local education authorities responsible for higher education were urged to establish youth committees composed of representatives of the education committee and voluntary organisations, together with individuals

---

[1] It is significant that the first move came not from the Board of Education but from the Home Office. At the end of the war the Board of Education took over the responsibility.

[2] Board of Education Circular 1486, *In the Service of Youth*.

concerned with the welfare of youth, and the Circular expressed the hope that 'in the Youth Committee the individual traditions and special experience of youth possessed by the voluntary organisations will be joined with the prestige and resources of the Local Education Authorities'. Underlying aims and administrative proposals were thus similar in 1916 and 1939, but in 1939 their implementation was pursued with greater vigour. Youth committees were set up, and organisers appointed in counties and county boroughs throughout the country, while in some areas these committees, as well as encouraging and assisting voluntary bodies, established youth clubs of their own in those parts of their districts where provision was inadequate.

Thus the first war-time reaction of those concerned about the welfare of young people was an attempt to protect them from the war's moral dangers, but soon a significant change occurred. In the stress of total war the services of youth were needed, it must share in the nation's struggle for survival. This resulted in the development of the pre-service organisations, the Ranger Home Emergency Service and other offshoots of existing organisations, and spontaneous efforts by boys and girls to organise themselves for useful service. The enthusiasm with which some young people who had remained indifferent to previous attempts to reach them responded to this new approach is significant, and suggests that some of the more spirited young people who refuse to respond to efforts made for their good, will do so if they can discover a common purpose with which they can identify themselves. This stimulus of a common purpose which the young people understood and shared operated during the war, but it appears to have been lost again,[1] and one of the serious difficulties of the youth movement to-day is the rootlessness and insecurity, and consequent cynicism and hostility, of many of the young people whose needs it is seeking to meet.[2]

The war years witnessed a rapid expansion of the youth service, both in the numbers of young people brought within the scope of its various organisations and in the range and variety of opportunities available for them. Their most important administrative legacy is the partnership between the Ministry of Education, the local authorities and the voluntary organisations which was established then. Since the passage of the Education Act, 1944, the terms of reference of this partnership have been widened. The service of youth now forms part of a comprehensive scheme of further education in connection with which it is the duty of local education authorities to secure full-time and part-time education

[1] Cf. L. J. Barnes, *Youth Service in an English County* (Report prepared for King George's Jubilee Trust), pars. 41–3.
[2] Cf. Ministry of Education, *The Youth Service in England and Wales*, Cmnd. 929 (the 'Albermarle' Report), par. 69, p. 18.

for persons over compulsory school age, and 'leisure-time occupations in such organised cultural, training and recreative activities
as are suited to their requirements, for any persons over school age
who are able and willing to profit by the facilities provided for
them'.[1] Thus the rigid upper age limit for L.E.A. assistance has
been removed and youth clubs are given wider scope.

During the years immediately following the passing of the
Education Act, the nature of the partnership, both ideal and actual,
between local education authorities and voluntary organisations
was under almost continuous review and the roles of the two partners
variously interpreted[2] and, in those early days, 'it was indeed an
achievement to produce a friendly and operative partnership between statutory and voluntary bodies'. Even now the nature and
cordiality of the relationship varies from area to area, but it is
becoming recognised that 'the important thing at present is to emphasise the unity of the whole work by whomsoever it may be done'.[3]

Youth organisations, whether statutory or voluntary, may be
divided into three main types. First, there are those which are
closely linked with some parent organisation, and which exist, not
as ends in themselves, but as means by which the younger generation are trained in the beliefs and principles of the parent body
and learn to identify themselves with it. The youth groups connected with the churches form the majority here, but this division
also includes youth movements sponsored by political parties and
the co-operative youth movement. Secondly, there are what are
sometimes called the uniformed organisations, such as the scouts,
guides and brigades, whose local units may or may not be attached to some adult organisation such as a church, but which
have their own definite aims, set out in clearly defined codes,
which not only outline the principles underlying the movement's
work, but designate the means by which they are to be carried out
in practice. Finally, there is the heterogeneous mass of boys', girls'
and mixed clubs and youth centres of all types and sizes. 'They
may be run by an *ad hoc* committee and be entirely a law unto
themselves, or they may be promoted by or affiliated to a national
youth organisation, or they may be entirely provided and "ser-
viced" by the L.E.A. They may exist to promote a variety of purposes and make certain demands on their members, or they may
exist for no purpose discernible by them, and one of their methods
may be to make no explicit demands on those who join them.'[4]

[1] Education Act, 1944, Section 41 (b).
[2] See, for example, L. J. Barnes, *The Outlook for Youth Work*, or, for a different
interpretation, B. H. Reed, *Eighty Thousand Adolescents*.
[3] King George's Jubilee Trust, *Citizens of To-morrow*, p. 101.
[4] Eileen Younghusband, *Employment and Training of Social Workers*, p. 118.

They vary very considerably in size, premises, frequency of opening, leadership and activities. Recreational facilities such as dancing, games and opportunities for social intercourse usually figure prominently in their programmes, but the clubs may also provide informal classes, possibly with the assistance of teachers supplied by the local education authority. Their characteristic feature is, however, that membership of the club is regarded as an end in itself, and more importance is attached to the group than to any purpose or activity to which it may lend itself, for it is maintained that membership of the group gives the adolescent freedom and opportunity to develop his own activities and interests.[1]

The variety of youth work is so great that it is neither easy nor safe to generalise about its achievements and limitations, its success or failure. There are some signs of disillusionment in recent surveys. Thus the Report of King George's Jubilee Trust quoted in an earlier paragraph continues, 'Unfortunately, it seems to be a fact that the Youth Service is being taken less seriously than it was. . . . There are serious doubts abroad as to the purpose of the Youth Service in these days of full employment and the claims it can make on the already over-pressed resources of the State and local authorities.'[2] A year or two earlier a team of investigators sponsored by the same body, having asked the question 'Has the Youth Service fulfilled the high hopes entertained at its inception in 1939?' felt compelled to reply 'That it provided material benefits was not in dispute: but what might have been a new and exciting experiment in the co-ordination of voluntary and statutory work seemed to have developed along prosaic and unimaginative lines.'[3] Interesting and worth-while experiments are being made by individual clubs and organisations, but the wartime inspiration seems largely to have disappeared from the movement as a whole.

It is suggested by the compilers of the report, *Citizens of To-morrow*, that perhaps the most important of the reasons for this disappointment is a stultifying doubt as to the relevance of traditional youth organisations to the life and outlook of the adolescents of to-day, boys and girls who, for the most part, have had wider educational opportunities, possess greater financial security and take for granted higher standards of material comfort and a wider choice of leisure time satisfactions than their forerunners for whose benefit youth clubs were started.[4] Even if it is accepted that youth groups have something to offer to this generation of young people,

---

[1] *The Service of Youth To-day*, p. 291.   [2] Op. cit., pp. 101 and 102.
[3] Pearl Jephcott, *Some Young People*, a Study of Adolescent Boys and Girls, sponsored by the King George's Jubilee Trust, p. 136.
[4] Cf. *The Youth Service Today*, Cmnd. 929, pp. 20–25.

there is still some doubt as to what their aims should be in a situation in which 'the most serious problem is one of emotional and spiritual poverty rather than lack of material substance'.[1] Is the youth service first and foremost 'a new and exciting form of informal education' offered to all who can profit from it and ignoring the rest, or is it primarily a therapeutic service, complementary and in some ways analogous to casework, reaching out to the delinquent, socially deprived and under-privileged but leaving the main body of adolescents to be catered for by evening institutes and, if and when they come into being, county colleges?[2] To set these two approaches in opposition to one another in this way is to stultify the all-round development of the movement, however. Since the needs and aspirations of children and adolescents are manifold and varied, the service needs the contributions both of those men and women whose approach is primarily educational and those more concerned to develop group work skills and techniques in such a way as to further the personal and social adjustment of their club members. Indeed the distinguishing mark of a good youth leader may well be that he is sufficiently balanced in his approach to be both educationalist and social worker. On the one hand, there is much truth in the observation that 'every human being, however deeply involved in emotional problems, wants to be made to develop his or her other abilities', and 'all welfare and sympathy, and no goading into purposeful activity can defeat the ends of welfare';[3] on the other it cannot be denied that the seriously maladjusted or delinquent child is likely to need help to overcome his personal and social problems before he can take real advantage of the educational opportunities which a well-run club or recreational institute has to offer him. Catering for these latter children may mean the wider provision of small selective clubs in which experiments can be made in the use of group work techniques to bring about their social rehabilitation, for reports of experimental work of this kind undertaken in the country of recent years indicate that it has been sufficiently successful to justify further expansion and wider public support.[4]

Another problem which faces the youth movement as a whole,

[1] J. McAlistair Brew, 'Group Work with Adolescents', ch. iv in *Social Group Work in Great Britain*, p. 89.

[2] Cf. J. McAlistair Brew, 'Hence, one of the most interesting features of group work among adolescents in Great Britain to-day is the unresolved conflict between those who still regard the work as a social palliative and those who regard it as a new and exciting form of informal education.' *Social Group Work in Great Britain*, p. 89.

[3] G. W. Jordan and E. M. Fisher, op. cit., p. 165.

[4] See, for example, M. Lloyd Turner, *Ship Without Sails*, and J. B. Mays, *On the Threshold of Delinquency*.

SOCIAL SERVICES FOR CHILDREN AND YOUNG PEOPLE

and the individual organisations within it, is that of relating the adolescent's opportunities and experiences in the club and its standards of conduct and relationships to those of his home, neighbourhood and conditions of employment. In the opinion of one experienced girls' club leader, 'To-day's youth organisation is, in many cases, external to the girl's working life and to the social activities in which the people of her family take part,'[1] and youth organisations, even more than schools, have always had to face the difficulty that the youngster's parents and neighbours regard them as something apart. The club which remains an alien institution with different standards and norms from those of the surrounding neighbourhood may well fail to exert much influence over more than a minority of its members, but it is not easy for the workers and leaders of an institution in a near-delinquent neighbourhood to overcome this isolation, and, at the same time, avoid the opposite danger of becoming so closely identified with the lives and outlook of the people living there that the club ceases to be effective in raising the standard of its members.[2] It is to the credit of leaders and workers in the movement that so many of them have succeeded in winning the co-operation of families and neighbours, while maintaining their own integrity and sense of purpose.

In spite of the adolescent's search for interests and activities as a member of a group of his peers and apart from his family, a search which the youth movement sets out to meet, the real centre of his life remains his home, and of all the neighbourhood links which the youth club or centre should establish, those with members' parents are most important. What may be accomplished when the club is closely linked with the home has been demonstrated by the first three years' work of a junior club for delinquent and near-delinquent boys in a dockside area, one of the features of which was the close and continuous contact maintained with the parents of the boys who attended. No boy was admitted into membership without his parents' consent, the home was visited if the boy ceased to attend regularly or was excluded for serious misconduct, and a real attempt was made to help the parents to realise that the club was a joint enterprise between themselves and the social workers to prevent their children developing wrong habits and attitudes. At the end of three years, while it was difficult to arrive at firm conclusions, and the degree of success varied from family to family, its sponsors were satisfied that, 'whatever the shortcomings of the workers associated with the club and whatever the weaknesses of their technique and method there is no doubt that some parents

[1] Pearl Jephcott, *Rising Twenty*, p. 166.
[2] This problem is discussed by J. B. Mays, *Growing Up in the City*, p. 135.

have been helped and that some children, who were straying dangerously across the threshold of delinquency, have been guided back into happier ways, safer activities and healthier relationships.'[1] They considered that the experiment had also demonstrated that while the support and help given to families whose parents were deeply and genuinely concerned with their children's welfare was completely justified, there was a hard core of seriously disturbed boys, often the products of parental rejection and lack of affection, for whom its healing influence was ineffective. For these, 'the answer, if answer there is, would appear to be in a more thorough going attempt to improve the conditions of family life and relationships that has yet been assayed in our culture.

Apart from the scouts and guides, which have always attracted, and from their earliest days made special provision for, young children, youth organisations have devoted most of their attention to young people above school-leaving age, but the needs of the younger brothers and sisters are equally, if not more, urgent, for in a crowded neighbourhood, the younger child, as well as learning to imitate the delinquent or semi-delinquent exploits of his older brother and sister, is exposed to traffic dangers and continually frustrated in his efforts to find somewhere where he can play naturally and happily.[3] It was Mrs. Humphry Ward who, before the end of the last century, gave the lead in the movement for the provision of play centres to meet the needs of these children. At first provided entirely by voluntary organisations, they can now also be sponsored by local education authorities, but in spite of the requirement of Section 53 of the Education Act, 1944, which makes it a duty of local education authorities to provide adequate facilities for recreation and social and physical training in their areas, and empowers such authorities, with the approval of the Minister, to establish, or assist in establishing, camps, holiday classes, playing fields, play-centres, and other places where these are available, the number of such centres and of junior clubs is still woefully inadequate to meet the need. The position is equally unsatisfactory with regard to play spaces, while it is only here and there that adventure playgrounds, which originated in Scandinavia with the purpose of giving the city child opportunities 'to

[1] J. B. Mays, *The Threshold of Delinquency*, p. 232.
[2] Ibid., p. 229.
[3] 'Despite the commendable impetus of the rehousing programme, thousands of children for many years to come will grow up without adequate living, growing, playing space. . . . Hordes of youngsters play among dangerous, tottering ruins on bombed sites and partially demolished buildings. One hundred and eighty-seven children have been injured on our busy streets during the past three years—some fatally.' Annual Report of the Victoria Settlement, Liverpool, year ending March 1957.

SOCIAL SERVICES FOR CHILDREN AND YOUNG PEOPLE

build, to construct, to improvise, to pull up and pull down', and of teaching him 'to use his hands and imagination in coping with whatever simple materials he finds',[1] have been established. The problem here, as in the work with older boys and girls, is not only sites or premises or even money, it is man and woman power to provide the skilled and understanding leadership which is necessary if the children are to use constructively the provisions made for them. Finding the right leader is, moreover, a problem not confined to play centres and junior clubs. It is the quality of its leadership which, more than any other factor, finally determines whether any club or institution for young people, of whatever nature or age range, will finally fail or succeed, 'and in the long run the youth service will stand or fall, not by the magnificence of the premises provided by the church or local education authority, or by the generositg of the Ministry of Education, but by the degree to which men and women of ability are prepared to give themselves in friendship to young people'.[2] There is, unfortunately, a real shortage of good youth leaders, and although considerable thought has been given to the possibilities of recruitment and training, it still remains. Professional youth leadership involves exacting work at awkward hours, the financial rewards are not great, and it is not generally regarded as a profession in which a person should spend the whole of his working life. Hence men and women interested in young people are more likely to be attracted by one of the many alternative openings in educational or social work. The possibility of interchange between youth leadership and professions such as teaching, youth employment and other forms of social work have been considered from time to time and recommendations made, but little appears to have been accomplished and the shortage remains.

The recruitment and training of sufficient leaders of calibre and enthusiasm is probably the most urgent of the problems facing the youth service to-day,[3] but there are other needs to be met if the quality of the service is to be such as will satisfy the sophisticated and critical young people of the mid-twentieth century. Too often premises are inadequate and old-fashioned, 'battered and paint-

[1] J. B. Mays, *Adventure in Play*, pp. 6 and 7.
[2] Bryan H. Reed, *Eighty Thousand Adolescents*, p. 166. Compare this with the concluding sentence of *Some Young People*, 'Whatever the nature of the agent to be employed in the future, the inquirers were unanimous on one point, that the spark which first lights up the possibilities of leisure, more often than not comes from the friendly concern of an older person for an individual boy or girl.'
[3] Cf. Seventh Report from the Select Committee on Estimates, Session 1956–7. *The Youth Employment Service and the Youth Service*, p. ix. 'Leadership is accepted by everyone concerned with the Service as an acute problem.'

268

less without, cold and comfortless within',[1] failing to keep pace with rising standards of homes, schools and factories with which the majority of the youngsters are familiar, not to speak of the commercial organisations such as cinemas and dance-halls with which the clubs are competing. It may be argued that through its fellowship a good club has something intangible to offer which, in the end, will more than compensate for its dreary premises and inadequate equipment, but this 'something' is not immediately obvious, nor can the restricting influence of ugly and inconvenient premises on the members range of activities, and their deadening effect on the leader's enthusiasm, be discounted. An energetic and resourceful leader will create an active club with a varied programme despite poor premises and equipment and the financial anxieties and stringencies which frequently cause and accompany them, but the cost in overwork and worry may be high. The less persistent and enterprising leader will use deficiencies of premises and equipment as an excuse for contenting himself with a programme, limited in aims and low in standards of achievement, which is unlikely to attract more than a minority of young people.

One of the most common reasons for the inadequacy and unattractiveness of many youth club premises is lack of funds, a perpetual source of anxiety to youth organisations and leaders. This is particularly true of the voluntary organisations, and the nature of the evidence given to the Select Committee on Estimates, 1957,[2] showed how widespread was the feeling that the money allocated to the youth service from central and local authority funds was both inadequate and badly distributed, and that this was having adverse psychological as well as material effects. While giving due weight to the Ministry of Education's contention that the youth service had not suffered any worse cuts as a result of the financial stringency than other educational services such as nursery schools, the Committee said in so many words that they were 'not satisfied' that the Ministry of Education was properly exercising its responsibility for the money voted, and their general impression was that 'the Ministry is little interested in the present state of the Service and apathetic about its future'. 'Your Committee considers,' they continued, 'that this apathy is having a deeply discouraging effect on the valuable work done for the Service, much of it voluntary and unpaid, and must thereby be reacting unfavourably on the value for money obtained from the Grants'.[3] This is a serious situation, and not easily remediable

[1] Pearl Jephcott, *Some Young People*, p. 124.
[2] Seventh Report from the Select Committee on Estimates, Session 1956–7. The Youth Employment Service and Youth Service Grants.
[3] Ibid., p. x.

as long as existing financial policies continued but as the Committee urged, a considered and forward looking policy with regard to youth work on the part of the Ministry of Education would do much to counteract discouragement and help organisations and clubs to plan more confidently for the future.

The following year the Minister of Education showed that he was neither unaware of or indifferent to the parlous situation by appointing a committee under the chairmanship of the Countess of Albermarle to review the position, and 'to advise according to what priorities best value can be obtained for the money spent' on the youth service. The Committee reported in February, 1960 and in presenting the report to Parliament the Minister took the almost unprecedented step of recommending its immediate acceptance and implementation. The most important recommendation was that 'the Minister of Education should initiate a ten-year development programme' divided into two stages of five years each, and should appoint a small advisory committee, the Youth Service Development Council, 'composed of men and women who have special qualities and experience to offer' for that period. The composition of Council was announced at the end of February, 1960.

The Minister's principal task, however, was recognised as being that of tackling the long-standing problem of the shortage of leaders, particularly of full-time professional leaders, for 'a strong body of such skilled workers is indispensable if the standards of the service are to be raised'. In order to furnish a corps of trained and professional leaders, teachers, social workers and 'mature persons with a natural gift for leadership' are to be encouraged to come forward for training. Various kinds of training are suggested to meet the needs of recruits of differing age, background and interest,[1] but it is considered that persons trained in recognised courses of all kinds should rank as qualified youth leaders.

Only second in priority to leadership is the improvement of facilities, and the committee recommends material improvements, planned and phased in every section of the youth service. But this cannot be brought about without cost, and 'the Minister should, at an early stage urge local education authorities to see that their expenditure on maintained and aided services is sufficient to sustain the momentum of development; and at the same time he should expand his own aid to national voluntary bodies, particularly in the form of special grants for pioneering work of direct significance to an expanding service'.[2]

[1] These are described in the Report, Chapter 6. The Committee recommendations that qualified teachers should be the main source of recruitment.

[2] Op. cit., p. 113.

It is hoped that much of the new provision made possible by this financial aid, and of the energies of the young men and women who may be attracted to a re-vitalised service, will be devoted to work of an experimental nature, for it is clear that whatever its virtues, and they are many, the youth service, as it is now, is attracting but one in nine of the young people whose needs it sets out to meet.[1]

It is true that many young people are 'unclubbable' because they have interests or hobbies of their own and are adverse to group activities, but there are others who appear to be in need of the companionship and occupation which a good club has to offer, but who fail to find their niche in any particular organisation. One of the most disquieting findings of the Birmingham survey was that a great many of the boys and girls found to be unattracted to any organisation were in fact lapsed members who believed, rightly or wrongly, that uniformed organisations catered primarily for children and that clubs on the whole are badly organised, that they dont do anything and that attendance is a 'waste of time'.[2] Experiments such as the 'Outward Bound' Centres and the Duke of Edinburgh award scheme have done much to counteract this purposelessness and help to raise standards, encourage outdoor pursuits and foster self-reliance and initiative, but they have no immediate appeal to the self-conscious and cynical street-corner boy, living in his own teen-age world and distrustful of all outsiders. For these youngsters, 'too wary or too deeply estranged to accept, at any rate initially even the slight commitment required by club-membership', the Albermarle Committee recommends such 'unconstrained' provision as the teen-age coffee-bar, and the drop-in club. They also suggest that experiments should be made with the appointment of perepatetic youth workers who would seek out and make contact with existing groups of young people, for 'only by going out to them shall we discover how to gain their confidence, to meet their needs and to make them aware of more genuinely rewarding pursuits'.[3]

Much can, and it is hope will, be done by an alert and expanded youth service to help young people to develop new friendships with both adults and contemporaries, find new interests, cultivate new skills, and come to a better understanding of the meaning and purpose of life, but, to quote the Albermarle Committee again, 'It is important not to encourage excessive hopes'. The problems of youth, are deeply rooted in the soil of a disturbed modern

[1] Ibid., p. 12.
[2] Reed, op. cit., p. 129.
[3] *The Youth Service in England and Wales*, p. 53.

world,[1] and cannot be solved by a specialised service working in isolation. They are problems of home and family life, neighbourhood patterns and mores, work standards and satisfactions, the community's contradictions and uncertainties as to goals and values. The youth service can only be effective in the context of a wider effort on the part of the general public to try and appreciate what it means to be adolescent in so changing and bewildering a world, the pressures of which bear most hardly on young people. In this setting the youth service can play its part in helping adolescents to make the difficult transition from childhood to maturity more easily and effectively.

[1] Ibid., p. 2.

PART FOUR

THE AGED AND HANDICAPPED

'How we treat our old people is a crucial test of our national quality. A nation that lacks gratitude to those who have honestly worked for her in the past, while they had strength to do so, does not deserve a future, for she has lost her sense of justice and her instinct of mercy.'—DAVID LLOYD GEORGE.

'The soul of a nation is revealed in its attitude to the unfit.'—GEORGE TOMLINSON.

CHAPTER XVIII

THE WELFARE OF OLD PEOPLE

COMMUNITY care for the aged is complementary to community care for children, and the welfare of old people, like that of children, is becoming increasingly a national as well as a family responsibility.

Old age is usually regarded as being synonymous with pensionable age, that is over 65 for men and 60 for women, but this division is an arbitrary one, and men and women beyond this age span a generation or more. It has been suggested, moreover, that it is the quinquennium from 70 to 75, not that from 60 to 65, in which the transition really occurs; 'before it the majority are potential donors, whereas after it they become debtors to the common effort'.[1] Hence, from the point of view of social policy it is important to have some idea, not simply of numbers, actual and potential, of persons of more than pensionable age, but also of changes taking place or likely to take place in the expectation of life beyond it, and particularly the likelihood or otherwise of the survival of large numbers of men and women to an extreme old age.

The fall in the birth rate, which, with minor fluctuations, continued from the seventies of the nineteenth century to the thirties of the twentieth, has combined with an increasing expectation of life in all ages, but particularly in the younger age groups, to change the age structure of the population as compared with Victorian times. Between 1911 and 1951 the number of men over 65 and women over 60 taken together increased from 2,750,000, or 6·7 per cent of the total population, to 6,620,000, or 13·5 per cent of the total population. Estimates as to the future age structure vary, but, assuming that over the period there will be a slight progressive decline in fertility, that the decline in mortality in each age group over the next twenty-five years will be at the same rate as over the past fifty, and that migration can be neglected, it is estimated that by 1979 the total number of elderly persons in Great Britain is likely to be about 9,500,000, or 18·2 per cent of

[1] J. H. Sheldon, 'The Social Philosophy of Old Age', Presidential address to the Third Congress of the International Association of Gerontology, London, 1954. *Old Age in the Modern World*, p. 17.

the total population.[1] This estimate is based on the assumption that the expectation of life for persons in their sixties and over, which has increased but little compared with that of younger persons during the last thirty years, will remain about the same[2] and discounts the likelihood of the 'medicated survival' of large numbers of men and women into extreme old age. Nevertheless the possibility that gerontological and other medical research may alter this situation cannot wholly be disregarded, and this might result in the survival of more men and women who will then die slowly in extreme old age of degenerative diseases with all the demands that this will make on the resources of the community.[3]

One of the issues of social policy arising from the changes taking place in the age structure of the population which has received considerable attention in recent years is that of the possibility and desirability of the more widespread employment of elderly persons beyond the minimum pensionable ages. Despite the conditions of full employment which have existed since the war, the numbers of both men and women still at work after reaching the present minimum pensionable age were considerably less in 1951 than in 1931, a year during which there was serious unemployment,[4] Moreover, while the Phillips Committee reporting in 1954 discerned signs of a reversal of this trend, both this Committee and the First Report of the National Advisory Committee on the Employment of Older Men and Women set up by the Ministry of Labour to consider the problem, believed that more should be done to encourage the widespread employment of elderly persons. This involves consideration not only of the capacity of elderly men and women for continued employment, but also of their attitudes to it, and the effect that such employment would have on the prospects of younger men and women.

Research into the effects of ageing on speed and accuracy in a

[1] Report of the Committee on the Economic and Financial Problems of the Provision for Old Age (Phillips Committee), Cmd. 9333, 1954, pp. 15–16. For a detailed discussion of the position by the Government Actuary, see Appendix II of this Report, 'Population Trends in Great Britain'.

[2] In 1910–12 the expectation of life for a man aged sixty-five was eleven years, in 1950–2 it was eleven years, nine months, a gain of nine months; for women the gain in thirty years was one year and three months. Figures from English Life Tables, No. 8, and General Registrar Quarterly Returns for England and Wales, quoted by R. M. Titmuss, 'Age and Society', *Old Age in the Modern World*, p. 47.

[3] J. H. Sheldon, op. cit., pp. 16–17.

[4] Report of the Committee on the Economic and Financial Problems of the Provision for Old Age, Cmd. 9333, 1954, Table IX, p. 54. In 1931, 47·9 per cent of men aged sixty-five and over were still at work and 11·0 per cent of women aged sixty and over. In 1951 the figures were 32 per cent for men and 8 per cent for women.

number of different skills and learning and memory processes has been, and is being, carried out by psychologists and the results of their investigations are becoming available.[1] A number of inquiries have also been made into the achievements of older workers in differing industries and occupations and the adjustments which have to be made to assist them to carry on.[2] It appears from these various investigations that older workers feel the strains imposed by the pace of the work, and in particular those imposed by striving to keep up with the pace set by machines, more acutely than those imposed by heavy physical work, especially if the worker has become accustomed to this and can carry it on at his own speed, eased perhaps by concessions made unofficially and unobtrusively by the management, and by assistance from his mates.[3] Hence for the older worker advances in speed and automation in industry may create as many problems as they solve.[4] Moreover, while continuance in work may be possible under favourable conditions to a later age than is sometimes realised, sooner or later the older docker, miner or industrial worker employed in similar heavy work will find the task beyond his physical powers, and either give up altogether or seek lighter work in the same industry. In this event his claims will have to be weighed against those of other groups, notably the disabled, for assignment to such relatively undemanding jobs as are available.

There is little available evidence as to the occupational fitness of those men and women who retire early compared with those who remain at work, but such as there is suggests that those who do retire of their own free will are frequently influenced in their decision by ill-health or consciousness of strain and failing powers. Thus according to the survey made by the Ministry of Pensions and National Insurance in 1953,[5] 25 per cent of the men retiring at sixty-five did so because of ill-health, including strain, and while, as pointed out by Mrs. Shenfield, this figure may have to be accepted with some reserve, 'This is not to suggest that there are not substantial numbers of older men and women whose retirement is

[1] *Old Age in the Modern World*, Report of the Third Congress of the International Association of Gerontology, 1955, ch. viii. A. T. Welford, *Ageing and Human Skill*, Report of the investigations made by the Nuffield Research Unit into Ageing, at the Psychological Laboratories, Cambridge, O.U.P., 1958.

[2] Several of these are mentioned in *Old Age in the Modern World*, ch. ix.

[3] Mrs. Pearson found that these concessions were made for the benefit of older workers in the manufacturing firm she investigated. Margaret Pearson 'The Transition from Work to Retirement (1)', *Occupational Psychology*, April 1957, p. 83.

[4] Cf. B. E. Shenfield, *Social Policies for Old Age*, pp. 50–4, where the suitability of light work for older persons is discussed at some length.

[5] *Reasons given for Retiring or Remaining at Work*, Report of an Inquiry by the Ministry of Pensions and National Insurance, H.M.S.O., 1954.

clearly dictated by failing health, which in effect compulsorily retires them.'[1] A detailed socio-medical study of 244 retired men made by Dr. I. M. Richardson of the Department of Social Medicine, Aberdeen University,[2] appears to confirm this in that it revealed that the men over seventy in the sample were, on the whole, slightly more fit than those aged 65–69, which, Dr. Richardson suggests, 'is likely to be caused to some extent by the retirement at sixty-five of the least fit men who had "hung on" in employment until eligible for retirement pension'. Similarly, after making allowances for the difficulties of determining the precise cause of retirement, Peter Townsend estimated that ill-health or disability played a part in the retirement of nearly four-fifths of the 45 retired men whose histories he studied in some detail, and was the main cause for nearly three-fifths.[3]

Important as ill-health is in bringing about retirement at the minimum age, it is not the only factor. 'It is usually a combination of circumstances which produces a "voluntary" decision on the part of the employee to retire,'[4] and the reasons for taking this decision at a particular time may not be clear to the person concerned. Once having broken the work routine and associations with the old firm there seems, however, to be considerable reluctance to take up new work. Men who have retired will express dissatisfaction, and tell the investigator that they would like to be working, but on further inquiry a discrepancy is frequently found between the numbers of those who express a wish to work and those who have actually tried to find it.[5] The conclusion of one investigator was that, before retirement the majority of men 'accepted the work situation and wanted to continue in it as long as they felt physically able to stand the strain; after retirement they settled down more or less contentedly. With very few exceptions, when once a man has retired from his regular work with his own firm, he would seem to be lost to industry.'[6] This finding was based on a study of a group composed mainly of unskilled men attached to a family firm, but it serves to confirm the view that 'the most hopeful chance of providing employment for older workers is to retain them after pension age in their former employment, if not exactly in the same job, at any rate in the same industry, and if

---

[1] Shenfield, op. cit., p. 64.

[2] I. M. Richardson, 'Retirement. A Socio-Medical Study of 244 Men', *Scottish Medical Journal*, Vol. I, No. 12, December 1956, pp. 381–91.

[3] Peter Townsend, *The Family Life of Old People*, An Inquiry in East London, p. 143.

[4] Shenfield, op. cit., p. 62.

[5] E.g. Richardson, op. cit., p. 386. Cf. M. Pearson, 'The Transition from Work to Retirement (II), *Occupational Psychology*, July 1957, p. 142.

[6] Margaret Pearson, ibid., p. 148.

possible, in the same firm'.[1] This depends on the policy of the firm as well as the attitude of the worker, however, and compulsory retirement at a specific age is common in some forms of employment, more so for clerical and administrative than for manual workers, although some firms make it a rule for all their employees.[2]

Fixed retirement ages are frequently associated with occupational pension schemes, and are often operated in occupations and industries in which promotion to more remunerative and responsible jobs may be blocked if older workers are retained. It is true that promotion will probably come eventually and the post thus obtained can be retained longer, but it is earlier in life, when the children are still dependent that the money is urgently needed. This difficulty is recognised by the National Advisory Committee on the Employment of Older Men and Women. They suggest that advisory or consultant posts may be found for the older employees, but acknowledge that there is no single or simple solution to the problem, and they fall back on recommending 'thought and experiment'.[3] The right of all adults, irrespective of age, to work if they so wish is, however, implicit in the general recommendation of the National Advisory Committee that 'all men and women employed in industry, commerce, the professions or elsewhere who can give effective service, either in their normal work, or in any alternative work which their employer can make available, should be given the opportunity, without regard to age, to continue at work if they so wish'. On the other hand, Mr. A. Roberts, speaking at the 1954 International Gerontological Conference, emphasised that in the trade union view this right still means particularly the right of adults under pensionable age to work. 'When there has to be a choice, it is in favour of the age group with greatest domestic responsibility.'[4] A fuller and happier life for the elderly should not be purchased at the expense of frustration for the young.

Hitherto in this discussion retirement has been taken to mean retirement from full-time remunerative employment, and it has been assumed that the transition is one from full-time work to a life of leisure. This is the pattern for the majority of working men and women, but the more gradual transition, with some form of part-time work as an intermediate stage, is an alternative possibility. Thus, in his Reservation at the end of the Phillips Report,

[1] Richardson, op. cit.

[2] This was the case in the Merseyside firm investigated by Mrs. Pearson, and several of the men interviewed expressed their approval of a system in which all were treated alike from the directors downwards.

[3] National Advisory Committee on the Employment of Older Men and Women. First Report, Cmd. 8963, 1953, p. 45.

[4] *Old Age in the Modern World*, p. 321.

Professor Cairncross writes, 'If a growing number of older people have to be helped to lead happy and useful lives I can think of nothing more important than that they should learn to retire slowly, continuing in work as long as possible, but for diminishing stretches of time, at a diminishing pace of work and with diminishing responsibilities.'[1] Dr. Richardson's Scottish study revealed that 93 per cent of the men doing some form of part-time work in their retirement were content with their lot, compared with 54 per cent of the wholly retired, and from this he concluded that 'part-time employment appeared to be a very satisfactory compromise between former job and retirement'. However, detailed investigation of the similarities and differences between the wholly retired and those doing part-time work led him to the more cautious observation that, 'opportunities apart, measures to extend part-time employment are unlikely to be successful until more is known about the motives and circumstances which actuate the wish for this compromise arrangement'.[2] Nor is this question only one of the attitudes of the retired persons themselves. While there are ample opportunities for part-time domestic work for elderly women, part-time or intermittent work for men is not so easy to organise, even if desired,[3] and is said to be unpopular with employers, perhaps because of their unfortunate if not wholly relevant experiences with part-time married women. Nevertheless, where offered and undertaken it has frequently brought satisfaction to both employer and worker, and its potentialities would appear to be by no means exhausted.[4]

Among the interesting experiments in old people's welfare work which have been made of recent years are the sheltered workshops where old people may find satisfaction in the performance of useful work for which they receive a small remuneration. The principle on which these experiments is based and their methods of working seem to be similar in some degree to those of the sheltered workshops for disabled persons. So far, they are limited in number and operating on a very small scale, and many difficulties might attend their extension, but, where they exist, they can

[1] Cmd. 9333, p. 89.   [2] I. M. Richardson, op. cit., pp. 385–6.

[3] Out of a group of 117 men between the ages of sixty and sixty-five employed by a Liverpool manufacturing firm who said that they would like to go on working after sixty-five, 71 or 61 per cent were ready to work a normal working week all the year round, 18 per cent wanted minor alterations, such as a slightly shorter working day, only 21 per cent wanted a greater reduction, some being prepared to work part of the week, some part of the year. Margaret Pearson, 'The Transition from Work to Retirement' (I) *Occupational Psychology*, April 1957, p. 88.

[4] National Advisory Committee on the Employment of Older Men and Women. Second Report, Cmd. 9628, H.M.S.O., 1955, p. 20. Cf. Shenfield, op. cit., p. 81.

claim to have done much to increase and maintain the contentment and self-confidence of the elderly men and women for whom
they cater.[1]

In addition to spanning a wide age range, men and women over
pensionable age form a cross-section of the whole population and
include persons of differing family backgrounds and economic and
social circumstances, and they cannot be considered apart from
the families and communities to which they belong. Traditionally
the care of the aged, like that of the young, is a family responsibility, and until 1948, when the National Assistance Act abolished the Poor Law, this obligation could, as a last resort, be
legally enforced. Since then, not only has the legal obligation to
maintain one's parents been done away with, but financial assistance from the National Assistance Board or residential care from
the local authority has largely ceased to be the reproach that once
it was. In consequence, the belief is widespread that in recent times
there has been a regrettable decline in family responsibility. The
findings of surveys into old people's welfare which have been made
over the past few years do not support this belief, however. Geographical mobility, more opportunities for work outside the home
for both married and single women, and the decline in size of the
family itself, so that the burden shared a generation back by four
or five children now has to be borne by one or two, all these may
result in a greater reliance on community services than was
accepted in the past. In general, however, the evidence so far
collected goes to support the conclusion that 'where it exists the
family tie is still strong and the sense of family responsibility
marked'.[2] This may impose serious strains, however, especially
when old age has brought with it mental or physical infirmity, and
the condition is long continued.[3] The community has a respon-

[1] A scheme of this kind started in Finsbury in 1951 is described in *Old Age
and the Modern World*, pp. 599–601.

[2] *Social Contacts in Old Age*. Report of a Liverpool Survey, 1953, p. 13. Cf.
Report of the National Assistance Board for the year ended 31 December
1954, Cmd. 9530, p. 20, and the Report Relative to the Complete Survey of
Elderly Citizens in Salford, 1957, p. 15. The strength and solidarity of the
kinship group is emphasised over and over again in the intensive study of the
family life of a sample of 203 old people in Bethnal Green, made in 1954–5 by
Peter Townsend at the Institute of Community Studies, and published under
the title *The Family Life of Old People* in 1957. The position is summed up
in ch. ix, pp. 108–19, the concluding sentence of which reads 'As members
of this [extended] family most old people in Bethnal Green found security,
occupation and interest day by day.' By an extended family is meant a group
of relatives who live in two or more households and see each other every day
or nearly every day.

[3] The Governors of the National Corporation for the Care of Old People
state in their Ninth Annual Report (p. 10) that they have had reported to
them cases where members of a family have so overtaxed their financial and

sibility for easing such burdens wherever possible, for example by arranging assistance with attendance and nursing care, and arranging for the temporary care of infirm old people so that their relatives may have a holiday. Moreover, while the family tie, if it exists, should be where possible preserved and strengthened, the needs of elderly persons who have no one to turn to for comfort or support, either because they have outlived their relatives or become estranged from them, should not be overlooked. These old people, like the children deprived of home care, have a special claim on society.[1]

For the purposes of community care old people may be divided into three groups: those able to live in their own homes or with relatives, those requiring residential accommodation, including care but not medical or nursing care, and the sick and infirm.

The first claim on the community made by old people no longer able to support themselves is for adequate pensions, so that they can live in reasonable comfort free from financial anxiety and without becoming dependent on children or other relatives. The provisions made by the National Insurance and Assistance Acts were designed to ensure this, but in spite of the later successive increases in scale rates, their effectiveness in securing freedom from want for old people is continually being threatened by the rising cost of living. Old people without other resources, if now spared the rigours of extreme poverty, often exist on the edge thereof, sometimes endeavouring to keep up traditions and appearances by sacrificing even the necessities of life and 'living almost entirely on bread, margarine, tea, potatoes and more bread'.[2] In many cases, the strain is increased by the wide difference between weekly income before and after retirement, a difference which may amount to as much as a half or two-thirds. Moreover, as age and infirmity increases, additional expenditure may well be incurred on such items as coal and bedding. The pensions now provided for elderly persons have already been discussed in Chapter III, together with proposals for improving them, and their cost to the nation both actual and potential. While, in considering pension rates and plans, economic costs and financial considerations must be borne in mind, so also must the fact that the maintenance of a minimum standard of living for old people has been accepted by

---

physical resources in looking after their old people that they may well, at some stage, break down and have to call upon the State for assistance for themselves.

[1] Professor R. M. Titmuss has calculated that 25 per cent of persons over pensionable age are either single or married but childless. *Old Age in the Modern World*, p. 49.

[2] James Roberts (Director of Civic Welfare), 'Report Relative to the Complete Survey of Elderly Citizens in Salford', p. 17.

the community as a statutory responsibility, and this should not be allowed to go by default, nor should the standard be so low as to permit the continuance of serious hardship.

Suitable living accommodation is almost as important to old people as financial security. In some areas it is difficult to secure, and many old people are either unsuitably housed or obliged to share accommodation with younger families. In this respect they are but sharing in hardships common to all age groups, and living as part of the same household may involve greater discomfort for the young couple than for the old,[1] but hardship exists neverthe-less. It has been found that on the whole, however, old people are more likely to have too much accommodation at their disposal than too little, often because they are reluctant to leave or even sub-let the family house with all its associations, or to move away from the neighbourhood with which they are familiar.[2] If they are prepared to move, then provided there are family contacts, the move should not entail making these more difficult, since the happiness and domestic efficiency of the old person may well depend on their maintenance.[3] The new accommodation pro-vided should be compact, easy and inexpensive to run and accept-able to the person concerned. These conditions may not be easy to fulfil at a reasonable cost, and the local housing authority has to balance the needs and demands of its older citizens with those of young families, though the two are not necessarily in direct competition, since the provision of flats and bungalows for elderly persons may well free family houses for married couples with children. Taking into account the numbers of one- and of two-person householders among elderly persons and the needs of young married couples together, Mrs. Shenfield suggests the allocation of 10 per cent of new housing accommodation to small units, 6–7 per cent being devoted to the needs of the elderly, but emphasises

---

[1] P. Townsend, op. cit., pp. 155–6. This is suggested by Mrs. Shenfield, op · cit., p. 151, who points out that in the majority of cases the old person remains head of the household.

[2] A survey conducted by the National Assistance Board into the circum-stances of 139,279 persons over eighty in receipt of National Assistance revealed that less than one in ten were living and cooking in one room, two-thirds in three or more rooms. Cmd. 9530, 1954, p. 17. Cf. *Social Contacts in Old Age*. p. 8, where it is also stated that it was the younger pensioners, those in their sixties and early seventies, who were willing to move.

[3] In his survey made for the Nuffield Foundation in 1947 into the health and welfare of 552 old people in Wolverhampton, Dr. Sheldon found that this was the case in about 40 per cent of his sample. *Social Medicine of Old Age*, O.U.P., 1948, p. 141. This is confirmed by Peter Townsend as the result of his survey in Bethnal Green. He criticises L.C.C. housing policies as tending to separate families and make mutual aid between old people and their relatives more difficult. Op. cit., pp. 194–6.

that each area should make its own estimates, having regard to the numbers, age and marital status of its older inhabitants and the amount of suitable accommodation already available.[1]

The statutory provision of a sufficient number of new houses to meet the needs of all the older men and women now badly or unsuitably housed is unlikely to come about for many years, if ever, and in different parts of the country voluntary organisations and public utility companies are doing what they can to relieve the shortage by the conversion of old houses into flats. Many such schemes include the services of a caretaker or even the provision of a main meal each day, and in this way enable frail elderly people—women especially—to retain their independence without being wholly isolated and uncared for.

Financial security and suitable accommodation are fundamental to old people's welfare, but by themselves are insufficient to ensure contentment in old age. Retirement from active work means more than loss of income, it means loss of purpose and significance and of membership of a working group. Like Charles Lamb, the retired worker walks 'about', no longer 'to and from'.[2] Having done his task he has the rest of the day to himself, and has to make what he can of his remaining ten to fifteen surplus years.[3] This adjustment may be extremely difficult for a man with no or few interests outside his work. With the ending of his working life he may well feel that he has lost his prestige and significance as well as all the companionship and fulfilment that his work brought him. Many of the men in the Bethnal Green sample spoke of their retirement as a tragedy, as indeed it was, for their life had become 'a rather desperate search for pastimes or a gloomy contemplation of their own helplessness, which, at its worst, was little better than waiting to die'.[4] If such tragedies are to be avoided action should, if

---

[1] Shenfield, op. cit., pp. 152–4. Circular 18/57 of the Ministry of Housing and Local Government reminds local authorities of the importance of making adequate provision to meet the needs of old people. In its Eleventh Annual Report (1958) the National Corporation for the Care of Old People estimates that the proportion of dwellings suitable for the aged built by local authorities since the last war is 8·3 per cent of the total dwellings built. The Corporation regards this as inadequate and says that few local authorities have made any real attempt to assess present and future demands for old people's housing in their areas.

[2] *Last Essays of Elia.* Cf. the comment made by Margaret Pearson as the result of her investigations: '. . . it is symptomatic of the lack of interest and purpose in the lives of many retired persons that several of the men interviewed spent much of their time wandering aimlessly round the city to pass the time away,' Margaret Pearson, 'The Transition from Work to Retirement', *Occupational Psychology*, vol. 31, No. 3, July 1957, p. 151.

[3] 'For more and more people, work and death are becoming increasingly separated by a functionless interregnum. What is the individual and society to make of this enlarging span of twelve to fifteen "surplus" years?' R. M. Titmuss, *The Times*, 29 December 1954.   [4] Townsend, op. cit., p. 148.

possible, be taken during the first months and years of retirement when the new routine is being established and new habits formed. In America, and to a more limited extent over here,[1] attention is now being paid to the possibility of preventive measures by encouraging older men and women to prepare for retirement by developing new interests and occupations in which they can employ their approaching leisure, perhaps as members of groups.

Membership of a group may be vital, since old age is often a period of increasing isolation and loneliness,[2] and much of the energy of individuals and organisations concerned about the welfare of old people is directed to alleviation of these conditions, mainly through friendly visiting schemes and clubs. The value of such work has received statutory recognition, notably in the National Assistance Act, Section 31, of which empowers local authorities to make contributions to the funds of voluntary organisations whose activities 'consist in or include the provision of recreation or meals for old people'. A subsequent circular, 'Welfare of Old People', issued by the Ministry of Health in 1950, drew attention to the value of the regular friendly visiting of lonely and house-bound old people, and emphasised the need for its extension and organisation, not simply as a means of mitigating loneliness, but also as a way whereby an isolated old person might be made aware of, and helped and encouraged to accept, the statutory and voluntary services available to him. Since then extensive developments have taken place in many areas mainly through old people's welfare committees and councils acting in co-operation with local authority welfare departments, churches, clubs and other voluntary organisations, and in a further Ministry circular issued in 1957 it was stated that 'experience has confirmed the great importance of an effective voluntary home visiting service'. Local authorities were urged to consider 'whether in many areas the time is not ripe for renewed contacts between themselves and voluntary bodies working in the area with a view to further encouragement of voluntary help and efforts on the lines laid down in Circular 11/50'.[3] Useful as these organised visiting schemes are, they are but an inadequate substitute for the more informal contacts with relations, neighbours, friends and fellow members of associations of all kinds on which happiness in

[1] The National Old People's Welfare Committee has set up a small Committee to consider the question of preparation for retirement.

[2] Various attempts have been made to gauge the numbers of old people in particular areas who are seriously isolated from normal social contacts, and estimates vary, perhaps because social isolation is not easy to measure. The findings of various local surveys are summarised and commented on by Mrs. Shenfield, op. cit., p. 171.

[3] Circular 14/57, par. 17, p. 5.

old age so greatly depends, for it is the knowledge that they are sought out because they are regarded as belonging to a group to which the visitor also belongs, and not simply because they are lonely and friendless, which does so much to maintain and restore self-respect.

Friendly visiting of a relatively informal nature may be all the community care that many old people require, at any rate for the time being, but there are those whose social and psychological problems cannot be satisfactorily dealt with in this way, and who need the counsel and skill of a trained social case worker. Such help and advice may also be required by families whose old people present serious problems. Many local authority social welfare departments employ social workers who are available to give this kind of assistance, but the coverage is by no means universal. Workers who are both appropriately trained and have the personality and interest required for this often difficult and exacting work are not easy to come by.

Old people's clubs, which have now been formed in centres of population all over the country, vary widely in sponsorship, size and character from semi-political pressure groups, such as the branches of the National Federation of Old Age Pensioners and the National Old Age Pensions Association to centres sponsored and run by voluntary organisations with the active support of the local authority.[1] Some are no more than weekly or monthly socials held in a church hall or other hired building with a Christmas party and summer outing thrown in for good measure, others are quite elaborately equipped day centres; some are run by the old people themselves, with their own officers and committee, in others the old people sit passively while voluntary helpers perform even the simplest tasks; some do much to encourage activities such as handicrafts, drama and singing, in others meetings consist of a third-rate entertainment followed by a cup of tea. In areas where old people's welfare committees are active they do much to extend the clubs in their districts and to encourage them to be more enterprising in the range of activities they undertake and more democratic and businesslike in the management of their affairs. The success which has attended even those clubs functioning under difficult circumstances in unsuitable premises testifies to the difference they make to the life of many old people, but their range is limited. Those old people who do attend do so with enthusiasm, sometimes joining two or three clubs meeting on different days, but they form a limited proportion of the population and it

[1] The local authority may even provide the premises as, for example, at the Riverview Centre, Liverpool, or the All-Purpose Social Welfare Centre, formerly a library, in Salford.

appears that the vast majority of old people are either not attracted by the clubs in their area or ignorant of their existence and the facilities they provide.[1]

Friendly visits and clubs are two ways of helping old people living at home, but they are not the only possible ones, and attempts are continuously being made to meet other needs. Domestic help and, where required, nursing attention can be provided by local authorities under the provisions of the National Health Service Act.[2] Meals-on-Wheels, where they are provided, are a boon to old people with inadequate cooking facilities in their own homes, while chiropody services which, formerly outside the National Health Services may, with the approval of the Minister, now be established by local health authorities,[3] can make all the difference to the comfort and mobility of the old people.

The majority of old people prefer to remain in the general community living in their own homes as long as possible, and it is generally accepted that this is desirable, though some recent investigations by the National Corporation for Old People have shown that the cost in both money and manpower of providing domiciliary services is not necessarily less, and may in extreme cases be considerably more, than that of providing institutional care.[4] It is not always easy to decide when the reasonable limits of home assistance have been reached, and the alternative of institutional care should be urged on the possibly reluctant old person. Much will depend on the availability of assistance from relatives or neighbours and friends, and the attachment of the old person to his home and neighbourhood. In extreme cases, where an old person is really incapable of looking after himself and is not receiving the care and attention he needs from others, he may be

[1] An investigation made in Liverpool in 1955 revealed that 'the most optimistic estimate of total membership of old people's clubs could not put the total number of members higher than 15,000 or about 16 per cent of the approximately 90,500 persons of pensionable age in the city'. Forty-one per cent of a sample of club members interviewed held membership in two old people's clubs, 6 per cent in three. G. Worthington, *Clubs for Elderly Persons* (unpublished M.A. thesis). Cf. the findings of the survey discussed by Mrs. Shenfield, op. cit., Appendix III, p. 229. Only 6·8 per cent of the persons visited mentioned clubs and 35·1 per cent said they had no interests outside their homes.

[2] Sections 25 and 29.

[3] Ministry of Health Circular 11/59 (April 1959). The circular suggested that priority be given to the elderly, the physically handicapped and expectant mothers. Reasonable charges may be made for the service.

[4] Ninth Annual Report, pp. 10–14. Data collected about 21 cases where differing services were provided showed that the cost per case varied from £2 14s. 0d. to £9 15s. 10d., compared with the average weekly cost of institutional care in 1954–5 of £6 12s. 8d. for chronic sick hospitals and £4 9s. 8d. for local authority homes.

compulsorily removed to residential accommodation where he will be properly cared for, but local authorities exercise this power (which is given them, subject to adequate safeguards, in Section 47 of the National Assistance Act, 1948, as amended by the National Assistance (Amendment) Act, 1951), very reluctantly and only after all preventive measures and attempts at persuasion have proved useless.[1]

Until 5 July 1948 local public assistance committees were responsible for the residential accommodation of those aged persons in their areas who needed it, and they had inherited from their predecessors, the boards of guardians, the large mixed workhouses of the nineteenth century, institutions designed to deter from entering them all but those in desperate need. Of recent years, and particularly since the passing of the National Assistance Act, local authorities, now acting through their social welfare committees and departments (which may be directly responsible to the Council or may form one of the responsibilities of the local health committee), have done much to improve these institutions by the introduction of amenities and the relaxation of rules, but the design of the buildings, the large numbers to be accommodated and the necessity of accepting all 'in need of care and attention not otherwise available to them',[2] however difficult or unpleasant, have combined to slow down improvements. It is now recognised that, except perhaps for the minority needing special care or discipline, small homelike hostels are to be preferred to large institutions. For many years voluntary organisations both religious and secular, have been running small homes where personal loving care is given to the residents, and in so doing, have not only helped the old people for whom they are directly responsible, but also by their example have helped to raise the general standard of residential care for old people throughout the country. Some local authorities were also experimenting along these lines before 1948, and the evacuation hostels established during the war, both by voluntary organisations and under the auspices of the Ministry of Health, further demonstrated the advantages of small hostels.

As already indicated, the National Assistance Act imposed a duty on county councils and county borough councils to make accommodation available in their areas for all persons 'who by reason of age, infirmity or any other circumstances are in need of

[1] For instance, Mr. Roberts in his 'Report Relative to the Complete Survey of Elderly Citizens in Salford', claims that as a result of the patience and tact of his staff, only one person had been made subject to such an order during the period covered. The Report of the Ministry of Health for 1955 gives the number of orders made during the previous year as about 280, and adds that numbers do not seem to vary significantly from year to year.

[2] National Assistance Act, 1948, Section 21 (a).

care and attention not otherwise available to them'. Such accom-modation is paid for by the user according to his means, for the aim of those who planned the service was 'that the local authority will cease to be merely a reliever of destitution, and will be-come the provider of comfortable accommodation with care and attention for those who owing to age and infirmity cannot wholly look after themselves'.[1] The Act also empowers local authorities to make arrangements with voluntary organisations for the use of accommodation in their hostels, payments being made at an agreed rate, while a useful clause[2] ensures the maintenance of at least minimum standards by requiring that all homes for old people, whether managed by voluntary organisations or by private individuals, shall be registered and inspected. Since the passing of the Act, both local authorities and voluntary organisations have been active in the establishment of hostels of differing types and sizes, mainly by the conversion of large houses, and it has been estimated that there are about 44,000 beds available in local authority accommodation in England, while voluntary organisa-tions provide another 18,000. Despite the efforts that have been made, however, 62 local authorities still have more than half their accommodation in former public assistance institutions, efforts to provide alternatives having been hindered because of financial and other controls.[3]

Until recently institutional care of one kind or another was regarded as the only alternative to continued independence or residence with relations or friends, but the old people's welfare committees at both Exeter and Plymouth have experimented successfully with the boarding-out of old people in private families, and small-scale experiments have begun in other areas also. Suc-cessful boarding-out of old people is no easier than that of chil-dren, however. Careful matching of the old people with the families with whom they will make their homes, clear understanding as to the extent and limits of the family's responsibilities in the event of sickness or increased infirmity and adequate supervision are all essential, and entail the working out of a well-organised scheme in which a number of statutory and voluntary bodies will co-operate.[4]

Among the most serious problems of old age are increasing in-firmity and recurrent or chronic sickness. With advancing years

[1] Summary of the Provisions of the National Assistance Bill, Cmd. 7248, H.M.S.O., 1947.

[2] Section 37.

[3] National Corporation for the Care of Old People, Ninth Report, p. 8.

[4] This means of caring for elderly persons is discussed in an article by Mar-jorie Bucke (Secretary, National Old People's Welfare Council), 'Foster Care for the Elderly', *Social Service Quarterly*, Vol. XXX, No. 1, June-August, 1956, pp. 19–22.

THE AGED AND HANDICAPPED

the margin between sickness and health narrows, the burden on
relatives who are caring for the old person increases, independent
existence becomes less possible and even the domestic care given in
ordinary hostels may cease to be adequate. The placement and
care of the infirm, and particularly of the mentally infirm, aged
has proved to be the most intractable of all the old people's
welfare problems. The position is still far from satisfactory, and is
further complicated by the difficulty of making a clear line of division between the responsibilities of regional hospital boards and
those of local authorities. These problems have been considered
both by the Guillebaud Committee[1] and, with particular reference
to the mentally infirm, by the Royal Commission on the Law
Relating to Mental Illness and Mental Deficiency,[2] while in 1954
the Ministry of Health made a special survey of the services available to old people throughout England and Wales in order to obtain
a more accurate assessment of the quantity and quality of the hospital and local authority services available to the chronic sick and
elderly and to discover in what areas and in what respect these
services could be improved.[3] For the purposes of the survey the
Ministry made a demarcation which, broadly speaking, confines
the responsibility of the local authority to persons for whom the
nursing care required is of the type which could be given by relatives with the help and advice of the home nurse if the old people
were living in their own homes. This is the kind of care which can
be given by attendants assisted or advised by a visiting nurse in
a small welfare home, or by a small staff with nursing experience
or qualifications in a large one. Persons already in a welfare
home who require nursing care during their terminal illness, but
'whose removal to hospital away from familiar surroundings and
attendants would be felt to be inhumane', should also be retained there. Hospital authorities are expected to accept responsibility for the chronic bedfast requiring prolonged nursing care,
even though they may need little or no medical treatment, the
convalescent care of the elderly sick not yet ready for discharge,
and the care of the senile, confused or disturbed patient who is
unfit to live a normal community life in a welfare home. The
Guillebaud Committee accepted this as an adequate clarification
of the position and deprecated any widespread extension of the
provision of 'half-way' houses for long stay patients too infirm for
ordinary hostels, a provision which had been made by voluntary

[1] Cmd. 9663, 1956, pp. 214–17.
[2] Cmnd. 169, 1957, pp. 214–17.
[3] Ministry of Health Reports on Public Health and Medical Subjects, No.
98. *Survey of Services available to the Chronic Sick and Elderly, 1954–1955.* Summary
Report prepared by C. A. Boucher, H.M.S.O., 1957.

organisations in some areas. In this Committee's view it is the 'inadequacy' of the service and not the form of administrative organisation which is the root cause of the problems relating to the care of the aged, and they do not wish the notion to be allowed to develop that there is a gap between hospital and local authority services for the treatment and care of the aged which only 'half-way houses' can fill. They consider that 'What is most important is that the statutory authorities concerned should have a clear conception of where their duties lie in the provision of accommodation for the aged, and should plan to make good the present deficiencies as and when their resources will permit.'[1] The Royal Commission also accepted the Ministry's division of responsibility as valid, but at the same time emphasised the need for more accommodation for persons who suffer from some degree of mental infirmity but who do not require care or treatment under specialist supervision. They laid the responsibility for the provision of such accommodation squarely on the shoulders of the local authorities, and a Circular issued by the Ministry[2] following the publication of the Royal Commission's Report included 'the elderly mental infirm who do not need the services and resources of a hospital' among the categories for whom it is considered accommodation should be provided. That this provision is a local authority responsibility is made clear by the Mental Health Act, 1959, which includes the provision, equipment and maintenance of residential accommodation among the specific services which local authorities are required to undertake in connection with their general responsibility for the care of the mentally disordered. Hostels of this kind and similar accommodation which the local authorities might consider necessary for the physically frail or intermittently ill, would, in effect, provide intermediate accommodation between the hostels now provided for the generality of old people in need of care and attention and hospital geriatric units, and an old people's welfare service without accommodation of this nature would hardly seem to be giving adequate coverage. Voluntary organisations, by experimenting with 'half-way houses', have pioneered in the provision of this accommodation and helped to draw attention to the need. In October 1957 the Ministry of Health issued two circulars, one to regional hospital boards, boards of governors of teaching hospitals and hospital management committees,[3] and one to local health authorities,[4] drawing attention to the Boucher Report and to the demarcation of responsibilities

---

[1] Cmd. 9663, p. 215. It differed in this respect from the Phillips Committee which, although it made no specific recommendations, appeared sympathetically inclined towards these experiments. Cmd. 9333, pp. 73–4.
[2] Ministry of Health Circular, 9/59.   [3] H.M. (57) 86.
[4] Circular 14/57, par. 8.

made in connection with it, and emphasising the importance of maintaining 'close and constant liaison between the two authorities so that there may be the greatest possible interchange of cases, that all accommodation be used to the greatest advantage and that maximum use is made of outpatient facilities'.[1] Even so, deficiencies are likely to remain and the voluntary organisations have still a valuable part to play in meeting these as other needs.

One of the most important manifestations of the current interest in old age is the rapid growth of the branch of medicine known as geriatrics and its repercussions on the care and treatment of the aged, particularly the sick and infirm aged. The transformation of the chronic wards of the erstwhile poor law infirmaries into geriatic units where treatment is designed to restore, and to maintain for as long as possible, activity and interest in life, is now the accepted procedure. This change has often required courage, enterprise and patience, but it has brought renewed life and hope, and new willingness to co-operate in their own rehabilitation, to many sick and infirm old people. The difficulties, not least of which is the uneven distribution of the available accommodation with accompanying shortages of hospital beds in many areas,[2] are formidable, and while much can be done to maintain activity in what were formerly regarded as hopeless cases, there remain those for whom little beyond nursing care can be given. Hence, if possible, geriatric units should include long-stay annexes for such cases, staffed by nursing attendants under the direction of a qualified sister. Attachment to the active treatment unit, and periodical reviews by the geriatrician of the condition and progress of the old people detained here, would prevent them from being left to linger, half-forgotten, in such annexes.

The ten years which have elapsed since the National Health Service came into operation and the National Assistance Act abolished the Poor Law have been years during which the community has recognised more fully than ever before its responsibility for the welfare of what the Americans would describe as its 'senior citizens', and provisions for their welfare are now comprehensive if not always adequate. These developments have taken place under differing statutory auspices, with the voluntary organisations playing an active and significant part. Hence co-operation and co-ordination are essential if there is not to be overlapping and waste, or, more important, neglect or hardship, arising from misunderstandings or failure to apportion responsibility clearly. The

[1] Circular 14/57.
[2] The findings of the Ministry Survey indicate that the problem is one of maldistribution of beds between regions and cases between different kinds of care rather than one of overall shortage. Op. cit., pp. 13–16, pp. 16 and 51.

need for co-operation is becoming increasingly recognised and, steps are being taken to further it in different parts of the country.[1] It was to further this co-operation that the National Old People's Welfare Committee, later renamed the National Old People's Welfare Council, was established under the auspices of the National Council of Social Service in 1940, Miss Eleanor Rathbone being the first chairman. Since its foundation it has consistently encouraged the establishment of local and regional committees whose objects are to co-ordinate the work in their own areas and promote new ventures where these are needed. As well as promoting local effort the Old People's Welfare Council acts as a clearing house for information about old people's welfare and is consulted by Government departments and voluntary organisations, as well as by interested people from abroad.

The National Corporation for the Care of Old People was founded in August 1947 with the assistance of a generous grant from the Nuffield Foundation and a substantial donation from the Lord Mayor's National Air Raid Distress Fund. It was constituted to meet the need for a central body, able, not only to make grants to schemes for the welfare of old people, but also to accept gifts and hold property in trust, to obtain and maintain an expert advisory and consultant service and to set up a central record of needs and provisions, and it has already done much useful work along these lines. It sets out not to replace, but to reinforce the work of voluntary agencies seeking to further the welfare of old people and to complement rather than to compete with the National Old People's Welfare Council. To these two bodies has since been added the King George VI Foundation whose particular contribution so far has been that of helping to improve the standard of voluntary work among old people by grant-aiding schemes for the training of workers. Together these agencies can do a great deal to encourage statutory and voluntary bodies to make further constructive efforts to meet the many and varying needs of elderly men and women and to grapple with the problems of an ageing population.

[1] For example, in 1954 the Lancashire County Council Health Committee adopted a scheme the objects of which were 'to encourage and assist old people to continue to live in their own homes by the use of all available statutory and voluntary services; and at the same time it aims at co-ordination and liaison between the statutory services and the voluntary organisations, and fostering and encouraging the latter's activities among the aged'. After a year's trial in three divisions, its extension to the rest of the county was recommended. Lancashire County Council, Report of the Medical Officer of Health for the year 1955, p. 89.

CHAPTER XIX

THE PERMANENTLY HANDICAPPED

'THERE are no such people as "the handicapped", there are handicapped individuals, all of them different',[1] each with his own psychological and social problems to meet as well as his own particular physical disability to overcome. For example, the handicapped person 'born that way' has a different outlook from and a different adjustment to make compared with the one who has experienced normal life before being disabled by disease or injury. This is brought out by Mr. J. D. Evans' comparison between the 'deaf', that is those who were either born deaf or were deprived of hearing powers so early in infancy that they never absorbed a language in the natural imitative manner, and those deafened in later life. 'Between the psychological attitudes of the deaf and the deafened to the world in general', he writes, 'there is an almost unbridgeable gulf . . . at the beginning of their lives the deaf are abnormals, shut off from that stream of verbally conveyed ideas which moulds the individual mind to the general sameness with the mental pattern of society, and throughout their lives the deaf are struggling towards full normalcy. The deafened, on the other hand, are normals threatened with the horror of abnormalcy. To the change in their state, and particularly to the change in the behaviour of other people towards them, they are particularly sensitive—the least tendency on the part of the public to treat them as different from normals fills them with acute distress, in some cases indeed amounting to torment.'[2] Further, the disabled, like the old, are drawn from all sections of the community. They differ in age, although in certain categories, such as the blind and the deafened, the higher age range predominates[3] intelligence,

[1] Saying by an almoner quoted by Jean Simeon Clarke, *Disabled Citizens*, p. 19.

[2] J. D. Evans, 'Voluntary Organisations for the Welfare of the Deaf', ch. v, pp. 73–74, in *Voluntary Social Services: Their Place in the Modern State*. Ed. A. Bourdillon.

[3] In 1954 68·9 per cent of persons newly registered as blind were seventy years of age or more, compared with 43·4 per cent in 1937, the first year in which the age distribution of the newly registered blind first became available. The proportionate increase was also a numerical increase (7,848 in 1937, 12,491 in 1954). The increase may in part be accounted for by the activity of the National Assistance Board in referring cases of old people who had come to their notice but not sought medical aid. For further discussion of this point, see Ministry of Health, *Blindness in England*, 1951–54. Report by Arnold Sorsby, pp. 27 and 44–5.

education, home background and social class. Moreover, each handicap has its own different type and degree of frustration and isolation, so that, for example, the adjustment problems of the home-bound cripple are in many respects different from those of the blind or the deaf, whose problems are those of communication with their fellows. Whatever the disablement or the disabling circumstances, however, the handicapped person becomes at the same time more dependent on, yet set apart from, his fellow men and this combination of dependence and isolation, together with the frustrations of impaired strength, mobility or communication, may easily lead to resentment and suspicion, or what may be even worse to combat, apathy and despair. The aim of the rehabilitation services provided by the community is to assist the disabled person to overcome his physical handicap and psychological and social difficulties, and to take his place as a self-supporting and self-respecting member of the community, sharing as fully as possible in its economic and social life.

The use of the term 'rehabilitation' is, in itself, evidence of the more constructive approach to the treatment of handicapped persons which has become increasingly evident in recent years. It first found expression in voluntary effort, but State action followed, stimulated by the two world wars which both accentuated the need for devising measures to save young disabled persons from years of hopeless dependence and frustration, and at the same time created a situation in which all available manpower, however unpromising, had to be made fit for use and used. Hence, in 1941, Mr. Ernest Bevin, then Minister of Labour, started a scheme for the training and resettlement of disabled persons, and two years later set up an Interdepartmental Committee, under the chairmanship of Mr. George Tomlinson, to consider, and make proposals for, the introduction of a comprehensive scheme for the rehabilitation and employment of disabled persons.

The recommendations of this committee, which were published in 1943,[1] were embodied in the Disabled Persons (Employment) Act, 1944. This Act provided the legislative framework for extensive schemes designed to promote both the rehabilitation of the disabled worker, that is his restoration to working capacity, and his 'resettlement' or establishment in suitable work. Nine years after the passing of the Act, the Minister of Labour and National Service, the Minister of Health and the Secretary of State for Scotland jointly appointed a Committee under the chairmanship of Lord Piercy to 'review in all its aspects' existing provision for the 'rehabilitation training and resettlement of disabled persons'.

[1] Report of the Inter-Departmental Committee on the Rehabilitation and Resettlement of Disabled Persons. Cmd. 6415.

It is a tribute to the vision and acumen of their wartime predecessors that the committee was able to record at the conclusion of its investigations that it considered that 'the facilities for enabling disabled persons to get suitable employment are comprehensive and well established, needing little change or development'.[1] Criticism might be necessary and modifications called for, but, in the opinion of the Piercy Committee, the foundations of a comprehensive rehabilitation and resettlement service have been well and truly laid.

The scope of the scheme is wide. The Act defines a disabled person as 'a person who, on account of injury, disease or congenital deformity, is substantially handicapped in obtaining or keeping employment, or in undertaking work on his own account, of a kind which, apart from that injury, disease or deformity would be suited to his age, experience and qualifications'.[2] This definition covers disablement of all kinds and causes, surgical, medical and psychiatric, and includes congenital disablement as well as that brought on in later life by war service, disease, accident or industrial injury.

Persons registered as disabled under the Act numbered 715,825 in April 1959, compared with 936,196, the highest total, in 1950.[3] Since registration is voluntary and is made with the express purpose of increasing a person's chances of obtaining suitable work, this figure does little more than indicate the number of disabled persons who feel themselves to be in need of assistance in obtaining employment, and no reliable figures giving the number of persons who would benefit from the provisions of the Act, should they be aware of them and willing to utilise them, are available. The Piercy Committee suggests that an inquiry be set on foot to ascertain how many persons receiving sickness benefit for more than six months would be assisted to return to work if suitable facilities were made available.[4] and also that, wherever regional medical officers and medical referees of the Ministry of Pensions and National Insurance, the Ministry of Labour and National Service or the National Assistance Board are of the opinion that the person referred to would benefit from rehabilitation facilities they should include a statement to this effect in their report.[5] These measures would do something to bring persons unaware, or not making use of, the rehabilitation and resettlement services, within their scope, but in the long run it is the quality of the services

[1] Report of the Committee of Inquiry on the Rehabilitation, Training and Resettlement of Disabled Persons. Cmd. 9883, 1956, p. 85.
[2] Disabled Persons (Employment) Act, 1944, Section I (i).
[3] Ministry of Labour Gazette, October, 1959.
[4] Cmd. 9883, par. 23, p. 6.   [5] Ibid., par. 64, p. 17.

THE PERMANENTLY HANDICAPPED

provided and their obvious advantage to the disabled person that is likely to lead to their wider use.

The increased effectiveness of the rehabilitation and resettlement scheme will depend on many factors, not least of which is the recognition that rehabilitation is essentially a single continuous process, although the emphasis at the beginning may be on its medical, and the emphasis at the end on its work aspects,[1] and only if planned as such, can the patient derive full benefit from the varying services provided. The possibility of rehabilitation should be emphasised even in the early stages of the patient's illness or disability, for even if at that stage, little but medical care can be given, the effect of this on his whole attitude and outlook may be decisive. For example, the complete rest, which is an essential part of the treatment of tuberculosis, leaves the patient all too much leisure in which to brood anxiously over his family, his affairs and his prospects, and although 'While rest is paramount, rehabilitation can only consist of tentative planning, the attitude of mind engendered by such planning can help the patient immeasurably.'[2] The almoner has an important part to play here, as she is the person likely to be most knowledgeable about the patient's home background and social and economic problems, but the nature and emphasis of the treatment is finally determined by the doctor, and the Piercy Committee points out that 'the key to the full development of rehabilitation in the hospital service is the attitude of the hospital medical staff. Comparatively few patients need special measures of rehabilitation, but all of them benefit from hospital treatment to the fullest extent only where that treatment is conceived and planned from the outset by a doctor who has in mind, all the time, the terminal result and its effect on the patient's working capacity and home life.'[3]

If this rehabilitation process is to be realistic a proper assessment of the patient's capabilities on discharge from hospital or domiciliary medical care is essential. This may indicate full recovery, or permanent but static disability such as blindness or the loss of a limb. On the other hand the disease may be such that, even when discharged apparently cured, the patient may break down if subject to strain, as may occur with tuberculosis. Finally, as with disseminated sclerosis, the progressive character of the disease may make rehabilitation and final settlement extremely difficult. But the nature of the disability is not the only factor to be considered,

[1] Ibid., par. 80, p. 20.
[2] Dorothy Hicks (Almoner, The Churchill Hospital, Oxford). Paper on 'The Rehabilitation of the Tuberculous' in the *Welfare of the Disabled*, N.C.S.S., 1957, p. 77.
[3] Report, par. 41, p. 10.

the patient's abilities, temperament, intelligence, industrial experience, home background, and family relationships will all affect his readjustment to community life. Hence assessment is more than a medical procedure, and in recent years 'resettlement clinics' or case conferences at which persons concerned with the case, including such members of the medical team as the consultant in charge of the case, a senior member of the hospital staff, the almoner and the psychotherapist, together with the disablement resettlement officer or youth employment officer, confer with each other and with the patient about his future, and 'endeavour to integrate the medical and social aspects of his disability'.[1] Such clinics are, of course, expensive, both in time and manpower, and can only be utilised for the more difficult cases, but for these cases a clinic discussion may well make all the difference between successful and unsuccessful rehabilitation and adjustment, and the Piercy Committee endorses the recommendation of the British Medical Association and the British Association of Physical Medicine that in each major hospital a clinic of this kind should be set up as a normal feature of the hospital's work. It should meet regularly and deal not only with patients from the sponsoring hospital, but also with those from neighbouring hospitals or referred from other sources.[2]

From the point of view of their occupational resettlement, disabled persons may be divided into three main groups; first those who with or without special training, and, if necessary, with mechanical aids, can be found employment alongside normal persons and successfully hold down the jobs they obtain; secondly, those who, while they are unable to stand up to ordinary working conditions can be usefully employed in special 'sheltered' workshops; and thirdly those who, owing either to the exceptional severity of their disablement, old age, or some other complicating factor, can never become self-supporting and may need continuous care and attention. Wartime experience demonstrated that, given proper training and conditions, even quite severely disabled persons could successfully engage in industrial work alongside the non-disabled, and the Tomlinson Committee's recommendations were based on the belief that 'the only satisfactory form of resettlement for a disabled person is employment which he can take and keep on his merits as a worker in normal competition with his fellows'.[3] This is desirable not only because it enables the

[1] I. M. Richardson, 'The Aberdeen Resettlement Clinic', *The Almoner*, September 1954, p. 213. This is the first of four articles describing the work of a clinic with case illustrations, and is continued in the October, November and December issues.
[2] Op. cit., pars. 51–8, pp. 13–15.   [3] Op. cit., par. 9, p. 6.

disabled person to be economically independent, but because it assists him to make a better social adjustment. As the Working Party on the Employment of Blind Persons expresses it, 'One of the most desirable consequences of placing a blind worker in factory employment is that his social horizon is immeasurably extended. He is able to partake in social activities . . . and meet people with whom he has interests and not merely blindness in common.'[1] Most of the evidence submitted to the Piercy Committee supported this view which, the Committee stated, had been confirmed by the experience of the Ministry of Labour. This was that 'with careful assessment of individual capacity and correspondingly careful selection of employment, most disabled persons are capable, or can be rendered capable by training and rehabilitation, of taking their place in industry or other employment.'[2] The restoration of a sorely disabled person's confidence and capacity, so that he can do this, may not be easy, however, particularly if he is not able to return to work with his old firm, alongside his known workmates; and the Disabled Persons (Employment) Act, following the recommendations of the Tomlinson Committee recognised that the first step in industrial rehabilitation might be the restoration of general fitness, confidence and willingness to tackle an ordinary day's work. Hence the establishment under the Act[3] of industrial rehabilitation units, the aim of which has been described by the Piercy Committee as 'to restore the rehabilitee's confidence in his ability to return to work, to toughen him up physically, to assess his capacity for various kinds of work, and to advise him, where a change of job is desirable, on the choice of a new occupation or on a suitable form of training'.[4] Fifteen such units have been established so far, of which one (Egham, Surrey), is fully residential, two partly so, and the remainder non-residential, though suitable lodgings may be found for those coming from a distance. They are managed by the Ministry of Labour and the Piercy Committee comments favourably on the realistic atmosphere of the units. Here, away from the protection of hospital or convalescent home, or even, in some cases, of his own home, the disabled person learns or relearns the industrial virtues of punctuality, regular attendance, care of tools and the completion of a full day's work, meanwhile being studied and assessed by the staff with a view to further vocational guidance or general advice.[5] Important as it is that the emphasis should be on industrial rehabilitation, the continuity of the rehabilitation process should not be lost, and the evidence given to the Piercy Committee indicates that although it is

[1] Op. cit., p. 45.   [2] Cmd. 9883, par. 182, p. 45.
[3] Section 3.   [4] Op. cit., par. 68, p. 18.
[5] Ibid., par. 73, p. 19.

important for their essentially industrial character to be retained, increased medical provision and closer liaison with medical units is desirable.[1]

In modern conditions of industry and employment only a minority of disabled persons either need or desire training in a skilled trade, but for the minority such opportunities are very valuable. They are provided in various ways. The Ministry of Labour is responsible for sixteen training centres set up to assist able-bodied as well as disabled persons, and, while special courses limited to the disabled may be provided, and in other classes the curriculum adjusted to their needs, such persons are, as far as possible, trained alongside the fit, a valuable preparation for establishment in normal work. The more seriously disabled are catered for at residential colleges run by voluntary organisations, with financial help and technical advice from the Ministry, examples being St. Loyes' College for the Training of Disabled, Exeter, and Queen Elizabeth's Training College, Leatherhead; while those disabled persons who would benefit from technical or professional training provided elsewhere, for example, in technical colleges or universities, may be given grant-aid for the purpose.

When rehabilitation and training is complete, placement assumes paramount importance, and there may be difficulties, some foreseen, others unsuspected, before this last obstacle to independence can be overcome. These difficulties include practical problems such as suitable accommodation within easy reach of the place of employment, and transport to and from work, the attitude of prospective employers and fellow-workers, and, not least important, the willingness and determination of the disabled person himself. The possibility of accommodation with help, where necessary, with such operations, as dressing and undressing may prove to be decisive.[2] Increased housing and hostel provision by the local authorities would do much to ease the present situation.

The most fortunate of the disabled are those for whom a place has been retained in their old firm. Some firms make special provision for the rehabilitation and reabsorption of their own workers who are disabled by sickness or injury,[3] but this is not always possible, especially in the case of persons employed by small undertakings, and a disabled person unable to return to his

---

[1] A discussion of the work of I.R.U.'s based on an analysis and follow-up of the 9,608 disabled persons who entered the units in 1956 is to be found in the Ministry of Labour Gazette, August 1958.

[2] Cf. Dame Georgina Buller, 'Through the Gates of Opportunity,' article in *The Welfare of the Disabled*, N.C.S.S., 1957, p. 3. She goes so far as to say that 'the finding of a job may be the least difficult problem to solve'.

[3] The provisions made by the Ford Motor Company at Dagenham are described in *The Welfare of the Disabled*, pp. 89–92.

old firm: may find others reluctant to employ him. After due consideration the Tomlinson Committee decided that this reluctance was often based on a serious underestimate of the potentialities of the disabled, combined with largely groundless fears of the risks which their employment would entail, and these difficulties could only be overcome by some measure of statutory obligation to employ such persons.[1] The Disabled Persons (Employment) Act both instituted a scheme for the registration of disabled persons at the local offices of the Ministry of Labour and established a quota scheme whereby every employer of twenty or more workers is required to employ a quota (at present 3 per cent) of persons so registered.[2] Since their inception these two related schemes have been subject to a certain amount of criticism. An applicant for inclusion on the disabled persons register must provide evidence that he is substantially handicapped by his disablement in getting or keeping suitable employment or work on his own account, but that his disability is such that his prospects of getting and keeping a job are reasonable. Further, it must appear likely that the disablement is likely to last at least twelve months.[3] A disabled person may be registered from any period from one to ten years.[4] Despite these conditions some witnesses giving evidence to the Piercy Committee believed that persons with trifling disabilities were registering as disabled, and that the regulations governing registration should be tightened so that only disabled persons who needed and could benefit from its provisions should be included in it. The Committee made various recommendations to ensure this, but evidently considered that no fundamental changes are required.[5] They were even more favourably disposed towards the quota scheme and considered that this should be retained almost unchanged despite the criticism that in times of full employment it is unnecessary, and, in periods of serious economic depression, unenforceable. In the estimation of the Committee, the quota has served, and continues to serve, a useful educational purpose in publicising the industrial potentialities of disabled persons and in building up a sense of public responsibility for them. Hence they consider it worth continuing.

The designated employment scheme, also initiated by the Disabled Persons (Employment) Act, makes it possible for the Ministry

---

[1] Cmd. 6415, pars. 63–89, pp. 24–34.

[2] Special percentages can be fixed for industries specially suitable or unsuitable for disabled persons, and a specially low percentage has been fixed for ships' crews in the shipping and fishing industries.

[3] Disabled Persons (Employment) Act, 1958, Section 2 (1). A person's name may be removed from the register by written request to the Minister of Labour.

[5] Op. cit., pp. 39–41.

of Labour to limit certain employments to disabled persons, but this measure has been used by the Ministry with extreme caution, as such designation may give the impression that disabled persons are, in the main, only fit for comparatively low-grade work. The only employments so far designated are those of car-park attendant and electric passenger-lift attendant, and the Piercy Committee, while recommending that the designation of these two employments be retained, considered that, if at any time there should be need for more pressure on employers to employ disabled persons, this should be done through the quota scheme rather than by any extension of designated employments.[1]

The provisions discussed so far are intended to facilitate the re-settlement of the disabled worker in employment where he will be working alongside normal persons and, as already indicated, both the Committees which have investigated the problem of the re-settlement and placement of disabled persons and the Ministry of Labour itself takes the view that this is the goal which should be aimed at in the majority of cases. There are, however, a minority for whom conditions in open industry are unsuitable, or on whom they impose too serious a physical or psychological strain, and the Disabled Persons (Employment) Act empowered the Minister of Labour to set up a special company to provide sheltered employ-ment for such persons. In 1945 the Disabled Persons Employment Corporation Ltd., which later changed its name to Remploy Ltd., was established, and since then 92 Remploy factories em-ploying about 6,000 disabled workers have been brought into production. The men and women employed in them work at their own pace at specially selected trades, including, for example, furniture-making, cardboard-box making, knitwear, industrial glove manufacture, light engineering, bookbinding and printing, and receive a weekly wage at an hourly rate, travelling expenses in excess of sixpence a day being paid by the company. The goods made are placed on the commercial market or are manufactured in response to orders by public authorities.

The company is financed by public funds on the basis of direct payments to cover its trading losses and by loans to cover capital expenditure. Since its inception Remploy's losses have been heavy, rising from £68,659, or £277 per disabled person employed, in 1947, when as yet only six factories were in production, to £2,466,000, or £402 per head (estimated), in 1955–6.[2] It is not surprising, therefore, that the company's methods of working have

---

[1] Ibid., par. 178, p. 44.
[2] Figures taken from the Fourth Report from the Select Committee of Estimates, 1951–2. Training, Rehabilitation and Resettlement, p. xi, and the Piercy Report, par. 209, p. 52. In 1958–9 the operating loss was £2,812,000.

been subject to a good deal of criticism, criticism which is epitomised in the Fourth Report from the Select Committee on Estimates, Session 1951–2.[1] This Select Committee, while it admitted that the organisation was doing valuable work, evidently did not consider that this exonerated either the Company or the Ministry of Labour from blame for the serious loss of public money which they considered had been incurred, in part, at least, by faulty and inadequate direction and management.

The Piercy Committee, reporting four years later, were much more appreciative of the work done and strongly emphasised the benefit to both individual and community resulting from the social service for the disabled which the company operates, a service which, the Committee pointed out, 'seeks to demonstrate that, given suitable conditions of work, even the badly disabled person may find a place in industry and feel that he is making some effective contribution to the country's production'.[2] They admitted the losses, but regarded some financial loss as inevitable in view of the many difficulties and, in any case, these losses should be set against the likelihood that many persons employed by Remploy would otherwise have to be supported out of public funds. They pointed out that, in recent years, the Company's organisation has been examined by the Organisation and Methods Division of the Treasury and in the main their recommendations have been accepted, while its management has been strengthened. Hence the Committee hoped that it may consolidate its position in the future, even if no expansion is envisaged. Not the least of the benefits of Remploy, in the Piercy Committee's estimation, is that for approximately 250 disabled persons each year, employment by the company affords preparation and training for work in normal industry rather than permanent placement. The Committee considered that transition from sheltered to open employment should be encouraged in all suitable cases, even if this makes things more difficult, as thereby the company is continually losing its best workers, since, in the Committee's opinion, 'nothing could be worse than the prospect of a group of disabled people, some of them young on entering a workshop, remaining the whole of their working lives in a sheltered environment as a matter of course, and, incidentally, perhaps causing others with far better claims to sheltered work to be excluded'.[3]

Created by statute and with the resources of the State behind it, Remploy has become the largest and most important of the organisations providing sheltered employment for disabled persons, but

[1] Op. cit., pp. xi–xvi.
[2] Op. cit., par. 213, p. 53.
[3] Ibid., par. 199, p. 49.

it is not the only one. Voluntary organisations such as John Groom Crippleage and the Lord Robert Memorial Workshops are also undertaking valuable work of this kind and may receive financial assistance from the Ministry of Labour, while some local authorities continue to be responsible, either directly or through the agency of a voluntary society, for the organisation and management of long-established workshops for the blind.

The provisions made for the rehabilitation and resettlement in employment of the disabled person are thus extensive and varied, but if he is to take full advantage of them he may well need individual help and guidance, guidance which will take into account his temperament and intelligence, his home circumstances and social and educational background as well as the nature and extent of his disability and the employment opportunities of the area in which he lives. Since 1941 the Ministry of Labour has employed special officers called disablement resettlement officers to give this individual guidance, and the success of the resettlement schemes depends in no small measure on the understanding of the individual, knowledge of available facilities for training and employment, and degree of co-operation with the medical and social personnel also working on the case, which is shown by these officers. The social work content of their work is thus frequently high, but little recognition seems to have been given this by the Ministry, as they are selected for their work from amongst others in its employment service and receive only a short initial training. Representations were made to the Piercy Committee that disablement resettlement officers might more fitly be recruited from the ranks of trained social workers, but elicited the reply that such representations arose from a misconception of the role of the disablement resettlement officer. His role, the Committee considered, 'is primarily that of an employment officer as his main concern is with the placing of disabled persons in suitable employment . . . and while he must appreciate the special needs of the disabled, he should not be regarded as a social worker in the specialised sense of the term.'[1] While it is true that the D.R.O. is primarily a placement officer, the disabled person's social and psychological problems are so closely bound up with his placement possibilities and success and happiness in work that the possibility of successful placement in difficult cases is likely to be seriously impaired unless the officer has been trained so that he can realise both the nature and importance of these problems and co-operate fully with the social workers specially fitted to deal with them. The Committee recommend more training than is given now if the officers are 'to take their place and co-operate with other qualified

[1] Op. cit., par. 183, p. 45.

members of the rehabilitation scheme', but the emphasis is on in-training and no suggestion is made that an officer should seek to obtain a wider background to his work, for example, by taking part in general courses along with others engaged in social and related work.[1]

So far disablement has been considered almost entirely as a problem of employment, and rehabilitation and resettlement as processes directed towards fitting the handicapped person for this and ensuring that he obtains the type of work in which he will best be able to exercise the maximum skills of which he is capable. This is perhaps the most important aspect of community concern for the disabled, but it is not all that is needed. The handicapped person must be integrated socially as well as economically with the normal community. This is not easy and he may need a good deal of help and encouragement in his struggles to find a place in a world in which he is regarded as 'abnormal', different from his fellows. In this struggle, he may gain much from the support of those who are similarly placed, that is from membership in a group in which he conforms to type and in which his difficulties are shared by all and taken as a matter of course.[2] He may also need individual help and understanding from someone he has learned to know and trust, someone who understands his difficulties and hesitations and helps to link him with the normal community. The various associations for the handicapped endeavour to meet these needs. They vary their techniques to meet the special problems of the categories of disabled persons with which they are particularly concerned, but all of them would, no doubt, endorse Mr. J. D. Evans' description of the aims of a centre for the deaf. 'It is', he writes, 'at once the buffer between the deaf and the hearing world, and the gateway into that world.'[3]

Among those for whom adjustment to their disability is most difficult are the gravely disabled, permanently confined either to home, hospital or hostel. These include tragic cases of young 'chronics' who may need prolonged or permanent nursing care, which in the present state of hospital provision may mean con-finement for life in a ward with elderly or even senile cases, since the hospital has not enough young chronics to make a group by themselves.[4] Voluntary homes for severely handicapped help to

[1] Ibid., par. 190, p. 46.
[2] The success of such organisations as the Infantile Paralysis Fellowship and the Invalid Tricycle Association is an indication of this.
[3] *Voluntary Social Services in the Modern State*, p. 78.
[4] Cherry Morris, 'The Problem of the Young Chronic', in *The Welfare of the Disabled*, p. 47. In this paper Miss Morris points out that of recent years much attention has been given to the needs of the elderly, but relatively little to those of young incurables.

fill the gap, but there are too few of them to meet the need. The need for providing special accommodation for such cases and the difficulties connected with providing it are recognised and discussed in the Ministry of Health circular to regional hospital boards and management committees, issued in the autumn of 1957.[1] It is recognised that 'It is wholly unsatisfactory for such patients to be nursed for, perhaps, the greater part of a lifetime in the company of older patients in all stages of terminal illness, or of much greater age.' On the other hand, however, to gather them together in one hospital where they can be looked after on their own may, except in very large centres of population, make it difficult to preserve the necessary contacts with their own families. Regional boards and committees are asked to find out how many younger chronic sick patients they are caring for and in which hospitals and 'to consider at once whether it would not be practical to group them together in one or more hospitals'. 'The Minister considers this is a development which should, wherever possible, be introduced as a matter of urgency'[2]—which indeed it is.

Those badly disabled persons who live at home, while, in some respects more fortunate than those in hospital, have their own problems. Among the most serious of these are isolation, which may be accentuated by acute self-consciousness; lack of occupation, with its attendant apathy and boredom; and the knowledge of the burdens and restrictions which their disability necessarily imposes on relatives, even if this burden is willingly carried. One of the best ways of helping such home-bound cripples is the provision of occupation which, if possible, should be remunerative even if only to a limited extent. This is by no means easy, for it may involve the organisation providing it in considerable trouble and expense, the range of goods which can be produced is limited, and it is doubtful if much expansion of this type of provision is feasible in these days of increasing mass production.[3] At present Remploy has its own home-workers employment scheme covering about 130 home-bound persons, some local authorities have used their powers under Section 29 of the National Assistance Act to provide instruction in handicrafts as a therapeutic rather than remunerative activity, while some voluntary organisations such as the British Red Cross Society operate schemes which, whatever their limitations, may make all the difference to those severely disabled persons who have been reached and are profiting from them.

[1] National Health Service, *Geriatric Services and the Care of the Chronic Sick*, H.M. (57) 86.
[2] Op. cit., pars. 35 and 36.
[3] Cmd. 9883, pars. 223–39, pp. 56–9. Cf. J. S. Clarke, op. cit., pp. 174–6.

THE PERMANENTLY HANDICAPPED

Until the passing of the National Assistance Act, 1948, the social care of the handicapped was, in the main, left to voluntary effort, except for the provisions made for the education of handicapped children which have already been described. The only handicapped adults for whom there was statutory provision were the blind. Under the National Assistance Act the provision of welfare services for the handicapped became a local responsibility along with the social care of the aged. The intention of the Act appears to be to extend to all who are permanently handicapped the services hitherto available to the blind alone, and to allow the same flexibility in administration of the proposed general welfare schemes as had been allowed in blind welfare. Thus Section 29 of the Act empowers county councils and county borough councils 'to make arrangements for promoting the welfare of persons who are substantially and permanently handicapped by illness, injury or congenital deformity or such other disabilities as may be prescribed by the Minister' (of Health). This power becomes a duty 'to such an extent as the Minister may direct'. In Circular 87/48, he directed that it should become a duty in relation to blind persons ordinarily resident in the council's area, and in a further circular, issued in 1951,[1] he explained that, while at that time he had no intention of giving any similar direction in respect of other categories of handicapped persons, he was ready to consider schemes submitted by local authorities who desired to exercise their powers under Section 29 to provide welfare services for handicapped persons other than the blind or partially sighted, and authorities proposing to exercise their powers must do so in accordance with such a scheme. Outline schemes covering the deaf and dumb and other handicapped persons respectively were appended to the circular. The Act itself[2] makes it possible for the local authority to employ a registered voluntary organisation as its agent for carrying out these provisions, and in the circular already referred to the Minister expresses the opinion that 'much benefit would accrue to handicapped persons of all classes covered by the outline schemes if the voluntary effort which abounds for their welfare were properly co-ordinated and directed in close co-operation with the Council's Health and Welfare Department'.[3] In some areas committees, which are broadly comparable to the more numerous old people's welfare committees, have been formed to bring together representatives of the statutory and voluntary

---

[1] Circular 32/51. Welfare Services for Handicapped Persons other than the Blind and Partially Sighted.   [2] Section 30.

[3] For a discussion of the part played by voluntary services see J. H. Nicholson *Help for the Handicapped*, an enquiry into the opportunities of the voluntary services, National Council of Social Service, 1958.

agencies dealing with the welfare of the physically handicapped. They act as consultative or co-ordinating bodies, some covering county areas whilst others are under the aegis of local councils of social service. The committees thus provide opportunities for common consultation and discussion of mutual problems and undertake the collection and dissemination of appropriate information to statutory departments and voluntary organisations, to disabled people themselves and to supporters of work for the physically handicapped. At the same time their member organisations are carrying out their own particular work for disabled people.

Representatives of such committees from various parts of the country are brought together by the Central Council for the Care of Cripples, which, besides convening periodic meetings of senior officers of the committees, is also responsible for a national standing conference which brings together a large number of delegates from statutory departments and voluntary organisations concerned with the welfare of the disabled.

The welfare provisions included in the Ministry's schemes as set out in Circulars 87/48 and 32/51 are based on the recognition that the needs of disabled persons vary according to 'the nature of the handicap and the degree of personal adjustment which the individual has achieved or can be expected to achieve', and aim at ensuring that 'all handicapped persons, whatever their disability, shall have the maximum opportunity of sharing in and contributing to the life of the community, so that their capabilities are realised to the full, their self-confidence developed, and their social contacts strengthened'.[1] They include, in particular, provisions for guidance and advice on personal problems, and for social and recreative activities, opportunities for sheltered and home employment and assistance in marketing the products of such employment, and help in acquiring skill in diversional handicrafts, and the provision of both long and short stay hostels. An important basic provision which is obligatory on all local authorities adopting schemes is the compilation of classified registers of all handicapped persons who, in however informal a way, indicate their need for assistance.

Given imaginative understanding of the social and psychological needs of disabled persons and willingness to co-operate on the part of both local authorities and voluntary bodies, the Act and its attendant circulars make possible the development in each area of comprehensive and constructive services for the handicapped. Many local authorities have been active in investigating conditions in their areas and getting their schemes under way, but, reporting in November 1956, the Piercy Committee sadly ad-

[1] Ministry of Health Circular, 87/48.

mitted, in a somewhat doubtful metaphor, that 'It is clear that only the fringes of the field have yet been touched.'[1] They suggested that this is, in part at any rate, due to the fact that such services attract no grant aid from Exchequer funds and recommended that this be remedied. Another problem which local authorities have to face is that of the recruitment of suitable personnel for work with disabled persons and their families. The adoption of the Younghusband Committee's proposals for general social work training with opportunities for detailed study of particular kinds of work, for example, with the blind or deaf, should help to meet this need.[2]

Important as local developments are, there are services for the handicapped which can only be adequately provided on a national scale, and nation-wide voluntary organisations such as the National Institute for the Deaf, the Central Council for the Care of Cripples and their kindred organisations have still valuable services to perform for their own people. They endeavour to maintain contact with all organisations in their particular field, watch over the legislation affecting the category of persons in which they are particularly interested, and initiate and maintain services which cannot be provided locally, such as specialised education, training and employment schemes covering the whole country and services for special categories of persons such as the Home of Recovery for the newly blinded, and hostels for the deaf-blind.

On the whole, the outlook for the handicapped person of this generation is more hopeful than it was in the past, for the attitude of his fellow men is changing from pity for his helplessness to encouragement to him to make the most of his powers. This change is coming about slowly, however, and much remains to be done to educate public opinion to a real understanding of this new approach. Mistaken ideas still continue to be held and influences 'unfavourable to full and healthy development' continue to retard progress towards independence of all categories of disabled persons, not only of the blind about whom these words were written.[3] Nor is it only the attitude of society that is the determining influence. Despite all that is and can be done, the response of the handicapped individual and his family remains decisive. 'Her disability certainly was physical, but the cause of her disablement lay in her disturbed attitude to others,' wrote the Superintendent of the Aberdeen Resettlement Clinic about a deformed girl who had been over-protected in childhood and failed to settle

[1] Op. cit., par. 106, p. 26.
[2] Report of the Working Party on Social Workers in the Local Authority Health and Welfare Services, H.M.S.O., 1959.
[3] Report of the Working Party in *The Employment of Blind Persons*, p. 8.

in any of the jobs found for her.[1] Against this can be set the adjustments made and the successes achieved by persons suffering from the most grievous disabilities, with the aid of their own courage and will-power and the understanding and encouragement of their families and friends.[2] What the community can and should do is to make such victories over disablement easier for the strong and possible for the weak.

[1] I. M. Richardson, Cf. 'The Aberdeen Resettlement Clinic', *The Almoner*, September 1954, p. 217.
[2] The stories of several such courageous men and women are told in *Disabilities and How to Live with Them*, a book published by *The Lancet* in 1952.

CHAPTER XX

THE MENTAL HEALTH SERVICES

In the chapter immediately preceding this we have been considering the provisions made by the community to help persons handicapped by some more or less permanent infirmity to overcome their difficulties and to achieve as great a measure as possible of economic independence and social adjustment. Many of these services, together with those provided under the National Health Service Act, are available to, and used by, persons who are mentally subnormal or who suffer from mental ill-health, but additional special legislative and administrative provisions are needed if they are to be properly cared for and treated. From the administrative point of view the crux of the problem is that mental illness or subnormality may, and in the more serious conditions does, involve either failure to achieve the understanding and self-control required of a responsible person managing his own affairs, or their loss or impairment, either temporarily or permanently. Hence a mentally sick or subnormal person may require control as well as care, for his own sake as well as that of others. The imposition of such control, without the full understanding or consent of the person concerned, is a serious infringement of the liberty of the subject, and must needs be hedged about with adequate safeguards. The difficulties of framing laws which will provide these safeguards, encourage early and effective treatment where this is possible, and at the same time maintain adequate control where this is needed, have proved considerable. Our latest attempt to solve them, the Mental Health Act, 1959, places the emphasis on early and effective treatment, freely given and accepted with 'no more restriction of liberty or legal formality than is applied to people who need care because of other types of illness, disability or social difficulty'. Compulsory powers are reserved for those cases where their use is 'positively necessary to override the patients' unwillingness or the unwillingness of his relatives for the patients' own welfare and the protection of others'.[1] The passing of this Act epitomises the change in outlook with regard to mental disorder which has taken place over the years.

When we trace the history of provisions made for the care of

[1] Report of the Royal Commission on the Law relating to Mental Illness and Mental Deficiency, 1954–1957, Cmnd. 169, pp. 3–4.

THE AGED AND HANDICAPPED

mentally disordered persons, however, we find that historically control preceded care, and care treatment. 'In the eighteenth century, madmen were locked up in madhouses; in the nineteenth century lunatics were sent to asylums; and in the twentieth century the mentally ill receive treatment in hospitals.'[1] For generation after generation ignorance, fear and superstition resulted in harsh restraint and ill-usage, whether the patient was confined in Bethlem Hospital, London, shut away in a private asylum, or maintained as a pauper lunatic in his parish workhouse. During the eighteenth century increasing enlightenment and the growth of public concern resulted in the first tentative reforms. In 1774 the Act for Regulating Private Madhouses, ineffective as it was, established principles including the licensing of private premises, their visitation by Commissioners, whose method of appointment was prescribed by Parliament, their inspection to ensure that the wrongfully detained were released, the supervision of their inmates by the medical profession, and notification of the reception of persons alleged to be insane, which have been retained in subsequent legislation. Along with these tentative administrative reforms went new experiments in treatment, of which perhaps the most famous English one was 'The Retreat', York, a 'retired habitation' founded in 1792 at the instance of a Quaker tea and coffee merchant, William Tuke, where patients were kindly treated and well cared for, and occupations encouraged. The success of the methods used at this small institution 'removed the final justification for neglect, brutality and crude medical methods. It proved that kindness was more effective than rigorous confinement.'[2]

Meanwhile the need for lunacy reform, involving both better provision and more effective state control, was increasingly realised, and an Act passed in 1807 encouraged the establishment of county asylums, the forerunners of the mental hospitals of to-day. In 1828 a further step forward was taken by the appointment of the Metropolitan Commissioners in Lunacy. This was followed in 1845 by an important Act, the Lunatics Act, which established a permanent Board of Commissioners in Lunacy with general jurisdiction over the whole of England and Wales, and with wide powers to investigate conditions in asylums, gaols, workhouses and licensed houses, that is houses licensed for the reception of persons of unsound mind, run by private persons for profit. At the same time rules were made for the reception of both private and pauper patients. During the succeeding half-century the gains won in a century and a half of effort were consolidated in the Lunacy Act, 1890, which made provision for the proper

[1] Kathleen Jones, *Lunacy, Law and Conscience, 1744–1845*, Introduction.
[2] Kathleen Jones, op. cit., p. 65.

312

THE MENTAL HEALTH SERVICES

certification, care and control of persons of unsound mind, and the provision and inspection of asylums and licensed houses.

The provisions of the Lunacy Act governing certification and compulsory detention remained in force until their repeal by the Mental Health Act, 1959, but in the main these provisions rested on a concept of mental disorder which was already beginning to be out of date when the Act was passed. As the twentieth century advanced and new psychological discoveries, resulting in a new approach to the whole problem of mental illness, were made and new treatment adopted, it was gradually realised that in some respects at least the legislative provisions made in 1890 were hindering advance and must be supplemented by new legislation. In particular, the elaborate legal safeguards against wrongful detention which the Act contained militated against early diagnosis and treatment, while the position was further complicated by the close association between lunacy provisions and the Poor Law, a feature of nineteenth-century legislation which the Act confirmed. After the First World War the position was reviewed by the Royal Commission on Lunacy and Mental Disorder, 1924–6, and their recommendations, embodied in the Mental Treatment Act 1930, marked a new departure in mental health legislation. They were based on the principle that, 'the treatment of mental disorder should approximate as nearly to the treatment of physical ailments as is consistent with the specific safeguards which are indispensable when the liberty of the subject is impinged',[1] and the Act's most important provisions were those which made it possible for two categories of patients to be treated in mental hospitals without certification, namely 'voluntary' patients and 'temporary' patients. The former entered hospital at their own request and could take their discharge at seventy-two hours' notice, but were required to sign a written application at the time of admission. The provisions with regard to 'temporary' patients were designed to cover patients who had lost volition, and could not themselves apply for admission, but who were likely to make a speedy recovery. Despite their limitations the provisions with regard to voluntary patients in particular were found to be very valuable in that they did much to facilitate the treatment of the neuroses, that is those milder forms of mental illness in which the patient is able to co-operate in his own treatment. Similarly useful were those which authorised the establishment of psychiatric out-patients' clinics in connection with either mental or general hospitals, and those which recognised the value of after-care by empowering local authorities to make provision for the after-care

[1] Report of the Royal Commission on Lunacy and Mental Disorder, Cmd 2700, 1926, p. 157.

of any persons who had undergone treatment for mental illness, and to contribute to the funds of voluntary associations formed for that purpose.

The Lunacy Act dealt largely, and the Mental Treatment Act solely, with the problems presented by mental illness; equally far-reaching were those presented by that incomplete or arrested development of mind hitherto designated 'mental defect', but now described as subnormality. The distinction between disease and defect has been recognised since the fourteenth century when different provisions were made with regard to the control and disposition of the property of a 'born fool' or idiot and that of a 'lunatic', that is a person 'who hath had understanding, but by disease, grief or other accident hath lost the use of his reason'. These provisions recognised that the lunatic might recover his sanity or have lucid intervals, but assumed that the idiot was incurable. In spite of this early legal distinction it was not until the nineteenth century that separate provisions were made for the care of mental defectives, in the first instance by voluntary associations,[1] and the first comprehensive legislation for their benefit was the Mental Deficiency Act, 1913.

The Mental Deficiency Act, 1913, was passed following the report of the Royal Commission on the Care and Control of the Feeble-minded, 1904–8. It defined mental deficiency and divided mental defectives into four categories, idiots, imbeciles, feeble-minded, and moral defectives, and apart from slight modifications introduced in 1927, these definitions remained in use until after the passing of the 1959 Act. The 1913 and 1927 Acts taken together defined 'mental deficiency' as 'a condition of arrested or incomplete development of mind, existing before the age of eighteen years whether arising from inherent causes or induced by disease or injury'. Those persons whose defect was so great that they could not guard themselves against common physical dangers were graded as idiots, those able to do this but incapable of managing their own affairs, or in the case of children being taught to do so were classed as imbeciles, while the category 'feeble-minded' covered persons more intelligent than idiots or imbeciles but suffering from a mental defectiveness so pronounced that they required care, supervision and control for their own protection and that of others.

As the Royal Commission 1954–7 has pointed out,[2] these definitions are, in each case, a combination of a medical descrip-

---

[1] For a description of the pioneer work undertaken by the voluntary associations for the care of mentally defective persons, see Madeline Rooff *Voluntary Societies and Social Policy*, pp. 99 ff.

[2] Cmnd. 169 par. 160 p. 49.

tion of an underlying mental disorder and a sociological description of its practical effects, and, in the last resort, the measure of
defectiveness is based on social adaptation. As the Joint Committee
appointed by the Board of Education and the Board of Control
put it in 1929, 'in short, the only really satisfactory criterion of
mental deficiency is the social one, and if a person is suffering from
incomplete mental development which renders him incapable of
independent social adaptation and which necessitates external
care, supervision and control, then that person is a defective'.[1]
This raises the question as to how far it is permissible to regard as
defective, and to bring within the scope of mental health legislation which sanctions the use of compulsion in certain circumstances, not only persons with sub-normal intelligence, but also
persons whose intelligence is near, or even above the average, but
who are seriously emotionally immature and show this in abnormal or anti-social behaviour. For some time now increasing attention has been paid to these personality disorders and their attendant behaviour difficulties, and the word 'psychopath' has come
into use to describe persons who display these characteristics.
According to the Royal Commission the word is used in different
ways by different psychologists and psychiatrists, but is often used
in connection with mental disorder or subnormality which manifests itself in behaviour which is self-centred, unrestrained, showing
complete lack of foresight or consideration for others or capacity
to learn from experience. The actions of such persons may be, and
frequently are, anti-social or even criminal, and they fail to
respond to ordinary treatment or punishment,[2] but generally
speaking they did not come within the scope of pre-1959 mental
health legislation. The proposals for re-definition and re-classifica-
tion set out by the Royal Commission, and subsequently incorporated with modifications in the Mental Health Act, 1959, are
intended, among other things, to rectify this omission.

An important proposal made by the Royal Commission was that
a new term, which they proposed should be 'mental disorder'
should be introduced to cover all forms of mental ill-health or
disability. This was a corollary to their contention that the existing
clear-cut legal distinction between mental illness and mental subnormality which had grown up during the previous half-century
was undesirable, since, while it might be useful to draw a broad
distinction 'between disorders which affect the course or extent of
a person's mental development and which are likely to affect his
personality throughout life, and mental illness which often lasts

[1] Report of the Mental Deficiency Committee, 1929, Part 1, p. 13.
[2] Cmnd. 169, pars. 165–70, pp. 51–4.

only a short time', that such a distinction is 'only of limited validity, even for administrative purposes'. Some adults whose abnormal behaviour is due to a defect in development but whose intelligence is not seriously impaired may benefit from treatment not dissimilar from that given to persons suffering from mild forms of mental illness, while elderly mentally infirm persons may require similar treatment as persons who have been mentally inadequate all their lives. The community services which are needed to help the feeble-minded are not dissimilar from those needed to help the patient recovering from an acute mental illness or left with some residual mental disability after such an illness.[1] These considerations, the Commission felt, should lead to more flexible and unified administration than hitherto and hence the value of the overall term, but some differentiation between patients needing different types of services would still be required, and so, in addition to the inclusive term 'mental disorder', specific designations for certain categories of such disordered persons were also needed.

The designations finally adopted by Parliament are set out in Section 4 of the Mental Health Act. Mental disorder is defined as 'mental illness, arrested or incomplete development of mind, psychopathic disorder and any other disorder or disability of mind', and, in addition to the generally recognised forms of mental illness, the Act sets out three categories of mental disorder: 'severe subnormality', 'subnormality' and psychopathic disorder. 'Severe subnormality' is defined as 'a state of arrested or incomplete development of mind which includes subnormality of intelligence and is of such a nature or degree that the patient is incapable of living an independent life or of guarding himself against serious exploitation, or will be so incapable even when of age to do so'. 'Subnormality' means 'a state of arrested or incomplete development of mind (not amounting to severe subnormality) which includes subnormality of intelligence and is of a nature and degree which requires or is susceptible to medical treatment or other special care or training of the patient. Psychopathic disorder is defined as 'a persistent disorder or disability of the mind (whether or not including subnormality of intelligence) which results in abnormally aggressive or seriously irresponsible conduct on the part of the patient and requires or is susceptible to medical treatment'. The two categories 'subnormality' and 'severe subnormality' can be matched in preceding legislation, although it is significant that the need for 'care, supervision and control for their own protection and that of others' contained the earlier definitions of feeble mindedness is replaced by 'requires or is susceptible to

---

[1] Ibid., par. 185, p. 60.

medical treatment or other special care or training' in the new
definition of subnormality, but the inclusion of 'psychopathic disorder' as a mental disorder, the sufferer from which may in the
last resort be subjected to confinement and treatment without his
consent is new and has not been accepted without question.

The anxiety expressed about the inclusion of the psychopath
among the mentally disordered appears to result from the difficulty
there is in discovering criteria other than that of his general
behaviour by which his mental condition may be diagnosed. As
the Royal Commission themselves recognised, 'if one concentrates
on the patients' behaviour rather than on the mental condition
which lies behind it, one comes very close to making certain forms
of behaviour in themselves grounds for segregation from society,
which almost amounts to the creation of new "criminal offences",'[1]
but in the present stage of our knowledge it is very difficult to
isolate independent symptoms, and a psychopath has been described as being *'par excellence*, and without shame or qualification,
the model of the circular process by which mental abnormality is
inferred from anti-social behaviour while anti-social behaviour is
explained by mental abnormality'.[2] The framers of the Mental
Health Act have tried to avoid this unsatisfactory situation by
including both 'abnormally aggressive' or 'seriously irresponsible'
conduct on the part of the patient and susceptibility of the condition to medical treatment as joint criteria by which the issue as
to whether he is or is not suffering from psychopathic disorder is to
be decided, and the latter criterion is a matter of medical judge-
ment. As an additional safeguard a sub-section has been included
in the section of the Act which defines categories of mental disorder which states categorically, 'Nothing in this section shall be
construed as implying that a person may be dealt with under this
Act as suffering from mental disorder, or from any form of mental
disorder described in this section, by reason only of promiscuity or
other immoral conduct'.[3]

Important to the satisfactory functioning of a service as definitions undoubtedly are, they are but preliminary to action, and at
the heart of the Mental Health Act are two general principles
governing treatment both of which were enunciated by the Royal
Commission, and both of which have been endorsed by Parliament. The first of these guiding principles is that mental disorder
is an illness and mentally disordered people should be treated as
nearly as possible in the same way as persons suffering from bodily

[1] Ibid., par. 338, p. 119.
[2] Barbara Wootton, *Social Science and Social Pathology*, p. 250.
[3] Mental Health Act, 1959, Section 4 (5).

sickness; the second that, as far as possible, long hospitalisation should be avoided and community care take its place.

As we have already seen, important steps towards the approximation of the treatment of the mentally disordered to that of the physically ill or handicapped were recommended by the Royal Commission on Lunacy and Mental Disordered 1924–6, and incorporated in the Mental Treatment Act, 1930, and the administrative provisions of the National Health Service Act, 1946 took the process a stage further. The improvement of the 'mental' as well as the 'physical' health of the people of England and Wales is stated as the objective of this Act[1] and at both central and local government level, steps were taken to bring about a closer integration between the general and mental health services. At central government level supervisory functions hitherto exercised by a semi-independent body called the Board of Control were transferred to the Ministry of Health, but the Board retained both its powers of inspection and its very important quasi-judicial functions in connection with the admission and discharge of certified patients. At the local authority level it was made clear that the responsibilities for the prevention of illness, care and after-care which local authorities were to exercise under Section 28 of the Act included both mental illness and mental defectiveness, and a circular issued by the Ministry of Health[2] recommended the setting up in each authority of a Mental Health Sub-Committee which would be responsible for providing and controlling all the mental health services for which the authority was responsible, whether these services were for mentally ill or mentally defective patients, and whether provided under the National Health Service Act or under the Lunacy, Mental Treatment or Mental Deficiency Acts—the Acts in operation at that time.

The Royal Commission 1954–7 reviewed these administrative arrangements in the light of the two major changes in the character and emphasis of the service which they were recommending, namely that compulsion should be reduced to a minimum, and that as far as possible, community care in the patient's own home should replace incarceration in an institution.

The medical and administrative considerations and the social factors which have led to change in emphasis from institutional to community care of which the recommendations of the Royal Commission and the provisions of the Mental Health Act are the culmination, are summed up in the Report of the Ministry of

[1] National Health Service Act, 1946, S. 1.
[2] Mental Health Services to be provided by Local Health Authorities, Ministry of Health Circular 100/47.

Health for the year 1958, Part II.[1] The administrative considerations have centred round the problems posed by serious overcrowding in hospitals, changed economic and social conditions have meant that housing has improved, and industry has become more active so that there is now a place and a job for many patients able to leave hospital, but 'more important than any of these has been the gradual realisation that kindly care in a hospital or institution removing all responsibility from patients can be just as damaging as harshness'. Hence the intention is that, while 'the mental hospital remains and will remain a place for diagnosis, treatment, medical and nursing skill and of facilities for applying them, it is no longer a final and unalterable resting place for any but a small proportion of those who enter it'. It is recognised that there will be some who cannot leave, and that 'not every patient who can go home should go home; there is a limit to the disturbance, uncertainty and distress which a family can be expected to endure in order to keep a mentally disturbed relative out of hospital', nevertheless, it is hoped that as time goes on hospitals will be able more and more to limit their function to active treatment for those who can benefit from it. Care, as distinct from treatment, is to be the function of the community.

Community care of increasing numbers of mentally disordered persons will mean increased responsibilities for individuals, families and local authorities. It was realised by the Royal Commission that if their recommendations were carried out the general public would have to learn to tolerate in their midst persons with mild abnormalities of behaviour or appearance hitherto confined in hospitals, but they believed that there was increasing public sympathy towards mentally disordered patients which would result in a higher degree of tolerance in this regard.[2] But 'public sympathy by itself is insufficient to meet the needs of either the sick or subnormal person himself or of his family without planned and concentrated public action resulting in adequate and appropriate community provisions, and this is in the main the task of the local authority. This is made clear in Part II of the Mental Health Act 1959, which sets out the responsibilities of such authorities in some detail.

It is perhaps significant that the responsibilities of local authorities for the community care of mentally disordered persons as laid down by the new Act are to be discharged under Section 28 of the National Health Service Act. This emphasises both that they are an integral part of the local authority's overall responsibility for the

---

[1] Cmd. 871, pp. 120–1.
[2] Op. cit., par. 601, p. 207.

general health of the community, and that they are a continuation of existing responsibilities and not a new departure. What is new is that the Minister is exercising his power under the Act to make what have hitherto been powers, duties,[1] and that certain specific services are to be provided by local authorities, whatever they may or may not do in addition. These services include the provision, equipment and maintenance of residential accommodation, facilities for occupation and training, and the appointment of mental welfare officers.[2]

Mental welfare officers, both sufficient in number and of the requisite calibre are essential if community care of the mentally disordered is to be carried our effectively, and their recruitment and training is a major problem whose importance has been recognised both by the Royal Commission[3] and by the Younghusband Committee. Present staffs are inadequate and many of those now employed in the local authority mental health services are men and women who until 1948 were poor law officers and who are now nearing retirement age, and it will not be easy to find successors for them, let alone expand the service to the number which the Younghusband Committee consider is required if case loads are to be reduced sufficiently to permit of real preventive work.[4] Nevertheless the attempt must be made if community care is to be effective.

While the major responsibility for community care rests with the local authorities it is not intended that they shall operate in isolation. Co-operation with both general practitioners and with the hospitals is essential. Some local authorities have evolved joint-user schemes whereby the services of psychiatrists and social workers are shared between hospital and local authority,[5] and, while in certain areas difficulties in the way of co-operation may persist,[6] its possibilities and advantages are widely realised. Ideally, general practitioners, hospitals and local authorities should combine to create an integrated mental health service.

[1] Ministry of Health Circular 22/59.

[2] Section 6 (2).

[3] Par. 723, p. 244.

[4] Op. cit., pars. 784 and 785. The Committee estimated that, including officers who combined mental welfare and general welfare duties there were, in 1956, the equivalent of 'not far short' of 1,100 whole-time mental welfare officers in the country. They thought that 'in view of the very large additional commitments' local authorities would undertake if the recommendations were implemented, this number should be increased to about 2,000.

[5] Examples of co-operation between the hospital and local health authority services are given in the Report of the Minister of Health for 1958, Part II, pp. 126–9.

[6] In a discussion of some of the problems involved see Kathleen Jones, 'Problems of Mental After Care in Lancashire,' *The Sociological Review*, 1954.

Some of the most interesting developments which are taking place in the mental health service at the present time are connected with the hospitals. Some of these developments are aimed at making it possible for patients receiving hospital treatment to live at home, and include the extension and improvement of out-patient facilities, domiciliary visiting and treatment of patients in day hospitals. The changes that have received most attention are, however, those which relate to the admission and discharge of in-patients. As we have seen, the Royal Commission recommended that admission to hospital for mental treatment should normally be attended by no greater formality than admission for physical treatment and in January 1958 the Minister issued a circular[1] recommending that future admissions to mental deficiency hospitals and institutions should be on a voluntary basis in all suitable cases. It also asked superintendents to review cases already in care with a view to the orders under which they were detained being discharged. At the same time local health authorities were asked to make a similar review of cases under guardianship. In October 1959, the Minister brought into operation that part of the Mental Health Act which makes it possible for patients entering Mental hospitals to do so informally in the same way as general patients are admitted to general hospitals.

It is hoped that in future the vast majority of mental patients will enter hospital voluntarily and without formality. There still remain, however, a small proportion of men and women who are in urgent need of mental treatment but who are unwilling to enter hospital, and, both in the interest of these patients and for the protection of others it is necessary to include in mental health legislation provisions for compulsory admission and detention of recalcitrant patients should this become necessary. Part IV of the Mental Health Act sets out the circumstances in which compulsion may be used to secure admission for observation or treatment. Thus a patient may be admitted for not more than 28 days' observation on the grounds that he is suffering from mental disorder of a nature or degree which warrants his detention·in hospital for observation for a limited period and that he ought to be so detained in the interests of his own health or safety or with a view to the protection of others. Grounds for admission for treatment are that the patient is suffering from mental disorder of a nature or degree that warrants his detention for treatment, and that it is necessary in the interests of his health or safety or for the protection of others that he be so detained. Where a patient is suffering from mental illness or severe subnormality such compul-

---

[1] H.M. (8) 5.

sion may be exercised whatever his age, but it is limited in the case of psychopathic disorder and subnormality to persons under the age of 21. Older psychopaths can only be detained by court order following conviction for an offence.[1]

Compulsory detention in hospital or placement under guardianship deprives the person concerned of his liberty, and until the passage of this present Act it was necessary to obtain an order from a magistrate before this could take place. The Royal Commission considered that this reference to the judicial authority was open to objection and contained no real safeguard[2] and recommended it should be done away with. This recommendation was accepted by Parliament despite misgivings in some quarters, but, except in cases of emergency, application for compulsory admission, which may be made by the nearest relative or the mental welfare officer, must be based on two medical recommendations at least, one of the doctors making them being a practitioner approved by a local health authority as having special experience in the diagnosis or treatment of mental disorder, the other, if practical, being a doctor with previous knowledge of the patient.[3]

The abolition of judicial certification is one respect in which the Mental Health Act departs from well-established tradition, the other is the dissolution of the Board of Control, which, itself inheriting the powers of the Commissioners in Lunacy, has, since 1913 sought to safeguard the liberty of the subject by watching over the admission and discharge of patients, making sure that compulsory powers are only used as and when allowed by law and with adequate documentary authority for their use in each individual case. The Royal Commission considered that these functions could be more effectively discharged by local Mental Health Review Tribunals, the Minister of Health holding reserve power.[4] The Mental Treatment Act makes provision for the constitution in each hospital region of a Mental Health Review Tribunal, which shall consist of three groups of persons—legal members appointed by the Lord Chancellor, medical practitioners appointed by the Lord Chancellor after consultation with the Minister of Health, and persons having 'such experience in administration, such knowledge of social services or such other qualifications or experience as the Lord Chancellor considers suitable'.[5] The Commission placed high hopes on the effectiveness of such tribunals, but recognised that their success will depend very largely on the experience

[1] The procedure is set out in Part V of the Act.
[2] Op. cit., par. 438, p. 148.
[3] Mental Health Act, Section 28.
[4] Op. cit., par. 454, p. 153, and par. 790, p. 272.
[5] Mental Health Act, 1959, S.3 and First Schedule.

and calibre of their members, in particular the regional chairman.[1]

The Mental Health Act is being implemented stage by stage and at the time of writing[2] its implementation is not yet complete. Local authorities are formulating their schemes for community care, Mental Health Review Tribunals being appointed, the new designations are beginning to be used, the new procedures adopted. Like the National Health Service, of which it is a part, the Mental Health Service is likely to be handicapped for some time to come by shortages of accommodation and personnel, and unless these shortages are overcome the hopes raised by the legislation cannot be fulfilled. Hostel accommodation of all kinds is inadequate, more training centres are needed, more sheltered workshops, and perhaps most urgent of all, more men and women to staff these institutions and provide the social workers for what is intended to be an expanding community service.

Among the mental health workers for whom the demand is far greater than the supply are the psychiatric social workers.[3] The majority of those who deal with adults are attached to hospitals or clinics, where they undertake work in connection with treatment and after-care in direct co-operation with the psychiatrist. Some are employed in the community care services developed by the local authorities, but the evidence presented to the Younghusband Committee indicated that the position with regard to such employment is not always satisfactory and the Working Party pointed out that, 'Psychiatric social workers, almoners and family case-workers are in short supply. They are much needed in the health and welfare servcies, but they will not be easily attracted if their contribution is better recognised elsewhere'.[4] One way which the Younghusband Committee suggests their skills might be used to advantage is by encouraging them to provide casework consultations for the less highly trained mental welfare officers.[5]

In this necessarily general description of the mental health services an attempt has been made to show how the emphasis has shifted from custody to care and from care to treatment. But the present position in which treatment is central cannot be regarded as final, and the general tenor of the Report of the Royal Commission and the Mental Health Act are indications of the importance attached to prevention. We must not only treat those who are

---

[1] Op. cit., par. 454, p. 153.

[2] May, 1960.

[3] 'A psychiatric social worker is a social worker who, in addition to her general social work training, has received special training designed to fit her for work with children or adults suffering from mental illness or problems of personality.' Noel K. Hunnybun in *Social Case Work in Great Britain*, p. 100.

[4] Op. cit., par. 745, p. 210.

[5] Ibid, par. 746.

sick, but also endeavour to safeguard and improve the mental, as well as the physical health of the people. The roots of mental ill-health, both in the individual and in society, go deep and it may well be that only a re-ordering of men's relationships with each other and with the natural and spiritual worlds to which they belong can bring about the wholeness for which they crave. This involves, among other things, a deeper understanding of ourselves and of society. Further progress in psychological and social research should help bring this about.

PART FIVE

COMMUNITY SERVICE

What life have you if you have not life together?
There is no life that is not community,
And no community not lived in praise of God.

When the Stranger says: 'What is the meaning of this city?
Do you huddle close together because you love each other?'
What will you answer? 'We all dwell together
To make money from each other', or 'This is a community'?—T. S. ELIOT.

CHAPTER XXI

SETTLEMENTS AND COMMUNITY CENTRES

THE Temporary Social Committee of the United Nations set up immediately after the war laid it down that the standard to be attained in a social welfare programme is 'the well-being of the community so as to enable each to develop his personality . . . and at the same time to enjoy, from youth to old age, as full a life as may be possible'. This statement epitomises a conception of social service which, although it has always been present in some degree, is becoming increasingly emphasised now that the worst evils of poverty and preventible ill-health are being overcome. It rests on the assumption that the universal provision of services to maintain minimum standards of health and decency, although important, is insufficient in itself. Even if these universal basic provisions are accompanied by patient individual care designed to help those with personal handicaps to reach the level of the majority there is still more to be done, for a society which truly seeks the welfare of its members is not only concerned that they shall live, but that they shall have opportunities for more abundant life.

One of the pioneers in the provision of such opportunities for those who conspicuously lacked them was Canon Barnett, who became vicar of St. Jude's, Whitechapel, in 1873, and his work had far-reaching consequences. At that time this East End parish consisted almost entirely of a network of insanitary courts and alleys in which lived a degraded population of casual labourers, hawkers, beggars and thieves, and when he came to know his parishioners, Canon Barnett became increasingly sensitive not only to their material poverty and to the physical squalor of their surroundings, but also to their spiritual, intellectual and cultural poverty and the drab monotony of their lives. Hence, he not only sought to overcome the worst of the housing and kindred evils by every kind of influence he could muster; he not only sought to restore people to some measure of self-respect and independence by reorganising the relief giving connected with his church on C.O.S. lines; but, secure in a belief in 'the equal capacity of all to enjoy the best', he provided opportunities for the people of the neighbourhood to hear good music, to have access to books and pictures[1] and make good some of the educational opportunities they had missed.

As Canon Barnett pursued his self-appointed task of restoring their heritage to the culturally disinherited inhabitants of Whitechapel, he came to believe that the 'poverty of life', as he described it, of his parishioners could be relieved by continued contact, leading on to friendship, between these people and people of culture and education. Hence he conceived the idea of 'bringing the life of the university to bear on the life of the poor' by founding 'settlements' in working-class areas. In a settlement men of university standing and education would live as members of a community; from here they would go out and learn to know the people of the neighbourhood, help them in any way for which they were suited by character and inclination, and gain from them a fuller understanding of social conditions. In this way the immense gap between the privileged few and the poverty-stricken many would be bridged, and through friendship they would realise their common citizenship.[2]

The first settlement founded was Toynbee Hall in Canon Barnett's own parish of Whitechapel. He himself was largely instrumental in getting it started and became the first Warden. Soon numerous others were founded in various parts of London, chiefly by men and women associated with the universities and public schools, and the idea spread to the provinces, to America, and to all parts of the world.

Individual settlements have developed along different lines, according to the needs and circumstances of the neighbourhoods they set out to serve, and the predilections of their founders and workers. Play centres for young children and clubs for people of all ages from older boys and girls to men and women over sixty are usual, and educational classes, now often held in conjunction with the local education authority or the Workers' Educational Association, are provided where there is a demand. Settlement premises are also frequently centres of individual welfare work, and house such organisations as the local legal advice centre, citizens' advice bureau or branch office of the Invalid Children's Aid Association.

From the first certain settlements have regarded the study of social conditions as an important part of their task, and some of the social investigations undertaken in connection with settlements

[1] This in spite of the fact that he was himself both colour blind and tone deaf!

[2] The idea was first set out in a paper read by Canon Barnett at St. John's College, Oxford, 17 November 1883. This paper is printed as an appendix in J. A. R. Pimlott, *Toynbee Hall*, 1938. See also Henrietta Barnett, *Canon Barnett, his Life, Work and Friends*.

have been of far-reaching importance. Thus, 'It was from researches conducted as a Toynbee Hall settler that William Beveridge hammered out his thesis that unemployment is primarily a problem of industry rather than a problem of personal character or particular misfortune. It was from personal encounters between the sweated workers of East London and a group of Oxford settlers that the sweated industries campaign generated the impetus which led to the tentative reappearance of statutory wage regulation in 1909, and the Manchester Settlement produced the man (J. J. Mallon) who carried that campaign to fruition. There is indeed scarcely any field of social legislation or any statutory instrument of social service which does not owe something of its inception or direction to the recorded observations or voluntary experiments of settlers who, year by year, followed the call of Samuel Barnett to those mean streets where their fellow-citizens led anxious, meagre lives.'[1]

A valuable tradition which many settlements have built up over the years is that they have established a continuing link with certain families of the neighbourhood. Provisions are made to meet the needs of all age groups and both sexes, and so the different members of the family all come to be known, and while each follows his particular interest, the life and atmosphere of the settlement is shared and felt by all. Moreover the transition from one age group to another is easy, and the individual can progress from childhood to maturity or even old age without severing his link with the settlement, while his children follow in his footsteps and he takes an interest in their pursuits and progress. 'It is not that the family is treated as a unit, which might be undesirable, but the continuity of interest in each individual establishes a family connection between him and the settlement.'[2] The settlement thus becomes the centre round which much of the family's social life revolves, an example of the way in which a community service can help keep a family united.

While much of the work carried on at or in connection with the settlements is as necessary and valuable now as when they were first started, in some respects the movement, like the C.O.S., was a product of its time, a child of the age in which it was born. At that time the social cleavage between the classes was marked; there had hardly been time for the effects of universal education to make themselves felt, and until the last decade of the century trade

[1] Mary Stocks, *Fifty Years in Every Street*, the story of the Manchester University Settlement, 1945, p. 3.

[2] P. J. O. Self, 'Voluntary Organisations in Bethnal Green', ch. xiii, in A. Bourdillon, *Voluntary Social Services in the Modern State*, 1945, p. 238. Compare this point of view with that of those responsible for the policy of the Peckham Health Centre. See Innes H. Pearse and L. H. Crocker, *The Peckham Experiment*.

unions, Co-operative societies and other workers' organisations, with their demands for corporate self-reliance, scarcely touched the unskilled labourer. Hence it seemed both right and natural to both givers and receivers that schemes for relieving distress and raising standards in a poor neighbourhood should be promoted, financed, and largely carried out, by people of a different background coming into the area from outside. To-day we live in a society which is both better educated and more self-consciously egalitarian, and settlements throughout the country are facing the task of adapting themselves to changed conditions without losing much that is valuable in their tradition. To do this they have had to become both more democratic and more truly part of the life of the local community. 'Their work is no longer so much helping those who cannot help themselves as providing a framework within which people can use their own initiative.'[1] This re-orientation is not always an easy task. Some settlements are saddled with constitutions which reflect the conditions and spirit of the age in which they were founded, and there may also be some difficulty in accustoming the people of the neighbourhood to a change from 'dispensation' to 'co-operation'. They must learn to shoulder the burden of general financial responsibility, and instead of having things done for them learn to do them for themselves and for others, and 'this volte-face is bewildering and will take time to assimilate'.[2] If these difficulties can be overcome, and the transition accomplished, settlements can continue to do much valuable social and educational work in their neighbourhoods and the newer community centre movement will be enriched by the tradition they will be able to carry over to it.

Settlements came into being as the result of the concern of a sensitive and educated man about his neighbours' lack of opportunities for sharing in the rich cultural heritage of the society of which they were nominal, but to a great extent disinherited, members. Although material conditions were much better, this same cultural poverty characterised the housing estates built between the wars, and to it was added the social isolation of many of the families who came there to live.[3] It was on these housing estates and in response to the needs of the inhabitants that community associations came into being and community centres were built.

The origins of the first community associations and centres were varied. Some arose spontaneously, while others were inspired by interest and leadership from without, as when an old-established

[1] P. J. O. Self, op. cit., p. 248.
[2] Harvey Sheppard, Head of Cambridge House Settlement, 'Settling in a New World', *Social Service*, Vol. XVII, No. 4, March–May, 1949, p. 179.
[3] See above, Chapter VI.

settlement in a slum area started a branch or sent some of its workers to live on an estate to which a number of its families had moved.[1] Where and when associations arose as a result of the efforts of the tenants themselves, it is doubtful if, in the early days at any rate, their aims were as abstract and self-conscious as they have since become. These people formed gardens guilds because it was cheaper to purchase seeds and fertilisers collectively in bulk rather than individually in small quantities, tenants' associations because they wanted to protest about the inadequacy of the local bus service, the iniquity of the electricity charges or the inefficiency of the grates which had been installed, or social clubs because they wanted to hold whist drives and provide treats for their children; that is they came together because there were certain things they wanted done which could only be done in association. In pursuit of these common interests they learnt to know each other, and slowly, and often only as the result of outside influences or the outstanding leadership of one of their own number, they began to realise that such activities could interlock and fit into the wider conception of a community association. Moreover, many associations, although they might pay lip-service to the high-sounding objectives of the community associations movement, never really made them their own and remained little more than social clubs.

The associations started as the result of inspiration from without, for example, through the influence of a settlement, were more deliberately planned, and from the start often included a variety of activities for different age groups. These ventures made valuable contributions to the development of social life on the estates, particularly perhaps on slum clearance estates where conditions were most difficult and internal leadership lacking. There have been instances, however, where, in spite of the efforts made to train local leaders, the work has flagged and died when the support from outside was withdrawn. It seemed as though the people could accept what was offered, but could not make it their own.

The history of the community associations movement has thus been a chequered one, with its disappointments and failures as well as its successes, but in many areas considerable progress has been made and strong associations maintained over a number of years. Moreover, the movement has spread, not only to housing estates in all parts of the country, but to other types of area as well. This progress has been furthered by the encouragement and help given by

[1] For early histories of community centres and associations, started between the wars, see Terence Young, *Becontree and Dagenham*, 1944; Ruth Durant, *Watling, a Survey of Social Life on a New Housing Estate*, 1939; Mary Stocks, *Fifty Years in Every Street*, 1945; M. P. Hall, *Community Centres and Associations in Manchester*, 1946.

the National Council of Social Service. In 1929 the Council formed a New Estates Community Committee and obtained a grant from the Carnegie U.K. Trust for the development of social work on new housing estates. Gradually the scope of the Committee widened to include the encouragement of associations and the provision of centres in areas other than housing estates. At the same time representation of the associations themselves on the central committee was encouraged, and ultimately an autonomous body, the National Federation of Community Associations, emerged. To-day this forms a link between centres and associations throughout the country.

Whatever the origins or activities of a community association its first need is for suitable premises, and in its early years much of the energy of an association may be directed to finding, building or adapting premises or to raising money for this purpose. Working for a tangible objective which is obviously beneficial to all members may have, and in many cases has had, a stimulating effect on the association concerned, and has helped to bind the members more closely together. Moreover, when the building is obtained and ready for use the members can really feel that it is their possession and their pride. Hence it is generally inadvisable, even if it be financially feasible, for a local education or housing authority or a private benefactor to rob the people of the neighbourhood of this opportunity for initiative and common action by building premises without expecting any contribution or effort on their part, or consulting them about its plans. Where this has been done the results have not always been good. On the other hand years of delay and frustration may stifle enthusiasm and result in apathy.

Statutory powers with regard to the building or adaptation of premises for community centres are contained in the Education Act, 1944;[1] the Physical Training and Recreation Act, 1937[2], and the Housing Act, 1936.[3] Local authorities thus have powers under a number of different acts to provide or assist in the provision of community centres. In 1949, however, the Ministry of Education issued a circular limiting work on community centres to that of maintenance and for some years little could be achieved in the way of new building projects and the work of many centres was restricted and made more difficult. The position became easier when, as in December 1954, a new circular (Ministry of Education Circular No. 283) was issued. It stated that the Ministry proposed to relax existing restrictions on grants in connection with the capital cost of village halls, community centres and youth clubs. Building was again restricted by Circular 331/57, which stated that the Ministry would only grant-aid local authorities 'in exceptional

[1] Section 41 b.   [2] Section 4.   [3] Section 80.

cases of urgent need such as in a new town or a large housing estate'. This was before the 'block grant' which may well have affected the position in some areas.

When once a community association has become established, and acquired or hired premises of some kind on which to base its activities, the real test of its vitality and the contribution it has to make to the life of the neighbourhood begins. According to a booklet issued by the Ministry of Education immediately after the war community centres exist 'so that neighbours can come together on an equal footing to enjoy social, recreative and educational activities either as members of groups following particular hobbies and pursuits or on the basis of their common needs and interests as human beings living in the same locality'.[1] Their purpose is thus educational in its broadest sense, but the centre is also intended as a focal and growing point of community life. The assumption here is that individuals and families living in a locality will, by doing things together which they find to be worth while, develop a common loyalty to the centre and neighbourhood which will do much to create that sense of belonging together which transforms a geographical expression into a local community.[2] In pursuit of this objective the association will not only welcome individual members who will join in its own activities and help to create its own group life, but it will also encourage other groups in the neighbourhood to affiliate to it, and, if premises permit, hold meetings at its centre. In this way the centre will become 'a power house of community effort'.[3]

Such high ideals and far-reaching plans were characteristic of the community centre movement during the period of transition from war to peace. They were closely linked with those of neighbourhood planning, since the community centre was designed to be the focus of the neighbourhood unit. As we have already seen[4] neighbourhood planning has itself been subject to a considerable amount of criticism of recent years, and the community centre movement has not escaped it.

The main criticism which has been made is that too much is expected in the way of unification from one type of social relationship, the leisure-time interest group in a local setting. As the writer

[1] Ministry of Education, *Community Centres*, 1945, p. 6.
[2] Cf. 'Neighbourhood does not, of itself, necessarily constitute a social bond; but if, by grouping its leisure activities round a recreative and educational centre a neighbourhood can develop into a socially conscious community, learning through managing the affairs of a centre to participate intelligently in the work of local and national government, then education for democracy will have made a real advance', ibid., p. 4.
[3] National Council of Social Service, *The Size and Social Structure of a Town*, p. 17.   [4] Chapter VI, above.

of the P.E.P. pamphlet *Can Communities be Planned?* sees it, the danger is twofold. 'The first [danger] is to forget that local communities are not the only social relationships open to people in a modern society [the most important alternative bond of association is probably that of common employment]. The second is to exaggerate the importance in a local community of organised activities,' for while the provision of facilities which encourage communal activities can help to foster community life it cannot by itself create it. The influences which combine to create communities are more subtle, more far-reaching, slower and more secret in their working. At the same time, if exaggerated and diffuse claims be modified, and the community centre accepts the position that it is one of the many and various influences which combine to enrich the life of the neighbourhood, it can find its own special place and make its own special contribution.

The particular contribution a community centre has to make will vary from neighbourhood to neighbourhood according to social needs, and provision or lack of provision to meet them. In some areas the emphasis of the centre may be on providing facilities for common enjoyment of a more creative and sociable kind than the rather passive and individualistic pleasures of commercial entertainment, and this may lead some groups on to 'learning based on joy'.[1] In other neighbourhoods the most important contribution the association can make may be to give hospitality on the centre premises to struggling organisations frustrated for the lack of a place wherein to meet. Some centres may endeavour to cater for families rather than individuals, while others may regard themselves primarily as adult organisations and leave the provision of activities for children and young people to other bodies. Yet another centre may have a youth wing, but one 'insulated' from the remainder of the centre.[2]

Thus the vitality of the community centre movement may most clearly manifest itself in the variety of ways in which it adapts itself to meet differing circumstances, the needs of differing neighbourhoods.[3] This has been true of the settlement movement so that, for example, the educational settlements started in the Welsh mining valleys during the years of unemployment have developed along completely different lines from the early settlements in East Lon-

[1] The phrase is taken from David Hardman, 'New Pathways in Adult Education', *Social Service*, Vol. XXIII No., 1, June–August 1949, p. 17.
[2] This was the arrangement favoured by the Ministry of Education in its pamphlet on Community Centres, op. cit., p. 13.
[3] A development of this kind may be found in the tenants' common rooms provided in connection with some housing estates, for example, in London and Birmingham. This development is described in *The Neighbourhood Worker*, January 1958.

don. In both the settlement and community centre movements the distinguishing feature is, or should be, sensitiveness to the needs and wishes of the people of the neighbourhood in which the organisation is functioning. In these days of specialisation this is a particularly valuable contribution. At the present time many organisations and services are structured in such a way that particular interests and ideals of the organisation come first, the general interests of the locality second. A branch of such an organisation, which may for example be a political party or trade union or ex-serviceman's association, may serve those people who share particular needs or interests in an area, but its principal loyalties and activities go far beyond and outside this area, and may be dependent on or largely directed by a national committee which meets at the other end of the country. On the other hand, a community centre or association may cater for the particular needs and interests of special groups, but it is concerned with them not only as ends in themselves, but as elements enriching the life of the neighbourhood. The basis of such an association and centre is thus geographical rather than functional, and it is complementary to the organisations with a more definite purpose. If organisations of both types are found in an area its inhabitants will have opportunities of developing a rich and varied social life. Their very existence is indeed a sign of such abundant life. We have already suggested that such organisations are likely to be insufficient in themselves to create that sense of belonging which is the basis of community, but at least they help to break down the social isolation which is so marked a feature of the life of many people,[1] and make a real contribution to their happiness.

[1] A study of this characteristic of modern life was made in 1955–7 by a sub-committee of the Women's Group on Public Welfare, and has been published by the National Council of Social Service with the title *Loneliness*.

CHAPTER XXII

CO-OPERATION IN SOCIAL SERVICE

I F this book has done nothing else, it may perhaps have given the reader some idea of the range and variety of the social services. They all minister in some way to the personal well-being of individual members of the community, but they differ in scope, purpose, approach and method of administration. More-over, in the main, their growth has been haphazard, since they came into being one by one as the community, or at any rate the more sensitive among its members, became aware of personal needs to be met or social evils to be overcome. This process has given rise to an astonishing number and variety of voluntary and statutory social service organisations and, while consultations be-tween workers about individual cases or specific problems occur quite frequently and, in general, good personal relationships exist between social workers in a particular area, there is surprisingly little joint discussion on basic principles of social work and ad-ministration. Moreover, insufficient co-ordination between the different services has often meant overlapping, wasted effort, gaps and anomalies resulting in frustration and misery to the people whom the social workers and administrators are trying to help.

The undesirability of such a situation has, of course, long been recognised by those concerned with social policy, and, looked at from one point of view, the great series of measures of social recon-struction passed during the last years of the war and the period immediately following may be regarded as an attempt to bring order out of chaos, and to substitute planned development for haphazard growth. The call in the Beveridge Plan for a concerted attack on the Five Giants of Want, Squalor, Disease, Ignorance and Idleness[1] provided an objective which fired the imagination; such investigations as that of the Curtis Committee revealed the evils that arise when co-ordination is lacking; and wartime ex-perience had conditioned the people to national planning on matters affecting their daily lives. Hence the years between 1944 and 1948 witnessed the creation of a unified system of national insurance, a comprehensive national health service, a national assistance service, and a co-ordinated service for the care of

[1] Sir William Beveridge, *Social Insurance and Allied Services*, 1942, par. 8, p. 6.

deprived children. If we compare our present statutory social services with the corresponding provisions in 1939 it is clear that great steps forward have been taken in the direction of clarification and unification, but there is still much to be done. Not only do our present schemes contain gaps and anomalies,[1] they are also structured separately to meet classified social needs and this is bound to lead to difficulties since man 'is not a bundle of sticks each of which can be taken out and dealt with by different persons without affecting the rest',[2] but a living whole. Having gone a long way to meet specific social needs we realise we must now pay more attention to the ways in which they interlock, and at the present time considerable emphasis is placed on the need for the development of schemes of co-ordination and unification.

In furthering co-ordination, however, it is important to leave room for plasticity and spontaneity, for the social services have continually to adapt themselves to men's changing needs and ideas, and administrative efficiency can be purchased at too high a price if it results in rigidity and uniformity. Real co-operation, while it may be hindered or assisted by the legislative framework, is free rather than imposed. It is an expression of breadth of vision and understanding of the totality of human needs on the part of workers and administrators. For this reason we cannot expect, nor should we desire, to achieve over the whole wide field of social service the unification that has come about in the social insurance and allied services as a result of the implementation of the Beveridge Plan. Instead, we should examine some of the ways in which co-operation has developed freely in the past, and consider the means by which such free co-operation can be furthered in the present and future.

An old-established method of co-operation in case work is by means of Registers of Assistance and Care, which, started many years ago with the encouragement of the Charity Organisation Society and kindred organisations in London and some of the larger towns, had as their object the avoidance of overlapping in the giving of relief. Agencies making use of such a register supplied the names, addresses and relief given of cases assisted by them, and applied to the Registrar for information about the assistance given by other agencies to the families seeking their help.

In the past, when much of the work of voluntary organisations consisted of charitable relief, central registers of this kind helped to check wholesale cadging and served to let the different societies concerned with a particular case know which other registering agencies were in touch with it, but their potential usefulness in

[1] E.g. the unhappy position of the infirm aged described in Chapter XVIII.
[2] Una Cormack, 'The Welfare State', *Loch Memorial Lecture*, 1953, p. 24.

other directions was not developed and as emphasis in social work shifted and the problems associated with helping families to overcome the distress caused by poverty and destitution declined in importance, registers were thought to be unnecessary or redundant and only remained in operation in one or two areas. In these areas, for example, Liverpool and Manchester, the councils of social service operating them are encouraging the agencies using them to regard them as a means of facilitating co-operation at a casework level. There are difficulties in the way of this, however, for the free use of a mutual register raises the important issue of the responsibility of an agency to respect the confidence of its clients, and some statutory and voluntary bodies may refuse to register or simply consult the register without recording their own cases because they regard the full use of a register open to organisations of all kinds as a breach of confidence. In an attempt to overcome this difficulty the Liverpool Council of Social Service has divided the forty organisations and departments using its register into two categories. The seven casework agencies in Category A not only receive all relevant information submitted but, in addition, certain confidential information which is circulated only to them. At the time of writing the Council considered that during the two years in which the system had been in operation it had proved itself in practice, and it had been favourably commented on by the agencies concerned. In the Council's Annual Report for 1957 the number of 'Category A' reports issued by the register is reported to be 'a steady seven per cent of the total sent to the seven agencies and approximately five per cent of the grand total to all users'. The Report also notes that since 1948 the number of cases dealt with by 'relief' agencies had declined continuously while those dealt with by 'casework' agencies had increased, itself an indication of the greater concentration on the longer term casework problems which is characteristic of modern social work.[1]

As we have already seen,[2] it is in connection with long-term casework with families presenting multiple problems that the need for co-ordination is greatest and most clearly recognised, and various measures designed to foster it, such as the co-ordinating committees established by local authorities with ministerial encouragement to deal with cases of child neglect, have already been described. The emphasis in these and other similar case conferences and committees is on mutual consultation and agreement,

[1] Liverpool Council of Social Service, Annual Reports for 1956 and 1957. In 1956 a scheme was established for the co-ordinated development of the social services on the new satellite town of Kirkby and the 1956 Report states, 'The Register has been particularly valuable in establishing a good basis of co-ordination in the initial stages of social work at Kirkby . . .'.

[2] Chapters X and XIV.

and this may sometimes result in the major responsibility for visiting a particular family being entrusted, at any rate for the time being, to a particular agency or individual. This delegation raises the question as to how far and in what ways it is possible or desirable for a service or group of services to make use of an all-purpose social worker or general family visitor.

This possibility was discussed by the Working Party on Health Visiting and by the Younghusband Committee, and is, no doubt, under consideration by the Ingleby Committee, and it is symptomatic of the failure, at central government level, to grasp the importance of giving overall consideration to the problems of all the social services concerned, that it is being discussed by a series of self-contained working parties. What was, and still is, needed was a comprehensive review of the work carried out by all the different social workers concerned with discovering and meeting family needs, from whatever central government or local authority department or voluntary organisation they operate, and the closer co-ordination of the social services and the better distribution of function between social workers will continue to be frustrated until this is done.

Meanwhile, the suggestion that there might be room for a general family visitor raises a number of questions. The first of these is the level at which she will operate. As the Joint University Council for Social and Public Administration pointed out in their evidence to the Working Party on Health Visiting, the term could denote a person who, apart from exercising any specialist function (such as health visiting), 'would attempt little more than immediate practical help and would refer difficulties to an appropriate authority; or a general family caseworker, like those employed by the Family Welfare Association; or an exceptionally well-qualified worker able to co-ordinate and supervise a team and act as consultant in difficult cases'.[1] Until their status and functions have been further elucidated by the investigating committees, by local discussion and experiment, and by further research into the distribution and context of social work activity, any overall policy with regard to such workers would be difficult to formulate and unlikely to succeed.

An even more far-reaching suggestion than that of the employment of general family visitors, namely, the setting up of a comprehensive local authority family service, is now being canvassed by some individuals and organisations concerned with child care.[2] The case put forward in support of this proposal is that at present

[1] Report of a Working Party on Health Visiting, par. 71, p. 21. Cf. Report of the Working Party on Social Workers in the Local Authority Health and Welfare Services (Younghusband Committee Report), pars. 639–65.

[2] E.g. Council for Children's Welfare and the Fisher Group, *Families with Problems*, April 1958, D. V. Donnison and Mary Stewart, *The Child and the Social Services*, Fabian Research Series, No. 196, April 1958.

'there is no organisation which can assume continuing responsibility for ensuring that help will always be available for families in trouble—families whose troubles may not fit precisely into the statutory categories of need',[1] and that voluntary services cannot meet a nation-wide need. Such proposals are, as yet, inevitably still tentative, and need very careful consideration in both principle and detail before they can become practical policy, not least because they cut across the existing patterns of social service, patterns which have developed over the years. That there is need for a review of the whole situation is beyond doubt, however, and this review should be as comprehensive, careful and far-reaching as the Royal Commission on the Poor Laws of 1905–9.

Co-operation at the casework level between authorities and agencies undertaking some form of social casework or welfare work with individuals and families in need, important as it is, is not the only form of co-operation, however. There are other aspects of the problem of securing better co-ordination between the various statutory and voluntary social services. The furtherance of such wider co-ordination is the main function of the National Council of Social Service.

Founded in 1919, the National Council seeks to develop co-operation among voluntary agencies, and between them and the statutory authorities. It provides information on the social services, carries out research on problems of social work and social policy, encourages international co-operation in social work, promotes and sometimes undertakes, experiments in social service, provides a secretariat for a number of consultative groups of national social service agencies. The Council aims at bringing about two forms of co-operation, between organisations concerned with different forms of social and community service in the same area, and between organisations carrying out the same work in different parts of the country. Ideally, the two should supplement each other, so that, for example, an old people's welfare council in a particular area is linked on the one hand with its local council of social service, and, on the other, with its county or regional old people's welfare committee, and through this, with the National Old People's Welfare Council, which in its turn is linked with the National Council of Social Service, to which the local Council is affiliated through the Standing Conference of Councils of Social Service.

[1] D. V. Donnison and Mary Stewart, op. cit., p. 6. Cf. 'It was the view of the Fisher Group and the Council for Children's Welfare that the situation could only be effectively met by a local authority family service, available to any family who desired to use its help, whether for straightforward information or advice or for long-term skilled case-work with tangled family relationships.' *Families with Problems*, p. 9.

There are, of course, certain dangers to be guarded against in constructing such elaborate co-ordinating machinery. It may result in conformity at the expense of originality, or the dominance of the central administration, and there is always the danger of accepting the appearance of co-operation for its reality. Affiliation to a local or national body does not constitute co-operation if it means nothing more than the payment of an annual subscription, an invitation to an annual meeting, or the perusal of an annual report. If real co-operation is to be brought about, the National Council and its associated regional and local bodies must encourage individual statutory and voluntary agencies to lift their eyes from their own specialist tasks, must enable them to see these tasks in relation to the needs of their locality and the nation as a whole, and must inspire them to take co-ordinated action to meet these needs. Co-operation of this kind results not only in the smoother working of existing services, but in the promotion of new ones, for an alert council of social service or community council is sensitive to the developing needs of its area, and ready to discern the gaps left by existing organisations in their haphazard growth.

The chief means used by the National Council of Social Service to promote co-operation on an area basis are the rural community councils in country areas, the urban councils of social service in the towns, the county councils of social service and the area councils of social service which may cover areas greater or less than a geographical county. The Council has long taken a particular interest in the welfare of the countryman and the effects of the changes taking place in the countryside. It believes that 'the methods of consultation and working together for which it stands have special value in this country work, where the scope is large, and the pooling of resources is a very practical necessity'.[1] Its rural development policy has five main objectives, namely to establish in each county a representative council (the Rural Community Council) competent to survey the whole field of rural social life and to promote co-operation between statutory and voluntary agencies taking part in it; to help and encourage villagers to provide halls for themselves; to co-operate with other bodies in the provision of amenities; to increase the effectiveness of parish councils, and to support the country craftsman.[2] At present such co-ordinating councils are functioning in forty-six administrative counties, and the rural work of the Council is developing steadily with the encouragement of H.M. Development Commissioners and the appropriate local authorities.

[1] *A Challenge to the Citizen*, Annual Report of the National Council of Social Service, 1946–7.
[2] Ibid.

The promotion of urban councils of social service was the first task undertaken by the National Council, but it did not prove an easy or particularly rewarding one, and has tended to be over-shadowed by more spectacular activities. In October 1946, when an attempt was made to revive interest in this particular work, a Standing Conference of Councils of Social Service was set up. In 1958 forty-one local, four county and nine area councils of social service were members of the Standing Conference. Even in those towns and cities where bodies describing themselves as 'Councils of Social Service' exist, they vary greatly in the services they provide and the part they play in the life of the local community. According to the sponsors of the movement they should be centres of information about the differing agencies, statutory and voluntary, engaged in social work in their area; they should provide facilities for joint consultation and action; arrange conferences, lectures and exhibitions; and encourage new social experiments, either by assisting other agencies, or, where there is no one else able to accept responsibility, by undertaking the work themselves.[1]

The functions of an urban council of social service may thus be very varied, and its executive committee and officials have to be ever on the alert lest, on the one hand, it concentrates on one or two aspects of its work to the detriment of the rest,[2] or, on the other hand, allows itself to be saddled with the responsibility for a large number of unrelated services simply because no other body is able or willing to do anything about them. In either case the unity and sense of proportion which should be the characteristic of the Council's work may easily be lost, and it is in danger of sacrificing its role as a co-ordinating and promotional body, and of becoming one among many organisations specialising in certain types of social work. Ultimately the success of a council of social service depends on the extent to which it enjoys the confidence of the specialist agencies and of the central and local government departments in its area, so that they will consult it when new developments are envisaged, or new needs, for whose satisfaction joint action is required, become apparent. This will only happen if, as well as showing itself efficient in the ordering of practical affairs, and in the administration of those services for which it has assumed special responsibility, it continues to promote 'collective thinking' on current social problems, and this important activity should never be neglected in favour of what seem more urgent and useful tasks.[3]

[1] N.C.S.S., *A Local Council of Social Service*, 1944, pp. 8–9.

[2] This temptation is particularly great when a Council undertakes case work or runs a citizens' advice bureau, since the day-to-day demands of these activities are particularly insistent.

[3] Ibid., p. 12. Cf. Sir Herbert Thompson (General Secretary, London Council of Social Service): 'If, therefore, it is to fulfil its aim no Council of

CO-OPERATION IN SOCIAL SERVICE

Among the developments in co-operation between the various voluntary social services which have taken place in recent years, have been those in connection with raising the money required to enable them to carry on their work. Finance is one of the most serious problems facing voluntary organisations, and it has become increasingly clear that not only must new methods be found to extend the interest in and support of these organisations from the upper and middle to the working classes, but that this can only be done by carefully planned co-ordinated effort. In Liverpool the joint efforts of the Council of Social Service and the Personal Service Society have led to the setting up of a new organisation, United Voluntary Organisations, which, with the co-operation of the employing bodies and the trade unions, collects weekly pennies from between 60,000 and 70,000 persons working in approximately 550 firms and distributes the sum so collected annually among the local charities associated with the scheme. In the collection of the money care is taken to secure the goodwill and co-operation not only of the employers, but of the workers' representatives, and to keep subscribers informed about the work of the organisations they are supporting, for it is realised that 'if the population in general, as opposed to enthusiasts with a special interest or a particularly strong social conscience, are to subscribe regularly to voluntary organisations, the appeal must be rational rather than emotional'. They must also be convinced that 'none of the money is being wasted by inefficiency or overlapping and that it is being fairly distributed to the charities in proportion to their needs and their capacity for useful work'.[1] Distributions are made in accordance with a general scheme approved by the Council, the amounts for each charity being worked out by a Committee consisting of one of the city's leading chartered accountants and a leading actuary. As far as can be judged from four years' experience, the scheme seems to be working well. Manchester has started a similar scheme and preliminary steps are being taken in other towns and cities.

Local councils of social service are well fitted to take the lead in initiating experiments in their own areas, for such joint action is essentially an expression of a real sense of common purpose, showing itself in willingness on the part of all participating in it to substitute co-operation for competition, and to consider the claims

---

Social Service can be content with case work, however excellent, and co-ordination, however necessary. To serve the democratic body it must also think, weigh, study and inspire.' 'Councils of Social Service and Democracy.' *Social Service*, June–August, 1950.

[1] National Council of Social Service, *Finance of Local Voluntary Organisations*, An Experiment, United Voluntary Organisations.

of others as well as their own, and this is directly in line with the main objects of these Councils.[1]

Fostering co-operation between specialist agencies in particular areas by means of urban councils of social service and rural community councils is one function of the National Council of Social Service; complementary to it is that of promoting co-operation between people and agencies engaged in similar work in different areas. Examples of such work are the bringing together of local groups striving to foster the growth of community life through the National Federation of Community Associations, and the promotion of co-operation at all levels in the very different field of old people's welfare. Moreover, in these, as in other branches of the Council's work, such as the welfare work carried out among the unemployed during the depression between the wars, and the organisation of clubs for women of the lower income groups, the National Council has done more than foster co-operation between existing organisations. Much of its energy has been directed to the promotion of new services as the need for these has become manifest, and in this its task has been threefold, first, the encouragement and canalisation of local effort in different areas throughout the country, secondly, the linking of local committees by means of a national council or standing conference, and thirdly, the provision of specialist help and advice to ensure the maintenance and, where necessary, the improvement of local standards. Local committees dealing with special services remain autonomous and free to accept or reject the help offered by the Council, but in some fields of work it has been able to apply a powerful economic sanction, since it has been made the agency for the disbursement of certain government funds, and can, therefore, impose conditions and insist on the maintenance of certain minimum standards for those benefiting from this financial assistance. For example, in 1933, when the need for specialised social provision for unemployed persons and their families was at last widely recognised, the government of the day made an experimental grant for this purpose, and asked the National Council of Social Service to undertake its administration. By 1937 the amount of government money received by the Council had reached the impressive total of £317,688, namely, £102,757 from the Ministry of Labour and £214,931 from the Commissioner of Special Areas.[2] Similarly, during the war, the National Council was the agency through which the Ministry of Health gave grant-aid to citizens'

[1] For the history of one such Council which illustrates this point see H. R. Poole, The Liverpool Council of Social Service, 1909–59.

[2] *Voluntary Social Services since 1918*, ch. xii, 'The Finance of Voluntary Social Service', p. 192.

advice bureaux, and only bureaux 'approved' by the Council received this financial aid. Clearly an organisation entrusted with the disbursement of such large sums of public money carries a weight of responsibility and wields considerable power. It is to the credit of the National Council of Social Service that in general it administers these grants in such a way as to encourage local initiative and individual responsibility.

The use made of the National Council of Social Service in the disbursement of public funds raises the question of the relationship between the voluntary organisation for social service and the State, and no discussion of co-operation in social service would be complete without some reference to this question and to the related one of the respective spheres of the public and voluntary social services. Before considering these questions, however, it may be as well to define the term 'voluntary social service' a little more closely. It is used here to denote organised social service activity which is in the main independent of government control—'private enterprise in the service of mankind', as Lord Beveridge describes it.[1] This is not the same as 'volunteer service', which is service undertaken by individuals without remuneration. The volunteer helper may, and frequently is, to be found working in connection with a voluntary organisation for social service, but he may also be found as a school manager, member of an area advisory committee of the National Assistance Board, or hospital management committee, or serving on the local council. On the other hand, voluntary organisations may, and do, employ full- and part-time salaried workers, but this does not affect their essential character, which depends on the fact that they owe their existence to the initiative and continued support of individuals and groups and not to the State.

The question of the relationship between the voluntary and statutory social services is not a new one. During the latter part of the nineteenth and the early twentieth century the generally accepted theory as to the respective roles of private philanthropy and public relief was that enunciated by Mr. Goschen, the President of the Poor Law Board, in a Memorandum issued in 1869. This theory, designated by Beatrice and Sidney Webb as 'the parallel bars' theory,[2] divided those seeking help into two main categories, the one to be relieved by voluntary agencies, the other left to the functioning of a strict and deterrent Poor Law. Statutory and voluntary aid were to exist side by side, but there was to be no overlapping, and each case must be dealt with wholly by one or other means of assistance. Various criteria were tried as means of separating the sheep from the goats. In the original minute it

[1] Lord Beveridge, *Voluntary Action*, 1948, p. 322.
[2] S. and B. Webb, *The Prevention of Destitution*, 1911, p. 225.

was proposed that the wholly destitute be relieved by the Poor Law, those with some but not adequate means of subsistence by voluntary agencies. Later the Charity Organisation Society endeavoured to distinguish between the 'deserving' and 'undeserving'; helping the former and thrusting the latter back on poor relief, and when the impossibility of thus exercising the prerogative of the Almighty was made plain, they then tried to decide between those who could and those who could not be helped back to economic independence by the casework methods which they were slowly evolving. This attempt at segregation also broke down in practice, and although in 1906 the theory was still sufficiently influential to form the basis of the Majority Report of the Royal Commission on the Poor Law, it gradually became clear that the premises on which it had been constructed were false, and a new basis for demarcating the respective spheres of statutory and voluntary action must be sought.

The Webbs' alternative to the 'parallel bars' theory was that of 'the extension ladder'. This theory was based on an attempt to determine the respective strength and weakness of statutory and voluntary organisations, and is thus a division based on the character of the agency rather than the nature of the case. Voluntary organisations were regarded as being superior to public authorities in three main ways—in invention and initiative, in ability to lavish unstinted care on particular cases, and in the intensity and variety of the religious influences they could bring to bear on personal character; but public authorities were regarded as superior in that they alone could ensure provision that was universal, complete or continuous, and had the power to force the negligent or irresponsible to fulfil their responsibilities. Hence, the Webbs suggested that public authorities should be responsible for seeing that every individual born into the community was given the opportunity to reach a 'national minimum' of civilised life, and that his own obligation to maintain that standard was enforced. The role of the voluntary societies was to raise the standard of civilised conduct and physical health above the comparatively low level which could be enforced by the public authority. Voluntary service would thus be an extension ladder 'placed firmly on the foundation of an enforced minimum standard of life, but carrying onward the work of the public authorities to far finer shades of physical, moral and spiritual perfection'.[1]

The 'extension ladder' theory is more akin to present modes of thought on the relationship between the voluntary and statutory social services than the earlier 'parallel bars' theory, but the rapid growth of the welfare state during the last twenty years, and the

[1] S. and B. Webb, op. cit., pp. 240–52.

changes which have taken and are taking place in the scope and character of the social services, have led to a good deal of discussion of the whole subject, and the questioning of accepted ideas.

All discussions of the question stress the importance of the experimental work of the voluntary organisations, and pay tribute to those social pioneers who fought prolonged battles against apathy and prejudice in order to eradicate long-established social evils or provide new services for the benefit of their fellows. The history of the social services provides many instances of the ways in which voluntary effort may prepare the way for State action. For example, long before the appointment by a local authority of the first health visitor, the Manchester and Salford Ladies' Sanitary Reform Association arranged for the visiting of young mothers in their homes by an experienced woman especially appointed for the purpose. Joseph Lancaster founded his school for poor boys in Borough Road East many years before the government of the day considered the education of the children of the nation as a matter worthy of its attention. Similarly the court missionary preceded the probation officer. These are examples from the past, but such experimental work is still going on and some of the services described or mentioned in these pages are of this nature; for instance, the Family Service Units' intensive casework with problem families, the recuperative centres for neglectful mothers, the Marriage Guidance Council and the Family Discussion Bureau. Even experiments that fail, or are only partially successful, may contribute to social progress by showing that what may appear to be a clear way forward is but a blind alley, or that such a method of tackling a problem has unforeseen results and may, in the long run, do more harm than good. Voluntary organisations can more readily run the risk of failure than can the State or local authorities for these are answerable to the public and are custodians of public money. Thus, voluntary initiative has played and is still playing an important part in the development of the social services, and in some branches of social work its influence has been decisive.

Generally speaking, central and local government authorities have been slower in initiating wholly new experiments than the voluntary organisations, but they have often shown considerable imagination and enterprise in adapting and developing projects initiated by private enterprise or voluntary action. For example, when once the principle of government support for popular education was accepted, Sir James Kay-Shuttleworth could seek to raise its standards and widen its scope far beyond the rather limited ideas of the National Society and the British and Foreign Schools Society, while as soon as the necessary powers had been obtained Sir Arthur Newsholme and Sir George Newman built up the child health services on a national scale. In some instances, moreover, local authorities have themselves made the initial experiments, even if this has meant obtaining special powers for the purpose. Thus Liverpool may claim the credit for appointing the first medical officer of health, St. Helens for setting up the first infant milk depot, and Huddersfield for introducing the notification of births. Further, some services, to be effective, had to be universal and statutory from the start, and in these cases the work of the pioneer was so to influence public opinion that it sanctioned large-scale state experiment. That this may be a long and wearisome task is shown, for instance, by Eleanor Rathbone's twenty-year struggle to get Parliament to bring in legislation to provide universal family allowances, but such measures for the betterment of the people as old age pensions, the setting up of employment exchanges, and the regulation of wages in certain trades by means of trade boards (now wages councils), show what can be done by this means.

It would seem, then, that ultimately all social advance begins with 'the vision of an inspired individual',[1] but this vision may be translated into reality in more than one way, the precise method used being dependent on the nature of the reform to be brought about, the circumstances and spirit of the times, and the temperament and outlook of the individual who has been moved to set his hand to a particular plough. If progress is to continue it is essential that all concerned with social service in any form—statesmen, administrators, local government officials, as well as secretaries and organisers of voluntary associations—shall be sufficiently open to new ideas to give heed to the voice of the prophet, and enable the pioneer to make his experiments. Both statutory and voluntary bodies can too easily become stereotyped in outlook and method, and over-cautious in their attitude towards the original thinker, and in this way opportunities for further advance may be lost. The voluntary organisations have perhaps special responsibilities for encouraging new ideas and experiments, but in much of their pioneer work they can enlist the interest and encouragement, if not in its early stages the active support, of the State or local authorities. Then, if the latter respond, co-operation may be brought about from the beginning. Where this has been done[2] difficulties have been avoided, and greater progress has been made.

The special fitness of voluntary organisations for pioneering and experimental work is widely acknowledged, but the question as to whether they should confine themselves to this type of work, handing over those enterprises whose usefulness has become established to the State or local authorities, is a more debatable one. Such

---

[1] This phrase is taken from B. H. Reed, *Eighty Thousand Adolescents*, p. 147.
[2] E.g. in connection with citizens' advice bureaux. See Chapter IX.

self-sacrifice would oft-times seem to be the right course of action, although it may be hard for the voluntary organisation concerned, but there are some forms of social service for whose satisfactory operation voluntary organisations might appear to be intrinsically better fitted than the statutory authorities. Such services they should continue to operate. Thus, in an earlier chapter[1] it was suggested that the provision of an advice service, whether general or legal, is best left in the hands of a voluntary or professional organisation, and, for different reasons, voluntary organisations have a special contribution to make to the service of youth.[2]

Some social workers still hold with the Webbs that voluntary organisations are able to handle personal problems with greater delicacy and understanding than the statutory services, and that as far as possible, the various forms of social casework should remain within their province. It is, however, doubtful if this position can be maintained in the face of the recent developments of the statutory services and it is an attitude no longer as widespread as it once was. For example, the nationalisation of the hospitals has meant that numerous almoners and psychiatric social workers who, until July 1948, were working for voluntary organisations, now function within a statutory framework, but the change does not appear to have lessened their opportunities for real social casework,[3] while the Children Act has created new opportunities for personal work of a most intimate kind. These examples show that employment by a statutory authority does not necessarily mean that the social worker loses her personal touch. At the same time, the recommendations of the Denning and Harris Committees, the proposals of the Ministry of Health to local authorities for co-operation with voluntary organisations in the friendly visiting of old people,[4] and the same Ministry's concern that local maternity and child welfare authorities should seek the help of voluntary organisations in dealing with the personal problems of the unmarried mother and her child,[5] indicate a recognition, on the part of the statutory authorities themselves, that non-official bodies have a real contribution to make in dealing with personal problems, and that their help will sometimes be accepted by people who are suspicious of official visitors, however friendly and

[1] Chapter IX.
[2] See Chapter XVII.
[3] As pointed out in Chapter VIII the Ministry of Health regards the nationalisation of the hospitals, which has largely freed the almoner from the necessity of making assessments of the patients' incomes, as providing her with further opportunities for 'the important medical-social work for which she has been especially trained.'
[4] Ministry of Health Circular 11/50, *Welfare of Old People*.
[5] Ministry of Health Circular 2866, 1943, *The Care of Illegitimate Children*.

sympathetic. It would thus appear to be useless to try to demarcate rigidly the respective spheres of the statutory and voluntary social services in social casework. What is important is to seek to ensure that in so far as they undertake the intimate personal casework, at one time considered to be the special province of the voluntary organisations, the statutory authorities should also exercise those qualities which characterise voluntary social service at its best. Furthermore, where statutory and voluntary bodies are working in the same or related fields their relations should be based on mutual co-operation and respect, and not on 'primitive fears of other tigers in the jungle'.[1]

So far the main theme of this chapter has been the need for co-operation, but co-operation does not necessarily mean acquiescence in all that the partner does, and an important, and indeed necessary, function of the voluntary organisations is that of constructive criticism, both of the law itself and of its administration. Much can be done from within a statutory service, and the nation owes a great deal to those civil servants known and unknown, whose criticisms and suggestions, first embodied in departmental reports and minutes, have ultimately been incorporated in new legislation.[2] At the same time informed and constructive criticism from without may be a valuable stimulus and corrective to any tendency to inertia or complacency on the part of a government department. Hence the value of such voluntary organisations as the Howard League for Penal Reform and the Council for the Unmarried Mother and her Child, which are concerned not so much to help individual cases of distress as to try to bring about radical improvements in the laws and their administration. Moreover, as we have already seen, organisations such as citizens' advice bureaux, whose main work is that of dealing with individual difficulties, are by the very nature of their work in an especially good position to see where the shoe pinches, and have a real responsibility, not only for mitigating hardship in individual cases, but also for pressing for reform. This is an important additional argument for preserving their voluntary character.

Thus, even in a welfare state, there are tasks to which private individuals concerned to further the well-being of their fellows may still feel themselves called, but many such organisations have fallen on difficult times, and are hard-pressed to find the wherewithal to continue their work, since costs are rising, and sources of income drying up. Consequently, they are coming to rely more

[1] Roger Wilson, 'The Aims of Social Work'. Address given to the British National Conference on Social Work, Harrogate, April 1950.
[2] For example, the Factories Acts incorporate many suggestions first made by local inspectors as a result of their direct observation of conditions.

and more on grant-aid from local authorities and central government departments, and it may be that, except on a very limited scale in pioneer or very controversial work, the days of the strictly voluntary organisation—that is, an organisation, working absolutely independently without state or local authority assistance of any kind—are at an end. The emphasis to-day is on partnership, a partnership in which the central government, the local authority and the voluntary organisation all have their parts to play,[1] and in which the State, recognising the value of the work of the voluntary organisation, assists it to play its part. Hence the State and the local authority give financial support to the voluntary body and so help to establish its status as well as making its continued existence possible; in return they make use of the machinery it has built up, and benefit from the tradition it has established. It is an arrangement demanding mutual confidence, and is only possible in a society where the State has confidence in the free association of its citizens. It demands give and take on both sides. There is a danger that, on the one hand, over-reliance on grant-aid may make impossible that independence of thought and action which is the very life-blood of voluntary social service, on the other hand, that a voluntary body so assisted may establish a 'vested interest' in a particular form of social work, and perhaps delay its transfer to a more efficient method of administration.[2] If these dangers can be avoided, such State assistance to voluntary organisations has the advantage of encouraging variation and experiment while ensuring minimum standards, since aid from public funds necessarily carries with it some provision for seeing that standards are maintained.

Grant-aid is but one means by which the central government or local authorities can assist voluntary organisations concerned with social service. The provision of specialist advice and help, such as that often given by local education authorities to voluntary youth organisations is another, the loan of premises and equipment is a third. These may seem small things, but it is in the handling of concrete situations in particular localities that the reality behind high-sounding phrases about co-operation and partnership can, if it exists, find expression, and a sense of common purpose issue in action resulting in achievements of lasting value to the community.

[1] This is stated specifically in such pronouncements as Circular 1486, *The Service of Youth.*
[2] The effects of financial dependence and the general relationship between statutory and voluntary services are discussed in an article, 'Voluntary Social Service in the Changing Welfare State', by Professor S. E. Finer, Professor of Political Institutions, University College of North Staffordshire. *Social Service Quarterly,* June–August 1955, pp. 5–9.

CHAPTER XXIII

THE WELFARE STATE

IN the course of this book we have been considering, one after another, the public and voluntary social services functioning at the present time in England and Wales. For the most part the book has been descriptive rather than analytical, and this was its intention, but even the most straightforward description of the social services would be incomplete without some discussion of the assumptions on which they are based, the changes which they are expected to bring about, and the extent to which these assumptions and expectations have been fulfilled, or may be modified, as time has gone on and they have been put to the test. Some attempt to assess specific services in this way has been made in the chapters dealing with them; in this final chapter we shall seek to bring these discussions together, and inadequate and superficial as this concluding survey may be, it is hoped that it will provoke further thought and enquiry. As stated in the Preface, this book was written as an introduction to the study of the social services, and an introduction which does not lead to closer acquaintance has failed in its purpose.

One way of learning something about the social objectives of a particular period is to look at words and phrases in common usage at the time. A term characteristic of the reconstruction era which immediately followed the second world war was 'social security', a term which was used to express both an ideal and a particular method by which the ideal might be made an actuality, and which came into general use with the publication of the Beveridge Report. The need for both economic and psychological security was deeply and widely felt by a generation which had but exchanged the deprivations and uncertainties of a prolonged economic depression for the strains and stresses of total war. For many people, moreover, the most important aspect of social security was 'freedom from want'—assurance that sufficient income to purchase the necessities of life would be guaranteed at all times, even when the individual was unable to support himself and his family. Although the author made it clear that it was put forward as part of a general programme of social policy,[1] it was as a plan for social security

[1] Cmd. 6404, par. 8, p. 6 and par. 456, p. 170.

352

in this sense that the Beveridge Plan caught the imagination. It was in so far as they were regarded as accomplishing this objective that measures such as the National Insurance Act, 1946 were accorded widespread support, and a good deal of the resentment which has since been expressed, for example in connection with the treatment of widows and retirement pensioners, can be traced to the fact that these expectations have never wholly been fulfilled.[1]

The desirability of this limited goal of remedying the lack of food, clothing and other necessities of life by a universal scheme of mutual aid sponsored by the State has never seriously been questioned. Divergencies of opinion and differences of emphasis appear, however, when the question is raised as to how far, if at all, the State should go beyond this. Lord Beveridge expresses himself clearly and strongly on this issue: 'The Plan for Social Security,' he wrote in his Report, 'was designed . . . to establish a national minimum above which prosperity can grow with want abolished,'[2] and 'The plan is one to secure income for subsistence on condition of service and contribution. . . . It can be carried through only by a concentrated determination of the British democracy to free itself once for all of the scandal of physical want for which there is no economic or moral justification. When that effort has been made, the plan leaves room and encouragement to all individuals to win for themselves something above the national minimum. . . .'[3] Thirteen years later he reiterated the same point. 'The idea underlying the Beveridge Report,' he wrote in 1956,[4] 'was not that of a Welfare State providing everything that the citizen could desire. The idea was that of a minimum guaranteed by the State, without a means test, so that every man could safely spend or save for himself all that he and his family might desire to have beyond the minimum.' Nor is he alone in his contention that security in this sense should be the limit to which the state should go in its income maintenance provisions, since to do more would be to stifle opportunity and initiative. For example, Mr. Peter Goldman in his Preface to a booklet published by the Conservative Political Centre,[5] writes, 'It has lately become a cliché of Right-wing rhetoric to proclaim the need for an Opportunity State to match and sustain the Welfare State,' and a variation on the same theme is to be found in one of the *New Fabian Essays* where Mr. C. A. R. Crosland writes, 'The object of the social services is to provide a

---

[1] This has already been discussed in Chapter III.
[2] Cmd. 6404, par. 447, p. 166.
[3] Ibid., par. 455, p. 170.
[4] Foreword to *People in Need*.
[5] *The Future of the Welfare State*. Seven Oxford Lectures. Conservative Political Centre, 1958, p. 7.

cushion of security against hardship due to unavoidable misfortune. Once the essential cushion has been provided, further advances in national income should normally go to citizens in the form of "free" income to be spent as they wish, and not to be taxed away and then returned in the form of some free service determined at the fiat of the state.'[1] The corollary of these arguments is that as 'opportunity' increases, social security, in the narrow sense of state guaranteed income maintenance, should become less and less necessary. 'More and more people of working age are becoming capable of standing on their own feet; more and more can afford to make provision out of their earnings, either directly or through insurance, for the necessities and against the hazards of ordinary life,' and this they should be encouraged to do, so that public spending can be shifted, 'away from the crude services which working people ought increasingly to be able to provide for themselves and towards modern services crying out for community effort or finance; namely, the vigorous creation and maintenance by public authority of the finest environmental conditions for our people and the general application of public money to the subtle problems of personality, social adjustment and education in its widest sense'.[2] On this view the social security services, if not the social services as a whole, should be, in the long run, 'self-liquidating'.

But as the coiner of this phrase, Mr. Walter Hagenbuch, has himself pointed out,[3] the situation is a complex one, more complex than the above paragraphs would suggest. Not only is there the problem of rising standards which makes 'subsistence level' increasingly difficult to define in a way that is both meaningful and acceptable,[4] not only does inflation make a mockery of successive attempts to relate benefit rates and assistance payments to a clearly defined standard, but the whole issue is complicated by the question as to whether social security is in itself sufficient if it leaves out of account all considerations of social equality. Professor Titmuss' complaint that our present provisions for income maintenance in old age have created a situation in which 'it is possible to see two nations in old age, greater inequalities after work than in work' has already been quoted.[5] The plea implicit in this complaint and the article of which it forms a part,[6] namely that the social services

---

[1] Op. cit., p. 83.

[2] Peter Goldman, op. cit., p. 10.

[3] 'The Rationale of the Social Services', *Lloyds Bank Review*, July 1953, p. 9.

[4] 'May it not be that public opinion will never accept a definition of the subsistence level such that there will in fact be nobody below it?' Ibid., p. 10. This question has already received some consideration in Chapter IV.

[5] Chap. III, p. 39 above.

[6] 'Pension Systems and Population Change', *Political Quarterly*, Vol. 26, 1955.

should be regarded as instruments in the creation of greater equality as well as greater social security, he has a long tradition behind him. It is a tradition which one author[1] has traced back to the philosophic radicals who, by claiming that the common man, indeed the worst man, was equally entitled to happiness with the best, were not only contradicting the whole existing concept of human society, but promulgating a doctrine which was to have far-reaching practical consequences. 'Men like Edwin Chadwick,' writes this author, 'were the real fathers of the social service state in modern Britain. The integrated state acting through paternalist legislation and administration is, in Britain, the child of secular egalitarianism.'

To regard the development of the social services as both an expression of the ideal of greater social equality and as means by which this greater equality can be brought about is to introduce a concept quite different from the one of 'social security' which we have just been discussing. It changes them from minimum provisions designed to protect the user from otherwise irreparable disaster to optimum provisions which the citizens can and should avail himself of in order that he may live as full and happy a life as possible. Services with this objective are 'social rights' in the sense used by Professor T. H. Marshall[2] and as such should be universal in scope and entitlement. One of the most noticeable features of post-war social legislation was that by it all citizens became entitled to the free use of a wide range of services hitherto available only to those able to pay for them, or, if extended to the rest, extended as acts of private or public charity. The two Acts which have made the greatest changes in this direction are, undoubtedly, the National Health Service Act, 1946, and the Education Act, 1944. The changes brought about by the introduction of the National Health Service have already been discussed.[3] We have not attempted to survey the education service as a whole but a writer who has done so claims for the Education Act, 1944, that 'it marked a final departure from the tradition which had hitherto persisted throughout the whole of English history that education beyond the elementary stage is a privilege to be reserved for the dominant élite be it of wealth, power, intellect or whatever fashion might dictate'.[4] In their own limited sphere the provisions made for handicapped children which have been outlined here are also designed to give these children equality of opportunity with their more fortunate fellows. Thus the Scottish Education Department bases its argument

[1] David Thomson, *Equality*, pp. 22–23.
[2] *Citizenship and Social Class*, pp. 11 and 46 ff.
[3] Chapters V and VI above.
[4] H. C. Dent, *Growth in English Education*, 1946–52, p. 67.

for making special provision for the mentally handicapped child on the belief that 'The individual child, whoever he may be, has a right to enter into his social heritage and develop his powers as fully as possible. This right is not to be surrendered because the accidents of heredity or experience have reduced attainment or potentiality to less than the average, nor can we condemn to unhappiness or maladjustment those who are less richly endowed than their fellows with gifts of mind.'[1]

The aim of equality entitlement to optimum standards of social service brings its own problems, however, not the least of which is that of the costs incurred or likely to be incurred in making this provision. We have already noted Dr. Frangcon Roberts' forebodings about the increasing cost of the National Health Service,[2] in the course of which he points out that the progress of medical science means that there is no foreseeable upper limit to the amount we could spend on preventing and alleviating disease. Standards of other services also tend to rise as goals are attained and it becomes possible to see beyond them. The difficulties in the way of determining the basic minimum provisions the state should guarantee its citizens are formidable enough, but the assessment of what should be optimum provisions is virtually impossible, as the Guillebaud Committee recognized in their discussion of the 'adequacy' of the Health Service.[3] The position is further complicated by questions of priority both within the social services themselves and between the social services and other claimants to a share of the national income, and also by the fact that the country's economic situation and resources of manpower, money and materials are not constant but vary from year to year, from decade to decade. Nor is it easy to assess in economic or financial terms the gains that are likely to accrue to the country as a result of the improvements in health, efficiency and educational attainment the social services are bringing about, and which might be regarded as offsetting both the current cost of the services themselves and their economically more debateable consequences, such as the prolongation of the life of the aged and the seriously crippled and defectives, consumers rather than producers of the national wealth. The provision of 'optimum' services at community expense, equally available for all is the expression of a particular form of social idealism; their retention and development dependent partly on the continuing strength of the ideals which they embody,

---

[1] Scottish Education Department, *Pupils with Mental or Educational Disabilities.* Cmd. 8401, 1951, p. 10.
[2] *The Cost of Health.* This problem has already been referred to in the discussion of the cost of the National Health Service in Chapter VI.
[3] Cmd. 9663, pars. 94–98, pp. 49–50.

and partly on the continuance of the economic prosperity and stability necessary to sustain them.

Implicit in the concept of equality of entitlement to the best provisions the country can afford is the belief that each individual member of the community is of inherent worth, and this belief is manifest in the concept of 'welfare' which occurs and recurs in the modern social services. It is prominent in the National Assistance Act, both in Part II where the Board are instructed to 'exercise their functions in such manner as shall best promote the welfare of persons affected by the exercise thereof'[1] and in Part III where the local authorities are instructed to 'have regard to the welfare of all persons' for whom they provide accommodation[2] and later empowered to make arrangements for 'promoting the welfare of' handicapped persons.[3] Similarly, the phrase 'the welfare of the child' recurs like a refrain throughout the whole of the Children Act, and, it is, moreover, as Clarke Hall and Morrison remind us, clearly laid down as the principal consideration to be observed in all dealings with juveniles.[4] It is a difficult term to define, but if it means anything at all, it means individual treatment according to individual need, that is to say it may, and often does, involve unequal or at any rate, different treatment of persons with equal social rights. The need for individual treatment to balance general provision was recognized by R. H. Tawney in his classic discussion of the problem of equality thirty years ago,[5] 'It is true again,' he wrote, 'that human beings have, except as regards certain elementary, though sadly neglected matters of health and development, different requirements, and that these different requirements can be met satisfactorily only by varying forms of provision.' Equality is to be achieved 'not by treating different needs in the same way, but by developing equal care to ensuring that they are met in the different ways most appropriate to them.'[6] The equality described here is complementary to equality of entitlement; it is equality of regard for each individual manifesting itself in diversity of treatment, and it is the hall-mark of the social work which, as we have seen,[7] is now undertaken as a statutory responsibility in connection with many forms of social service provision, for example, that for handicapped persons and deprived children. This equality of regard raises its own problems, however, notably that of the extent to which individual treatment involves discrimination between

[1] National Assistance Act, Section 2 (2).
[2] Section 21.   [3] Section 29.
[4] Clarke Hall and Morrison's *Law Relating to Children and Young Persons*, p. 3.
[5] R. H. Tawney, *Equality*, p. 39.
[6] A modern social worker would probably add 'and to the people who have them'.
[7] Chapter VIII.

COMMUNITY SERVICE

citizens with equal rights. Not only is this a problem in itself, but there is always the risk that unless carefully safeguarded, such discrimination may become arbitrary or based on considerations other than those of differing need. Readers of *Mr. Lyward's Answer* may remember that his efforts to bring about the rehabilitation of each individual boy in his care quite often involved deliberate 'unfairness' and the author of the book quotes Mr. Lyward as saying 'It was one of my great joys when I discovered how quickly they sensed the dignity which "unfairness" gave them.'[1] This was in a relatively small community where personal relations were close, however. The 'dignity' of unfairness, though not of considerate individual treatment, is not so easy to appreciate and accept in the less personal atmosphere of, for example, a local office of the National Assistance Board or a juvenile court. In these and similar situations discrimination can only safely and justly be exercised within the framework of known and accepted equalities. Thus the National Assistance Board area officer can make discretionary payments, or even reduce allowances, but the scale rates on which basic payments are to be made and the methods by which need is to be assessed are both laid down in regulations approved by Parliament which must be observed in dealing with all applicants, and this is known to them. Similarly, although a juvenile court must have regard to the welfare of the child or young person brought before it,[2] 'this does not mean that the courts may travel outside the law in order to achieve what they believe to be welfare'.[3] Only if a young offender is proved guilty or the need for 'care or protection' established can the court proceed to exercise its powers. It is in that event it must have regard to 'welfare', and even then it has not a wholly free hand. For example, only if the young offender has been guilty of an offence 'punishable in the case of an adult with imprisonment' can the court order him to be sent to an approved school or commit him to the care of a fit person[4] however much it may consider such action to be for his welfare. 'The liberty of the subject, however small that subject may be, must be safeguarded by the courts and . . . the High Court will intervene where that liberty has been invaded without proper legal justification.'[5] Should the law be altered in such a way as to raise the age of criminal responsibility and to transfer to case committees some of the work now undertaken by juvenile courts, as some social workers hope, it would be vitally necessary to ensure that

[1] Michael Burn, *Mr. Lyward's Answer*, p. 72.
[2] Children and Young Persons Act, 1944, Section 44.
[3] Clarke Hall and Morrison, op. cit., p. 3.
[4] Children and Young Persons Act, 1933, Section 57.
[5] Clarke Hall and Morrison, ibid.

358

liberties would be safeguarded and the ends of justice as well as those of welfare preserved,[1] and this general principle is applicable to other situations also, for example, the compulsory treatment of the mentally ill, especially 'psychopaths'.

So far in this discussion we have considered three concepts which appear to find expression in varying degrees and in varying ways in our social services—social security, equality of entitlement and opportunity, the furtherance of the welfare of the individual. There is a fourth which might be mentioned since, as we have seen,[2] it has influenced housing and planning policies, and inspires such voluntary social services as settlements and community centres. It is the belief that economic inequalities, occupational differences, differences in social and educational standards and outlook need not prevent people coming together to develop community activities on a neighbourhood basis, and that such activities should be furthered, since they help overcome the social isolation with its accompanying loneliness which has come to be recognized as a real problem for many persons in our urbanised and geographically and socially mobile society,[3] encourage people develop their varied gifts and interests, and foster active participation in local developments.[4] Such investigations as have been made in this field[5] have revealed that social planning along these lines has so far largely failed to achieve its objectives. Community centres and associations attract a few enthusiasts, the remainder of the population retain their class consciousness,[6] cling to their privacy and remain generally indifferent towards communal activities and aspirations. Active and responsible citizenship is not necessarily or easily brought about by community planning, but this does not mean that the attempt to provide conditions which will encourage rather than hinder this objective should be abandoned, although both objective and means of achievement might well be subject to rigorous though sympathetic examination.

One of the features which distinguishes community centres and similar provisions from the other social services is that active

[1] This is clearly recognised in the discussion of this issue in the Fabian Society pamphlet *The Child and the Social Services*, p. 12.

[2] Chapter VI.

[3] The problem is discussed in a pamphlet issued by the National Council of Social Service, *Loneliness*.

[4] In the enthusiasm of the immediate post-war years the Ministry of Education hoped that each community centre would become a 'power house of community effort'.

[5] Examples are given in previous chapters.

[6] 'The most pervading concept in nearly all our interviews is status or a consciousness that society is made up of different social classes. . . . Its opposite, the equality of man, scarcely received more than a passing mention.' J. M. Mogey, *Family and Neighbourhood*, p. 139.

participation in their planning, management and control by those whose needs they are designed to meet is both a condition and a criterion of their success. In the majority of the social services, whether statutory or voluntary, there is a clear administrative distinction between those who administer the service and those who benefit from it, a distinction which is intensified by the increased professionalism of social work and the development of the nation-wide statutory services with their hierarchical structure, elaborate administrative machinery and often remote control. Nevertheless, as citizens, both administrators and recipients are members of the body which has created the statutory service, the nation state, and, as citizens, they have a common responsibility for the maintenance and improvement of all social services, a responsibility which is also shared by all their fellow citizens. Means to influence social policy and maintain a check on administration exist in the organs of democratic government at both central and local level, and tenuous though the link with the controlling body may be, circuitous the method of approach, and negligible the influence exercised by any one individual, yet the fact that these means exist and are known to exist and to be regarded, is one of the reasons which has given this nation the confidence to create a 'welfare' state at all. This is pointed out by Professor Evelyne M. Burns of the New York School of Social Work who contrasts the society which 'regards its organised government as a dangerous and uncontrollable authority whose powers and activities must be kept to a minimum, or which holds governmental agencies to be inherently inefficient or corrupt' and which will in consequence seek to organize its social security services in such a way as to keep government activity to a minimum, with 'countries such as Great Britain, which appear to regard Government merely as the most effective of several possible institutions for the administration of income security programmes or for the provision of services, and which believe that the public agency can be kept under control and responsive to the wishes of the citizenry'.[1]

One important means by which the 'public agency', or to use the English designation, 'statutory social service' is kept responsive to the wishes of the citizens for whose benefit it was created, is the retention of the ultimate administrative control of so many of our services in the hands of committees. Whether elected, as in all the local authority services, or appointed, as in the case of regional hospital boards and management committees, these committees consist of laymen and women chosen to represent and act on behalf of their fellows, and of these lay people the official, however great his responsibility, is the servant. Such committees may range

[1] Evelyne Burns, *Social Security and Public Policy*, New York, 1956, p. 274.

in influence and importance from a school management committee responsible for a small primary school to a regional hospital board responsible for the hospital and specialist services over an extensive and diverse area; they may be slow, ignorant, biased or prejudiced in the way they handle the problems with which they are faced, or they may exhibit sound judgment, considerable understanding, great humanity and marked common sense; relationships between the committee chairman and permanent officials may vary in the degree of co-operation achieved or dominance exercised. Nevertheless, by their very existence such committees constitute an important safeguard against the overgrowth of bureaucracy, and are a means whereby an intelligent and responsible citizen can bring his knowledge and experience to bear on matters of public interest and concern. A question which is of grave moment to the future of public administration, as the Acton Society Trust has stressed in its discussion of the administration of the hospital service,[1] is the question as to whether enough people of the right calibre and motivation are coming forward prepared to take on the responsibilities involved in committee membership and particularly in committee chairmanship. Economic and social factors beyond the scope of this book affect the likelihood of this, but to a considerable extent it will depend on the degree to which the objectives of the social services can be regarded as those which busy and responsible citizens find it worth sacrificing time and trouble to achieve.

As we have seen, there is some divergence in emphasis and opinion with regard to the objectives of the social services, even among those most directly concerned with their creation and maintenance, and opinions also differ as to the extent of the danger that the pursuit of these objectives will lead to the sacrifice of some greater good. Differences of opinion of this nature and judgments on the social services generally, are partly subjective, dependent on the relative importance the individual attaches to particular values as compared with others, for example, how much freedom of individual choice he is prepared to sacrifice to secure economic security or greater equality of opportunity. They may also be partly dependent on his knowledge of the actual working of the services, knowledge which may be almost entirely governed by individual experience direct or indirect, and consequently biased or incomplete.

Generalisations made by individuals or groups on the basis of inadequate or incomplete knowledge may be wide of the mark or no more than partially true, yet exercise a considerable influence

[1] *Hospitals and the State*, 4, Part II, p. 50. This question has already been considered in relation to the hospital service in Chapter VI above.

on public opinion and policy. An example of this is the widespread belief that the cost of maintaining and improving the nation's health rose out of all proportion with the introduction of the National Health Service. The careful investigations into the cost of the service made by Professor Titmuss and Mr. Abel-Smith and accepted by the Guillebaud Committee showed, however, that contrary to public opinion, 'the net diversion of resources to the National Health Service as a whole since 1949–50 has been of relatively insignificant proportions'.[1] Even more of a generalisation than this misapprehension with regard to the cost of the health service is the widespread belief that the overall effect of the development of the social services has been to weaken family ties and responsibilities. This indictment contains an element of truth, but it is far from being the whole truth and ignores the complex social and economic changes which have been and are taking place, and which affect not only family structure and relationships but our whole manner of life. The relationship between specific social changes brought about by specific events and family needs, is brought out in a study made by Sheila Ferguson and Hilde Fitzgerald of the impact of the Second World War on family life and the developments which took place in the social services in response thereto.[2] The opening chapter of the book, after discussing the changes in family size over the previous twenty-five years and the effect of this on the ability of the family to become and remain responsible for the well-being of those of its members in need of help, goes on to consider the disruption of both the family and neighbourhood caused by the War and the gaps left by these changes. It was to plug these gaps that existing social services were expanded and new ones created. 'What the family and neighbourhood could now no longer do for themselves the State had to help them to do,'[3] a summing up of the war-time situation which in many respects is still valid to-day.

The present position is one in which, for various reasons, such as increased geographical and social mobility, there seems to be a tendency 'for the more peripheral kinship relationship to become less important and more of a latent force'[4] and the development of social services has been both a consequence of and contributory factor in this tendency.[5] 'More and more tasks which formerly

[1] B. Abel-Smith and R. M. Titmuss, *The Cost of the National Health Service*, p. 67.
[2] S. M. Ferguson and H. Fitzgerald, *Studies in the Social Services*, H.M.S.O., 1954.   [3] Ibid., p. 7.
[4] John B. Mays, 'Cultural Conformity in Urban Areas', *The Sociological Review*, Vol. 6, No. 1, July 1958, p. 100.
[5] For an example of the social services as a contributory factor, see the discussion of the effect of housing policies on kinship ties in M. Young and P. Willmott, *Family and Kinship in East London*. This is referred to in Chapter VII above.

were the responsibility of the extended family have been taken over by both statutory and voluntary social services. It is becoming much easier for the nuclear family, not only to survive as a distinct unit, but also to live quite successfully unto itself, if it so desires, with the assistance of the social agencies, without being obliged to make frequent calls on kinsfolk for help, guidance and companionship.'[1] Nevertheless, such evidence as is available from the various social surveys so far undertaken in this field, goes to show that mutual aid between kinsfolk is still widely accepted as the natural thing and family responsibilities, even when long-continued and onerous, are frequently shouldered with a degree of good will and patience which can but move the outsider to respect and admiration.[2] In emphasising the need for preserving such values as mutual support and care resting on family affection the almost intolerable strains which these sometimes impose should not be lost sight of, and the community should not grudge the provision of such services as home helps, the home nursing service and the provision of holiday homes which enable the obligations imposed by family loyalty to be undertaken and maintained without too great a sacrifice on the part of the individual or family concerned.[3]

The provision of community services to enable an individual or family to undertake and sustain a burden which would otherwise be intolerable is one example of the use of the social services to maintain family solidarity and responsibility. A further contribution to the preservation and maintenance of healthy family life is made by those social services which, while they do nothing to abate the responsibility of the persons concerned, endeavour to inculcate, and help the family reach and maintain, higher standards of domestic and child care by means of expert advice and technical assistance. The maternity and child welfare service is a good example of this type of social service, but all caseworkers, whatever the particular administrative setting in which they work, would emphasise that their role is to help the family develop its strengths and to preserve its unity. Thus, the probation officer in his dealings with the parents of a young delinquent, the psychiatric social worker guiding the mother of a maladjusted child towards a better understanding of his difficulties, the marriage guidance

[1] Mays, ibid.

[2] For evidence on these issues see the three studies of Bethnal Green published by the Institute of Community Studies: M. Young and P. Willmott, *Family and Kinship in East London*; P. Townsend, *Family Life of Old People*, and Peter Marris, *Widows and their Families*, also Cyril S. Smith, *People in Need* and the various studies made of old people's welfare referred to in Chapter XVIII above.

[3] For examples of the extent to which individual lives can be sacrificed to the demands of the elderly and infirm, see J. H. Sheldon, *The Social Medicine of Old Age*, pp. 27–29 and 181–185.

counsellor advising a young couple who are finding adjustment to married life a more exacting task than they had anticipated, the family caseworker helping a problem family back to self-respect and independence, each and all of these social workers are deeply concerned to maintain, and if necessary, restore family life. Only as a last resort, when all their resources and techniques have failed, will they countenance measures which involve the separation of the marriage partners or alternative forms of care for children.

The same recognition of the family as a unit is present in some measure in income maintenance legislation. Indeed, the Family Allowances Act is a direct expression of this recognition. The emphasis in this piece of legislation is on the immediate rather than the wider family, however, and a similar emphasis is found in the National Assistance Act[1] which drastically reduced the legal obligations for maintenance hitherto laid on kinsfolk, limiting them to the spouses' responsibilities for each other and those of parents for their children under sixteen. This Act, at any rate, would thus seem both to recognise and encourage the tendency already mentioned for wider kinship ties to become less important than they were. However (as has been pointed out in an article by Mr. Peter Willmott in the *British Journal of Sociology*),[2] post-war legislation is not wholly consistent in this respect. Despite the contraction in legal liability brought about by the National Assistance Act, both the National Insurance Act and National Insurance (Industrial Injuries) Act recognise obligations voluntarily entered into to maintain kin in their provisions relating to dependants' benefits. Mr. Willmott considers that the most important reason for this is 'the simple fact that many people recognise a responsibility to assist certain relatives in need, and are likely to want to go on doing so; governments have not found it easy to resist the argument that such feelings of kinship responsibility should be officially recognised and encouraged'.[3] 'Whatever the explanation,' he continues, 'the fact is that, although official recognition of kinship *liability* has shrunk, the official recognition of kinship *dependency* has in some respects expanded,'[4] and 'the State is surely reflecting public opinion in its implied acceptance of the view that social policy should encourage, rather than discourage, the acceptance of such responsibility'.[5] Present provisions have grown up haphazardly, however, and, particularly if fiscal provisions such as income tax relief and inheritance on intestacy are taken into account as well as the provisions contained in social legislation, there is some inconsistency both as to what constitutes dependency

[1] Sections 42 and 43.   [2] June 1958, pp. 126 ff.
[3] Op. cit., p. 129.   [4] Ibid., p. 130. Author's italics.
[5] Ibid., p. 137.

and who is eligible, and Mr. Willmott concludes with a plea for 'more factual information about which obligations are actually undertaken in British society, so that social administration can be brought into line with customary practice'. This plea could well be extended to cover other aspects of social policy as it affects the family for there is a real need for further field studies into family relationships in contemporary Britain, studies which will cover different classes and different areas from those already surveyed. Only in this way can generalisations based on local studies, however careful, be put to the test.

The belief that the social services are 'taking away' family responsibility, is frequently encountered and appears to be widespread but as we have just seen is not necessarily or wholly true. Another assertion which is met with from time to time is that the values which the services enshrine are wholly hedonistic and material. For example, one contributor to the Conservative Political Centre pamphlet *The Future of the Welfare State*, Mr. George Schwartz, states quite categorically, 'Can we, may I ask you, clear our minds of cant on this particular subject, and admit that as far as practical politics are concerned, "Welfare" has only one significance and that is "material welfare"?'[1] Here again, as with the statements made about the effect of the social services on family responsibility, a close examination of the position fails wholly to support the assertion. The social services are concerned, in the first instance, with meeting basic material needs, with overcoming such evils as poverty, sickness, inadequate and low standard housing, but to suggest that they are limited to these ends is to do less than justice to both the framers and administrators of social policies. At least in its application to children, the very term 'welfare' itself is given a wider significance in law than that of material well-being, for a specific legal judgment has been made that 'The welfare of the child is not to be measured by money only or by physical comfort only. The word "welfare" must be taken in its widest sense. The moral and religious welfare of the child must be considered as well as its physical well-being. Nor can ties of affection be disregarded.'[2] Similarly, implicit in the present widespread concern that provisions for the prevention and treatment of mental disorder shall be as adequate and humane as those for the treatment of physical illness, in the present emphasis on the value of good relationships as well as good conditions in industry, and in

---

[1] George Schwartz, 'Work and Welfare', *The Future of the Welfare State*, p. 20.
[2] L.J. Lindley giving judgment in the case of *In re McGrath* (Infants) (1893). Quoted by Clarke Hall and Morrison in their commentary on S. 44 of the Children and Young Persons Act, 1933.

the recognition, inadequate though it still is, that families moved to local authority housing estates need more for their happiness than good-standard houses, is a broader concept of welfare and of the responsibilities of the 'welfare state' than that of the satisfaction of material needs. The degree of emphasis placed on the psychological as well as physical needs in social policy and administration, will, however, depend on two things. It will depend, firstly, on the degree of understanding and awareness achieved by the framers of social policies and the social workers and administrators whose duty it is to implement them, and secondly on the values implicit in the behaviour and aspirations of the community as a whole. These latter are crucial. A society whose goals and standards are solely, or almost solely, material will think of welfare in materialist terms, while a society whose values are distorted may even prostitute welfare to its own ends. Nor are the insights derived from psychology and sociology, valuable as these are in themselves, sufficient protection from this latter danger. 'No social scientist who has been closely in touch with the uses of social science in World War II . . . can doubt that awareness and understanding can be used destructively, that social science in itself carries no guarantee of good to mankind any more than theoretical physics does. . . . Pursued without responsibility either may lead to evil as easily as to good.'[1] Paradoxically, it may well be that only the continued recognition by both individual and community that there are ideals other than 'welfare' to be pursued and that there are loyalties which go beyond the state, will enable the welfare state to preserve the particular values of greater social security, greater equality of entitlement, and regard for individual need of which it is both the custodian and the symbol.

In the course of the last few pages we have drawn attention to some of the more general objectives which seem to be implicit or explicit in current social service legislation, and to some of the problems to which the pursuit of these objectives gives rise. Data which will help to answer some of the questions raised in the course of this discussion, and in other parts of the book also, can be obtained from empirical research such as that already being undertaken in some areas, for example the community studies in Bethnal Green which have been referred to several times. Answers to other questions, for example the question as to the kinds of care most appropriate to a particular group in particular circumstances, may best be discovered by experiment,[2] and the fact that much of the

---

[1] Margaret Mead, 'The Ethics of Insight Giving', Appendix II to *Male and Female* (Victor Gollancz Ltd., 1950), p. 432.

[2] An example of this is the experiments made into the kinds of care most appropriate for old people and children.

administration of the social services is in the hands of local authorities, and that voluntary organisations still play an active part in it, helps to make such experimentation possible. But important as such researches and experiments are as showing what is happening and helping us discover the best means of reaching particular goals, in the long run it is on the value judgments made on such general issues as those raised in the last chapter that the future of the social services will depend.

SUGGESTIONS FOR FURTHER READING AND REFERENCE

THIS book was written as a general introduction to the study of the social services and should be read in conjunction with government publications, reports of Parliamentary debates and specialist literature dealing with the topics dealt with here. The list which follows is not exhaustive, but it includes a number of published works likely to be of interest and use to the general student. Acts of Parliament and annual reports of government departments have not been included, but it is assumed that they will be consulted.

When consulting books, pamphlets or other references the date of publication should be carefully noted as literature dealing with social legislation and economic and social conditions quickly becomes out of date. At the same time a book or document should not be left unread simply because it was written some years ago. Even if out-dated in detail it may contain discussions on policy and principle which are still relevant, or describe conditions and events a knowledge of which is necessary for a proper understanding of the present situation. It may be possible to consult some of the books now out of print in one of the libraries. A list of periodicals which deal specially with, or frequently include articles on, social policy and administration has been appended to this bibliography, but articles in them have not been listed separately.

The Development of the Social Services
H. and M. Wickwar: *The Social Services, an Historical Survey*. Second Edition, revised. Bodley Head, 1949.
T. S. Simey: *Principles of Social Administration*. Oxford University Press, 1937.
Emmeline W. Cohen: *English Social Services, Methods and Growth*. George Allen & Unwin, 1949.
A. F. Young and E. T. Ashton: *British Social Work in the Nineteenth Century*. Routledge & Kegan Paul, 1956.
Betsy Rodgers: *Cloak of Charity—Studies in Eighteenth-Century Philanthropy*. Methuen, 1949.
J. L. and Barbara Hammond: *Lord Shaftesbury*. First published 1923. Pelican Books, 1939.
Frank Smith: *The Life of Sir James Kay-Shuttleworth*. John Smith, 1923.
S. E. Finer: *The Life and Times of Sir Edwin Chadwick*. Methuen, 1952.
Henrietta Barnett: *Canon Barnett, His Life, Work and Friends*. John Murray, 1921.

SUGGESTIONS FOR FURTHER READING

E. Moberley Bell: *Octavia Hill, a Biography*. Constable, 1942.

Beatrice Webb: *My Apprenticeship*. First published 1926. Pelican Book (two volumes), 1938.

Our Partnership. Longmans Green, 1948.

Una Cormack: *The Welfare State*. Royal Commission on the Poor Laws, 1905–1909 and the Welfare State. Loch Memorial Lecture, 1953. Family Welfare Association.

Lord Beveridge: *Power and Influence*. Hodder & Stoughton, 1953.

Mary Stocks: *Eleanor Rathbone*. Gollancz, 1949.

A Hundred Years of District Nursing. Allen & Unwin, 1960.

T. S. and M. B. Simey: *Charles Booth: Social Scientist*. Clarendon Press, 1960.

Richard M. Titmuss: *Problems of Social Policy*. History of the Second World War, U.K. Civil Services. H.M.S.O. and Longmans Green, 1950.

S. M. Ferguson and H. Fitzgerald: *Studies in the Social Services*. History of the Second World War. U.K. Civil Services, H.M.S.O. and Longmans Green, 1954.

Social Conditions

B. Seebohm Rowntree: *Poverty, a Study of Town Life*. Macmillan, 1901. *Poverty and Progress*. A Second survey of York. Longmans Green, 1941.

B. Seebohm Rowntree and G. R. Lavers: *Poverty and the Welfare State*. A Third Survey of York. Longmans Green, 1951.

P.E.P.: Poverty, Ten Years after Beveridge. *Planning*. Vol. XIX. No. 344. August 4, 1952.

Social Security and Unemployment in Lancashire, Vol. XIX, No. 349, December, 1952.

Michael Young & Peter Willmott: *Family and Kinship in East London*. A survey by the Institute of Community Studies. Routledge & Kegan Paul, 1957

A. M. Carr-Saunders, D. Caradog Jones and C. A. Moser: *A Survey of Social Conditions in England and Wales*. O.U.P., 1958.

R. M. Titmuss: *Essays on 'The Welfare State'*. George Allen and Unwin, 1958.

David C. Marsh: *The Changing Social Structure of England and Wales, 1871–1951*. Routledge & Kegan Paul, 1958.

Social Security

Karl de Schweinitz: *England's Road to Social Security*. University of Pennsylvania Press, 1943.

Lloyd George's Ambulance Wagon. Being the Memoirs of William J. Braithwaite 1911–12. Edited with an introduction by Sir Henry N. Bunbury and with a commentary by Richard M. Titmuss. Methuen, 1957.

Sir William Beveridge: *Report on Social Insurance and the Allied Services*. Cmd. 6404, 1942.

William A. Robson: *Social Security*. George Allen & Unwin. First published 1943, third edition, revised 1948.

SUGGESTIONS FOR FURTHER READING

Ronald Mendelsohn: *Social Security in the British Commonwealth.* Athlone Press, 1954.

E. M. Burns: *Social Security and Public Policy.* McGraw Hill, New York, 1956.

Eleanor Rathbone: *Family Allowances*—a new edition of *The Disinherited Family*, with an epilogue by Lord Beveridge and a new chapter on the Family Allowances Movement, 1924–47 by Eva M. Hubback. Allen & Unwin, 1949,

Peter Marris: *Widows and their Families.* Routledge & Kegan Paul, 1958.

Sir Geoffrey S. King: *The Ministry of Pensions and National Insurance.* Allen & Unwin, 1958.

The Health Services

W. M. Frazer: *A History of Public Health 1834–1939.* Ballière, Tindall & Cox, 1950.

J. M. Mackintosh: *Trends of Opinion about The Public Health 1901–51.* Geoffrey Cumberledge, 1953.

Sir George Newman: *The Building of a Nation's Health.* Macmillan, 1939.

C. Fraser Brockington: *The Health of the Community.* J. & A. Churchill, 1954.

J. S. Ross: *The National Health Service in Great Britain.* O.U.P., 1952.

Ffrangcon Roberts: *The Cost of Health.* Turnstile Press, 1952.

Brian Abel-Smith and R. M. Titmuss: *The Cost of the National Health Service in England and Wales.* Cambridge University Press, 1956.

Report of the Committee of Enquiry into the Cost of the National Health Service (Guillebaud Report). Cmd. 9663, 1956.

T. Ferguson and A. N. McPhail: *Hospital and Community.* Nuffield Provincial Hospitals Trust, O.U.P., 1954.

Acton Society Trust: *Hospitals and the State.*
1. Background and Blueprint, 1955
2. The Impact of Change, 1956
3. Groups, Regions and Committees, Part I, 1957.
4. Groups, Regions and Committees, Part II, 1957.

National Council of Social Service and King Edward's Hospital Fund for London, *Voluntary Service and the State.* A Study of the Needs of the Hospital Service, 1952.

J. P. Martin: *Social Aspects of Prescribing.* Heinemann, 1957.

Stephen Taylor: *Good General Practice.* O.U.P., 1954.

Ministry of Health, Department of Health for Scotland, Ministry of Education. An Inquiry into Health Visiting. H.M.S.O., 1956.

Harry Eckstein: *The English Health Service.* Harvard University Press (O.U.P.), 1959.

The Mental Health Services

Kathleen Jones: *Lunacy, Law and Conscience 1744–1845: The Social History of the Care of the Insane.* Routledge & Kegan Paul, 1955.

Report of the Mental Deficiency Committee, being a Joint Committee of the Board of Education and the Board of Control. H.M.S.O., 1929. Reprinted 1931.

2B*

SUGGESTIONS FOR FURTHER READING

Report of the Royal Commission on Lunacy and Mental Disorders.
Cmd. 2700, 1926.
Royal Commission on the Law Relating to Mental Illness and Mental
Deficiency 1954–1957. Cmnd. 169, 1957.

Disabled Persons

Report of the Inter-departmental Committee on the Rehabilitation
and Resettlement of Disabled persons (Tomlinson Committee).
Cmd. 6415, H.M.S.O., 1943.
Report of the Committee of Inquiry on the Rehabilitation, Training
and Resettlement of Disabled Persons (Piercy Committee). Cmd.
9883.
National Council of Social Service: *The Welfare of the Disabled.* Selec-
ted Papers, 1957.
Ministry of Labour and National Service: *Services for the Disabled.*
H.M.S.O., 1955.
Ministry of Health: *Blindness in England.* Report by Arnold Sorsby.
H.M.S.O., 1956.
Ministry of Labour and National Service: Report of the Working
Party on the Employment of Blind Persons. H.M.S.O., 1951.
Fourth Report from the Select Committee on Estimates, 1951–2:
Training, Rehabilitation and Resettlement. H.M.S.O.
T. Ferguson, A. N. McPhail and M. I. McVean: *Employment Problems
of Disabled Youth in Glasgow.* Medical Research Council Memor-
andum No. 28. H.M.S.O., 1952.
J. H. Nicholson: *Help for the Handicapped.* An enquiry into the oppor-
tunities of the voluntary services. National Council of Social
Service, 1958.

Maternity and Child Welfare

J. Spence, W. S. Walton, F. J. W. Miller, S. D. M. Court: *A Thousand
Families in Newcastle-upon-Tyne.* Nuffield Foundation and Nuffield
Provincial Hospitals Trust. O.U.P., 1954.
J. W. D. Douglas and J. M. Bloomfield: *Children Under Five.* Allen &
Unwin, 1958.
Leontine Young: *Out of Wedlock.* A study of the problems of the un-
married mother and her child. McGraw-Hill, New York, 1954.

School Meals

F. Le Gros Clark: *Social History of the School Meals Service.* National
Council of Social Service, 1948.
Ministry of Education. Report of an Inquiry into the Working of the
School Meals Service (1955–6). H.M.S.O.

Handicapped Children

Ministry of Education: *Education of the Handicapped Pupil, 1945–1955.*
Ministry of Education Pamphlet No. 30, 1956.
Ministry of Education: Report of the Committee on Maladjusted
Children, H.M.S.O., 1955.

SUGGESTIONS FOR FURTHER READING

Neglected and Deprived Children

Report of the Care of Children Committee (Curtis Committee). Cmd. 6922, 1946.

Scottish Home Department: Report of the Committee on Homeless Children (Clyde Committee). Cmd. 6911, 1946.

Home Office: Sixth Report of the Work of the Children's Department, May 1951.

Seventh Report on the Work of the Children's Department, November 1955.

Sixth Report from the Select Committee on Estimates session 1951–52, *Child Care*. H.M.S.O.

J. Bowlby: *Maternal Care and Mental Health*. World Health Organisation, 1951.

D. V. Donnison: *The Neglected Child and the Social Services*. Manchester University Press, 1954.

Hilda Lewis: *Deprived Children*. Nuffield Foundation, O.U.P., 1954

Jean S. Heywood: *Children in Care*. Routledge & Kegan Paul, 1959.

Gordon Trasler: *In Place of Parents*. A study of foster care. Routledge & Kegan Paul, 1960.

T. S. Simey: *The Concept of Love in Child Care*. National Children's Homes, 1960.

M. Kornitzer: *Child Adoption in the Modern World*, Putnam, 1952.

Report of the Departmental Committee on the Adoption of Children (Hurst Committee), Cmd. 9248, 1954.

Clarke Hall and Morrison's *Law relating to Children and Young Persons*. Butterworth, Fifth Edition, 1956.

Young People at Work and Leisure

Ministry of Labour and National Service: Report of the Committee on the Juvenile Employment Service (Ince Committee). H.M.S.O., 1945.

Seventh Report from the Select Committee on Estimates, Session 1956–57. *The Youth Employment Service and Youth Service Grants*.

H. Heginbotham: *The Youth Employment Service*. Methuen, 1951.

M. E. M. Herford: *Youth at Work*. Max Parrish, 1957.

Home Office, Scottish Home Department: *Health, Welfare and Safety in Non-industrial Employments. Hours of Employment of Juveniles*. Report by a Committee of Enquiry (Gowers Committee). H.M.S.O., 1949. Cmd. 7664.

J. B. Mays: *Growing up in the City*. University of Liverpool Press, 1954.

Adventure in Play, Liverpool Council of Social Service, 1957.

On the Threshold of Delinquency. University of Liverpool Press, 1959.

J. Macalister Brew: *Youth and Youth Groups*. Faber, 1957.

Pearl Jephcott: *Some Young People*. Allen & Unwin, 1954.

G. W. Jordan and E. M. Lister: *Self Portrait of Youth*. Heinemann, 1955.

Bryan H. Reed: *Eighty Thousand Adolescents*. A Study of Young People in the City of Birmingham. Allen & Unwin, 1950.

Citizens of Tomorrow. A study of the influences affecting the upbringing of young people. King George's Jubilee Trust, 1955.

373

SUGGESTIONS FOR FURTHER READING

Ministry of Education: *15 to 18*. Report of the Central Advisory Council for Education—England. Vol. 1 (Report). H.M.S.O., 1959.

Ministry of Education (Albemarle Report). *The Youth Service in England and Wales*. H.M.S.O., 1960. Cmd. 929.

The Welfare of Old People

Peter Townsend: *The Family Life of Old People*. Routledge & Kegan Paul, 1957.

B. E. Shenfield: *Social Policies for Old Age*. Routledge & Kegan Paul, 1957.

Old Age in the Modern World. Report of the Third Congress of the International Association of Gerontology, London 1954. E. & S. Livingstone, 1955.

J. H. Sheldon: *The Social Medicine of Old Age*. Report of an Inquiry in Wolverhampton. Published for the Nuffield Foundation by O.U.P., 1948.

Report of the Committee on the Economic and Financial Problems of the Provision for Old Age (Phillips Committee). Cmd. 9333, 1954.

Ministry of Labour and National Service, National Advisory Committee on the Employment of Older Men and Women. First Report, Cmd. 8963, 1953. Second Report, Cmd. 9628, December 1955.

Ministry of Health: Reports on Public Health and Medical Subjects No. 98. Survey of Services available to the Chronic Sick and Elderly (1954–55). Summary Report prepared by C. A. Boucher. H.M.S.O., 1957.

Ministry of Pensions and National Insurance. *Reasons given for Retiring or Continuing at Work*. Report of an Enquiry. H.M.S.O., 1954.

Housing and Town and Country Planning

William Ashworth: *The Genesis of Modern British Town Planning*. Routledge & Kegan Paul, 1954.

Peter Self: *Cities in Flood*. Faber, 1957.

J. M. Mackintosh: *Housing and Family Life*. Cassell, 1952.

Neighbourhood and Community. An Enquiry into social relationships on housing estates in Liverpool and Sheffield. University of Liverpool Press, 1954.

L. Kuper (Ed.): *Living in Towns*. Cressett Press, 1953.

J. M. Mogey: *Family and Neighbourhood*. Two Studies in Oxford. O.U.P., 1956.

Ministry of Housing and Local Government, Reports of the Housing Management Sub-Committee of the Central Housing Advisory Committee.

Fourth Report. *Transfers, Exchanges and Rents*. H.M.S.O., 1953.

Fifth Report. *Residential Qualifications*. H.M.S.O., 1955.

Sixth Report. *Unsatisfactory Tenants*. H.M.S.O., 1955.

Seventh Report. *Moving from the Slums*. H.M.S.O., 1956.

Report of the Flats Sub-Committee of the Central Housing Advisory Committee: *Living in Flats*. H.M.S.O., 1952.

Rosemary J. Rowles: *Housing Management*. Pitman, 1959.

SUGGESTIONS FOR FURTHER READING

Voluntary Organisations

A. F. C. Bourdillon (Ed.): *Voluntary Social Services, their Place in the Modern State*. Methuen, 1945.

Lord Beveridge: *Voluntary Action*. A report on Methods of Social Advance. Allen & Unwin, 1948.

Madeline Rooff: *Voluntary Societies and Social Policy*, Routledge & Kegan Paul, 1957.

Mary Morris: *Voluntary Organisations and Social Progress*. Gollancz, 1955.

S. Mencher: *The Relationship of Voluntary and Statutory Agencies in the Welfare Services*. Loch Memorial Lecture, 1954. Family Welfare Association.

Report of the Committee on the Law and Practice relating to Charitable Trusts (Nathan Committee). Cmd. 8710, 1952.

Social Work

Cherry Morris (Ed.): *Social Case Work in Great Britain*. Second Edition, Faber, 1955.

Peter Kuenstler (Ed.): *Social Group Work in Great Britain*. Faber, 1955.

Ministry of Health, Department of Health for Scotland. Report of the Working Party on Social Workers in the Local Authority Health and Welfare Services. (Younghusband Report). H.M.S.O., 1959.

Winifred P. Smith and Helen A. Bate: *Family Casework and the Country Dweller*. Family Welfare Association, 1953.

A. F. Philp and Noel Timms: *The Problem of 'The Problem Family'*. Family Service Units, 1957.

Elizabeth R. Glover: *Probation and Re-education*. Routledge & Kegan Paul, second edition, revised, 1956.

Joan F. S. King (Ed.): *The Probation Service*. Butterworth, 1958.

The Association of Psychiatric Social Workers: *The Boundaries of Casework*. Report of a Residential Refresher Course, 1956.

J. H. Wallis and H. S. Booker: *Marriage Counselling*. Routledge & Kegan Paul, 1958.

Family Discussion Bureau. *Social Casework in Marital Problems*. A Study by a group of Caseworkers. Tavistock Publications, 1955.

Barbara Wootton: *Social Science and Social Pathology*. Allen & Unwin Ltd.

Barbara N. Rodgers and Julia Dixon: *Portrait of Social Work*—A Study of social services in a northern town. Nuffield Provincial Hospitals Trust. O.U.P., 1960.

Periodicals

Political and Economic Planning, 16 Queen Anne's Gate, London, S.W.1: *Planning*. A fortnightly broadsheet.

National Council of Social Service, 26 Bedford Square, London, W.C.1: *Social Service*. A Quarterly Survey.

Family Welfare Association, Denison House, 296 Vauxhall Bridge Road, London, S.W.1: *Social Work*. A Quarterly Review of Family Case Work.

375

SUGGESTIONS FOR FURTHER READING

Case Conference. A Professional Journal for the Social Worker and Social Administrator, 8 Codicote Road, Welwyn, Herts.

Institute of Almoners, 42 Bedford Square, London, W.C.1: *The Almoner.* A Journal of Medical Social Work.

Association of Psychiatric Social Workers, 1 Park Crescent, London, W.1: *The British Journal of Psychiatric Social Work.*

National Association for Mental Health, Maurice Cray House, 39 Queen Anne Street, London, W.1: *Mental Health.*

Moral Welfare, the Quarterly Review of the Church of England Moral Welfare Council, Church House, Westminster, S.W.1.

Howard League for Penal Reform, Parliament Mansions, Abbey Orchard Street, London, S.W.1: *The Howard Journal.*

Institute for the Study and Treatment of Delinquency, 8 Bourdon Street, London, W.1.: *The British Journal of Delinquency.*

Society of Housing Managers, 13 Suffolk Street, London, S.W.1: *Quarterly Bulletin.*

Town and Country Planning Association, The Planning Centre, 28 King Street, Covent Garden, London, W.C.2: *Town and Country Planning.*

The Town Planning Review. Liverpool University Press, 123 Grove Street, Liverpool 7.

Institute of Public Administration, 76a New Cavendish Street, London, W.1: *Public Administration.*

The British Journal of Sociology. Published quarterly by Routledge & Kegan Paul Ltd., Broadway House, 68–74 Carter Lane, London, E.C.4, for the London School of Economics.

The Sociological Review. University College of North Staffordshire, Keele, Staffordshire.

INDEX

INDEX

INDEX

INDEX

Geriatrics, 292
 Geriatric Units, 69, 292
Glasgow, 89, 116, 125, 130 n.
Goldman, Peter, 353
Gonner, Sir Edward, 136
Gowers, Sir Ernest, 257
Graham, Allen, 217
Greenwood, Arthur, 30
Guides, Girl, 263
Guillebaud Committee—see Health

Handicapped adults—see Disabled Persons
Handicapped children—see Children
'Harris' Committee—see Marriage Guidance
Hastings, 68
Health
 Boards of, 62
 Centres, 81–2
 Education, 174–5, 176
 Insurance—see Insurance
 Industrial (see also Factories), 74
 Local Health Authorities, 70–1, 76, 85–7, 138, 189, 212, 215, 289
 Medical Officers of, 62, 63, 64, 89, 177, 322
 Minister (Ministry) of, 29, 72, 73, 74, 75, 76, 77, 78, 80, 89, 101, 138, 139, 144, 154, 161, 175, 178, 183, 199, 200, 221, 285, 288, 290, 295, 306, 307, 318, 344, 349
 Circular, *Health of Children: Prevention of Break-up of Families,* 161
 National Health Service, 52, 54, 66, 73–97, 292
 Act, 1946, 5, 31, 61, 66, 72, 73–97, 134, 138, 162, 173, 175, 178, 200, 202, 215, 218, 287, 311, 318, 319, 355
 (Amendment) Act, 1949, 80
 Administration, 73, 74
 Charges under the, 83–5
 (Contributions) Act, 1957, 96
 Co-ordination, 87–92

Cost, 83, 92–6, 356, 361–2
 Committee of Enquiry into the Cost of (Gillebaud Committee), 76, 77, 79, 80, 81, 82–3, 84, 90, 91, 93–6, 173, 290–1, 356, 362
 of School Children—see School Health Service
 of the Worker—(see also Factories), 74
 Public Health Act, 1848, 61
 Public Health Act, 1875, 63, 99
 Health Visitors and Visiting, 86, 91, 138, 161, 162, 173, 175–6, 202, 347
 Working Party on Health Visiting, 175–6, 201–2, 339
Health and Morals of Apprentices Act, 1802, 249
Health, Welfare and Safety in Non-Industrial Employments, Committee on (Gowers Committee), 257–58
Henley-in-Arden Re-establishment Centre at, 56–7
Herford, Dr. M. E., 256
Hill, Octavia, 4, 109, 110 131, 136
Hire Purchase, 58, 117, 132 n., 147
Holloway Prison, Governor of, 221
Home Helps, 86–7, 91, 287
Home Office, 154, 221, 222, 224, 229, 233, 253, 257
Home Secretary (Secretary of State for Home Affairs), 154, 229, 252, 326
Hospitals, 69–72
 General, 70
 Infectious Diseases, 70
 Municipal, 70–1
 Teaching, 75
 Voluntary, 70, 71, 75
Hospital Service, 74–9
 Management Committees, 75, 76–79, 291, 306
 Regional Hospital Boards, 75, 76–79, 86, 88, 89, 215, 216, 218, 291, 306, 321, 323, 360
 Training of officials for, 179
Howard League for Penal Reform, 350

INDEX

INDEX

INDEX

For Product Safety Concerns and Information please contact our EU
representative GPSR@taylorandfrancis.com
Taylor & Francis Verlag GmbH, Kaufingerstraße 24, 80331 München, Germany

www.ingramcontent.com/pod-product-compliance
Lightning Source LLC
Chambersburg PA
CBHW060134280326
41932CB00012B/1514

* 9 780415 868600 *